Preparing to Teach in Secondary Schools

Preparing to Teach in Secondary Schools

A STUDENT TEACHER'S GUIDE TO PROFESSIONAL ISSUES IN SECONDARY EDUCATION

Third edition

Edited by Val Brooks, Ian Abbott and Prue Huddleston

Open University Press

Open University Press
McGraw-Hill Education
McGraw-Hill House
Shoppenhangers Road
Maidenhead
Berkshire
England
SL6 2QL

email: enquiries@openup.co.uk
world wide web: www.openup.co.uk

and Two Penn Plaza, New York, NY 10121-2289, USA

First published 2004
Second edition published 2007
Reprinted 2008 (twice), 2010
First published in this third edition 2012

A catalogue record of this book is available from the British Library

ISBN10: 0 335 24632 X (pb)
ISBN13: 978 0 335 24632 8 (pb)
eISBN: 978 0 335 24633 5

Library of Congress Cataloging-in-Publication Data
CIP data applied for

Typeset by RefineCatch Limited, Bungay, Suffolk
Printed and bound in the UK by Bell & Bain, Glasgow.

MIX
Paper from
responsible sources
FSC® C007785

The *McGraw-Hill* Companies

Contents

SECTION 3

SECTION 4

Notes on contributors

Ian Abbott is Director of the Institute of Education at the University of Warwick. Formerly he was the coordinator of the PGCE Economics and Business Studies course and he has taught on a number of teacher education programmes. He has substantial teaching experience in several schools and colleges. His research interests include 14–19 education, vocational education and training, education business links, and initial teacher education.

Fay Baldry taught mathematics in a range of secondary schools before becoming a senior teaching fellow in mathematics education at the Institute of Education, University of Warwick, where she teaches the PGCE in secondary mathematics. Her research interests include the role of digital technologies in the teaching and learning of mathematics.

Liz Bills taught mathematics in secondary schools for ten years before moving to posts in higher education. She has been a tutor for secondary mathematics PGCE students and, more recently, has also taught and coordinated the Core Professional Studies element of the secondary PGCE course as well as being Director of Secondary PGCE at the University of Warwick. She has a particular interest in innovative approaches to initial teacher education and has been active in promoting flexible and alternative routes into teaching. Her research interests are mainly in mathematics education and in classroom discourse. She is now course manager for the PGCE at the University of Oxford.

Val Brooks taught English in secondary schools and a sixth-form college before she became a lecturer in the Institute of Education, University of Warwick, where she is Director of Postgraduate Taught Courses. Formerly, she coordinated the Flexible Postgraduate Initial Teacher Training programme. Her research interests include assessment and initial teacher education.

Cheryl Cane taught English, Drama, and Performing Arts in further and secondary education before becoming a senior teaching fellow at the Institute of Education, University of Warwick. She has worked within school senior leadership, is a former Director of Arts, faculty leader, head of department, coordinator of Gifted and

Talented Education, subject mentor for ITE and she also completed her NPQH in 2004. She is currently subject leader for the PGCE in English with Drama, coordinator for mentor training, and a Professional Studies tutor at Warwick University. Her current research interests involve perceptions and processes of effective mentoring in ITE and the impact of the 'learning detective' in the classroom.

Paul Elliott has been a Professor in the School of Education and Professional Learning at Trent University, Ontario since 2007. He formerly coordinated the Secondary Science PGCE course at the University of Warwick. His early research was in insect ecology after which he became a teacher, working for several years at an 11–18 comprehensive school in Wiltshire. His research interests include the interface between science and literacy and the development of biodiversity education. He has recently developed an eco-mentoring programme for student teachers and takes every opportunity to promote the conservation of bats.

Judith Everington began her career as a teacher and subject leader of religious education in Coventry secondary schools. She has been a lecturer and teacher trainer for 18 years and is currently Associate Professor at the Institute of Education, University of Warwick, where she established a Secondary PGCE in Religious Education course and more recently taught Professional Studies to mixed-subject PGCE groups. She now leads Teach First courses for RE specialists and, as a Professional Studies tutor, is responsible for university and school based teaching and support of a mixed-subject group. She has written several pupils' textbooks and teachers' handbooks. Her research and publications are concerned with the relationship between beginning teachers' personal and professional lives.

John Gordon taught English in secondary schools before joining the School of Education and Lifelong Learning at the University of East Anglia, Norwich. He is a Senior Lecturer in Education, and co-directs the Secondary PGCE(M) programme. He leads the English strand, and has published discussion and research pieces in *Changing English, The Curriculum Journal,* and *English in Education.*

Chris Hallett is a registered social worker and also holds a masters degree in public sector management. He spent 36 years with Warwickshire County Council in a variety of social work practitioner and management positions before retiring in 2010 as Assistant Director – Head of Service, covering social care and safeguarding. He now works as an independent social work and social care consultant. He is currently the Independent Chair of both Warwickshire Local Safeguarding Children Board and Solihull Adoption Panel. He has published chapters in books on developing good practice, partnership and participation in social care, and quality management. In 2008, he was co-contributor of 'Working with complexity: managing workload and surviving in a changing environment' to the book *The Critical Practitioner in Social Work and Health Care* (Open University Press). He is also an Associate Fellow at the School of Health and Social Studies at the University of Warwick.

Mick Hammond has taught in secondary schools both in the UK and overseas. He has worked on several curriculum development projects and carried out evaluations on the use of ICT. He lectures at the University of Warwick where he has responsibility for a specialist teacher as researcher programme as well as a research centre specializing in evaluation of new technology. He has written widely on early teacher development, including the book *Next Steps in Teaching* (Routledge/Falmer). He has contributed to debates on the use of ICT in numerous articles for academic and professional journals.

Terry Haydn is Professor of Education at the School of Education and Lifelong Learning at the University of East Anglia, Norwich. He was a head of history at an inner-city school in Manchester for many years before moving to the Institute of Education, University of London, to work in initial teacher education. For several years he was the Director of the Secondary PGCE course at UEA. His research interests are in the history curriculum, the use of ICT in schools, and the working atmosphere in the classroom.

Sean Hayes works for an educational organization providing data analysis to schools and local authorities. Previously he worked as Head of Research and Statistics in Greenwich Children's Services, the Cabinet Office and Hammersmith and Fulham Education Department. One of his main educational interests is in the provision of high-quality performance data analysis for schools. His research interests are largely in the school improvement area, focusing on educational attainment and the intersection of social class, race, and gender. He is a member of the British Educational Research Association (BERA) and has been on the BERA Executive Council since 2008, holding the Local Authority and Children's Services portfolio. He has been writing and presenting educational research papers for over 20 years and is a governor at a secondary school in West London.

Sandra Howard has taught pupils from minority ethnic backgrounds both in England and abroad over a period of many years. She is currently a programme coordinator for Race Equality and Ethnic Minority Achievement with Coventry Local Authority. In this role she provides advice and support to schools on all aspects of minority ethnic pupil achievement and delivers in-service training on inclusion, race equality, and English as an additional language.

Prue Huddleston is Professorial Fellow and formerly Director of the Centre for Education and Industry, University of Warwick. She has a particular interest in the 14–19 curriculum focusing on vocational qualifications, work-related learning, and the use of alternative approaches to schooling for those identified as under-achieving. Before joining the University of Warwick, she worked for many years within the further education sector and on community and outreach programmes. She has been involved in research and evaluation projects for the DfES, DTI, European Commission, British Council, Soros Foundation, companies, colleges, schools, and local authorities.

Chris Husbands is Professor of Education and Director of the Institute of Education, University of London, and was previously a board member of the Training and Development Agency for Schools. He taught in secondary comprehensive schools before working in higher education, and his teaching experience spans three continents. His research interests include curriculum issues, particularly in the teaching and learning of history, and education policy issues; he co-directed the national evaluation of Children's Trusts Pathfinders for the Department for Education and Skills between 2004 and 2007.

Jenni Ingram taught mathematics in secondary comprehensive schools before moving to the University of Warwick. She is currently subject leader for the PGCE in Secondary Mathematics and the course leader for the MSc in Mathematics Education. Her research interests include mathematical discourse and communication in secondary classrooms, assessment in mathematics, and initial teacher education.

Alison Kitson worked in three secondary comprehensive schools for eight years before moving into higher education. She was a lecturer in History Education and Teacher Development at the University of Warwick between 2000 and 2005 where she coordinated the History PGCE and undertook research into the teaching of history in divided societies. From Warwick she moved to the Training and Development Agency for Schools where she led a number of projects, including the revised professional standards for teachers, postgraduate professional development, and CPD leadership. She is now Faculty Director of Initial Teacher Education at the Institute of Education, University of London, and her new book, *Teaching History 11–18* (jointly authored with Chris Husbands) has just been published.

Daniel Muijs is Professor of Education at the University of Southampton. He has conducted a number of large-scale research projects and programme evaluations and has published widely in the areas of school effectiveness and school improvement, effective teaching and learning, and school leadership. With David Reynolds, he is author of the bestselling *Effective Teaching, Evidence and Practice* (Sage Publishers). He is editor of the journals *School Effectiveness and School Improvement* and *Educational Management Abstracts*.

Faith Muir is a Regional Director with the Centre for Education and Industry (CEI) at the University of Warwick. She has written national guidance materials for practitioners and undertaken research and evaluation in work-related learning and enterprise education, 14–19 curriculum development, and vocational qualifications for the DfE/DCSF, Ofqual, and QCDA. In particular, she has supported the development of PSHEE (Economic Wellbeing and Financial Capability) in primary and secondary schools, and at regional and national levels. Before joining CEI, she taught music for many years and was a TVEI coordinator before managing an Education Business Partnership. She regularly contributes to initial teacher education at the University of Warwick, and has recently become a tutor for the Teach First programme.

Andrea Pitt taught mathematics in secondary comprehensive schools, including leading a mathematics department, before joining the University of Warwick as a senior teaching fellow. Andrea was a teacher researcher on the Deep Progress in Mathematics project with Steph Prestage and Anne Watson. Her research interests include initial teacher education and curriculum development and innovation.

Lynn Reynolds taught secondary science for a number of years before moving to the University of Warwick where she worked across the secondary PGCE and MA in Educational Studies. She was involved in Becta-funded projects examining the relationship between deep learning and ICT and also looking at how trainee teachers use ICT in the classroom. She has since moved to the University of Birmingham where she is a lecturer in science education and has also returned to the classroom.

Kate Shilvock is a former Associate Professor at the Institute of Education at the University of Warwick where she was course leader for the Secondary PGCE in English with Drama and also led the Core Professional Studies course. A former Head of English in Warwickshire, she had substantial experience of teaching in secondary schools across the country. She also acted as both subject and professional mentor for ITE students in school. With David Wray, she is co-author of *Cross-curricular Literacy 11–14* (Letts Educational).

Jan Warner worked as a secondary school Special Educational Coordinator over a period of many years. She went on to become a Lead Adviser for SEN in a London borough. More recently, she has been employed as a freelance trainer and consultant in the field of special education and English. She has worked as a teacher trainer for Kings College, The Open University, and Warwick University. Her main area of interest and focus for research is training teachers to recognize the needs of SEN students in their classrooms and to be able to manage their needs effectively.

Nick Zafar is Assistant Director of Learning at Bedford Academy. He entered teaching after a career in accountancy and business spanning more than 25 years. He retrained as a teacher of business at the University of Warwick, and as Head of Business at Waseley Hills School, Birmingham, and Ousedale School, Buckinghamshire, he was actively engaged in mentoring and developing both trainee and newly qualified teachers. He completed graduate study at the University of Warwick in the area of the changing PSHEE environment.

Acronyms and abbreviations

A level	Advanced level
ACT	Association for Citizenship Teachers
ADHD	attention deficit hyperactivity disorder
AFL	assessment for learning
ALIS	A Level Information System
ARK	Absolute Return for Kids
AS level	Advanced Subsidiary level
BICS	basic interpersonal communication skills
BME	Black and minority ethnic
CAF	Common Assessment Framework
CALP	cognitive academic language proficiency
CASE	Cognitive Acceleration in Science Education
CAT	Cognitive Abilities Test
CEDP	Career Entry and Development Profile
CEM	(Centre for) Curriculum, Evaluation, and Management
CPD	continuing professional development
CRE	Commission for Racial Equality
CVA	contextual value-added
DART	directed activities for reading and thinking
DDA	Disability Discrimination Act
DfE	Department for Education
DfEE	Department for Education and Employment
DfES	Department for Education and Skills
EAL	English as an additional language
EMA	educational maintenance allowance
EMAG	Ethnic Minority Achievement Grant
EPD	early professional development
ESW	education social worker
EWB	electronic whiteboard
EWO	education welfare officer
FFT	Fischer Family Trust

FE	further education
FHEQ	Framework for Higher Education Qualifications
FTE	full-time equivalent
GCE	General Certificate of Education
GCSE	General Certificate of Secondary Education
GTCE	General Teaching Council for England
HLTA	higher level teaching assistant
ICT	information and communications technology
IDP	Inclusion Development Programme
IEP	individual education plan
IQ	intelligence quotient
ITT	initial teacher training
IWB	interactive whiteboard
KS	Key Stage
LAC	literacy across the curriculum
LAL	literacy and learning
LDD	learning difficulties and disabilities
LEA	local education authority
LSCB	Local Safeguarding Children Board
LSA	learning support assistant
MI	multiple intelligences
MidYIS	Middle Years Information System
NC	National Curriculum
NEET	not in education, employment or training
NFER	National Foundation for Educational Research
NNS	National Numeracy Strategy
NQF	National Qualifications Framework
NQT	newly qualified teacher
OECD	Organization for Economic Cooperation and Development
Ofsted	Office for Standards in Education
PE	physical education
PGCE	Post Graduate Certificate in Education
PLTS	personal, learning and thinking skills
PPA	planning, preparation and assessment
PSHEE	Personal, Social, Health and Economic Education
PTA	Parent–Teacher Association
QCA	Qualifications and Curriculum Authority
QCDA	Qualifications and Curriculum Development Agency
QCF	Qualifications and Credit Framework
QTLS	qualified teacher learning and skills
QTS	qualified teacher status
RAISE	Reporting and Analysis for Improvement through School self-Evaluation
RE	religious education
RPA	raising of the participation age
SCAA	Schools Curriculum and Assessment Authority

SEAL	social and emotional aspects of learning
SEN	special educational needs
SENCo	special educational needs coordinator
SENDA	Special Educational Needs and Disability Act
SIP	School Improvement Partner
SMART	specific, measurable, achievable, realistic and time-related
SMCD	spiritual, moral, and cultural development
SoW	scheme of work
SSC	Sector Skills Council
TA	teaching assistant
TDA	Training and Development Agency
TLA	Teacher Learning Academy
TPaCK	technological pedagogical content knowledge
UTC	University Technical College
VAK	visual, auditory and kinaesthetic
VLE	virtual learning environment
www	World Wide Web
YELLIS	Year Eleven Information System
ZPD	zone of proximal development

Figures and tables

Introduction
Val Brooks, Ian Abbott and Prue Huddleston

Content and organization

This book has been written for those individuals preparing to teach in secondary schools. It is intended to complement your subject studies by covering a range of core professional topics with which all teachers need to be familiar irrespective of their subject specialism. The teaching profession is at a point of considerable transformation: national policies designed to make initial training and continuing professional development increasingly school-based; shifting relationships with para-professionals and other adults in the classroom; new ways of relating to other children's services; fresh opportunities and threats created by technological advances; novel approaches to teaching in the light of brain-based research; new thinking on teachers' professionalism and teacher leadership; data-rich approaches to managing school and pupil performance; and initiatives designed to personalize learning. The origins of some of these developments are to be found in academic research. The impetus for others is policy initiative at government level – part of an ongoing drive to raise standards of education nationally. Taken together, these developments have greatly expanded the core curriculum for initial teacher training. Their implications for those about to enter the profession – the opportunities and challenges they present – are an important feature of this book.

The book is divided into four sections:

- Section 1: Becoming a Teacher
- Section 2: Core Professional Competences
- Section 3: Secondary Schools and the Curriculum
- Section 4: Making Schooling Work for All: The Inclusion Agenda

Those new to teaching may be most familiar with teaching as a classroom activity. The three chapters in Section 1 seek to broaden your perspective, placing teaching in its wider professional context and drawing attention to issues and challenges that student teachers will face. Chapter 1 addresses your most immediate challenge – that of learning to teach! It draws on research into teachers' early professional development to elucidate this process. Chapter 2 widens the context by exploring the legal and professional framework for teaching, and professional values and practice. Chapter 3 looks beyond your period of initial training to highlight the range of opportunities, issues and challenges that new teachers will encounter as they embark on their early professional development. A key theme in Section 1 is the importance of regarding initial teacher training not as an end in itself, but as the opening phase in a teacher's ongoing professional development.

Having set the scene in Section 1, the nine chapters in Section 2 adopt a classroom focus. They examine some of the core professional competences – the knowledge, skills, and understanding – that newly qualified teachers (NQT) need to acquire. Chapter 4 opens by exploring the fundamental question of how learning takes place. The remaining chapters consider how different aspects of teaching, such as planning and differentiation, can be used to support learning.

In Section 3, the focus shifts to the secondary school curriculum. The opening chapter, 'What should we teach? Understanding the secondary curriculum' (Chapter 13), provides a conceptual framework for the following chapters by discussing some of the basic concepts of curriculum thinking. The remaining chapters consider government initiatives across all three key stages of the secondary curriculum (ages 11–19). Ways in which schools provide for pupils' spiritual, moral and cultural development are also explored (Chapter 14).

Section 4 concludes the book by considering major components of recent government policy and the inclusion agenda, under the heading 'Making Schooling Work for All'. As well as examining some of the more enduring aspects of the inclusion agenda such as pastoral care (Chapter 24) and provision for pupils with special educational needs (Chapter 21), this section discusses some of the latest national initiatives, including provision for the introduction of new types of state secondary schools (Chapter 26).

As mentioned above, it is natural to adopt a narrow focus centred on oneself when learning to teach. However, education is not divorced from its broader social and political contexts and the impacts of social change and political reforms make themselves powerfully felt in schools. Thus, it is important to recognize the likely impact of these factors on your work as a teacher. In 1960, the then minister of education, Sir David Eccles, described the curriculum as a 'secret garden' (Hansard 1960). The notion of the curriculum, or indeed most other aspects of education, as the preserve of educationalists has long since faded in policy circles. This is evident throughout this book, which was revised in 2011, a year when many elements of the education system were subject to major reform following the election of a Conservative/Liberal Democrat coalition government in 2010. Throughout the book, you will find references to proposed changes. In some cases, the nature of the reform has already been determined; in others, the changes are still the subject of consultation, making the future uncertain. In all cases, the longer-term impact of this overhaul of the system remains to be seen. By the time you read this book, evidence of impact will be accumulating, enabling you to judge whether intended consequences are materializing.

Ways of using this book

This book can be read in more than one way. It is possible to read it in its entirety, for instance as an introductory text at the start of your training. However, it is really intended for repeated reference throughout a course of study. To this end, each chapter is a self-contained entity, focusing on a specific topic and designed to be read as and when appropriate. For instance, you may read the chapter on 'Planning for learning' when you first attempt to construct lesson plans, whereas you may consult the chapter on 'Using assessment data to support pupil achievement' as part of your preparation for a written assignment on this topic. Chapters are cross-referenced to related material elsewhere in the text to help you to pursue specific interests.

This book is intended primarily for postgraduate students who are preparing to teach in secondary schools. It assumes an educated but non-expert audience. Therefore, imparting basic factual information about topics with which readers may be unfamiliar is an important feature of the book. However, this text was not designed simply to be read to gain information. Reading is meant to be an active rather than a passive process, so readers are invited to engage with the text and respond to it. Various stylistic features are designed to encourage you to do this. For instance, each chapter opens with a set of objectives to be achieved by the end of the chapter. Where we hope to challenge you to think about complex, sensitive or contentious issues, we may ask questions or provide case studies for consideration. Where we want to help you to further your knowledge or skills, we may set tasks or direct you to websites, as well as making recommendations for further reading. Practical examples are used throughout to make abstract or unfamiliar ideas concrete and meaningful. Where appropriate, chapters provide a brief historical context or an outline of government policy to help make sense of a subject.

The text contains a mix of tasks, case studies, and scenarios designed to help you to address issues that are raised and the practical application of ideas. Occasionally, chapters open with a question or a task, requiring you to engage directly with a topic from the outset. The majority of tasks are designed to be *self-contained*, enabling you to complete them there and then, without the need for additional resources. For instance, if a task requires you to analyse pupil performance data, a suitable example will be provided for that purpose. You are, of course, welcome to use your own materials if you have some to hand, but being able to complete a task will not depend on this in most instances. Some of the tasks do, however, require access to a computer with internet access and several are school-based.

A note on terminology

Like all other professional activities, education has its own 'shorthand', which can appear as jargon to those who are unfamiliar with it. Terms that have a specialized meaning in education, separate from their everyday use, are explained at their first mention. Education also has its fair share of acronyms for the uninitiated to become acquainted with! When a commonly used acronym is introduced, it is spelt out in full on the first occasion it is used in each chapter, with the abbreviation used thereafter. Acronyms and abbreviations are also listed at the front of the book.

Many schools refer to their pupils as students. Trainee teachers are also sometimes described as students. To avoid confusing the two, we use the term 'student' to denote only those who are learning to teach. The young people who student teachers will teach are described as 'pupils' or 'children'.

The aim of this book is to promote a reflective approach to initial training among those who read it. We hope you find it a useful aid to your early professional development.

SECTION 1

Becoming a teacher

1

Learning to teach and learning about teaching

Val Brooks

1.1 Learning to teach: the challenge

Learning to teach may turn out to be the greatest challenge you have ever undertaken! This is the conclusion reached by many student teachers when they reflect on their experiences at the end of training. Most of them also describe it as one of the most rewarding things they have ever done. The effort required to achieve an ambition is generally in proportion to the personal satisfaction it brings. Goals that are easily achieved rarely bring a sense of real satisfaction, whereas hard-won successes are often deeply gratifying. An Ofsted overview report on *Quality and Standards in Secondary Initial Teacher Training* declared that, 'today's newly qualified teachers are the best trained that we have ever had' (Ofsted 2003b: 4), claiming that both the quality of their training and the standards student teachers had achieved by the end of training were higher than ever before. Again in 2009, the Annual Report of the Chief Inspector judged most training providers to be 'good or outstanding in their overall effectiveness', enabling most trainees to attain 'good or outstanding professional standards' (Ofsted 2009a: 57). This chapter explores the process of learning to teach, examines some of the reasons why teaching is a demanding profession and highlights approaches to teacher development that are enabling recent generations of new teachers to be so successful.

By the end of this chapter, you should:

- be more aware of some of the challenges you are likely to face during training; and
- know about approaches that you and those responsible for your training can use to support your professional development.

Many beginning teachers believe that behaviour management will pose their biggest challenge. Will they be able to command an adolescent audience? Get them to listen? Engage their interest? Obtain their compliance? Although the importance of learning to manage classrooms and pupil behaviour should not be underestimated, in reality the challenges are more subtle and wide-ranging than managing the behaviour of wayward adolescents! Indeed, poor behaviour is often a symptom of an underlying problem and improves once the problem is tackled. The following two sections examine some less obvious reasons why learning to teach is challenging.

1.2 The personal challenge

Identifying tacit influences on the way you think and behave

One of the more subtle challenges in learning to teach is that it may force you to examine your own values, beliefs, prejudices and assumptions. This sometimes involves the unwelcome discovery that cherished beliefs or long-held assumptions do not stand up to scrutiny. Becoming an effective teacher may involve revising personal theories about teaching and learning. Unlearning established opinions can be a difficult, even painful business especially if you have believed something for a long time or have developed a theory based on personal experience. As Claxton (1984: 169) observed:

> All students when they arrive at a teacher-training course have a personal theory about education, schools, children, teaching and learning; what is important and what is not ... They have their own intuitive, largely tacit, largely unexamined set of beliefs, attitudes and values that are variously idiosyncratic, partial, simplistic, archaic and rigid.

As Claxton notes, some of the ideas new teachers hold about teaching may be tacit. By this, he means that underlying values, prejudices and beliefs are sometimes so completely internalized that they are no longer part of our conscious thinking on a subject. This is especially true of long-held views or attitudes that have never been questioned. Although these ideas may be submerged, they nevertheless exercise a powerful influence on the way new teachers think and behave (e.g. Wubbels 1992). Section 1.4 describes two approaches to training that can help new teachers to examine their own tacit influences.

Case Study 1.1

Alan was a mature student on his first teaching placement. His mentors had become concerned about the lack of variety in his teaching. Most of Alan's lessons followed the same format: a lengthy introduction during which Alan lectured his classes followed by a written task that pupils were expected to complete independently, working in silence. Denied opportunities to interact with their teacher or each other, Alan's classes became restive. Alan agreed that his professional development targets should include experimenting with a wider range of teaching and learning styles. Nevertheless, in the classroom he continued to display a preference for whole-class, didactic teaching and written tasks to be completed independently and in silence.

What do you deduce about Alan's educational beliefs and preconceptions from this account?

Teaching and one's sense of self

Another reason why learning to teach is challenging is that it involves giving of oneself in a way that entering many other occupations does not. This is how Smith and Alred (1994: 106) put it:

> Learning to teach is also a process in which people's whole sense of themselves is involved. We are not denying that that there are classroom skills that can be learned . . . the point we are concerned to stress is that the experience of teaching . . . is one in which our feelings, our sense of our identity, our vulnerability as human beings are all involved . . . This, essentially, is what makes the business of learning to teach different from learning to be a gardener or a carpenter or a welder.

Thus, initial teacher training (ITT) is a period of heightened emotional sensitivity for many student teachers. Indeed, it is possible to leave a lesson feeling elated when a pupil remarks: 'That was really interesting. Thanks', only to be plunged into gloom by the adverse reaction of the next class to a carefully prepared lesson. Rapid fluctuations in mood can make learning to teach seem like riding an emotional roller-coaster!

There is also an important moral dimension to teachers' work (see Chapters 2, 14 and 25). During training, you are likely to encounter moral dilemmas that force you to wrestle with the rights and wrongs of situations. For instance, during a form group period you might overhear a child complaining to her neighbour about the behaviour of one of her teachers. Realizing that you have heard her, she tries to draw you into the conversation asking your opinion of the behaviour. She has described something that you regard as unprofessional conduct. How should you respond? Alternatively, you may find yourself disagreeing with your department's marking policy, which is inconsistent with what you have learnt from reading about this topic and during your provider's training sessions. Will you mark pupils' work in the way you believe to be best or adhere to the department's policy on this matter? Learning how to handle moral dilemmas will form an important part of your professional development. Chapter 2 explores the topic of professional ethics further.

I have started by identifying some personal challenges in learning to teach but the cognitive demands are equally rigorous.

1.3   The cognitive/intellectual challenge

Subject knowledge and understanding

A sound knowledge and understanding of the subject you are planning to teach is a prerequisite for teaching it competently and confidently (Shulman 1986; Bennett and Carré 1993). Most student teachers devote considerable time and energy to developing or consolidating their subject knowledge during training. Although good subject knowledge is the cornerstone of effective teaching, it is not enough on its own. You will need to develop what has been described as pedagogic content knowledge (Shulman 1986) by learning how to apply your knowledge to make the subject meaningful and accessible to children. You will need to learn how to make subject matter interesting for secondary pupils, what they find especially difficult and what the common misconceptions are.

There are also many generic topics about which all teachers need to know irrespective of their subject specialism – core professional skills, such as the ability to plan, and national policy initiatives likely to affect all teachers, such as Achievement for All (see Chapter 21).

Core professional skills

The ability to plan, to assess, to differentiate, to communicate effectively, to use questions skillfully and to manage behaviour are but some of the core professional skills required by all teachers. Research into the acquisition of skill has identified several phases through which learners typically pass. Tomlinson (1995: 44–5) summarizes them as follows:

- *Phase 1*: unconscious incompetence (learners start by not knowing what they don't know)
- *Phase 2*: conscious incompetence (learners come to recognize that they don't know how)
- *Phase 3*: conscious competence (at this stage, learners know in theory but apply only with difficulty)
- *Phase 4*: unconscious competence (involves knowing how to but not being fully aware of what you're doing).

You will certainly experience the first three phases during training, although you are less likely to reach the stage of unconscious competence in any of the skills that are new to you. However, there are many other areas of your life where you already display unconscious competence. These are things that you can do automatically but would find difficult to explain to someone else.

Task 1.1

Can you identify skills where you display unconscious competence? This could include programming a piece of equipment that involves a complicated sequence of actions to perform which you can undertake without thinking because you have done it so often before.

Another challenge you face involves your ability to make connections between the different learning experiences you have during training. You need, for instance, to be able to see the links between your work on planning and that on assessment or to appreciate the implications of taught sessions in your training institution for practical experience in the classroom. Emerging teaching skills need to be melded in the classroom. Classrooms are busy places, full of lively, young people, where lots of things happen simultaneously. In some respects, a teacher is like the conductor of an orchestra; she or he orchestrates a lesson, attending to the multifarious elements that need to be managed so that everyone starts together and proceeds harmoniously to a satisfactory end point. The way in which concepts are presented, timing, the pace of progression, who talks and for how long, use of resources, the emotional climate in the room, seating arrangements and noise levels are but some of the elements of a lesson that a teacher needs to manage. Doyle (1986: 394–5) identified six attributes that combine to make teaching uniquely complex and dynamic:

- *Multidimensionality*: the sheer number of people gathered in one place who participate in a large number of events and tasks; one event can have multiple consequences.
- *Simultaneity*: Doyle (1986: 394) illustrates the number of things that could be happening at once as follows: 'During a discussion a teacher must listen to student answers, watch other students for signs of comprehension or confusion, formulate the next question, and scan the class for possible misbehavior.'
- *Immediacy*: order in classrooms depends in part upon the maintenance of momentum and the flow of events; the pace of events is rapid, giving teachers little time to reflect before acting.
- *Unpredictability*: classroom events take unexpected turns and distractions and interruptions occur frequently; because events are jointly produced, it is difficult to anticipate how an activity will proceed on a particular day with a particular group.
- *Publicness*: 'Teachers act in fish bowls' (Lortie, in Doyle 1986: 395); events, especially those involving the teacher, are often witnessed by a large proportion of the pupils who will use them to make judgements about the teacher based on their handling of specific events.
- *History*: a class that meets regularly accumulates a set of common experiences, routines, and norms that form the foundation for classroom conduct; early meetings often shape events for the rest of the term or year.

These characteristics help to explain why learning to teach is not simply a matter of mastering a set of teaching 'recipes', formulae or rules that can be applied as a matter of routine. On the contrary, teaching involves making many decisions where the choices are neither straightforward nor obvious. As well as the deliberate decisions that can be made at the planning stage, there are on-the-spot decisions that have to be made as a lesson unfolds. All decisions have to be context-sensitive – sensitive to school policy and procedures, the ability of the group, your previous relationship with a group or individual, a child's personal circumstances, what has happened earlier in the day and so on. It is this complexity, and the centrality of a teacher's professional judgement, that makes teaching both challenging and stimulating.

One of the keys to managing complexity is good advance planning, which is the subject of Chapter 5. Although planning is only one aspect of a teacher's job, it has been described as being as 'complex and cognitively demanding as the practice of medicine, law or architecture' (Clark 1989: 312).

Task 1.2

Choose a topic that is taught in your subject at Key Stage (KS) 3 or 4. How many factors can you think of that are likely to influence your planning of a scheme of work for this topic?

Your list is likely to be a long one! However, it is one that you could undoubtedly extend as your training progresses and you become increasingly aware of factors that influence planning.

Clearly, the demands of learning to teach are multifarious: cognitive, intellectual, personal, moral, and emotional. So what types of training will help you to develop on so many different fronts?

1.4 Some of the ways in which teachers develop professionally

Reflection

Reflection is regarded as essential to professional development and explains many of the activities you will be asked to take part in during training. A written assignment that requires you to give a critical account of some aspect of your teaching; taking part in seminar group discussions; producing written evaluations of lessons; one-to-one tutorials with mentors following lesson observations: at the heart of all these activities is the ability to reflect upon experience and learn from this reflection. The value of reflection is illustrated by a proverb comparing two fishermen; one has had twenty years' experience and the other has had one year's experience twenty times over. Although both men have been fishing for the same amount of time, one has the accumulated wisdom of twenty years' experience whereas the other still fishes in the same way that he did as a novice because he has failed to learn from experience.

A lot has been written about the role of reflection in teachers' professional development. One of the most influential figures in this field is Donald Schön (1983), who developed ideas about the 'reflective practitioner' as a result of studying the thinking and practices of different professional groups. Schön's findings led him to challenge a traditional model of professional practice that entails applying knowledge and practising skills acquired during a period of initial training. He found that reflective practitioners continued to develop as they accumulated a store of relevant previous experiences which acted as reference points, guiding their thinking and practices. They also acquired detailed contextual knowledge, becoming increasingly sensitive to the importance of context. He developed two models of reflective practice: reflection-in-action (i.e. during the event) and reflection-on-action (i.e. after the event). These ideas have been very influential in shaping approaches to teachers' professional development. As was noted above, many of your training activities will be based on the importance of opportunities for reflection-on-action. Reflection-in-action may not be feasible for the reasons identified by Doyle (1986) above. Simply doing the job will probably demand all of your mental energy at the outset, leaving little mental 'space' for reflection-in-action. However, as you gain experience and start to develop unconscious competence, you will find yourself increasingly capable of reflection-in-action. This opens up the possibility of working on aspects of your teaching that can only be honed by focusing on them as you do them, for instance, allowing increased 'wait time' after you have asked a question (see Chapter 8).

Challenge and support

In some respects student teachers are like plants, needing appropriate growing conditions to thrive. Plenty of light but not enough water will not produce a sturdy plant any more than being kept in the dark but with plenty of water will help a plant to grow. Similarly, research into teacher development has focused on the importance of achieving an appropriate balance between challenging student teachers and supporting them. Elliott and Calderhead's (1993) two-dimensional model of the relationship between challenge and support (see Figure 1.1) shows how:

> In the quadrant where challenge and support are both low the *status quo* is likely to be maintained but when challenge is increased without comparative changes

	High	
Novice withdraws from the mentoring relationship with no growth possible	**C** **H** **A** **L**	Novice grows through development of new knowledge and images
Low	**L**	High
SUPPORT	**E**	
	N	
Novice is not encouraged to consider or reflect on knowledge and images	**G** **E**	Novice becomes confirmed in pre-existing images of teaching
	Low	

Figure 1.1 Elliott and Calderhead's two-dimensional model of the relationship between challenge and support (adapted from Daloz 1986)

in support there is likely to be no growth. In this case the student is likely to withdraw physically from the development programme or, at best, resort to using previously formed ideas . . . There is evidence to suggest that challenge is a necessary component for professional growth to occur.

(Elliott and Calderhead 1993: 171–2)

Many people will play a part in your professional development. Some, such as mentors and tutors, will have a designated responsibility and others, such as fellow students and other teachers working in a school, will play a more informal role. The notion of a 'critical friend' is useful for thinking about the contribution of others to your professional development. As the name implies, a critical friend offers warmth, support and encouragement but is also prepared to question and criticize constructively. For all those involved in your development, the principle of balancing challenge with support remains an important one. A mentor, for instance, who provides only challenge, thereby obliging students to seek support elsewhere, will not create optimum conditions for growth. You are, however, unlikely to require challenge and support in equal measures at all stages in your training. Research by Furlong and Maynard (1995) illustrates why this might be. Furlong and Maynard studied a group of primary student teachers and identified five broad stages in their development while on school placement:

- *Stage 1: Early idealism.* This was characterized by: 'clear, if idealistic, ideas about the sort of teachers they wanted to be, the kind of relationships that they would develop with their pupils, the physical appearance of their classrooms and the classroom atmosphere that they would create' (Furlong and Maynard 1995: 74).

- *Stage 2: Personal survival.* 'Once student teachers began their school experience, their idealism appeared rapidly to fade in the face of the realities of the classroom, and they became obsessed with their own personal survival. Personal survival meant detecting and "fitting in" with the teacher's routines and expectations, being "seen" as a teacher and, in particular, achieving some form of classroom control' (Furlong and Maynard 1995: 76).

- *Stage 3: Dealing with difficulties.* At this stage, students learnt to make personal sense of what was happening in the classroom, identified some of the difficulties they faced and gained some measure of classroom control.

- *Stage 4: Hitting a plateau.* 'Having gained basic competence and confidence in management and organization . . . there was a noted tendency for student teachers to "relax" a little; their learning seemed to "hit a plateau" . . . Having found one way of organising their teaching that worked for them – they were going to stick with it!' (Furlong and Maynard 1995: 89).

- *Stage 5: Moving on.* Students were most successful at this stage when they worked with trainers who helped them to understand the need for change. For many students, moving on represented an enormous challenge that was met with varying degrees of resistance.

Findings such as these suggest that student teachers who are at different stages in their development will need varying amounts of challenge and support. A student at the survival stage, for instance, will be in most need of support, whereas someone who is deemed to have 'plateaued' will benefit most from being challenged. At Stage 5 (moving on), challenge and support may need to be carefully balanced.

The role of reading in professional development

The ITT curriculum has expanded greatly in recent years but the length of courses has not increased. Consequently, courses have become increasingly intensive and incapable of covering topics in the depth or detail that would be desirable if the curriculum were not so heavily loaded. Independent study is essential to supplement what is covered by taught courses. However, reading is much more than a default mechanism, making good the detail a taught course is unable to supply. Reading provides access to a wealth of information, ideas, and alternative perspectives on a topic. Most important of all, it provides access to the wisdom of others, making it an ideal aid to reflection and professional development. In preparation for writing this chapter, I undertook a small survey of some student teachers to enquire into their reading habits. They reported that reading had played an important part at all stages in their training: before the course started; during university-based phases in preparation for seminars and written assignments; and while they were on school placements. They had used reading to deepen their knowledge and understanding; to suggest practical ideas for use in the classroom; to broaden their repertoire of teaching strategies; to seek solutions to problems; to meet targets for professional development; and to develop expertise in areas of special interest to them.

Having identified several approaches to professional development, the next question concerns how all of this reading, reflection, challenge, and support is to be managed so that it makes a genuine contribution to your development. It is possible to end up feeling overwhelmed by possible courses of action, not knowing where or how to start.

Adopting a systematic approach to professional development

One recommended approach to professional development is needs-led (DfES 2002a). It starts with a thorough audit of students' prior experiences, knowledge and skills against the requirements they are training to meet. These requirements include the statutory requirements for ITT that are specified in teaching standards that are currently under review, with new standards expected to take effect in 2012. The statutory standards, plus any additional requirements of a particular training course, form the basis for an initial audit that is used to create learner profiles, highlighting strengths and achievements that individuals can build on during training, as well as identifying gaps and weaknesses that need to be addressed. This type of baseline assessment allows training to be tailored to individuals' needs and aspirations, and establishes the priorities for immediate development. However, it is essential to go beyond general aims (Black and Wiliam 1998a) to develop specific targets and an action plan for achieving them. The notion of 'SMART targets' is useful because it emphasizes attributes that make target-setting practicable and meaningful (see Figure 1.2).

S	Specific	Specific targets relate to a defined area of competence – perhaps related to one of the standards for QTS
M	Measurable	Measurable targets are couched in terms which allow you to point to evidence that they have been achieved
A	Achievable	Achievable targets are do-able rather than vague aspirations
R	Realistic	Realistic targets are defined in relation to the context in which you are working and the standards to be achieved
T	Time-related	Time-related targets have clear dates for review and monitoring in relation to the timescale available

Figure 1.2 SMART targets (adapted from DfEE 1997b: 10)

It is helpful to distinguish short-term targets (e.g. learning how to use a piece of software) from long-term goals (e.g. improving subject knowledge in a 'multiple' subject such as science), which will, themselves, need to be broken down into a series of short-term targets. It is also important to work with a manageable number of targets at any given time. Regular, timetabled reviews where progress can be evaluated with a mentor or tutor, and next steps decided upon, are also part of a systematic approach to professional development. In fact, target-setting is one phase in a cyclical process that involves target-setting, action planning for the next phase, implementation of the plan, followed by a period of reflection and review to complete the cycle. This cyclical process should be ongoing so that the end of one cycle merges with the opening stage of the next cycle with a review signalling new priorities for target-setting.

This process does not end when training is completed. As Chapter 3 explains in more detail, continuing professional development (CPD) has become a priority for the teaching profession. The transition from ITT to induction is currently managed using a bridging document, the Career Entry and Development Profile (CEDP). Each newly qualified teacher (NQT) enters their first teaching post equipped with a CEDP, which provides the basis for planning early professional development during induction, a period normally lasting one year. Initial teacher training is, therefore, best viewed not as an end in itself but as the initial stage in a career-long process of CPD.

1.5 Conclusion

The three Rs traditionally viewed as the foundation of schooling – reading, [w]riting and [a]rithmetic – have recently been replaced by a new triad focused not on basic skills but on the learning capital that equips learners of all ages with attributes necessary to succeed – resilience (refusing to be daunted by difficulties or to give up easily), resourcefulness (making best use of what is available to you), and reflection (identifying the lessons implicit in personal experience). It is by fostering these qualities that you will equip yourself to join the next generation of newly qualified teachers who are deemed to be good or outstanding – those with the capacity to inspire pupils, making a real difference to their educational outcomes.

1.6   Recommendations for further reading and webliography

The educational press is useful for keeping abreast of developments, for instance,   the *Guardian* (Tuesday).

The *Times Educational Supplement*: in 2011 this weekly publication moved from a newspaper to a magazine format. As well as news and comments, it offers a section on resources and a pull-out guide to good teaching practice. A wider range of ideas and resources can be accessed from the online version at http://www.tes.co.uk/.

Schools Research News is a monthly publication, supported by the DfE, intended to keep practitioners up to date with research by publishing summaries of newly published findings that have implications for practice. *Research Bites*, an associated resource, is a series of 90-second PowerPoint presentations focused on practical classroom issues, designed as a stimulus to discussion. Both can be accessed at: http://www.education.gov.uk/schools/careers/traininganddevelopment/research-informedpractice/b0058454/2011-schools-research-news.

Note: Although the General Teaching Council for England will close in 2012, its Teacher Learning Academy (TLA) will continue, under new ownership, to support ITT and CPD, offering access to the TLA website, resources and research.

2

The professional framework and professional values and practice
Ian Abbott

2.1 Introduction

When you become a teacher, you do not just take up a new job, you acquire professional responsibilities and therefore need to understand the professional framework
within which teachers work. There are two interlocking elements to this: the legal
requirements and responsibilities laid on you as a teacher by the state; and ethical
responsibilities to uphold and to exemplify certain professional values. During your
preparation to become a teacher, you need to find out about these legal and professional requirements and to consider how your personal values fit with the common
values espoused by the profession.

This chapter is divided into three sections: professional values and practice;
teachers' legal responsibilities; and the role of school governors. These areas are inextricably linked to each other and form the statutory framework within which you will
work in school. By the end of the chapter, you will have:

- an understanding of the ways the legislative framework in which you work is
  evolving;
- an understanding of the duty of care that teachers have;
- an understanding of the developing roles and responsibilities of governors and
  how these might affect your early professional life.

2.2 Professional values and practice

Values underpin everything that a school does: the teaching of the formal curriculum
and the messages implicit in the hidden curriculum (see Chapter 13); provision for
teaching and learning and extra-curricular activities; the kind of relationships that are
formed between individuals. Nothing in schools, therefore, is value-free. However,
teachers and schools cannot afford to leave unexamined questions about what values
underlie their practices and how widely those values are espoused by the school
community.

New teachers face some difficult issues in relation to values. The first is to do with understanding the values that underpin teachers' and schools' responsibilities in the light of current legislative and policy frameworks. The second is to do with understanding how those values relate to the values – formally expressed or informally understood – of individual schools. The third is to do with examining the relationship between these elements and your own values, and developing strategies to resolve tensions and difficulties.

This section does not have any pretensions to explore general issues in the philosophy of education or to engage in an exploration of moral education upon which other chapters focus (see Chapter 14). What it does do is to encourage you to consider how your own values relate to those espoused by the profession. The meaning of values has also been debated in many arenas: here it is used in the sense of the definition in the *Oxford English Dictionary*: 'one's judgement of what is valuable or important in life'. In this case, we mean what is important and valuable in the teaching profession. In considering this, we cannot detach ourselves from schools and pupils.

It is unwise to embark on the profession of teaching without having reflected on the question, 'What is the purpose of a school?' In answering it, you will progress in answering the lifelong question, 'What are my values as a teacher?'

Task 2.1

Make a note of what you consider to be the three most important purposes of secondary schools in the UK today. In each case, identify one or two values that are implied by that purpose.

Because the values that you demonstrate in your actions are visible to pupils, there is a strong link to be made between the values you espouse as a teacher and the values that you promote to pupils. You do not exist in a vacuum; nor do the professional values you hold. For example, the 1988 Education Reform Act requires schools to provide a curriculum that pays attention to 'the spiritual, moral and cultural . . . development of pupils at school and in society' so that they may be prepared for the 'opportunities, responsibilities and experiences of adult life' (DES 1988: 1(2)a, b).

How will you as a teacher develop a coherent approach to professional values when the values of pupils, parents, employers, and the wider community may or may not match the codified statements of the statutory bodies' approach to professional values? The new Teachers' Standards (DfE 2011c), which will be effective as of September 2012, contain guidance on personal and professional conduct:

PART TWO: PERSONAL AND PROFESSIONAL CONDUCT
A teacher is expected to demonstrate consistently high standards of personal and professional conduct. The following statements define the behaviour and

attitudes which set the required standard for conduct throughout a teacher's career.

- Teachers uphold public trust in the profession and maintain high standards of ethics and behaviour, within and outside school, by:
  - treating pupils with dignity, building relationships rooted in mutual respect, and at all times observing proper boundaries appropriate to a teacher's professional position
  - having regard for the need to safeguard pupils' well-being in accordance with statutory provisions
  - showing tolerance of and respect for the rights of others
  - not undermining fundamental British values, including democracy, the rule of law, individual liberty and mutual respect, and tolerance of those with different faiths and beliefs
  - ensuring that personal beliefs are not expressed in ways which exploit pupils' vulnerability or might lead them to break the law.
- Teachers must have proper and professional regard for the ethos, policies and practices of the school in which they teach, and maintain high standards in their own attendance and punctuality.
- Teachers must have an understanding of, and always act within, the statutory frameworks which set out their professional duties and responsibilities.

(DfE 2011c: 8)

You will also already know that values are inherent in choices, and may be clear-cut in some situations but conflicting in others. One way of understanding your own values is to consider how you would react in situations in which different values make conflicting demands.

Task 2.2

Consider each of the following scenarios and think about how you would respond in each. What are the values that might drive you to act in a particular way?

Scenario 1
Your patience and tolerance have been tested for some months by a child in a challenging Year 9 class that you teach. His behaviour has been linked to a very dislocated home life and he is a fairly recent arrival in the locality. The special educational needs coordinator (SENCo) has established an Individual Behaviour Plan, but you know that an external assessment of his needs will not happen soon. His behaviour continues to be so disruptive to the class that parents of other children have complained that their children's education is being adversely affected by his presence in your class.

Scenario 2
In a tutorial, one of the Year 9 girls in your tutor group tells you that she is planning to leave school at the end of Year 12 because her parents think that further education is not appropriate for girls.

Scenario 3
One of your Year 11 tutor group asks to speak to you in private and complains to you that the class is, as she puts it, being bullied by another teacher. She says that they have been intimidated into staying at lunchtimes and after school to work on their coursework assignments, and that some pupils have been 'forced' to choose the subject for A level.

Scenario 4
Three Year 9 pupils have just been admitted to the school having recently arrived in the country as asylum seekers. Their education in their home country has been severely disrupted by conflict for many years and these pupils, as well as speaking very little English, are barely literate in their first language. For them to make any progress, they need a teacher to work exclusively with them full time. The funding received by the school to support these pupils does not cover this expense.

Scenario 5
You are working as a support teacher in a colleague's mixed-ability class. Part of your role is to support differentiation in the lesson and you spend time with the highest and lowest attainers in the group. At the end of the lesson, the class teacher asks you to spend more time in the next lesson with a particular boy who is one of the highest attainers in the class because 'after all, he's the one who will be contributing most to my pension in a few years' time'.

Depending on your view of the purpose of schools, you may have professional values additional to those identified in the Standards and you will certainly place more emphasis on some than on others. You will want to work in schools that generally have values that match your own. How will you know? Nothing in a school is value-free. You can get some sense of a school's collective values by reading what they say about themselves – the school's aims as laid out in their prospectus, for example. But you will also want to look, for example, at how resources are allocated, how decisions are made, how pupils and staff are valued and rewarded, and how pupils and staff relate to each other outside lessons.

So when you work in a school you will want to achieve a match. Student teachers often express a desire to work in a 'good school'. But how will you define a good school? You may want to work in a faith school or a selective school. You may want to work in a comprehensive school with strong expertise in special educational needs (SEN). You will want to work in a school where the teaching methods, content, and organization most fit your own professional views about achieving your aims (why are you becoming a teacher?). Your aims will be the result of your values. While you might want to work in a school where the way you dress, speak, and relate to pupils inside and outside the classroom matches the values of that school, this is not always possible.

Schools, by their nature, are places where individuals' exploration, development, and expression of their own values need to be tested against, and tempered by, their membership of a structured community. And this is as true of the teachers as it is of the pupils. Becoming a teacher may mean setting aside some of your personal values in favour of those of the community. How will you react if the school does things that conflict with your values? Even if you were to see yourself as just an employee, nothing you do or say as a teacher is value-free.

So the last question is: What is not for sale in your professional life? If you were to be, in Tim Brighouse's exhortation (*Times Educational Supplement*, 21 February 2003), 'lovingly disobedient', on what matters would you be prepared to disobey 'lovingly'?

2.3   Teachers' legal responsibilities

There is a great deal of legislation relating to teachers' work and it changes constantly. There were more Acts of Parliament between 1990 and 2012 than in the previous fifty years. Legislation reflects changing government policy. The autonomous nature of schools, their need to compete in a quasi-market, and the new statutory framework are all reflected in the legislation. The new Teachers' Standards (DfE 2011c), which will come into effect in September 2012, apply to all members of the teaching profession. If you are completing a Post Graduate Certificate in Education (PGCE) programme, you will be assessed against the Standards that are consistent with the level that can be reasonably expected at that stage of your training. Once you have completed your training and induction, other Standards will be used to assess performance.

With such a vast amount of legislation affecting your work as a teacher, you cannot be expected to know all the details of the laws that apply to you. There are areas that you need to know about, there are areas that you need to have an overview of, and there are areas where you will need to know where to get some advice from. What this section does is to explain the types of documents related to legal requirements that are published by the government, to outline the main areas of legislation that affect teachers specifically, and to discuss some of the issues involved in the interpretation of the law.

First you need to understand the difference between primary legislation, secondary legislation, guidance (or circulars), codes of practice, and case law:

- *Primary legislation* comprises Acts of Parliament.
- *Secondary legislation* includes regulations, statutory instruments, and orders made by the Secretary of State under powers invested in him or her by primary legislation. The Education Reform Act 1988, for example, gave the Secretary of State no less than 200 powers to make statutory regulations and orders.

- *Departmental guidance and circulars* come from the DfE. Up to 2001, the name for these documents was 'circulars' and they were numbered and dated. For example, Circular 4/98, which set out arrangements for teacher training, was the fourth circular issued by the DfEE in 1998. This numbering system was dropped by the department in 2002. These circulars, now called guidance, give advice on the meaning and implementation of specific Acts. They do not have the force of law and occasionally the courts find that the Department has given incorrect advice on an Act.

- *Codes of practice* are also issued for guidance. Although they do not have the force of law, codes of practice are similar to the Highway Code in that, while breach of a code is not in itself an offence, it may be used as evidence of negligence in a civil action; for example, if good practice advice in a code on a health and safety issue has been ignored and there has been an accident. The Secretary of State often has a duty to consult widely with the appropriate bodies such as local authorities and the teachers' professional associations before promulgating a code of practice.

- *Common law* is the interpretation of the law through cases in the courts.

In most areas, the primary and secondary legislation gives only the barest outline of what teachers and schools need to do, and what will be of most interest to you are the codes of practice and guidance that help you to make decisions and put the law into practice in your own situation. However, you need to be aware of some of the most important Acts that govern aspects of your work.

The Children Act 1989 sets out teachers' responsibilities to protect children from harm. This is a very wide-ranging piece of legislation and it is supported by a great deal of guidance. Among the most important topics in this guidance is the recognition of child abuse. Schools are required to designate a member of staff to liaise between the school and other agencies in cases of suspected child abuse (see Chapter 20). Before you begin work in a school, you will need to prioritize finding out who this member of staff is and what systems operate within the school for the communication of concerns.

The Health and Safety at Work Act 1974 sets the basic framework for health and safety both of pupils and staff. You will need to familiarize yourself with the requirements both of the Act itself and of the particular policy of the school in which you work.

A number of pieces of primary legislation govern a school's and teachers' responsibilities in terms of inclusion. The Race Relations Act 1976 and Race Relations (Amendment) Act 2000, the Sex Discrimination Act 1975, the Disability and Discrimination Act 1995, and the Special Educational Needs and Disability Act 2001 all cover very complex areas of provision and are discussed in the appropriate chapters in Section 4 of this book.

An area of law that frequently concerns new teachers is that which relates to pupil behaviour and discipline, in particular the physical restraint of pupils. There are a number of relevant pieces of legislation. The School Standards and Framework Act 1998 requires schools to have a behaviour policy and individual teachers need to work within that policy. The Human Rights Act 1998 requires that treatment of pupils should not be inhuman or degrading. The Education Act 1997 gives more detailed information about the legality of keeping pupils in detention after school and of the use of physical restraint. It gives guidance on what is meant by the use of 'reasonable force' and in what circumstances this might be deemed necessary.

You will obtain more detail about the law in each of these areas from the *Bristol Guide* (Document Summary Service 2011) listed under Further Reading, and from the teaching unions, which regularly publish updated guides to teachers' legal responsibilities. These are available direct from the unions or from their websites, listed in the webliography.

One area of the law that is especially open to legal interpretation is teachers' 'duty of care'. Teachers have a common law duty of care towards their pupils resulting from their position *in loco parentis* – in the place of the parent. This means that they are required to care for their pupils as a 'reasonable parent' would. There is no legal interpretation of this and judgments are based on the large amount of case law that has built up over time.

It is impossible to lay down hard and fast rules for every circumstance. A teacher must take the same degree of care that a reasonably careful parent would of their own children, taking account of the number of children in the class and the nature of those children. Regard must be paid to the likelihood of accidents in particular situations, such as in science experiments. Older children can be allowed more freedom and discretion providing that the pupils are in a well-ordered environment.

Task 2.3

Here are two contrasting examples in recent leading cases. In each case, try to decide whether you think the school would be considered liable and what aspects of the situation might have been taken into consideration in coming to these judgments.

During a lesson, an 8-year-old boy is excused to go to the toilet. He slides down the banisters and falls onto the floor below, injuring himself. Discipline in the school was good and there had been no similar accident (*Gough v Upshire Primary School,* 2001).

A 15-year-old boy is in the playground five minutes before school and is struck in the face by a heavy leather football. There had been similar incidents before. Heavy leather footballs had been banned but no steps were taken to enforce the ban. There were thirty or forty members of staff in the staffroom but nobody patrolling the playground (*Kearn-Price v Kent County Council,* 2002).

The decisions made by the courts were that, in the second case, the school was liable, but in the first it was not. In coming to these decisions they would have considered first whether the danger was reasonably foreseeable. In the primary school there had been no previous instances of pupils sliding down the banisters and, even at 8 years old, the pupil could reasonably be trusted to walk through the school building unsupervised. At the secondary school, however, there had already been similar incidents and so the danger was foreseeable. The second key question is whether the school had taken preventive action that was reasonably practicable. It was thought impracticable to insist that a pupil be accompanied each time they leave the classroom, but not impracticable for staff to be on duty in the playground before school.

As a professional teacher, you will:

- work within the legislative framework;
- know that acting 'reasonably' is the legal cornerstone of all you do;
- know that your school will have guidelines and policies lodged within the legislative framework;
- know that you can gain advice within your school on general and specific matters;
- know that you can gain advice from your professional association. These associations are experts in the application of the law to teaching. They produce general guidelines on the law and specific publications on certain issues and can offer, in cases where it is necessary, specific and specialized legal advice.

The law covers every aspect of schools. It changes frequently and, at this stage in your professional life, you do not need to know all the details but you do need to know those areas that affect your daily working life. Most of all, you need to understand and carry out the school policies.

When you take up your first post, there are some fundamental things you can do:

- read the staff handbook. If it is not clear on something – detention, confiscating property, confidentiality, health and safety, off-site visits – ask to see the policy concerned, which has to be available to staff and parents;
- study the departmental handbook for the same reason;
- study the scheme of work (SoW) and the assessment and reporting procedures;
- make sure you are a member of a professional association and receive their legal publication for new teachers;
- find out at an early stage who the people are, apart from your head of department and head of year, who can provide advice. For example, who is the expert in the school on copyright, information and communications technology (ICT), teaching assistants, health and safety, learning mentors, child protection and SEN?

2.4   The role of school governors

Since the mid-1990s, the development of the roles and responsibilities of governors has quickened relentlessly. Since the Education Act 1988, which gave governing bodies additional representation and unprecedented freedoms, and the advent of

Local Management of Schools, governors' responsibilities and powers have been radically strengthened, largely at the expense of local authorities. These changes mean that it is the governors who strategically manage the central legislative framework for their school. The growth in governor training and support, and the number of national and local governor publications, indicate the burden on 350,000 governors nationally. An increase in central direction over the last twenty years, as reflected in the increase in primary and secondary legislation, for example in areas such as the curriculum and intervention in schools causing concern, has required governors to become involved in considerable detail previously left to head teachers.

The changes to school organization introduced by the Coalition government have led to a wide variation in the composition of governing bodies between different types of school (see Chapter 26). Broadly there are six types of governor (DfE 2011c):

Parent governors. Parents, including carers of pupils, are eligible to stand for election as governors. Parent governors are elected by other parents at the school. If insufficient parents stand for election, the governing body may appoint parents.

Staff governors. The head teacher is a staff governor by virtue of his or her office. Other staff, both teaching and support, may become governors as long as they are paid (volunteers do not qualify). Staff governors are elected by the school staff. Any election that is contested must be held by ballot.

Authority governors. Local authorities are encouraged to appoint high-calibre governors to schools that need the most support and to appoint candidates irrespective of any political affiliation or preference. Authorities may appoint minor authority representatives (e.g. district and parish councillors) as authority governors.

Community governors. Community governors are appointed by the governing body to represent community interests. They can be individuals who: (a) live or work in the community served by the school; (b) are committed to the good governance and success of the school even though they do not work or live close to it. The definition of community governor is wide-ranging. People from a business or professional background and minor authority representatives can be appointed as community governors.

Foundation and partnership governors. Foundation governors are appointed by the school's founding body, church or other organization named in the school's instrument of government. If the school has a religious character, the foundation governors must preserve and develop this. They must also ensure compliance with the trust deed, if there is one. If a foundation school has no foundation or equivalent body, the foundation governors are replaced by partnership governors appointed by the governing body after a nomination process.

Sponsor governors. Sponsor governors are appointed by the governing body. They may be individuals who: (a) provide substantial assistance to the school, financially or in kind; (b) provide services to the school. If the governing body wants to appoint sponsor governors, it must seek nominations from the sponsor(s). The governing body can appoint a maximum of two persons as sponsor governors.

You need to be aware of the type of school you are working in to ensure you understand the composition of your particular governing body. There are also frequent policy changes in this area and the DfE website (www.education.gov.uk/schools/leadership/governance/becomingagovernor/types) provides useful updates.

The key responsibility of governing bodies is to provide a strategic overview for the school's development, albeit within the framework of national policy and guidelines. They have overall responsibility for the budgetary, staffing, curriculum, and disciplinary frameworks within which staff work. Although their powers are wide, they are constrained by legislative and policy frameworks. Nonetheless, their responsibilities are extensive and most governing bodies will have constructed an elaborate committee structure to discharge their formal responsibilities. Governing bodies typically work through curriculum sub-committees, which have responsibility for the development, quality, coherence, and assessment of the curriculum, a finance sub-committee, which sets budget parameters and monitors spending, a personnel sub-committee, which oversees the school's staffing plan and appointments, and a premises committee, which oversees the school's site development plan. Other committees deal with exclusions, disciplinary hearings, and appeals. It should be clear from this list that governors often have to deal with sensitive, contentious, and difficult issues, such as grievance, discipline, and occasionally dismissal. Effective governing bodies depend on the commitment of their members to discharge their responsibilities and undergo continuous training to update themselves on legislative changes.

Governors are unpaid volunteers drawn as widely as possible from all sections of the community. Schools depend on their governors and good governors can be effective sources of support and expertise for their schools – many governors bring their own experience in business, industry, public service or the voluntary sector to bear on their role. Nonetheless, governors do not have day-to-day responsibility for the management of the school, or of individual staff or curriculum areas: these responsibilities rest with the head teacher and senior staff. Governors' roles are strategic rather than directly managerial. Whether governors have the time or the capacity for the detailed work now required of them is an issue that has not been seriously addressed by successive governments. Recruitment and retention of governors is a major focus of the work of local authorities. In some areas of the country, they are very hard to recruit. Recruitment of governors from minority communities is a particular issue.

As a new teacher, you will have a different perspective on the governing body. You may see the big picture of their roles as removed from the reality of your life. They do, however, have formal and informal connections – though some of them only potential connections – with you. For example:

- they have responsibilities to you as a newly qualified teacher (NQT); they are required to satisfy themselves that your induction is being conducted properly so that you are being given every opportunity to succeed;

- at least one governor may be involved with your appointment;
- they will establish policies and procedures that will have implications for you as a member of staff;
- one of the governors will be identified as a 'link governor' for your department and may be quite closely involved in the department's strategic development.

When you go into school, find out what type of school you are in and ask for a list of the governors by category. Ask to see agendas and minutes of the meetings of the governing body. Also ask to talk to one of the teacher governors about the work of the governors in your school and how you are represented at meetings.

Most governors are very supportive of the school they serve and act fairly towards the school and the staff. They show a genuine interest in the workings of the school and are keen for it to succeed. New teachers can feel vulnerable if they are teaching the child of a governor, or if a governor comes to spend time in their department, but you should remember that in the vast majority of cases the governors are there to play a positive, supporting role.

2.5 Recommendations for further reading and webliography

Department for Education (DfE) (2010) *Guide to the Law for School Governors*. Available online at: http://www.education.gov.uk/schools/leadership/governance/ guidetothelaw.
Department for Education (DfE) (2011) *Teachers' Standards*. London: HMSO. Available online at: www.education.gov.uk.
Document Summary Service (2011) *Professional Responsibilities and Statutory Frameworks for Teachers and Others in Schools: The Bristol Guide*. Bristol: University of Bristol Graduate School of Education.

Teaching union websites
www.atl.org.uk (The Association of Teachers and Lecturers)
www.nasuwt.org.uk (The National Association of Schoolmasters and Union of Women Teachers)
www.professionalteachers.org/ (The Professional Association of Teachers)
www.teachers.org.uk/ (The National Union of Teachers)

3

Key issues, opportunities and challenges for new teachers
Val Brooks

3.1 Introduction

Governments around the world are involved in the business of major educational reform, poring over international comparative data to identify those features of high-performing education systems that appear to explain their success. Even though there are few certainties about the ability of educational policy to secure higher performance from the educational system, the arguments for investment in teachers and teaching remain powerful and compelling. While the educational challenges are considerable, and the route to reform is complex, the potential of individual teachers to influence pupil and school performance is unquestionable. It has been shown consistently that the motivation of teachers and the quality of teaching that takes place in classrooms have a direct impact on school and pupil performance (Muijs and Reynolds 2002). In short, whatever else is disputed, teachers continue to make a significant difference to the life chances of young people.

Although the work of teachers is acknowledged to be socially and economically important, it is also intellectually and ethically complex. Teaching is fundamentally about upholding certain key values: what to teach; how to deploy resources; what constitutes success; how to engage and to relate to young people. Teaching is not just about teaching a subject, having good classroom control or obtaining good examination results. There are wider moral and social purposes. As Day (1999: 11) notes: 'Teachers cannot limit their work to the classroom only, leaving the larger setting and purposes of schooling to be determined by others. They must take active responsibility for the goals to which they are committed, and for the social setting in which these goals may prosper'.

In summary, as you learn to teach you will be engaged in thinking about the moral, ethical, political and instrumental issues that will impact on your everyday practice, on your processes of decision-making and on the pupils you teach. Reflection of this kind is important to all professionals in order to exercise responsibility and accountability for the decisions that they make. Being a teacher is more than demonstrating a narrow set of classroom skills or competences. It is about engaging more broadly with the many issues that impact on pupils' attainment and learning. As you get to know your pupils and the community in which they live, you will inevitably be aware of a range of social, political and economic influences that affect them and their potential to learn. Schools do not exist in isolation from the community they serve; neither do teachers. Consequently, as a teacher, you will need to engage with that wider community and the issues that influence it either directly or indirectly.

This chapter explores some of the opportunities and challenges facing new teachers today. It is not possible to talk about what teaching is like, when the experience of teaching varies so widely between schools, localities and across careers. Moreover, the pace of educational change is such that it is always dangerous to try to capture a contemporary picture of teaching. By the time you read this book, there will be new initiatives, strategies, and expectations that are not reflected in these pages. Moreover, any change in education may prove to be an opportunity or a challenge, depending on how it is implemented, funded, supported and evaluated. It is perhaps wiser to think about the opportunities and challenges inherent in some of the facets of teaching today that look set to endure.

As a qualified teacher you will be part of an increasingly diverse school workforce. You will be working alongside a wide range of others professionals who support children's welfare and learning. Together with other agencies of support for young people, teaching has been restructured or remodelled (see Chapters 7, 20, and 21). Most importantly, this includes para-professional support in the shape of teaching assistants. Teachers in the twenty-first century are supported by a new layer of professionals who, although not qualified to teach, have taken an increasing role in supporting classroom teaching. Teachers are also expected to work more closely with other professions that contribute to children's wellbeing, in health and social care for instance.

The increased expectation that teachers will take responsibility for their own continuous learning and contribute to the learning of colleagues is evident, for example, in the introduction of teaching schools in 2011. Teachers today are subject to multiple accountabilities, as individuals, as staff of their employing institutions, and as members of a profession subject to a professional accreditiation body, the Teaching Agency. Some of the opportunities and challenges of these dimensions of teaching today are explored in this chapter following an initial discussion of what is meant by teacher professionalism. By the end of this chapter, you should:

- recognize that initial teacher training (ITT) represents the opening phase in a process of continuing professional development (CPD);
- understand how and why the teaching profession has been remodelled.

3.2   Teaching as a new professionalism?

Historically, specific characteristics have distinguished 'professions' from other occupational sectors. These have frequently include: registration with a self-governing professional body; the definition of entry standards and standards of accomplishment; the specification of expectations regarding competence and conduct; and a commitment to use and develop a body of complex specialist knowledge in the client interest. Teaching shares many but not all of the characteristics of established 'professions' and would make a strong claim to 'professionalism' in the broader sense of undertaking work in a manner that is demonstrably competent and diligent. However, it might be argued that teaching should forge a new, fit-for-purpose definition of professionalism, to avoid the allegations of self-interest and elitism that have been levelled at some established 'professions', and to articulate values that place the learner at the heart of professional practice. Teaching also needs to define 'professionalism' in a way that takes account of the wide range of people involved in teaching, not all of whom will be qualified, registered teachers.

Teachers campaigned for over a century for the introduction of an independent body to represent their profession similar to that enjoyed by established professions such as medicine and law. The General Teaching Council for England (GTCE) finally started work in 2000 as the independent professional body for teaching in England. It is one of numerous quangos that have been abolished as part of economic austerity measures introduced by the Conservative/Liberal Democrat coalition government. Although short-lived, the GTCE contributed to teacher professionalism by developing a Code of Professional Practice, advising the government on revisions to the framework of standards for teaching and hearing cases related to professional conduct and competence. Some of its functions will be taken on by a new Teaching Agency due to take office in 2012.

Task 3.1

Note down your ideas about the characteristics of good professional practice. Now try to organize them into categories with sub-headings. Compare your own list with the Standards for Qualified Teacher Status (http://www.education. gov.uk/). To what extent are they similar? How do they differ?

3.3 An increasingly diverse workforce

As noted above, the current climate is one in which the idea of teaching and who teaches is evolving and changing, with a particular emphasis on the role of adults other than teachers within schools. It could be argued that there has always been a range of people involved in the processes of teaching and learning in schools who do not have qualified teacher status (QTS). These include unqualified instructors, often meeting a particular curricular need, such as language assistants or dance tutors. In addition, schools have employed staff to support the learning of particular groups of pupils, such as those with special needs or English as an additional language (EAL), and staff such as technicians and librarians may play an indirect role in learning in some schools, but a very direct role in others. The role of the teaching assistant has developed considerably in the last few years from performing lower-order practical tasks in the classroom to undertaking unmistakably pedagogical work with individuals or groups of pupils. It is also recognized that training must address the needs of both teachers and their assistants, and there is now a coherent career and qualifications structure for teaching assistants and other school support staff.

If there have always been people without QTS involved in teaching, legislation has made more radical changes in the composition of the school workforce possible. For instance, in 2006 secondary schools were required to redefine their staffing structures in such a way that responsibility allowances for qualified teachers were awarded only for work related closely to teaching and learning and not for administrative tasks, such as supervising external examination entries. These tasks were to be undertaken by administrators rather than teachers. In addition, higher level teaching assistants (HLTAs) now receive training in areas of the 'QTS curriculum' and are able, for example, to cover classes under the supervision of a qualified teacher. Non-teaching staff are also playing an increasing role in the provision of pastoral care, particularly in the case of vulnerable children who are at risk of social (and school) exclusion (Edwards et al. 2010).

Task 3.2

Compile a list of the other adults who work in schools.

Look at the following school staff lists to get a sense of the range of other adults employed: http://www.banbury.oxon.sch.uk/wholeschool/contacts/staff.php
http://www.stjosephs.uk.net/New/Staff.htm

Changing aspirations for schooling are the third factor that suggests a need for new configurations of staff. Parents arriving at the gates of their child's school in the middle of the previous century may have been greeted with a notice declaring, 'No parents beyond this point'! The message of exclusion contained within such notices contrasts starkly with the current policy of extended schools. Extended schools are open for longer than a traditional school day and provide a core offer of extended services, including: wraparound childcare (in primary schools); parenting and family support; a variety of out-of-school activities such as breakfast clubs, after-school clubs, sporting, and musical activities; and community use of adult and family learning plus information and communications technology (ICT). These schools are also expected to make an important contribution to the protection and support of children at risk of harm, disaffection, and under-achievement, in conjunction with other professions that play a role in the lives of young people (see Chapter 20). Swift and easy referrals to specialist services are expected. Some schools have responded by increasing provision from the fields of social work, counseling, and psychology, perhaps having an enhanced presence of other professionals on the school site. A multi-agency approach to supporting young people could include family services co-located on school premises.

Task 3.3

Use Appendix A from the following report to produce a list of the different professional groups that may be encountered by teachers working in extended schools (available at http://eprints.uwe.ac.uk/12563/).

Davies, J., Ryan, J., Tarr, J., Last, K., Kushner, S. and Rose, R. (2009) *Preparing Teachers for Management and Leadership of Multi-agency Assessment of Vulnerability: Building Capacity in ITT, TDA. Project Report.* Bristol: Teacher Development Agency.

As a new teacher you are entering the profession at a time when the boundaries between teachers and non-teachers are less clear than ever before. New teachers have every right to feel that their professional status is hard won, and that they are uniquely qualified to undertake certain teaching tasks. Conversely, they may feel that the role requires them to undertake too many activities that do not require the time of a qualified teacher, and that they could deploy their growing expertise more effectively if more support was available from other sorts of staff.

New teachers may be better prepared than some of their experienced colleagues for working with other adults within and beyond the classroom, as there are QTS standards relating to workforce diversification. However, you may find the business of deploying older or more experienced support staff challenging (see Chapter 21). Moreover, research (e.g. Clegg and McNulty 2002; Milbourne et al. 2003; Tett et al. 2003) suggests that while the opportunity to collaborate with other children's services has the potential to improve the lot of children, in practice working with other professional groups is often a tricky business. Other professions may operate within an unfamiliar culture characterized by a shared language and priorities that differ from those in schools. Their management systems, goals and working practices may also be incompatible. Thus, although 'joined-up' working involving multi-agency teams is essential in supporting some young people, the training, time and effort required to secure effective collaboration should not be under-estimated.

Diversification of the school workforce may turn out to be an opportunity for new teachers only if certain conditions are met. Clarity about where teaching responsibilities lie will be important, as will the development of new and effective models of collaborative working. However, if you as a teacher can spend less time on administrative and practical tasks, and more time on planning, reflection and collaboration, pupil learning will benefit.

3.4 Career-long professional development

Teaching is by far the largest area of graduate recruitment in the UK. Graduate recruiters point to the increasing sophistication with which graduates assess various career options. Salary and status continue to be significant, but other qualitative factors such as work–life balance and development opportunities are also significant. New entrants to the profession have many reasons for choosing teaching, but CPD is an important factor in retaining the best teachers within the profession.

The international research literature has consistently shown that teachers' professional development is an essential component of successful school-level change and development (Day 1999). It has confirmed that where teachers are able to reflect, access new ideas, experiment and share experiences within school cultures and with leaders who encourage appropriate levels of challenge and support, there is greater potential for school and classroom improvement. Improving schools invest in the development of their staff and create opportunities for teachers to collaborate and to share best practice (Harris 2002). Evidence also suggests that attention to teacher learning can impact directly on improvements in pupil learning and achievement. Where teachers have clear professional identities and have intrinsic as well as extrinsic rewards for their work, they are more satisfied and committed to their work. In addition, where teachers are able to expand and develop their own teaching repertoires, they are more likely to provide an increased range of learning opportunities for pupils (Joyce et al. 1998). In short, the research literature demonstrates that CPD has a positive impact on curriculum and pedagogy, as well as teachers' sense of commitment and their relationships with pupils (Muijs et al. 2004).

Continuing professional development is increasingly seen, then, as a key part of the career development of all professionals but particularly teachers. The concept is often left ill-defined, however, being in many cases conflated with the related concepts of in-service training and on-the-job learning. Both are more limited than CPD, as CPD can encompass a wide variety of approaches and teaching and learning styles in a variety of settings (inside or outside of the workplace). Continuing professional development is also distinguishable from lifelong learning, which is a broader concept in that it can include all sorts of learning, whereas CPD is seen as related to people's professional identities and roles and the goals of the organization they are working for (Galloway 2000).

In this chapter, Day's (1999: 4) definition of CPD is used, which encompasses formal and informal learning: 'Professional development consists of all natural learning experiences and those conscious and planned activities which are intended to be of direct or indirect benefit to the individual, group or school, which contribute, through these, to the quality of education in the classroom'.

One of the most striking findings from research into school improvement is that improving schools are marked by constant interchange and professional dialogue at both a formal and informal level (Harris 2002). Similarly, schools that are improving invest in professional development and are able to engage teachers in various forms of professional learning. It has long been argued that creating a collaborative professional learning environment for teachers is the single most important factor for successful school improvement and the first order of business for those seeking to enhance the effectiveness of teaching and learning (Little 1993). A particularly significant shift in the school improvement field in the last few years has been the burgeoning of network initiatives where teachers work closely together. As Hargreaves (2003: 9) proposed:

A network increases the pool of ideas on which any member can draw and as one idea or practice is transferred, the inevitable process of adaptation and adjustment to different conditions is rich in potential for the practice to be incrementally improved by the recipient and then fed back to the donor in a virtuous circle of innovation and improvement. In other words, the networks extend and enlarge the communities of practice with enormous potential benefits.

Consequently, it would seem imperative that teachers engage in collaborative forms of CPD that meet both the needs of individual teachers and the pupils they teach.

There are certainly opportunities and challenges associated with gaining access to professional development in teaching. In theory, it is inconceivable that a profession dedicated to promoting learning should not itself be a learning profession. In practice, it is fair to say that teachers' access to professional learning is still too variable, and too dependent on factors such as availability of funding and the priority attached to professional development by individual school leaders. There is an expectation that teachers will continue to learn and develop beyond their initial training, which is captured in professional standards for new and experienced teachers. Nevertheless, this expectation is most likely to be met in a supportive environment. This might mean one in which teachers are supported to develop evaluative skills and to talk about teaching and learning; where time is made for observation, reflection and feedback; where teachers have access to research and evidence and the skills to interpret them accurately and draw on them in their practice; where performance management genuinely facilitates teachers' identification of their own development needs as well as allowing managers to pursue their needs of staff.

There are many schools with these characteristics, but it is possible for new teachers to find themselves in schools that do not attach sufficient importance to creating a culture that supports teachers' own continual learning. New teachers are perhaps of particular value to these schools because they come to teaching with expectations with regard to their own development. They may be joining schools in which expectations among experienced teachers are similarly buoyant, or they may encounter cultures where expectation has been dampened by thwarted aspirations or poor CPD experiences. It is essential for the health of the profession that new entrants retain high expectations in this area. If some schools are better at meeting such expectations than others, there are always other avenues beyond the school to explore. Local authorities, unions and subject or specialist associations may offer professional development opportunities, and a school might be part of a networked learning community. Many ITT courses now award credits at Masters level offering smooth progression from ITT to Masters qualifications and beyond to research degrees. Thus, new entrants should also be aware of professional development opportunities offered for qualified teachers by their ITT provider or other local higher education institution. For instance, it may be possible for projects completed during ITT to count towards other awards. Local schools may have been designated to play a role in the development of teachers beyond their own workforce, such as through the Teaching Schools initiative.

The government is more attuned today to teachers' CPD needs than it has been in the past. However, even the best school leaders who are committed to CPD may feel pressure to raid the CPD budget when finances are tight, if the alternative might be to increase class sizes or leave unfilled posts vacant. But most school leaders see professional development as an investment that will not only improve the quality of teaching and pupil learning, but also help to retain and motivate staff.

An assessment of CPD provision needs to consider the quality of the learning as well as the extent of teachers' access to it. The term 'continuing professional development' may cover a diverse range of experiences from the traditional notion of a training day or a course, to participation in themed classroom observations, to touching base each week with a mentor. The Teacher Learning Academy (TLA; see Chapter 1) offers professional recognition and academic accreditation for those who seek it for teacher learning in a range of forms, placing a particular emphasis on collaborative approaches.

The work of the GTCE highlighted the benefits of peer development – teachers' involvement in the learning of their colleagues. New entrants to teaching will be acutely aware of learning from colleagues; they may be less aware of the extent to which experienced colleagues are learning from them. There will be topics on which students and newly qualified teachers (NQTs) have up-to-date knowledge of benefit to serving teachers, and new teachers will bring a fresh gaze to school practice. Most importantly, working alongside new entrants encourages experienced teachers to revisit and articulate their own pedagogy – to be confident and clear about the why and the how of teaching.

When applying for first teaching posts, one of the factors to take into consideration is opportunities for CPD available through the school, local authority, a teaching school or nearby higher education institution. This might be achieved by requesting a copy of the staff development policy, talking to the CPD coordinator, or asking about the school's approach to in-service training. Student teachers can prepare for this task by finding out about CPD in their placement schools.

Increasing attention is being given to teachers' CPD, starting with an induction period to which NQTs are entitled. The statutory induction period was introduced in 1999 to provide resources for CPD and designated non-contact time. New teachers must pass induction standards at the end of the period, usually a year, to maintain their qualified teacher status. To help them achieve this, they are currently entitled to a reduced timetable, the support of an induction tutor and a programme of observation and feedback on their teaching. At the time of writing, proposed changes to the induction regulations are the subject of consultation. It is worth becoming familiar with the revised induction arrangements before starting the induction period so as to be able to take early action if they are not properly in place. Consult the DfE or Teaching Agency website for details of the roles and responsibilities associated with induction. One of the most important ways of making this period of development effective is to make meaningful use of the Career Entry and Development Profile (CEDP), or any alternative bridging documentation that replaces the CEDP. The CEDP is designed to help you to think about your professional development at key points towards the end of ITT and during induction, thereby supporting the transition between the two, as well as preparing the way for the next phase of professional development.

Initial teacher training is an intensive undertaking and NQTs could be forgiven for breathing a sigh of relief when they gain QTS, and consider their development over for a while. It may be a challenge to think of induction as anything other than a further hurdle to jump. Nevertheless, in reality ITT and induction represent consecutive phases of development. Although there are expectations placed on NQTs undertaking induction, it may be helpful to think of induction as an entitlement to time, resources and support to consolidate and enhance professional practice.

3.5 Multiple accountabilities

New teachers are entering the profession at a time of debate about the nature and extent of accountability. This is not a debate unique to teaching but common to all professions. It is customary for debates about accountability to suggest that the professions were once subject to too little accountability and that the pendulum has now swung so far in the other direction that processes of accountability can impede and curtail the activity for which people are being held to account (see, for example, O'Neill 2002).

Teaching takes place in a complex network of accountability. Teachers are individually held to account through performance management, which is the responsibility of their line manager working within a framework set by school policy. Ofsted inspection also passes judgement on the quality of teaching. Schools are expected to instigate their own processes of self-evaluation rather than relying solely on external judgements about the quality of their work, and teaching is scrutinized as part of these processes. Local authorities may also operate quasi-inspectoral processes, often in preparation for or in the wake of Ofsted inspections. Head teachers are accountable to school governing bodies and, through them, to stakeholders in the school. Finally, teachers are accountable to a professional body, the Teaching Agency. In addition to these structural accountabilities, teachers are acutely aware of feeling accountable or responsible to pupils, parents and colleagues. They may also describe more abstract but no less binding loyalties to, for example, their subject or their locality.

Making sense of complex accountabilities is a challenge for new teachers, and for their more experienced colleagues. Teachers' representative bodies seek a more streamlined, less labour-intensive system of accountability with an emphasis on supporting improvement. New entrants to teaching may find it helpful to think of accountability as giving an account of one's practice. This is a process with which trainees and NQTs are very familiar – it forms an important part of their formative professional learning. It is no less important for seasoned practitioners to be able to account for the multiple decisions taken while teaching – about curriculum content and organization, pedagogy, classroom organization, management and assessment. Teachers' best defence of their practice is an articulate, evidence-informed account of it, and the evidence on which teachers can draw is improving all of the time. Within the field of educational research there is a stronger emphasis on accessibility and, where appropriate, usability of research by practitioners and policy-makers; and schools' interrogation of pupil and school level data is increasingly sophisticated (see Chapters 10 and 15). There is an emphasis on teachers being central to the process of school development and reform.

In conclusion, although you are entering teaching during a period of economic austerity and extensive change, teaching has always been a dynamic profession that can reward its members with a rich variety of experiences, within and beyond the classroom and school. Notwithstanding the importance for each generation of pupils and teachers of their own unique social, political and economic context, successive generations of pupils have reason to be grateful for teachers' ability to turn challenges into opportunities – to make extraordinary things happen without the benefit of an ideal environment, resources or policy frameworks.

3.6 Recommendations for further reading and webliography

Earley, P. and Porritt, V. (eds.) (2010) *Effective Practices in Continuing Professional Development: Lessons from Schools*. London: Institute of Education.

Hopkins, D. and Harris, A. (2001) *Creating the Conditions for Teaching and Learning: A Handbook of Staff Development Activities*. London: David Fulton.

Joyce, B., Calhoun, E. and Hopkins, D. (1998) *Models of Teaching: Tools for Learning*. Buckingham: Open University Press.

Muijs, R.D. and Reynolds, D. (2010) *Effective Teaching: Evidence and Practice*. London: Sage.

Websites

Teaching Agency website (to be announced)

Teacher Learning Academy website (to be announced)

SECTION 2
Core professional competences

4

Understanding how pupils learn: theories of learning and intelligence
Daniel Muijs

4.1 Introduction

In this chapter, we will discuss the main theories on how children learn. This is, of course, an important issue in teaching, as to be effective we need to try and teach in a way that reinforces how people naturally learn. Theories of learning and intelligence are many and diverse, and we cannot look at all existing theories in one chapter. What we will do instead is to focus on some of the theories that have been most influential in education over the years.

By the end of this chapter you should:

- know about the main theories on how pupils learn:
  - behaviourism
  - Piagetian and Vygotskian learning theories
  - socio-cultural theories of learning
  - IQ theory
  - the theory of multiple intelligences
  - cognitive and brain research;
- be able to make judgements on the relevance of these different theories to teaching and learning;
- be able to reflect on the extent to which these theories contradict or build upon one another.

4.2 Behaviourism

The first major theory of learning we will discuss is behaviourism, which was developed in the 1920s and 1930s by psychologists that included Skinner, Pavlov, and Thorndike. While somewhat outdated now, this theory still has a strong influence on educational practice, if not theory.

Behavioural learning theory emphasizes change in behaviour as the main outcome of the learning process. Behavioural theorists concentrate on directly observable phenomena using a scientific method borrowed from the natural sciences. The most radical behaviourists, such as B.F. Skinner, considered all study of non-observable behaviour ('mentalism') to be unscientific (Hilgard 1995; O'Donohue and Ferguson 2001). In the later twentieth century, however, researchers and psychologists in the behaviourist tradition, such as Bandura (1985), expanded their view of learning to include expectations, thoughts, motivation, and beliefs. Learning, according to behaviourists, is something people do in response to external stimuli. This was an important change to previous models, which had stressed consciousness and introspection, and had not produced many generalizable findings about how people learn.

As I mentioned above, behaviourists imitated methods used in the natural sciences, especially experiments conducted with animals like rats and dogs as well as humans. This is because, being against 'mentalism', behaviourists think that it is largely external factors that cause our behaviour. The basic mechanism through which this happens is conditioning. According to behaviourists, there are two different types of conditioning:

Classic conditioning occurs when a natural reflex responds to a stimulus. An example of this comes from another behaviourist's (i.e. Pavlov) experiments with dogs. To process food, dogs need to salivate when they eat. As all dog owners will know, what happens is that dogs will start to salivate even before eating, as soon as they have smelt or seen food. So, the external stimulus of food will cause the dog to salivate. It has become a habit: that is the response that is conditioned. When confronted with particular stimuli, people as well as animals will produce a specific response.

Behavioural or operant conditioning occurs when a response to a stimulus is reinforced. Basically, operant conditioning is a simple feedback system: if a reward or reinforcement follows the response to a stimulus, then the response becomes more probable in the future. For example, if every time a pupil behaves well in class they get a reward, they are likely to behave well next time. (Note that while animal behaviour follows reliably from a stimulus, this is not so certain among humans.)

Rewards and punishments are therefore an important part of behaviourist learning theory. Initial experiments with dogs and rats convinced the behaviourists of the importance of the use of rewards and punishments to elicit certain desired behaviours, such as pushing a lever, in these animals. Over ensuing decades these findings were further tested and refined with humans, and became highly influential in education. Pleasurable consequences, or *reinforcers*, strengthen behaviour, while unpleasant consequences, or *punishers*, weaken behaviour. Behaviour is influenced by its consequences, but it is influenced by its antecedents as well, thus creating the A(ntecedents)–B(ehaviour)–C(onsequences) chain. Skinner's work concentrated mainly on the relationship between the latter two parts of the chain (Skinner 1974; O'Donohue and Ferguson 2001), and these findings still form the basis of many behaviour management systems in schools, as well as much of the research on effective teaching (e.g. Muijs and Reynolds 2003).

While this movement remains highly influential, behaviourism has come to be seen as far too limited and limiting to adequately capture the complexity of human learning and behaviours. The idea that learning occurs purely as a reaction to external stimuli has proved to be inadequate. Activities such as recognizing objects (this is a ball), sorting objects (this is a rugby ball, this is a football), and storing information are clearly 'mentalist' activities; they occur in the head. Although an external stimulus (perception of an object) is present, behaviourist theory cannot account for the information processing that occurs when we are confronted by stimuli. Behaviourism also cannot account for types of learning that occur without reinforcement; for example, the way that children pick up language patterns (grammar) cannot be explained using a behaviourist framework. Behaviourism also presents problems when the learner is confronted with new situations in which the mental stimuli they have learnt to respond to are not present. The fact that behaviourists do not study the memory in any meaningful way (they only talk about acquiring 'habits') is another major problem if we want to explain learning. If we want to really understand how people learn, we have to be 'mentalists' and look at what is going on inside the brain as well as measuring reactions to external stimuli.

Should we totally discount behaviourism? As mentioned above, behaviourism has been heavily criticized over the years. Much of this criticism is justified. Behaviourism is clearly too limited a theory of learning to account for how we actually learn. Not all the criticism is justified, however. Some of it seems to emanate from a dislike of the findings rather than a close look at the evidence. Behaviourism has little place for the role of free will and human individuality. This is never a popular view and, as we have seen, this determinism is clearly overdone in behaviourist theories. However, that does not mean that it is entirely inaccurate. While we always like to believe that we are entirely free, our behaviours can to an extent be predicted, in some cases by behaviourist models. That this is true is attested to by the continued usefulness of behaviourist methods in teaching, such as the use of rewards. Not liking certain research findings does not make them wrong, and it is not the job of research and science simply to tell us what we want to hear. Recently, it is fair to say that neobehaviourist theories have become popular among scientists looking at the role of evolution in the way we behave. If you read the work of Richard Dawkins (1989), for example, there are clear links with behaviourist psychology.

Task 4.1

Can you think of anything you can do or know that you have learnt in a way that conforms to behaviourist learning theory? Can you think of anything that you learnt in a way that clearly is not behaviourist? What does that tell you about behaviourist learning theories?

4.3 Piaget and Vygotsky

Jean Piaget: learning as qualitative change

As well as the behaviourists like Skinner and Watson, two other pioneering psychologists have had a continuing influence on how we view learning – Piaget and Vygotsky.

Jean Piaget was a Swiss psychologist, who started his important work on how children develop and learn before the Second World War. In contrast to the behaviourists, who developed most of their theories using laboratory experiments and rarely looked at the real-life behaviours of children, Piaget's theories were developed from observation of children.

What these observations taught him was that to understand how children think, one has to look at the qualitative development of their ability to solve problems. Cognitive development, in his view, is much more than the addition of new facts and ideas to an existing store of information. Rather, children's thinking changes qualitatively; the tools that children use to think change, leading children and adults, and indeed children at different stages of development, to possess a different view of the world. A child's reality is not the same as that of an adult (Piaget 2001).

According to Piaget, one of the main influences on children's cognitive development is what he termed *maturation*, the unfolding of biological changes that are genetically programmed into us. A second factor is *activity*. Increasing maturation leads to an increase in children's ability to act on their environment, and to learn from their actions. This learning in turn leads to an alteration of children's thought processes. A third factor in development is *social transmission*, learning from others. As children act on their environment, they also interact with others and can therefore learn from them to a differing degree depending on their developmental stage.

According to Piaget (2001), learning occurs in four stages:

The sensori-motor stage (0–2 years). A baby knows about the world through actions and sensory information. He or she learns to differentiate him or herself from the environment. The child begins to understand causality in time and space. The capacity to form internal mental representations emerges.

The pre-operational stage (2–7 years). In this stage, the child takes the first steps from action to thinking, by internalizing action. In the previous stage, the child's schemes were still completely tied to actions, which meant that they were of no use in recalling the past or in prediction. During the pre-operational stage, the child starts to be able to do this, by learning how to think symbolically. The ability to think in symbols remains limited at this stage, however, as the child can only think in one direction. Thinking backwards or reversing the steps of a task are difficult. Another innovation that starts to take place during this phase is the ability to understand conservation. This means that the child can now realize that the amount or number of something remains the same even if the arrangement or appearance of it is changed (for example, four dogs and four cats is the same amount). This remains difficult for children in this phase. Children in this phase still have great difficulty freeing themselves from their own perception of how the world appears. Children at this age are also very egocentric. They tend to see the world and the experiences of others from their own standpoint.

The concrete operational stage (7–12 years). The basic characteristics of this stage are: (1) the recognition of the logical stability of the physical world; (2) the realization that elements can be changed or transformed and still retain their original characteristics; and (3) the understanding that these changes can be reversed. Another important operation that is mastered at this stage is classification. Classification depends on a pupil's ability to focus on a single characteristic of objects and then to group the objects according to that single characteristic (e.g. if one gives a pupil a set of differently coloured and differently shaped pens, they will be able to pick out the round ones). Pupils can now also understand seriation, allowing them to construct a logical series in which A is less than B is less than C, and so on. At this stage the pupil has developed a logical and systematic way of thinking that is, however, still tied to physical reality. Overcoming this is the task of the next phase.

The formal operational stage (12+). In this stage, which is not reached by all people, all that is learned in previous stages remains in force but pupils are now able to see that a real, actually experienced situation is only one of several possible situations. For this to happen, we must be able to generate different possibilities for any given situation in a systematic way. Pupils are now able to imagine ideal, non-existing worlds. Another characteristic of this stage is adolescent egocentrism. Adolescents tend incessantly to analyse their own beliefs and attitudes, and often assume that everyone else shares their concerns and is in turn analysing them.

Piaget's theory has been hugely influential, but has been found wanting in a number of areas. His stages of learning are clearly too rigid. A number of studies have found that young children can acquire concrete operational thinking at an earlier age than Piaget proposed, and that they can think at higher levels than Piaget suggested, even to the propositional stage that Piaget believed only adolescents or adults could use. Piaget also underestimated the individual differences between children in how they develop, and the fact that some of these differences are due to the cultural and social background of the child. Piaget also did not take much notice of the way children can learn from others, seeing learning as largely dependent on their stage of development. Notwithstanding that, Piaget's theories have stood the test of time well, and are still a useful way of looking at children's development.

Vygotsky: the social side of learning

Vygotsky was a Russian psychologist, who worked at around the same time as Piaget (although he died younger) and was influenced by Piaget's work. During his lifetime he was not well known in the West, but after his death (in particular since the 1960s) he has become increasingly influential.

Vygotsky's main interest was the study of language development, which he believed develops separately from thought initially, but starts to overlap with thought more and more as the child grows up. According to Vygotsky, a non-overlapping part still remains later in life; some non-verbal thought and some non-conceptual speech remains even in adults (Vygotsky 1978; Moll 1992).

A major disagreement between Piaget and Vygotsky was that Vygotsky did not think that maturation in itself could make children achieve advanced thinking skills. Vygotsky, while seeing a role for maturation, believed that it was children's interaction with others through language that most strongly influenced the level of conceptual understanding they could reach (Vygostky 1978).

Vygotsky strongly believed that we can learn from others, both of the same age and of a higher age and developmental level. One of the main ways this operates is through *scaffolding* in the *zone of proximal development* (ZPD). This latter concept, one of Vygotsky's main contributions to learning theory, refers to the gap between what a person is able to do alone and what they can do with the help of someone more knowledgeable or skilled than themselves. It is here that the role of teachers, adults and peers comes to the fore in children's learning, in that they can help bring the child's knowledge to a higher level by intervening in the ZPD. This can be done by providing children's thoughts with so-called scaffolds, which, once the learning process is complete, are no longer needed by the child. Children are not all equally *educable* in this respect, some being able to learn more in the ZPD than others.

Thus, for Vygotsky, it is *cooperation* that lies at the basis of learning. It is *instruction*, formal and informal, performed by more knowledgeable others, such as parents, peers, grandparents or teachers, that is the main means of transmission of the knowledge of a particular culture. Knowledge for Vygotsky, as for Piaget, is embodied in actions and interactions with the environment (or culture), but unlike Piaget, Vygotsky stresses the importance of *interaction* with a living representative of the culture.

While Piaget has been criticized as being too strongly focused on developmental learning, Vygotsky's work is seen as suffering from the opposite problem. Vygostky wrote little about children's natural development and the relationship of that to their learning (Wertsch and Tulviste 1992). Vygotsky's theories are also in many ways rather general and overarching, and have not been fully worked out (that Vygotsky died at the age of 37 is one reason for this). Vygotsky's contribution lies mainly in his attention to the social aspects of learning, which clearly need complementing by what current research is teaching us about brain functions.

This view of learning as socially constructed strongly influenced the so-called constructivist theories that have followed since, and has influenced classroom practice. His ideas about pupils' learning in their ZPD have been influential in the development of collaborative learning programmes.

Task 4.2

How do you think the theories of Piaget and Vygotsky influence teaching? What can teachers do to take into account both Piagetian stages of learning and the importance of the ZPD?

4.4 Socio-cultural theories of learning

As we have seen above, Vygotsky emphasizes the social aspects of learning and the role played by others in our learning processes. This emphasis on social processes has recently been taken forward in the so-called socio-cultural theories of learning.

Socio-cultural theories of learning emphasize the ways in which we develop 'tools for learning' through our interaction with others (both teachers and other learners). An important element of socio-cultural theories is that learning encompasses the ways we interact around particular learning. So we don't just learn, for example, the topics of the curriculum, but also ways of speaking, gesturing, and so on that go with learning in a particular context such as a classroom (Wertsch 1985). The focus of socio-cultural theory is therefore on the roles that participation in social interactions play in influencing learning. Importantly, these interactions occur in *culturally organized* settings (such as schools, but of course also various out-of-school settings like the home), and characteristics of these cultural settings affect learning. For example, classroom settings run along a range of culturally constructed paths, with expected behaviours (such as waiting to be picked to answer a question) that are as much a part of the child's learning as is the content of the lesson.

The importance of the setting to learning in socio-cultural theory has led researchers and practitioners to consider ways in which settings can be optimized for learning. A key development was the idea of creating *communities of practice*. The concept of a community of practice was first developed to study professional learning rather than classroom processes, and refers to a diverse group of people engaged in real work over a significant period of time during which they build things, solve problems and learn. Learning as part of a community of practice is also a matter of developing identity as a learner (Lave and Wenger 1991). The teacher is then not so much the repository of knowledge that he or she teaches children, but is seen as an expert in the practices of a particular community, for example a history classroom. What the teacher does is exemplify for the learner how to legitimately participate in these practices (for example, how to speak, move, ask questions, as well as what constitutes legitimate 'classroom history'). That classrooms form their own communities is an important insight that allows us to think of ways in which, for example, school history is different from history as done by academic historians, and also the reasons why what is learnt in the classroom doesn't necessarily transfer to other situations, and vice versa (Muijs and Reynolds 2010).

As learners, we are all part of a variety of communities of practice (different classrooms, social settings, and so on), in which we may play different roles, being more or less expert, and more or less central to proceedings. We learn best through fully participating in these communities, becoming *situated learners* in the process. That this view has consequences for classroom practice (requiring a more learner-centred approach, for example) is clear. However, a key difficulty for putting socio-cultural theory into practice is the fact that classrooms are not voluntary communities in the way some of the groups of professionals studied by Lave and Wenger (1991) were. This means, as all teachers know, that pupils are not always brought together by a common interest in the subject or topic, and that therefore creating this interest is a prerequisite for creating an effective community of practice.

A controversial part of socio-cultural theories of learning is the view that learning proceeds from the general to the particular, and from the abstract to the concrete. Most concepts we learn, like a word for something, are already abstractions of our actual experiences and feelings when interacting with the world. What this means, for example, is that many socio-culturalists would dispute the view that we first need to teach basic skills before moving on to higher-order thinking skills. Rather, getting students to think about abstract concepts may come before the teaching of operations (Renshaw 1992). This view, however, is not necessarily that well supported by research into teaching (Muijs and Reynolds 2010).

Socio-cultural theories clearly provide us with a lot of food for thought, especially how we configure classrooms as spaces for learning and as communities of practice. These theories also provide a lot of insight into the social influences on learning. Where socio-cultural theory is weak, however, is in its almost exclusive focus on these social factors. Individual differences and internal cognitive processes are also important, and learning is not a purely social matter.

Task 4.3

To what extent do you think a classroom is a community of practice? How can the specificity of learning environments affect transfer to other subjects and contexts?

4.5 IQ theory

Another theory that has had a lasting influence in education (whether this has been for the good is debatable) is Intelligence Quotient (IQ) theory. This theory is mainly interested in the concept of intelligence, which is seen as determining people's ability to learn, to achieve academically and therefore to take on leading roles in society. IQ theorists, such as William Stern, who was one of the developers of the theory in the early part of the twentieth century, claimed that core intelligence was innate. Many psychologists in America and England supported that conclusion. Using tests of intelligence, often developed for specific purposes such as screening for the US Army or screening of immigrants, psychologists such as Terman and Binet developed instruments designed to test people's innate 'intelligence', which were analysed using the most recent statistical methods such as factor analysis, developed by Thurstone and Spearman. These analyses showed that all the items (questions) in those tests essentially measured one big factor, called G, or 'general intelligence'. Therefore, the theory states that people have one underlying general intelligence, which will predict how well they are able to learn and perform at school (Howe 1997).

A major point of discussion is whether intelligence as measured by IQ tests is innate or learned, and to what extent. The initial theories largely stressed the innate nature of intelligence, seeing it as an inborn property. Subsequent research, however, has clearly shown that IQ can be raised through educational interventions, which means that it cannot be totally inborn. The successful Cognitive Acceleration in Science Education (CASE) programme in the UK, for example, does just that (Adey and Shayer 2002). Another fact that points to the mutability of IQ is that average IQ test scores have increased steadily over the past decades, in all countries where they have been studied (Flynn 1994). When we are testing someone's IQ, we are therefore testing his or her education level at least as much as (if not more than) whatever innate ability they may possess. Also, it has become clear that children's IQ test scores are strongly influenced by their so-called cultural capital, that is their cultural resources (how many books they read, what media they access, and so on). This in turn is strongly determined by their parents' socio-economic status, or their position in the social class system (Gould 1983; Howe 1997; Muijs 1997).

As well as the issue of whether IQ is innate or acquired, the whole theory of IQ has been heavily criticized for many years now. These criticisms focus on a number of areas. The first of these is the methods used to measure intelligence, which produced G. Although we will not go into a discussion of statistics here, it is fair to say that the factor analysis method these researchers developed was specifically designed to come up with one big underlying factor, and usually does. If you use different methods, you are likely to find far more factors. Therefore, in many ways it is pre-existing theories that led to the development of methods designed to confirm these theories (Muijs 2004). The theory of intelligence also focuses purely on 'academic' intelligence, and so disparages other skills and abilities. As we will see, recent theories have taken a different approach to these matters (Gardner 1983). The idea that there is one measurable factor that distinguishes people has also been widely misused. One of the earliest uses of IQ tests was to look at differences in intelligence between particular groups in society, which were then said to be differently intelligent (and by implication more or less suitable to take on leading roles in society). The findings of these studies tell us far more about the societies in which they were carried out than about the 'intelligence' of different groups (which as a matter of fact does not differ significantly). Thus, in the USA, research concentrated on finding differences between racial groups, in France on differences between the sexes (men scoring higher than women) and in the UK on differences in social class (the higher classes coming out as more intelligent than the working class; Blum 1980; Gould 1983).

Notwithstanding these criticisms, it would be wrong to reject wholly IQ theory. There is evidence that an underlying general aptitude influences how well pupils perform on a variety of subjects. There is a far stronger correlation between pupils' performance in maths and English than is often realized, for example. As we will see later, if conceptualized as just one of a number of possible 'intelligences', the study of the kind of intelligence measured by IQ tests may have some merit.

Task 4.4

Do you think there is such a thing as intelligence? Is it inborn, acquired, or both? In what ways do you think IQ theory has influenced educational practice?

4.6 The theory of multiple intelligences

As we saw in the previous section, the theory of IQ stresses the existence of one overarching intelligence, a view that has become increasingly controversial over time. For many decades, however, no alternative theory was able to overcome the dominance of

IQ theory whenever ability and intelligence were studied. This changed in 1983 with the publication of *Frames of Mind* by Howard Gardner, in which he set out his theory of 'multiple intelligences' (MI).

Gardner takes a view that is very different from that of IQ theory. According to him, people do not have one general intelligence, but are characterized by a range of intelligences instead. So, rather than being globally intelligent, I may be particularly strong in certain areas, for example mathematics, while someone else may be particularly strong in another area, for example physical sports.

Gardner (1983, 1993) distinguishes nine main types of intelligence:

1. *Visual/spatial intelligence.* This is the ability to *perceive the visual.* Visual/spatial learners tend to think in pictures and need to create vivid mental images to retain information. They enjoy looking at pictures, charts, movies and so on.

2. *Verbal/linguistic intelligence.* This is the *ability to use words and language.* These learners have highly developed auditory skills and are generally elegant speakers. They think in words rather than pictures. This is the ability that can be measured by the verbal part of IQ tests.

3. *Logical/mathematical intelligence.* This is the *ability to use reason, logic and numbers.* These learners think conceptually in logical and numerical patterns, making connections between pieces of information. They ask lots of questions and like to do experiments. The non-verbal portion of traditional IQ tests largely measures this intelligence.

4. *Bodily/kinaesthetic intelligence.* This is the *ability to control body movements and handle objects skilfully.* These learners express themselves through movement. They have a good sense of balance and hand–eye coordination. Through interacting with the space around them, they are able to remember and process information.

5. *Musical/rhythmic intelligence.* This is the *ability to produce and appreciate music.* These learners think in sounds, rhythms and patterns. They respond strongly to music and rhythm. Many of these learners are extremely sensitive to sounds that occur in their environment.

6. *Interpersonal intelligence.* This is the *ability to relate to and understand others.* These learners can empathize and see things from other people's point of view in order to understand how they think and feel. They are good at sensing feelings, intentions and motivations. Generally they try to maintain peace in group settings and encourage cooperation. They can be manipulative.

7. *Intrapersonal intelligence.* This is the *ability to self-reflect and be aware of one's inner states.* These learners try to understand their inner feelings, dreams, relationships with others and strengths and weaknesses. Their strength lies in the ability to be self-reflective.

8. *Naturalist intelligence.* This is the *ability to recognize and categorize plants, animals and other objects in nature.* Learners with strong naturalist intelligence are good at recognizing, categorizing and drawing upon certain features of the environment.

9. *Existentialist intelligence.* This is the *sensitivity and capacity to tackle deep questions about human existence, such as the meaning of life, why we die and how we got here.* Existentialist learners tend to have strong spiritual leanings and be interested in deeper underlying issues (Gardner 1983, 1993, 2003).

A misconception that exists is that one intelligence is necessarily dominant. This is not really the case, as all of us will possess all intelligences to some extent. It is also important to remember that doing something will usually require us to use more than one intelligence.

To some, it might seem that this choice of different intelligences is somewhat arbitrary. Gardner's theories are sometimes seen as unscientific, a seemingly random selection of intelligences. This is a misconception, arising mainly from vulgarization and low-level application of his theories in education. In fact, Gardner (2003) uses a number of quite stringent criteria for defining an intelligence, taken from a variety of disciplines, including developmental psychology and cultural anthropology:

- *Isolation as a brain function.* A true intelligence will have its function identified in a specific location in the human brain. This can increasingly be determined using the latest brain-imaging techniques.
- *Prodigies, idiots savants and exceptional individuals.* To qualify as an intelligence, there must be some evidence of specific 'geniuses' in that particular area, such as the footballer, Maradona (bodily kinaesthetic).
- *Set of core operations.* Each true intelligence has a set of unique and identifiable procedures at its heart.
- *Developmental history.* A true intelligence is associated with an identifiable set of stages of growth, and with a 'mastery level' that exists as an end state in human development.
- *Evolutionary history.* A true intelligence can have its development traced through the evolution of our species as identified by cultural anthropologists.
- *Supported psychological tasks.* A true intelligence can be identified by specific tasks that can be carried out, observed and measured by clinical psychologists.
- *Supported psychometric tasks.* Specifically designed psychometric tests can be used to measure the intelligence in question.
- *Encoded into a symbol system.* A true intelligence has its own symbol system that is unique to it and essential to completing its tasks.

Gardner's theory has proved both popular and controversial in education, and the two conditions are closely linked. As often happens in education, valid psychological theories are taken on board by educators or commercial consultants who do not understand them well and produce a low-level vulgarized version for use in schools. Gardner himself for a long time remained silent on the use of MI theory in the classroom, but more recently has pointed to a number of misuses he sees of his theories in education:

1. Sometimes it is inferred that all subjects or concepts need to be taught using all nine intelligences. According to Gardner (1995), while most topics can be taught in a number of ways, it is usually a waste of time to try to teach a topic using all nine intelligences.

2. Going through the motions of using an intelligence does not in itself lead to learning. Gardner gives the example of some teachers getting children to run around as a way of exercising bodily/kinaesthetic intelligence!

3. Gardner (1995) also does not believe that the use of materials associated with MI as background (e.g. playing music in the classroom) will do anything to aid learners who are strong in that area.

4. Sometimes teachers claim they are exercising pupils' MI (in this case musical/ rhythmic intelligence) by getting them to sing or dance while reciting something like a times table. While this may help them remember it, Gardner (1995) describes such a use of MI as trivial. What educators should encourage instead is thinking musically or drawing on some of the structural aspects of music to illuminate concepts in other fields (e.g. maths).

5. The use of various measures or instruments that grade intelligences is seen by Gardner as being directly in opposition to his views of intelligence as something that occurs when carrying out activities within cultural settings.

All this does not mean that Gardner sees MI as irrelevant to classroom teaching. The consequences he sees are the following (Gardner 1995):

1. The curriculum should be broadened so that schools cultivate those skills and capacities that are valued in the community and in the broader society, not just traditional academic school subjects.

2. Rather than going for a broad but shallow curriculum, schools should focus on key topics, which can be explored in depth. Exploring key ideas in depth and in a lateral way should allow teachers to address different intelligences (although not all at once!).

3. Individual differences should be taken seriously. Education is most effective when it takes into account the different strengths and ways of thinking of different individuals.

One issue for teachers here is that they themselves will tend towards preferring certain intelligences and will, as a result of this, be likely to teach towards those intelligences, which may not correspond to those of their pupils. Being aware of what different learning styles exist among pupils, what one's own learning style is and how to teach to different learning styles are therefore important skills in this area (see Chapter 6).

While Gardner's theory has been widely influential in education recently (although, as mentioned above, not always in the most helpful way), it has also been subject to criticism. One criticism focuses on what is seen as a lack of testability of his theory. This is seen to result from an ambiguity of the theory, in that it is not clear to what extent the intelligences are supposed to operate separately or interconnectedly. The fact that the existence or not of an intelligence is not testable experimentally and cannot be accurately psychometrically assessed is also critiqued (Klein 1997), although Gardner would argue that this critique misunderstands the theory, which sees intelligences as operating in cultural action. The lack of a clear definition of what intelligence is has also come under fire, with some authors stating that what Gardner is studying are in fact cognitive styles rather than intelligences (Morgan 1996). The criteria he uses have been described as somewhat arbitrary (White 1998), and Gardner is seen as not providing a clear explanation as to why these and not other possible criteria were chosen (Klein 1997). The fact that the number of intelligences he proposes regularly increases has reinforced these criticisms. Further evolution in brain science may allow us more accurately to assess the validity of the theory; what seems clear already is that in moving education on from traditional IQ theory, Gardner has done us a big favour.

Task 4.5

Thinking about the teaching you have done, or experienced, do you think the different intelligences of pupils have been addressed? Which ones were and which were not? What could be done to address more intelligences?

4.7 Cognitive theory and brain research

What many of the older learning theories (like behaviourism and the theories of Vygotsky) were not able to incorporate was any theory of how the brain works (due to limitations in research methods at the time). More recently, however, brain research and the neurosciences have progressed greatly, and are informing learning theory and education to an ever greater extent. To some extent, these new methods are confirming theories that we discussed earlier, like Vygotsky's views on learning, but they are also offering us important new insights.

One of the first major theories of learning that explicitly based itself on our emerging knowledge of the brain was cognitive information processing theory. Especially important in this theory is the role of memory in learning processes. The memory consists of three parts: the sensory buffer, the working memory and the long-term memory (see Figure 4.1).

One's memory works as follows: one's experiences (tactile, visual or auditory) are registered in the sensory buffer, and then converted into the form in which they are employed in the working and long-term memories. The sensory buffer can register a lot of information, but can only hold it briefly. Some parts of the information in it will be lost, while other parts will be transmitted to the working memory. The working memory is where 'thinking gets done'. It receives its content from the sensory buffer and the long-term memory but has a limited capacity for storing information, a fact that limits human mental processes. The working memory contains the information that is actively being used at any one time.

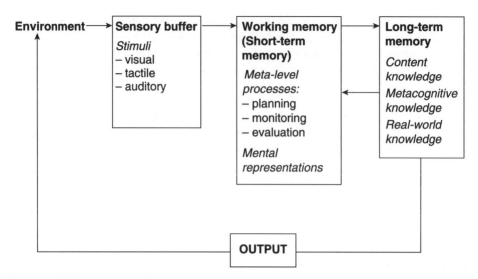

Figure 4.1 The structure of memory

The long-term memory has a nodal structure, and consists of neural network representations, whose nodes represent chunks in memory and whose links represent connections between those chunks. As such, nodes can be equated with concepts, and links with meaningful associations between concepts. Together these form schemata, or clusters of information. Activating one item of the cluster is likely to activate all of them (Best 1999). This means that memorization and making connections are two crucial components of learning, according to cognitive information processing theory. Making connections is particularly important. The brain has literally millions of neurons that can be linked in neural nets in an almost unlimited number of ways.

These structural characteristics of the brain have some important pedagogical consequences. In particular, if working memory is where information processing happens, the limitations of working memory are of great importance to learning. This, indeed, is the basic thesis of the so-called *cognitive load theory*, which suggests that the limited capacity of the working memory places a limit on the amount of information that can be processed at any one time. These limitations only apply to new information that has not been stored in the long-term memory. This type of information can only be stored for a short period of time. This is not the case for information from the long-term memory, which can be retrieved for an indefinite time and in large quantities. That makes it important that learning tasks do not overload working memory, something that is often a problem with individual and discovery learning approaches (Kirschner et al. 2006). Rather, a structured approach, akin to mastery learning, or an approach whereby cognitive load is limited through collaborative group work (with different pupils taking on different parts of the load) is more appropriate. The capacity of the short-term memory is itself not independent from the long-term memory. The more information about a specific area or skill that is contained in the long-term memory, the easier it will be for the working memory to retrieve the necessary information for quick processing. The capacity of the working memory is influenced by the extent and speed with which prior knowledge (in the broad terms defined here) can be accessed. The capacity of the working memory is therefore in part determined by prior knowledge, as well as the extent to which prior knowledge is organized in a way that makes it easily accessible. This capacity is open to change, and practice and learning can increase capacity, which in turn is linked to achievement in maths and reading (little research exists on other subject areas) (Molfese et al. 2010). Of course, this potential for change means that popular sayings on the actual number of chunks of information that can be processed simultaneously are not very helpful.

Brain research is also telling us that the brain is a pattern maker. The brain takes great pleasure in taking random and chaotic information and ordering it. The implications for learning and instruction are that presenting a learner with random and unordered information provides the maximum opportunity for the brain to order this information and form meaningful patterns that will be remembered. Setting up a learning environment in this way mirrors real life, which is often random and chaotic (Lackney 1999). The brain, when allowed to express its pattern-making behaviour, creates coherency and meaning. Learning is best accomplished when the learning activity is connected directly to physical experience. We remember best when facts and skills are embedded in natural, real-life activity. We learn by doing. The implications of applying the findings of neuroscience related to coherency and meaning suggest that learning is facilitated in an environment of total immersion in a multitude of complex, interactive experiences that could include traditional instructional methods as part of this larger experience (Kotulak 1996; Lackney 1999).

An interesting finding concerns the modular nature of the brain. This means that brain functions are made up of small sub-systems (modules) that can perform specific functions independently. This is particularly useful as it allows some compartmentalization, which reduces the interdependence of components, and leads to greater robustness. For example, the hippocampus, a structure located within the medial temporal lobe of the brain and long associated with memory function, appears to be critical for everyday episodic memory (our record of personal events), but is not necessary for semantic memory (our lifetime accumulation of universal factual knowledge) (Eichenbaum 1997).

This modular organization of the brain also allows flexibility, which enables the brain to adapt existing brain functions to new situations and learning (Bassett et al. 2010). This flexibility and modularity is implicated in the effectiveness of learning, since, according to Bassett et al. (2010), flexibility of a participant in one session could be used as a predictor of the amount of learning in the following session. This flexibility and plasticity of the brain has important consequences for teaching, in that it clearly implies that there is not one single 'pathway to learning'. Rather, the brain grows and reconfigures according to different stimuli presented. In other words, views of learning as determined by fixed learning 'styles' receive little support from brain architecture, and in all likelihood each individual will be able to learn in several different ways.

Another important finding relates to the strong evidence of individual differences between the brain functioning of different learners. While the basic brain architecture is essentially the same, brain scans have shown that, for example, 'while most people, when they recognize an object visually, show increased activity in the back part of their brains, the exact magnitude, location, and distribution of that increased activity varies quite a bit' (Rose and Meyer 2002: 64). Similarly, learners differ in the strategies they employ to make connections in the brain (Dall'Alba 2006). This is important for teachers, as it means both that, as constructivist educators have long claimed, each learner will construct knowledge in a slightly different way, and that teaching should be varied to address the different needs and strategies of learners, a finding that confirms the views of those who take a 'multiple intelligences' approach. This is not the same as saying that there are different 'learning styles', or that these can easily be categorized. An example of an idea based on learning styles is the use of the VAK categorization, very popular in England, not least following its support by the DfES (2004a). 'VAK' stands for visual, auditory and kinaesthetic, the three main learning styles that are claimed to differentiate learners. It is claimed that learners predominantly use one of three 'sensory receivers' to process information, and that teachers should therefore make sure that their teaching addresses all three types (Dunn 1990). While using a variety of teaching methods is always sensible, there is very little evidence for the existence of the VAK styles, or indeed of many other learning styles that have been developed, and basing teaching methods on these is therefore not recommended (Cofield et al. 2004).

The final critical finding from brain research relates to the importance of emotion in learning. Emotions can both help and hinder learning. On the positive side, emotions help us to recall information from the long-term memory, by allowing any information received through the sensory buffer to be perceived as positive or a threat. Research suggests that the brain learns best when confronted with a balance between high challenge and low threat. The brain needs some challenge to activate emotions and learning. This is because if there is no stress the brain becomes too relaxed and cannot actively engage in learning. Too much stress is also negative, however, as it will lead to anxiety and a 'fight' response, which are inimical to learning. A physically safe environment is particularly important in reducing especially high levels of stress (Sousa 1998; Dias-Ferreira et al. 2009).

Brain research is a constantly developing field of research, and it is highly likely that further developments will in future strongly inform our views on learning, and our teaching strategies. However, one caveat does apply: while I have presented a number of basic findings, this research area is diverse. Findings from different studies do not always agree with one another, and are usually far more subtle than I have been able to outline here. Also, it is dangerous to try to directly translate findings from brain research into the classroom. This type of research should clearly inform us, but we need to take into account that it has been conducted for very different purposes, and will always need to be matched to educational research findings on effective classroom teaching before it can be translated into effective classroom strategies.

4.8 Summary

In this chapter we have looked at some educationally influential theories of learning and intelligence.

Behaviourism was mainly concerned with how we learn from external stimuli. Using experimental methods, behaviourists looked at how behaviour can be conditioned, for example by providing rewards and punishments.

Piaget used observation to come to his theories of learning. His key concept is *maturation*, the unfolding of biological changes that are genetically programmed into us. A second factor is *activity*. Increasing maturation leads to an increase in children's ability to act on their environment, and to learn from their actions. An important finding of Piaget's is that growing up does not just mean knowing more, but also entails a change in how we think.

Vygotsky concentrated on the fact that learning is a social process, and that we learn through interaction with others, both of the same age and of a higher age and developmental level. This process operates through *scaffolding* in the ZPD. The ZPD is the gap between what a person is able to do alone and what they can do with the help of someone more knowledgeable or skilled than themselves. Scaffolding refers to the way others can help us to bridge that gap.

IQ theory focuses on the concept of intelligence. According to IQ theorists there is one underlying, general intelligence that determines our capacity for learning. More recently, Gardner developed his theory of *multiple intelligences*. Rather than just the one intelligence, according to Gardner there are nine: visual/spatial, verbal/linguistic, logical/mathematical, bodily/kinaesthetic, musical/rhythmic, interpersonal, intrapersonal, naturalist and existentialist. For most tasks, we need to deploy more than one intelligence.

Brain research is a fast developing area in psychology that is producing valuable findings for educators. One of these is that we learn best when challenged but not stressed. Another is the importance of *pattern-making* in the brain. This implies that we need to provide children with the opportunity to create patterns. Finally, brain research confirms that while we can learn throughout our life, early childhood is a key period in developing (the capacity for) learning.

4.9 Recommendations for further reading

Eysenck, W. and Keane, T. (2005) *Cognitive Psychology: A Student's Handbook*. New York: Psychology Press.

Gardner, H. (2006) *Multiple Intelligences: New Horizons in Theory and Practice*. New York: Basic Books.

O'Donohue, W. and Ferguson, K.E. (2001) *The Psychology of B.F. Skinner*. Thousand Oaks, CA: Sage Publications.

Piaget, J. and Inhelder, B. (2000) *The Psychology of the Child*. New York: Basic Books.

Vygotsky, L., Vygotsky, S. and John-Steiner, V. (eds.) (1978) *Mind in Society: The Development of Higher Psychological Processes*. Cambridge, MA: Harvard University Press.

5

Planning for learning
Paul Elliott

5.1 Introduction

Planning is the activity that underpins success. This chapter will first explore the journey that teachers facilitate, from where the pupil is and has been (prior learning) to where they need to be (learning outcomes). Appreciating the range of approaches that can be used to help different types of learners on this journey is important, as is the ability to make conscious decisions about which are most appropriate in particular circumstances. Guidance will be given on how to construct a lesson plan and you will be shown how planning, at a very practical level, can help pupils' learning. Effective planning is also the best way to reduce the stress and anxiety you will feel in the classroom and maximize the chances of things going smoothly for you. Only good planning will give you the confidence and clarity of purpose that will encourage the pupils to view you as someone in whose lessons they can learn. Since virtually all pupils want to learn, good planning will help you to build good relationships.

When you observe an experienced and successful teacher at work, it can be hard to appreciate how difficult teaching is. The lesson will proceed smoothly, all necessary resources will be at hand, and the pupils will be interested in and engaged with the work. It is only when you try to emulate this performance that you are likely to discover how much experience the teacher was drawing on and/or how much effort they had put into planning their lesson. Great lessons do not just happen and they are not a product of good luck. Great lessons are a product of great planning, plus a little bit of inspiration and a tiny amount of good fortune. You can aspire to teach great lessons, but only if you are prepared to put time and intelligent effort into planning.

By the end of this chapter, you should appreciate that good planning:

- starts with establishing 'where your pupils are';
- is driven by the learning that needs to happen;
- involves being clear about what you want pupils to achieve by the end of the lesson;
- requires you to think about how you can help pupils make progress;

- is something you can best demonstrate by producing a detailed written record of your thinking.

The principles of good planning discussed in this chapter are relevant to lessons at Key Stage 3 (KS3), KS4, and post-16.

5.2 Establishing where pupils are

The success of your teaching is judged by the learning that your pupils do. Your first task is to establish what they already know, understand or can do: 'where they are now'. Two analogies can make the reason for this clear.

Bus stops. Think of yourself as a bus driver. You need to be clear about your destination. However, you also need to make sure that you stop at the right bus stop to pick up passengers. If you do not stop, very few of your passengers will be able to run fast enough to catch the bus.

Building bridges. Imagine that some of your pupils are standing on one bank of a river; other pupils are further back from the river; while others are in midstream. The opposite bank is where you would like them to be. How are you going to get them there? Only a few will be capable of jumping across. The rest will need some help getting there. You need to build a bridge, or a number of bridges, to cater for the needs of all pupils. The bridges need to start where your pupils are and end up where you want them to be. The bridges need to be built carefully and probably in collaboration with your pupils, otherwise some will fall into the river and be lost. Some scaffolding would be useful to construct the bridges.

It should be clear from both of these analogies that your lesson plan needs to take account of what your pupils already know, understand and can do. This applies at the start of a new topic, but is also likely to be the case at the beginning of lessons. You may think the content of the previous lesson will be clear in your pupils' minds, but remember that since they last saw you they will have been to several other lessons on different subjects.

How can you find out where pupils are starting? There are a number of tactics that you can use:

Outside of the classroom
- Check what they have already studied by looking at the scheme of work (SoW) and the topics they have been taught prior to you taking the class. Cross-reference this information to the National Curriculum/examination specification(s).
- Look at pupils' exercise books to check the subject matter they have encountered and find clues about the level at which they have been learning and the range of support you will need to give.
- Ask to see assessment data for the members of the class.

Inside the classroom

- Question pupils on aspects of the topic with which they may already have some familiarity. Listen carefully to their responses (see Chapter 8).
- Set tasks to find out what they can do before you start (see Chapter 9). These could include pre-tests, quizzes, concept-mapping exercises, sorting games, and so on.
- Talk to pupils. Each individual will bring a different level of understanding to your lesson.

Try to avoid making assumptions about what a class will know or can do. If you do this, or misjudge where they are, you risk losing them by making too big a leap for them to follow, or boring or patronizing them by covering work they have done before.

5.3   Identifying learning objectives and outcomes

Once you have established where your pupils are, the next step is to decide where they need to go next. Think in terms of what the pupils need to know, understand or be able to do at the end of a lesson or series of lessons, rather than what you are going to *teach* them. The input that you make should be determined by the objectives you have identified and by the outcome that is desirable. This approach is sometimes referred to as 'backward design' and the implication of this approach is that you should not be tempted to go with the methods, sources or activities with which you are most comfortable, but with the ones that maximize your chances of meeting your objectives. As Wiggins and McTighe (2005: 14) say: 'We must be able to state with clarity what the student should understand and be able to do as a result of any plan and irrespective of any constraints we face'. It is also crucial that you think in terms of how you will know that you have succeeded. What will characterize success and how will you *measure* it?

Planning can be based upon the behaviours that are the desirable outcome of learning. The intended learning outcome for a lesson can be framed in a way that describes a behaviour, preferably a measurable one. However, there will be differences between, and within, subject areas. For example, planning in religious education (RE) might be more concerned with non-behavioural objectives, which are more difficult to measure. This might involve introducing objectives related to values, attitudes or beliefs.

It would be easy to devise a learning objective for a history lesson on the English Civil War that read something like:

- *Understand the reasons for the rise of the parliamentarian movement.*
  While this may be a desirable outcome for the lesson, it is incredibly difficult to measure whether you have been successful. Whereas, by contrast:
- *Be able to describe at least three factors that gave rise to the parliamentarian movement.*
  This allows you to use questioning, output from class work, homework activities or testing to judge your success. The second version becomes part of the assessment cycle (see Chapter 9) and allows you to evaluate your own performance in terms of what your pupils have learned.

Bloom's Taxonomy (Bloom et al. 1956) is a useful way of categorizing the levels of demand in thinking and learning represented by different types of task. The taxonomy categorizes learning outcomes into three domains: cognitive, affective, and psychomotor. The cognitive domain is broken down into six areas:

- knowledge
- comprehension
- application
- analysis
- synthesis
- evaluation.

It is helpful to draw on this approach during planning, to ensure pupils are being given opportunities to demonstrate what they have learned. For instance, in addition to the word 'understand', mentioned in the English Civil War example above, there are other terms that can be used when phrasing intended learning outcomes that provide only a poor indication of what outcomes might be expected. Examples include:

know   *memorize*
become familiar with   *appreciate the significance of*

Figure 5.1 shows a range of terms that can be much more useful when trying to identify appropriate learning objectives. Note that these are in themes, related but not

Draw	State	Record	Recognize	Identify	
Sort	Describe	Select	Present	Locate information from text	
Decide	Discuss	Define	Classify	Explain what...	
Devise	Calculate	Interpret	Construct	Clarify	
Plan	Predict	Conclude	Solve	Determine the key points from...	
Formulate	Explain why	Use the pattern to...	Reorganize	Explain the differences between...	
Link/make connections between...	Use the idea of... to...	Use a model of... to...	Provide evidence for...	Evaluate the evidence for...	

General increase in demand

Figure 5.1 Useful words to use for defining intended learning outcomes (DfES 2002a)

identical to Bloom's Taxonomy. The terms demonstrate a general increase in demand or difficulty as you go down the table.

Task 5.1

Choose a topic from your subject that might be taught in one lesson or a short series of lessons. Use the National Curriculum, exam specification or Qualifications and Curriculum Development Agency (QCDA) SoW to work out what relevant prior learning pupils might have. Identify the learning that you would expect to take place when you teach the topic and try to devise statements that describe the outcomes in behavioural terms, using Figure 5.1 for guidance. What techniques could you use to assess whether the teaching had been successful?

5.4 How can you help your pupils get there?

Having established where your pupils are starting from (prior learning and attainment) and where you need to get them (intended learning outcomes), you need to determine a number of other things if you are to plan effectively.

First, you need to be clear how long you have with the class:

- the length of lessons will be determined by the school;
- the department's SoW will almost certainly specify the number of lessons to be devoted to the topic.

These factors will set the framework within which you work. Most departments have a SoW in place for most topics and do not expect a trainee to create one from scratch. The SoW is normally the result of collaboration by a group of teachers to identify a route through the syllabus or curriculum that takes account of the learning that should take place, the resources and time available, and the ideas and enthusiasm of the staff. However, you will have some flexibility in how you interpret a SoW and should certainly aim to personalize aspects so that you can take ownership of it when you translate it into real lessons. You would be wise to plan to use slightly less time than the SoW indicates, because some of the learning may take longer than you anticipate and things like school trips, epidemics, and tests can eat into available time. Time might also be needed to incorporate actions in response to feedback from formative assessment (see Chapter 9).

Pupils can be more efficient at learning early in the morning and earlier in the week, so check when lessons are and plan accordingly. Also, check what the pupils have done immediately before your lesson, since this will affect their attention and energy levels. Homework should be integral to your planning and, used carefully, can allow you to devote time in the classroom to collaborative rather than individual learning.

Before progressing too far with your plans, you need to check what resources are available. Resources include props, information and communications technology (ICT) hardware and software, access to specialist teaching rooms, and the human support of technicians, librarians, learning assistants, and even external speakers. In some cases, you may have the chance to plan learning opportunities off the school site; for example, theatre visits, geography or science fieldwork, and visits to businesses or religious sites.

How are you going to assess how successfully pupils learn during the topic? You will almost certainly be preparing them for some sort of summative assessment, be it an end-of-topic test, a modular exam or coursework assignment, and you need to be aware of the attendant requirements and expectations. You need to ensure that your pupils are properly prepared, but should avoid 'teaching to the test'. Concurrently, a major part of your planning should focus on how you are going to formatively assess pupils' progress during the topic. This should be guided by the intended learning outcomes, since you and your pupils require feedback on how effectively these are being met. It is also useful if you have some idea of where pupils are meant to be 'going next', since no topic that you teach will stand alone. Even if the factual content is not directly linked to any other part of the course, the development of pupils' skills will be. You need to know how the topic you are to teach will contribute to pupils' progression.

Really effective planning will also take account of what pupils are doing in other subject areas, especially where the learning in one subject supports pupil learning in another. For instance, work on graphs in maths should have some bearing on the graph work that is expected of pupils in science lessons. In this case, both science and maths teachers should be aware of each other's requirements and take account of these in their planning.

5.5   Planning for success

A great amount of time during training is spent planning lessons. At times this will frustrate and exhaust you, but it is central to your success as a teacher. Carefully planned lessons are more likely to succeed. All your plans must exist in written form to provide evidence of the process you have been through. Mentors, tutors, and external examiners will draw on them to inform judgements about your progress towards qualified teacher status (QTS). Your lesson plans will also be scrutinized if the school you are working in, or the course you are training on, is inspected. It can be difficult to reconcile the amount of time you spend putting your plans down in writing when more experienced teachers seem to get away with something far briefer. The truth is that good, experienced teachers are far more practised at teaching than you are and they automatically internalize aspects of the planning process. Even they have to put detailed plans on paper when producing a portfolio of evidence to cross the pay threshold, or to achieve Advanced Skills Teacher status, or when their school is being inspected.

The experienced teachers who you work with in school will give you assistance with lesson planning, but ultimately the plans need to be yours. Avoid trying to teach someone else's lesson, unless as a deliberate learning tactic. Some websites are listed at the end of the chapter from which you can download lesson plans, but you have to process the plans to tailor them to suit your pupils and your needs and strengths. If the plan is not really yours, you will not have engaged with all aspects of the planning process and will not feel fully committed to it.

Planning lessons is a complex business. Let us consider some of the fundamental processes that you need to engage in when planning a lesson.

Subject content and skills

First, you need to be clear what it is that your pupils are supposed to be learning. This will relate not only to specific subject-based information, but also to relevant skills, including those of literacy, numeracy, and ICT. You then need to check that you have sufficient personal subject knowledge to help your pupils learn. If there are deficits in your knowledge, you will have to address them in advance of the lesson. At the same time you need to consider how you are going to make your personal knowledge accessible to Year 7, Year 10, and so on; you need to 're-shape ideas to represent knowledge in different ways' (Ellis 2002: 34). This is one of the most challenging aspects of planning for new teachers.

Planning for progression

Make sure you understand what pupils already know and be clear where they need to get to (intended learning outcomes). How will you take account of the different learning preferences or multiple intelligences possessed by pupils in your class? How will you differentiate your teaching and your expectations so that lower attaining pupils can still achieve something because of the support you give and the manageable tasks you set? Some pupils may have individual education plans (IEPs), which you will need to consider (see Chapter 21). How will the more able in your class be challenged and stimulated by your lesson? It helps to consider what you want all, most or some pupils to be able to do (see Chapter 6).

Resources

You will need to think about resources at least three times in your planning!

1. Identify the resources available to you that *could* be used to help your pupils meet the objectives and the intended learning outcomes.
2. Decide which of these is most appropriate.
3. Make absolutely certain that the resources you want to use will be available. Some you may need to order (e.g. science equipment), some you may have to book (e.g. ICT suite or drama studio), and some you may have to collect for yourself (e.g. fresh fungi for an art lesson or leaflets from a medical centre for a Personal, Social, Health, and Economic Education [PSHEE] lesson). An oversight in these areas is easy to make, but could be disastrous and very stressful. Check the minutiae: have you got the key to the room, your flash

drive, whiteboard pens, spare pens to lend pupils, something to light the Bunsen burners with?

Resources may need organizing well in advance of your lesson.

Safety should be incorporated into all planning, but for some subjects (e.g. physical education, science, technology) this is a big issue and needs to be done overtly, in writing. In such subjects, you will probably receive specialized training in risk assessment. In all cases, the responsibility for safety in lessons lies with the normal class teacher, so it is in their interests to check your plan in advance of a lesson. You should have your plan ready sufficiently in advance of a lesson for the class teacher and/or mentor to check.

5.6   Structuring a lesson

So far, we have considered planning in a general sense, as it applies to any defined period of learning. For much of your time, however, you will be preoccupied with the planning of specific lessons, and the rest of this chapter will be devoted to this.

The underlying sequence of events when planning a lesson should be based on backward design:

Identify your objectives and what the learning outcomes should be.
⇓
Identify and choose activities that help deliver the learning outcomes.
⇓
Determine what you have to do to facilitate these activities.

Be clear about the learning that needs to take place in the lesson and then investigate what activities might successfully bring this about, rather than trying to think of a justification for using an activity you have come across or had suggested to you. Next, think carefully about the lesson's exact structure. By adopting a clear structure for your planning, you will find the task of helping pupils meet the learning objectives more manageable. You will also find that your pupils respond more positively if you have planned the learning as a set of discrete 'chunks' that will not test their powers of concentration for too long. If you make your pupils do any activity for too long, for example listening to you, writing, discussing, watching a video, you will start to see diminishing returns. By incorporating variety, you stand a good chance of maintaining their interest, motivation, and momentum.

Lessons should have clear beginnings, middles, and ends. It is surprising how many student teachers get bogged down with the 'middle' and neglect to plan for an effective start to their lesson or a discernible end. In recent years, teachers have been encouraged to re-focus attention on lesson planning and to define 'beginning, middle, and end', as 'starter, main activity(ies), and plenary'. A lesson should not necessarily contain only three phases, but these components are a useful tool in planning. Figure 5.2 represents various ways of structuring a lesson, but each is built on the principle of starter, main activity, plenary.

Lesson plan structure 1

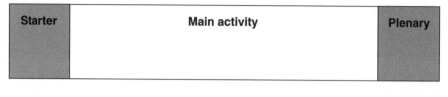

Lesson plan structure 2

Starter	1ˢᵗ main activity	Short plenary	2ⁿᵈ main activity	Longer plenary

Lesson plan structure 3

Starter	Whole class same task	Plenary 1	Whole class same task	Plenary 2	Whole class different task	Plenary 3

Lesson plan structure 4

Starter	Main activity Groups working on different tasks or circus of tasks	Plenary

Figure 5.2 Model lesson structures (adapted from DfES 2002b)

5.7 Starting a lesson

Before your lesson, your pupils may have been stimulated to the extent that their adrenaline is flowing and they find it difficult to settle. At the other extreme, they may have come from a stuffy, overheated classroom in which they were being bored to tears. If they have come to you after a break, anything is possible! You may not have seen them for days, in which case the topic of the last lesson with you may have dimmed in their memory. In all of these cases, your challenge is to get them learning. Some experienced teachers have their class so well trained that calling a register is an effective way of creating a calm, ordered start to a lesson. For a student teacher, starting a lesson this way can present a class with an opportunity to challenge their authority. Even if you can do it effectively, it is still a pretty boring way to start a lesson! It is much easier to take a register once pupils have engaged with a motivating task.

In most circumstances, it is wise to reassure your pupils that you have a plan by sharing your agenda and the objectives of the lesson. Since you cannot guarantee that all pupils will be paying attention, it is worth reinforcing this visually. The learning objectives you have identified for the lesson are unlikely to be in a suitable format for sharing with pupils, but can easily be translated into pupil-friendly language, displayed on a board, and explained to them. You can also flag up any new or recently introduced key words at this stage. Pupils will also respond better if you give them this overview of the structure of the lesson, so that they understand better what is expected of them.

It is in your interests to start your lesson in a way that focuses attention quickly on the main theme of your lesson. Plan something that:

- you can start quickly;
- will stimulate your pupils' interest;
- will build bridges between relevant prior learning and today's lesson.

There are many tactics that can be used to start a lesson in a way that quickly engages pupils' attention, helps them to focus on the theme or purpose of the lesson and its objectives, but which do not take too much time. Table 5.1 offers a range of activities that can be employed to start lessons in ways that will achieve these

Table 5.1 Examples of starter techniques

Technique	Features
Sequencing	Put something on paper that has a sequential order to it. Give pupils envelopes containing the cut-up sequence for them to order.
Card sort	Prepare sets of cards that can be paired up. Pupils work in small teams to see who can correctly pair them fastest.
Continuum	Pupils position themselves on an imaginary line representing the range of views from one extreme to another (e.g. from *Personal firearms should be banned* to *Anyone has a right to carry arms*) or level of skill (e.g. from *extremely competent with spreadsheets* to *not sure what a spreadsheet is*)
Traffic lights	Pupils each have three coloured cards: red, amber and green, respectively. The teacher asks a question and provides a possible answer. Pupils hold up the relevant card: red = false, green = true, amber = uncertain.
Mini-whiteboards	Teacher asks questions and pupils have to write the answer quickly on mini-whiteboards and display them to the teacher.
Five things	*Give me the five key questions/key things/most interesting things/most important things about …* Teacher (or pupil) records the answers, which can then be used to recap prior learning.
Visual/audio stimulus	The teacher shows something thought-provoking (e.g. a piece of art, an artefact, a short science demonstration, a YouTube clip, a newspaper headline) and asks pupils to provide an immediate response or to raise questions about it.

aims. Try to employ a variety so that the starts of your lessons do not become predictable.

Task 5.2

Identify appropriate intended learning outcomes for a single lesson in your subject. Identify some of the tactics in Table 5.1 that could be used to get the lesson off to a good start. Choose two contrasting alternatives from the table and prepare in detail, identifying any necessary resources. When you come to teach the relevant topic, choose which starter activity to use and on the second occasion you teach it, use the other starter. Compare the responses.

5.8   Main activities

The main activity or activities in a lesson provide a time when you are probably not centre-stage. Activities with the greatest educational value are very often not teacher-led, but teacher-facilitated. The teacher is then free to check that pupils are on-task and give them highly valuable individual attention. The activities need to be carefully planned so that they enable pupils to meet the intended learning outcomes of the lesson and are accessible to all. Having identified a suitable activity ('task'), you need to think about how long pupils will need to complete it ('time') and whether you want them to work as individuals, in pairs, in groups of three or more or as a whole class ('team'). These are crucial decisions because they will affect the type of learning that takes place and have implications for classroom management and behaviour. Once you are clear about the activity, how long it will take, and how pupils will be grouped, you need to plan how all this is going to be communicated to the pupils. It may be useful to remember the task–time–team triangle while planning to make sure that you have considered all three aspects (see Figure 5.3).

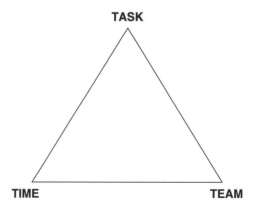

Figure 5.3 The planning triangle

Remember to make use of a wide variety of techniques to suit multiple intelligences and the range of preferred learning styles in your class (see Chapter 6). You need to develop empathy for those pupils who learn in a different way from yourself, so that they are not disadvantaged in your lessons.

You should also consider the nature of evidence the activity will generate and how it can demonstrate whether learning and progression have occurred. Evidence may come from the way in which pupils engage with the activity, the output or both. The quality and quantity of evidence you collect will be influenced by:

- the way in which you communicate with pupils during the activity (see Chapter 8);
- the subject that you teach. This will influence the range of opportunities for pupils to demonstrate what they have learnt, but you should plan to incorporate activities within lessons and across a series of lessons that enable pupils with different learning styles and aptitudes to show you what they can achieve (see Chapter 6).

Once the structure of your lesson is in place, you need to review timing. Some student teachers find it really difficult to get this right. The most common problem is running out of time. There are various causes, the most common of which are:

- Underestimating how long pupils will take to complete a task. Until you get some experience of the speed at which pupils can be expected to work, this is difficult to get right, but observing lessons and practice will help.
- Failing to give pupils a clear indication of task–time–team parameters, leading to confusion, uncertainty, and lack of pace. This problem can therefore be avoided by good planning.
- Failing to plan for all aspects of the lesson, for example, clearing away, setting homework, having a plenary.

5.9 Bringing a lesson to a close

How you end a lesson or a discrete portion of a lesson can have a profound effect on the overall quality of the learning that takes place. If you plan carefully how you will finish your lesson, or a portion of it, you can maximize the chances of pupils meeting the intended learning outcomes. The term 'plenary' is now widely used to describe this phase of a lesson.

Plenaries have a number of uses, including:

- an opportunity to draw the whole class together;
- a chance to review what has been learnt so far, including progress against intended outcomes;
- a time to direct pupils to the next stage of learning (signposting);
- a time to help pupils reflect on how they have learnt (metacognition);
- an opportunity for the teacher to make formative assessments, identify and explore misconceptions.

Successful lessons do not end with the teacher calling over the noise of pupils packing away, 'That's all we've got time for today, don't forget to bring your homework in next lesson'. As you can see from Figure 5.2, even if there are other plenary phases during a lesson, there should certainly be one at the end. In your lesson plan you should allow time for reflection, so that pupils leave your classroom with a feeling that they have completed something and gained from the experience. This will build their confidence in you as someone who can help them learn. Yet ending lessons effectively is something that even many experienced teacher struggle with. Table 5.2 shows some plenary pitfalls and possible solutions.

Table 5.2 Plenaries: common pitfalls and possible solutions

Pitfall	Suggested solutions
The class runs out of time and never gets round to a plenary	1. Ask a pupil to be a timekeeper 2. Stick to your planned times, even if some activities have not been completed 3. Plan the plenary in detail
Pupils feel the lesson is over when the main activity finishes and do not take the plenary seriously	1. Signpost what will be expected of pupils in the plenary 2. Involve pupils in delivering the plenary 3. Do not allow main activities to run until the bell rings
'All I need to do is get them packed away, sitting in their seats and repeat the objectives and set the homework'	1. Over a course of lessons, vary your plenaries to re-engage attention 2. Set homework at the beginning of the lesson
'It's become dull because it's always the same routine'	1. Plan for variety 2. Design each plenary to fit the lesson and use it to revisit the objectives 3. Use it to whet the pupils' appetites for the next lesson
You end up repeating everything and nothing is gained	1. Ask pupils to articulate the key points or consequences of the lesson 2. Ask pupils to apply the learning to a new context 3. Ask different groups to apply the learning in different ways
The learning is implicit in what has been covered	1. Ask pupils to identify the factors that have helped to achieve the lesson's objectives

Adapted from KS3 Strategy training materials (DfES 2004f)

5.10   Other planning issues

As well as planning your lesson so that it starts effectively, consists of appropriate main activities, and has a purposeful ending, there are several other factors that you need to consider and incorporate into your planning:

- The need to accommodate the special needs or exceptional ability of one pupil. Overlooking this can undermine your plans for the whole class.
- Opportunities for pupils to develop generic skills within the lesson, especially those relating to literacy, numeracy, and ICT.
- Opportunities for your lesson to contribute to relevant cross-curricular themes, such as education for sustainable development.

5.11   The best laid plans . . .

Ideally, by the time your lesson starts, your plan should be so familiar to you that you do not need to consult it during the lesson. If you need subject knowledge crib sheets, keep them separate, for example on index cards, so that they are easy to consult. Try to keep to your planned timing, in particular allowing time for the end-of-lesson plenary. You may need to modify the plan during the lesson to take account of rates of progress, rates of learning, management issues caused by behavioural problems, interesting inputs from pupils, and so on. Good planning will give you the confidence to deviate from your plan.

5.12   When it's all over . . .

Once a lesson is over, it is tempting to transfer your attention to the next. First though, you should try to learn from the experience you have just had. Part of this evaluation should focus on the lesson you planned as well as the lesson you delivered. How suitable did the plan turn out to be? Which parts of your planned lesson worked and which did not? Did you deviate from your plan and, if so, why? Were the objectives met and do the outcomes support your verdict? To develop your practice you need to make the time to ask these questions and answer them honestly.

5.13   Recommendations for further reading and webliography

Brown, K.J. (2009) *Classroom Starters and Plenaries: Creative Ideas for Use across the Curriculum.* London: Continuum.

Haynes, A. (2010) *Complete Guide to Lesson Planning and Preparation.* London: Continuum.

Wiggins, G. and McTighe, J. (2005) *Understanding by Design.* Alexandria, VA: Association for Supervision and Curriculum Development.

Wright, T. (2008) *How to be a Brilliant Trainee Teacher.* London: Routledge.

Websites

www.bbc.co.uk/schools/teachers (a variety of resource types, including lesson plans, worksheets, and ideas for making use of BBC media)

www.tes.co.uk/secondary-teaching-resources/ (lesson plans and other resources submitted by teachers)

www.lessonplans4teachers.com/ (a North American site where teachers share lesson plans for a wide range of topics)

6
Using differentiation to support learning
Val Brooks and Liz Bills

6.1 Introduction

It is a truism to say that all pupils are different and have different needs. Yet the comprehensive system aims to provide the best possible education for all its pupils and the teacher has to plan to teach them in groups of around thirty. Whereas traditionally differences between pupils have been seen principally in terms of academic attainment, there is an increasing understanding that pupils also have legitimate differences of learning style and that helping pupils to fulfil their potential involves catering for these kinds of differences. This chapter will help you to understand your role as the class teacher in this process.

By the end of this chapter, you should:

- know what differentiation is and why it is an essential element of effective teaching;
- be aware of its role in national policy;
- be familiar with different ways of differentiating in the classroom and at school level;
- be aware of issues raised by differentiation.

6.2 Case studies

To set the context for what follows in the rest of the chapter, here are three case studies. The following are descriptions of three pupils from the same Year 9 tutor group.

Case Study 6.1

Aisha is a high achiever in most areas of the curriculum. She performs particularly well in mathematics and science, and also has very good literacy and language skills. She achieved a level 6 in English, maths and science in Year 6. Aisha grasps new concepts very quickly, however the material is presented, and she can be impatient with what she perceives as repetition. She likes to establish basic principles and to work from definitions; she is less interested in anecdotes or personal responses. Her strong analytical skills mean that she is often in a position to take a lead in group work, but she finds it difficult to work with those who grasp theoretical ideas more slowly or have priorities that are different from hers.

Case Study 6.2

Daniel generally gets on well with people and is popular with his peers. Teachers find that he is happy to make constructive verbal contributions in lessons but that his attitude changes and he 'acts the fool' when they set a written task. In Year 7 he got off to a bad start with some teachers because he was invariably the last to arrive at a lesson and would usually give some excuse about being lost or having forgotten what time it was.

Daniel's difficulties stem from the fact that he suffers from dyslexia. His difficulties with literacy were recognized early in Key Stage 2 (KS2) and most of his teachers were sympathetic and supportive, with the result that he did much better in his end of KS2 tests than originally expected. Provision was made for a reader/scribe in his maths and science tests and for part of English. He only managed to achieve level 3 in English but gained secure 4s in maths and science.

Daniel finds it difficult to read from the board, especially if he is some distance from it, and cannot copy from the board at any speed. He finds it difficult to communicate his ideas in writing and gets frustrated when this is the only way to demonstrate his understanding. Structuring a piece of writing is particularly difficult for him. He reads competently but slowly and often stumbles if asked to read aloud.

Case Study 6.3

Ben's performance data on entry to secondary school indicated that he was working below the expected level in key areas of the curriculum. He had achieved level 3 in English and maths and had a reading age 14 months below his chronological age. He did, however, gain a level 4 for science. His Year 6 primary school report described Ben as a quiet child who needed to develop greater confidence in his own abilities. Ben has been placed in low sets for maths and English and a middle set for science. His reading age is now 10 months behind his chronological age following an intensive reading course in Year 8. Although Ben has made progress in KS3, he is unlikely to attain level 5 in the core subjects at the end of KS3.

Ben finds it difficult to concentrate during teacher expositions and doodles when required to listen for any length of time. He responds positively when visual stimuli are used to help him understand new concepts. Ben is left-handed and writes slowly and awkwardly, producing poorly formed script. In subjects that require extensive reading and writing, Ben is poorly motivated, slow to start tasks and gives up easily when he encounters difficulties. Written work is rarely completed. Ben does not seek help either from his peers or his teachers. In fact, he is at pains to avoid drawing attention to himself and always appears to be working assiduously whenever a teacher approaches. Ben does not enjoy group tasks, especially group discussions, and contributes little when he is obliged to work in a group. Although Ben's fine motor skills are poor, making intricate tasks difficult, he nevertheless enjoys practical activities. Ben likes investigating how things work and designing and making things.

Ben has an older brother, an able, confident boy in his final year in the sixth form. Throughout his school career, his parents and teachers have had expectations of Ben based on his brother's achievements. Unfavourable comparisons have dented his self-esteem.

Task 6.1

Analyse the aptitudes and needs of each case-study pupil. Now pick a topic that is taught at KS3 in your subject. Imagine that you will be teaching this topic to a mixed-ability group containing the three pupils described above. How might you adapt your basic scheme of work/individual lesson plans to cater for the needs of Aisha, Ben and Daniel?

Spend some time thinking about the characteristic features and demands of your own subject. (For example, English literature involves reading closely and reflecting on texts to analyse features such as theme, imagery and characterization. Mathematics involves solving problems by thinking logically and sequentially about the application of general principles.)

Identify the following:

(i)   distinctive features/demands of your subject;
(ii) types of learners who may be well suited to studying your subject;
(iii) types of learning difficulty or learning style preference that are likely to provide particular challenges for learners in your subject.

The exercise you have just completed replicates the kind of thinking required to plan for differentiation. Differentiation is the provision teachers and schools make to help each child to achieve their full potential. It entails teachers developing insight into individuals' learning style preferences, their needs and difficulties. It involves identifying the barriers to learning faced by some children and devising means of removing, or at least minimizing, them. It also entails identifying potential: the strengths and interests that each child brings to learning and finding ways to capitalize on these. Skilful differentiation relies on a sound diagnosis of what is required to improve learning and this is why differentiation and assessment are best viewed as twin activities that work in tandem. The best way to build a detailed picture of a child's learning profile is through formative assessment (see Chapter 9). Assessment helps a teacher to understand where a pupil currently is with their learning and to decide on next steps: what kind of experience, support or challenge will help them to progress. Information derived from assessment provides the basis for action and that is why differentiation and assessment are closely related processes. Differentiation is a set of strategies which aim to ensure that each pupil leaves a lesson having moved on with their learning: knowing more; understanding more and in more depth; confidently applying skills and wanting to learn more.

6.3 Differences between learners

All pupils are unique and it is easy to identify differences between any pair of pupils. However, not all differences between pupils are relevant to their lives as learners. It is helpful to have some idea about categories of difference that might affect the way you plan for pupils' learning.

Educational differences

At a very obvious level, pupils' learning in any lesson is affected by what they have already learnt in previous lessons. This will be influenced both by the teaching that they have experienced and by the way in which they responded to it. Pupils in your class will have:

- attended different schools at KS2;
- been in different classes for your subject last year;
- been absent from lessons, worked with different partners, paid different degrees of attention both in class and to homework, and attended to different aspects of the lesson;
- been more or less successful in achieving the learning objectives.

So even without taking account of differences in pupils' cognitive make-up, there are strong reasons to expect that pupils will come to the new topic differently equipped to learn it.

Most of the information about pupils' prior achievement that is mentioned above is available to you as the class teacher if you know where to look for it and are prepared to spend a little time interpreting it. Some is not, no matter how assiduous you are in collecting assessment information, and so there will always be a need to make ongoing assessment during the lesson and to adapt your plans accordingly. For example, you may need to provide support during the lesson for Ben when you find that he did not complete a unit of work from last year that you were relying on as background for the current topic. You may need to provide a more challenging task for Aisha when you find that she has encountered all the ideas in your introductory exercise already.

Psychological differences

It is a common shorthand in schools to speak of pupils with 'high ability', 'low ability' or 'middle ability'. However, this terminology masks a great number of uncertainties and complexities about pupils' learning potential. The very existence of a character-istic that can be termed 'general ability' or 'intelligence' is hotly contested (see Chapter 4). Humans begin to learn as soon as they begin to exist and recent research into brain function has confirmed that, even more than was previously thought, the ability of the brain to learn is developed through its learning activity. In other words, cognitive ability is not set at birth but is developed through use. In this context, although it is possible to make statements about what pupils can do now (i.e. their attainment), it is not possible to be certain what they will be able to do in the future. For this reason, it is more acceptable to describe a pupil who has been successful in their learning to date as a 'high attainer'. The use of this terminology is a reminder that there is nothing either innate or inevitable in a pupil's level of achievement.

In terms of differentiation at the classroom level, the notion of general ability, or even that of attainment in a general sense, is not particularly useful. It may help you to predict who will achieve a high score in the end-of-year assessment, but it doesn't tell you how to provide for the high or low attainer. What kind of learning do they prefer? Can they work effectively on their own or do they need a lot of input from an adult? What kind of problems or tasks will they excel at or find difficult?

Differences in learning style

Ability to learn might be characterized in terms of speed or capacity, but there is also much interest currently in different learning styles.

Learning styles have been conceived differently by different authors. However, two common distinctions are between *wholists* and *analysts*, and between *verbalizers* and *imagers* (see Riding and Cheema 1991). Wholists like to get an overview of what is to be learnt before they begin to fill in the detail, whereas analysts like to understand the detail before integrating the parts into the bigger picture. Verbalizers are most comfortable learning from words, whether spoken or written and can assimilate infor-mation most easily in this form. Imagers prefer to receive information in diagram-matic or pictorial form. There is a good deal of evidence that people have styles of learning that are common to the individual across different areas of learning. There is some debate regarding whether an individual's learning style remains constant or can be developed over time.

Learning styles differ from Gardner's multiple intelligences (see Chapter 4) in that an individual's learning style goes across all the domains in which they learn; for example, a verbalizer will prefer to learn using words whether they are learning about chemical reactions or poetry, whereas somebody with a strength in a particular intelligence will show an aptitude for associated areas of activity, for example a pupil with high musical intelligence will excel in music.

It may seem obvious that the best strategy for teachers is to try to adapt their teaching style to the learning style of their pupils to allow them to learn more efficiently. However, there is some evidence that a teaching style that is slightly different from pupils' preferred styles can help them to expand their repertoire of learning styles. The most effective differentiation strategy in these circumstances is to cater for different learning styles by making opportunities for wholistic thinking and analytical thinking, for verbalizing and using images. Schools tend to cater best for analytical thinkers and for verbalizers, so it makes sense to think about how that balance might be redressed. For example, it would be important to offer opportunities to Ben to learn through access to visual representations (diagrams, videos, posters) and to teach him methods of setting his ideas down in visual form, perhaps through 'mind maps' and annotated diagrams.

Social, cultural and gender differences

There is little evidence that particular learning styles are more common for boys than for girls, or for pupils of some cultural backgrounds rather than others. There are some claims that girls tend to be wholistic rather than analytical thinkers (Head 1995) and that minority groups in America value particular forms of information (Guild 1994). However, it is very clear that differences within groups are much greater than differences between groups. So, for example, if you guessed that a pupil was a wholistic thinker on the grounds that she was a girl, you would be only slightly less likely to be wrong than if the pupil were a boy. Paying too much attention to statistical links between certain learning styles and pupil characteristics can lead to dangerous stereotyping.

However, there are differences between pupils' interests and cultural experiences that can be linked to their sex and ethnic background. The teacher has the difficult task here of being continuously aware, in particular, of how these interests and experiences might differ from their own. For example, a mathematics teacher who had based a probability lesson on examples using a pack of playing cards found that the lesson was inaccessible for a number of pupils. Some pupils in the class were unfamiliar with playing cards and others found them offensive on religious grounds because of their association with gambling.

Specific needs

Some pupils have been identified as having learning needs that make special provision necessary, or as having 'special educational needs' (SEN). Such pupils benefit from early identification of potential barriers to learning and differentiation strategies designed to remove or minimize their impact. For example, the school's special educational needs coordinator (SENCo) has provided the following advice to Daniel's teachers:

> It is recommended that Daniel sits near the front in lessons where he can more easily read from boards and is more likely to build a positive relationship with the teacher through verbal interactions. Daniel will particularly benefit from opportunities to consolidate and demonstrate his understanding in ways that do not require a written response. Where possible, written tasks should be short and employ techniques such as writing frameworks to help him organize his response. Teachers should avoid asking Daniel to read in class, because he is very embarrassed about his difficulty with this. Giving homework well before the end of a lesson will give Daniel time to copy it down correctly.

Special educational needs can take a great many forms and it is not possible to do justice to the range of needs in a chapter of this nature. You will find more information in Chapter 21, which looks at SEN in greater detail.

6.4   Differentiation and planning

It is sensible to consider how differentiation affects the types of planning undertaken by student teachers: the medium-term planning of units and scheme of work (SoW) and the short-term planning of individual lessons. Some aspects of differentiation are best planned for in the medium term. For instance, it may not be possible to cater for a wide range of learning styles and preferences within a single lesson, and to attempt to do so would fragment the planning. Therefore, it is helpful to think about catering for different learning styles and preferences as part of your overall planning for a SoW rather than attempting to tackle this on a lesson-by-lesson basis. Similarly, as well as having objectives for individual lessons, it is important to clarify longer-term aims for a SoW, distinguishing between essential knowledge, skills and concepts that all pupils will be expected to learn, additional materials that most pupils will assimilate, and more advanced ideas and skills that some learners might master. This will result in a set of differentiated aims specifying what pupils must, should and could attain:

- all pupils MUST;
- most pupils SHOULD;
- some pupils COULD.

A similar process should take place at the level of individual lessons where it can be useful to distinguish between key, support and extension materials:

- *Key material* refers to information, concepts and activities that it is essential for all learners to address in some way.
- *Support material* refers to provision that supports pupils who find the key materials difficult for physical, psychological, emotional, behavioural or linguistic

reasons. Support materials are not necessarily easier but they will have been developed with access in mind.

- *Extension materials* take the key materials to a higher or more complex level and are developed for those who find the key materials insufficiently challenging.

Differentiation can be considered in relation to lesson content, processes and products. The most commonly used differentiation strategies are described below.

Differentiation by task. Pupils use similar resources but complete different tasks. For example, all pupils use the Internet to research a topic but high-attaining pupils such as Aisha compile a report that requires them to synthesize and evaluate their findings, whereas lower-attaining pupils with SEN such as Daniel follow structured guidelines and search for answers to specific questions. Pupils with learning difficulties often find tasks more manageable when they are analysed into a series of small steps rather than them being required to take one large step.

Differentiation by resource. Pupils do similar tasks but use different resources. For instance, all pupils produce a descriptive account of weathering during a geography lesson, but some base their account on reading about the process in written sources and others, such as Ben, base their account on watching a video.

Differentiation by time. Similar tasks are undertaken but pupils have more or less time to complete them. Any subsequent tasks need to be purposeful and engaging to avoid acting as a disincentive to finishing promptly!

Differentiation by support. In-class support could be provided by you or by assistants. At the planning stage, decide how your own time and that of assistants will be deployed (see Chapter 7). Some pupils will need help at the beginning to get going with tasks, others will need help intermittently and others still will need support throughout.

Differentiation by outcome. Pupils work on similar tasks but the tasks are open-ended to allow for different outcomes. For instance, in a science lesson pupils are required to present the arguments for and against gas-fired power stations but a choice of presentational formats is offered, including a poster, an audio recording of a speech and a written report.

These strategies can, of course, be used separately but they are more often used in conjunction with one another. Indeed, differentiation often involves a cluster of interventions designed to support and challenge children in their learning. For instance, Daniel's teachers make a point of monitoring his progress closely whenever he has to follow written instructions, a task that is made easier by seating Daniel near the front of the classroom. Teachers also find that it helps if instructions are printed on pastel-coloured paper, using a large font size and simplifying the language. In science and mathematics, Aisha often works with a small group of high-attaining pupils focusing on open-ended, investigative tasks where there is scope for taking risks in learning and devising creative solutions to problems.

Clearly, differentiation as part of lesson planning focuses on the detailed provision teachers make to meet the specific needs of individuals and groups within a class.

Therefore, the requirements of all children have to be considered at the lesson planning stage with differentiation embedded in the process – and not seen as the addition of a few support and extension activities that can be tacked on after a lesson plan has been finalized. Thus, when Daniel's teachers set written tasks, they have to consider whether it would be appropriate for him – and other children who find writing difficult – to complete the same basic task by working in a different medium, possibly by word-processing a response or by producing an audio version. Alternatively, such children may be provided with a writing frame to enable them to complete the task or they may annotate a diagram rather than producing an extended prose response.

There are various organizational considerations to make, too. For instance, Daniel benefits from sitting near the front of classes where he can more easily read from boards and has frequent opportunities to interact with teachers. Giving homework well before the end of a lesson gives Daniel time to copy it down correctly. Differences in temperament and attainment make it difficult for Aisha and Ben to cooperate on group tasks so the composition of groups needs careful consideration.

Differentiation at lesson level is also shaped by feedback from ongoing formative assessment (see Chapter 9). For instance, before they started their work on addition of fractions, a class completed a pre-test. The results of the test suggested three broad starting points for this new topic. The understanding of equivalence of fractions needed to address addition was in place for over half of the group. However, over a quarter of the group had misconceptions that would need to be eliminated before they could tackle the work and a small group were already competent in addition of simple fractions with similar denominators and needed to extend their understanding. Pupils were assigned to groups based on their results in the pre-test and completed tasks tailored to their needs. The use of feedback to set individual and group learning targets is another example of the close relationship that should exist between assessment and differentiation. It is important to remember that where lesson objectives and learning targets have been differentiated, assessment criteria should also be adjusted so that different outcomes are recognized and valued.

Task 6.2

Consider these common methods of instruction. How many ways can you think of to differentiate them?

- Teacher exposition
- Question and answer
- Modelling/demonstration
- Worksheets
- Reading a text
- Watching audio-visual material
- Internet research

6.5 Differentiation beyond the classroom

So far we have focused on what teachers can do inside their classrooms to help pupils to achieve their full potential. However, in the first decade of the twenty-first century, differentiation became subsumed by a policy initiative: personalized learning. Personalized learning was identified as a national priority in the Labour government's Primary and Secondary National Strategies; associated materials are now available through the National Archives.

Personalized learning is a nebulous concept that has been variously defined. The name seems to suggest that each pupil should follow an individualized learning programme. However, teachers have been urged to view personalized learning as a 'philosophy' that has been embraced by some schools for many years. It entails:

> . . . tailoring education to individual need, interest and aptitude so as to ensure that every pupil achieves and reaches the highest standards possible, notwith-standing their background or circumstances, and right across the spectrum of achievement . . . giving every single child the chance to be the best they can be, whatever their talent or background.
> (www.standards.dfes.gov.uk/personalisedlearning/about)

Thus, although personalized learning addresses the needs of all children, including those who are gifted and talented, it has been promoted as playing a particular role in raising the aspirations and attainments of disadvantaged children. The Gilbert Review (DfES 2007a: 6) suggested that:

> Put simply, personalising learning and teaching means taking a highly structured and responsive approach to each child's and young person's learning, in order that all are able to progress, achieve and participate. It means strengthening the link between learning and teaching by engaging pupils – and their parents – as partners in learning.

Figures 6.1 and 6.2 provide frameworks and sets of tools intended to help schools to improve their own practice. They depict personalized learning as a multi-facetted initiative, combining in-class provision with whole-school approaches.

The five components in Figure 6.1 are listed below with examples of what these might mean in practice.

1. *Assessment for learning* and the use of evidence and dialogue to identify every pupil's learning needs.
   - Teachers use feedback to plan lessons matched to needs and pupils are given individual learning targets.
   - Teachers use questions designed to stretch pupils, providing adequate think-ing time for pupils to provide well-considered responses.
   - Pupils are trained to understand assessment criteria so that they can use them to assess their own and their peers' work.

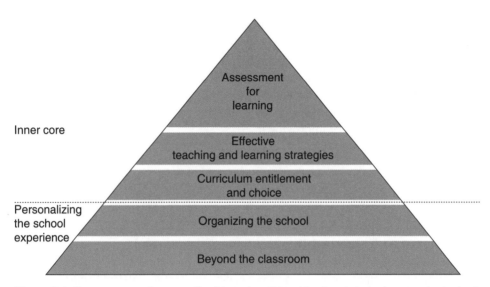

Figure 6.1 Components of personalized learning (http://nationalstrategies.standards.dcsf.gov.uk/print/83149)

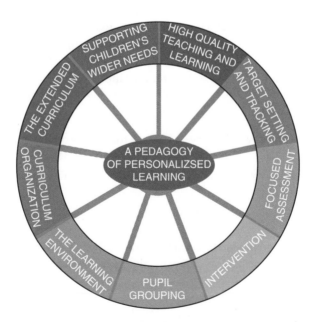

Figure 6.2 Pedagogy of personalized learning (http://nationalstrategies.standards.dcsf.gov.uk/node/156770?uc=force_uj)

2. *Teaching and learning strategies* that develop the confidence and competence of every learner by actively engaging and stretching them.

   - Teachers use a wide repertoire of teaching strategies including whole-class interaction, guided group work and focused, one-to-one tuition for those who are experiencing difficulties.

   - Pupils engage with learning by reflecting on their own performance and identifying ways of improving it.

   - Peer tutoring schemes train same-age or older pupils to support the learning of other pupils.

   - Cognitive acceleration programmes focus on improving pupils' thinking skills.

3. *Curriculum entitlement and choice* that delivers breadth of study, personal relevance and flexible learning pathways through the system.

   Groups of schools form consortia to provide greater curriculum choice at 14–19 years, with pupils moving between sites to access different parts of the curriculum.

   Vocational options in subjects like engineering, and health and social care.

4. *A student-centred approach to school organization* with school leaders and teachers thinking creatively about how to support high-quality teaching and learning.

   - Pupils are given a voice in decision-making by, for example, more effective use of school councils, allowing pupils a bigger role in setting agendas.

   - Pupils are given a real say in their learning, by being consulted about the effectiveness of teaching and learning and by providing feedback to teachers.

   - The use of information and communications technology (ICT) to create a 'virtual school' that provides online materials and support to pupils outside normal hours.

5. *Strong partnerships beyond the school* to drive forward progress in the classroom, to remove barriers to learning and to support pupil well-being.

   - Collaboration with employers to provide pupils with commercial and industrial experience.

   - Creative partnerships that involve local artists or creative institutions working with pupils.

   - Strengthening partnerships with parents and carers by, for instance, running workshops where parents can work alongside teachers and pupils to improve participation and progress.

Although the research community has broadly welcomed this policy, its response has been cautious and a number of questions have been raised. For instance, Pollard and James (2004) emphasized the capacity of external and contextual factors to subvert the practice of schools, teachers and pupils, arguing that: 'If Personalised Learning is to be introduced successfully, national government agencies . . . will need to align their policies appropriately' (p. 23). Schools also have a part to play in recognizing pupils as individuals and ensuring that their provision caters for different learning needs. Traditionally, differentiation has been seen as a response to ability, and so at school level it has involved the use of organizational strategies, 'setting' and 'streaming' being the most common. Streaming involves allocating children to a stream for all or most parts of the curriculum. It is an approach grounded in the notion of ability as 'general', that is that pupils will perform at a similar level in the various subjects that make up the curriculum. This is an outmoded view in the twenty-first century and streaming is a relatively unusual strategy in schools currently. Where it is adopted, this is often for pragmatic reasons to do with ease of timetabling. Setting involves allocating pupils to ability groupings on a subject-by-subject basis, allowing for variations in performance from one subject to another. Higher sets will, in theory, be set more demanding work using more sophisticated learning materials and more complex tasks. The 1997 White Paper, *Excellence in Schools* (DfEE 1997a), marked a shift in official thinking about organizational differentiation strategies, requiring schools to consider setting unless alternative approaches could be shown to be more effective. Despite this official endorsement, concerns about setting remain. There are dangers that pupils placed in lower sets will be 'labelled' by themselves, their peers and teachers. Pupils can lose motivation when they are placed in the 'bottom set' and disaffection quickly spreads throughout the group creating an almost unteachable class. Setting can unfairly limit teachers' expectations for pupils in lower sets and sometimes leads to inequitable distribution of resources, both financial and human. Whatever mechanism is used for allocating pupils to classes, it is important to recognize that every group, however finely set, will contain children with a range of prior attainments and learning preferences. The only difference between a school practising 'setting' or 'streaming' and one using 'mixed ability' groups is in the spread of attainments and needs to be found within a group. Some researchers have raised doubts about the effectiveness of setting precisely because it allows teachers to assume that pupils in the class will work in the same way and at the same pace (see, for example, Boaler 1997).

Although school approaches to differentiation traditionally focused on ways of grouping pupils according to attainment so that pupils of similar ability could be taught together, some schools have experimented with grouping pupils according to learning style preference or, in response to different learning styles observed among boys and girls, by gender. Schools have also become increasingly responsive to pupils as individuals and the approaches listed below demonstrate this. This list is intended to convey some of the main ways in which schools are currently responding to the challenge of differentiation.

Target-setting

Target-setting takes place at different levels in schools. Chapter 9 considers target-setting as a feature of classroom life – the individual learning targets that are negotiated by teachers with pupils on an ongoing basis to enable children to progress in a subject. This day-to-day target-setting takes place within a framework of whole-school target-setting. Many schools run target-setting days where the timetable is collapsed to provide time for individual consultations between subject teachers, pupils and their parents. The aim of such meetings is to review a child's progress and potential and to establish targets for the medium term (e.g. the end of a Key Stage or year). Once individual targets have been agreed, the information is collated and shared among relevant staff. Overall progress can then be monitored, for instance by a pupil's form tutor, year head, and school assessment coordinator. Continuous monitoring allows schools quickly to detect when an individual's progress exceeds or falls below expectations and to agree an appropriate intervention strategy.

Mentoring

Many people perform the role of mentor for secondary pupils, including older pupils in a school, members of a school's senior management team, university students and business mentors from local workplaces. Although the role and responsibilities vary from scheme to scheme, mentoring represents an attempt to identify underperforming individuals whose learning may benefit from involvement in a mentoring relationship.

Support for the curriculum

The National Curriculum established pupils' entitlement to a broad and balanced curriculum. You will encounter a host of initiatives designed to support a broad and balanced curriculum by removing barriers and facilitating access for children with learning difficulties. For pupils who require additional challenge, the curriculum is extended in various ways. For instance, enrichment programmes may supplement the curriculum for high-attaining pupils whereas low-attaining pupils may be provided with in-class support from a teaching assistant. Alternatively, pupils may be withdrawn from classes either for parts of the week or for certain subjects, and taught by specialist SEN teachers or assistants. Sometimes pupils are withdrawn for several weeks at a time during which their education takes place in a special unit attached to a school. Chapter 7 explains how the work of other adults in the classroom may be organized.

6.6   Conclusion

This chapter has provided a brief introduction to the many ways in which differences between individuals impact on their learning and to some of the approaches adopted by individual teachers and by schools in response to these differences. Responding to individual differences is possibly one of the most difficult aspects of a teacher's role and, if taken seriously, will provide you with challenges for the rest of your career.

6.7 Recommendations for further reading

Adey, P., Fairbrother, R., Wiliam, D., Johnson, B. and Jones, C. (1999) *Learning Styles and Strategies: A Review of Research*. London: King's College, London.

Department for Children Schools and Families (2008) *Personalised Learning: A Practical Guide*. Nottingham: DCSF.

Kerry, T. (2002) *Learning Objectives, Task-setting and Differentiation*. Cheltenham: Nelson Thornes.

McNamara, S. (1999) *Differentiation: An Approach to Teaching and Learning*. Cambridge: Pearson.

Pollard, A. and James, M. (2004) *Personalised Learning: A Commentary by the Teaching and Learning Research Programme*. London: DfES. Available at: wwwfitlrp.org/documents/ESRCPerson.pdf.

Weston, P., Taylor, M., Lewis, G. and MacDonald, A. (1998) *Learning from Differentiation*. Slough: NFER.

7
Working with parents and other adults
Prue Huddleston and Liz Bills

7.1 Introduction

As a teacher you will take sole responsibility for groups of pupils right from the start of your career. However, you will also need to be a team worker in many aspects of your professional life. As well as working alongside other members of the teaching profession, you will need to work in partnership with a wide range of other adults who have an interest in the education of the young people in your care. To be effective in teaching young people, you will need to understand the roles and interests of these other adults and to liaise with them to share information and make decisions. The key adults in a young person's life are their parents or carers. The first part of this chapter is devoted to looking at the means by which teachers and parents meet and communicate about individual pupils. In addition, teachers have dealings with a variety of other professionals. In the second part of the chapter we look in some detail at the skills needed for working with other adults in the classroom, and briefly at the roles of other professionals with whom you may come into contact in school.

This chapter aims to introduce you to good practice in reporting to parents and carers and in working with other adults in the classroom. By the end of this chapter, you should:

- understand the principles of good report writing;
- feel more confident in taking part in a parents' consultation event;
- understand the role of specialist support teachers and assistants and how the class teacher can most effectively work with them;
- be familiar with the roles of some other professionals who work with schools.

7.2 Parents and schools

In September 2006, Rawmarsh School in Rotherham made headline news because of a dispute between the head teacher and parents of some pupils at the school. Following the introduction of new 'healthy eating' rules about the content of school meals, parents began delivering hot food from local take-aways and passing it to their children through the railings around the school grounds. The two mothers at the centre of the story were said to be providing food to as many as sixty children who did not like the new menus in school. Yet a few years before, Ofsted had been able to say of the school that it was responsive to parents who approached it with questions or concerns and that the school worked well with parents to support pupils' learning.

Relationships between home and school vary enormously from school to school, from home to home, and over time. They are, however, a vital part of the context in which pupils achieve or fail to make progress. The nature of the home–school partnership and the extent of the responsibilities of each to the other are frequently areas of contention.

Parents also play a key role in the development of the school in general, rather than just in the education of their own child. As an illustration of this, the National Confederation of Parent–Teacher Associations (PTAs), which is an umbrella body for individual schools' PTAs, with over 13,000 members across the UK, reported that in 2009, PTAs helped state schools to raise £79 million.

Task 7.1

Which aspects of their child's life in school would you expect parents to be most concerned with? What are a parent's sources of information about school and the child's experiences of it? Note down your answers to these questions and then think about how this impacts on your role as a subject teacher and as a form tutor.

Since 1999, schools have been obliged by law to set up a home–school agreement which they should seek to have acknowledged by the parents or carers of all pupils.

A home–school agreement is a statement explaining:

- the school's aims and values;
- the school's responsibilities towards its pupils who are of compulsory school age;
- the responsibilities of each pupil's parents;
- what the school expects of its pupils.

(DfE 2011d)

Such agreements should include school policies on:

- the standard of education;
- the ethos of the school;
- regular and punctual attendance;
- discipline and behaviour;

- homework;
- the information schools and parents give one another.

These agreements have been shown to be most effective when they are arrived at in consultation with both parents and pupils, and take account of the circumstances and value systems of different groups of parents. (More details are given at http://www. education.gov.uk/parentalinvolvement.)

7.3   Parents' consultation meetings

Parents' consultation meetings take a variety of forms. Parents may be invited to meet all their child's teachers on one evening, or to have a longer appointment with the pupil's form teacher who, in preparation, has received reports from all the child's subject teachers. The meetings may be timed during the school day, possibly with pupils off timetable to facilitate this, or in twilight or evening hours. Pupils may be invited to attend with their parents or asked to stay away.

Task 7.2a

As a parent, what might you hope to gain from a consultation event? Information, advice, reassurance? Or to show support for your child and the school? To express concern to the teacher(s)? Below are four parents' stories. Read through each in turn and ask yourself what this parent would be hoping to get from the consultation.

1. You are very concerned about Amir, who started secondary school this year. At primary school he was always very keen on science and usually got good marks. Since he started Year 7, he has been put in set two, which upset you, and he seems to be showing little interest in the subject now. When you ask him about his homework, he says he has already done it. He still spends quite a lot of time looking at the night sky through his telescope, though. Science is your own area of interest and you hope that Amir will make a career in it too.

2. Brenda is in Year 13 and has always enjoyed school. She has plenty of friends and has recently had a major part in the school drama production. She sings in a rock group as well and is very keen on a career on the stage. She doesn't talk much about school work, apart from her drama lessons, but you've no real reason to be concerned except that she does seem to get very tired. You wonder whether you ought to be firmer with her about being home at a reasonable time on week nights.

3. Carl is in Year 9 and finds all school work difficult. You left school yourself at 16 and have never been keen on reading, so it is hard to help him. You know

he needs to gain some qualifications to be able to go to college and eventually, you hope, to get a job, but you are not very clear about what to expect. He seems to like his English teacher so you decide to ask her.

4. Danielle is in Year 8 and is in the top set for maths. It has always been her favourite subject and last year's teacher said she had a real flair for it. This year she seems to have become disillusioned with the subject. She says the lessons are slow and boring and that a lot of the other pupils 'mess about'. She often has no homework because she has finished it during the lesson.

Task 7.2b

Now imagine that you are about to meet one of these parents. The notes below will give you the teacher's perspective on each pupil. What would your priorities for the meeting be as a teacher? How would your actions meet their expectations? What are the likely difficulties in each conversation and how could you, as the professional, deal with them?

1. Amir is in your class for science in Year 7, in the second set out of five. He achieved a good level four for science in Year 6 that put him among the highest achievers in the small primary school that he attended. He seems to be having some difficulty adapting to the secondary school context and, although he is keen to answer questions in class, his written work is not as good and his homework usually appears rushed.

2. Brenda is in your Year 13 tutor group and is a very outgoing and lively personality. Recently, she has been involved with the school production and that seems to have taken up a lot of her time. You have encouraged her in this as you know she is very keen on drama. However, in the last fortnight you have had notes from four different subject teachers saying that Brenda has been late handing in A level coursework, and you need to tell her parents about this at the consultation meeting. You have also noticed that she is often tired in the mornings during the tutor period and you wonder whether the new boyfriend that her friend keeps teasing her about has anything to do with this.

3. You teach Carl in your Year 9 English group, set five out of five. He has struggled with literacy ever since primary school and has particular problems with spelling, punctuation and grammar. His reading and writing skills are both at level three. He seems to like English though, perhaps because you always

go out of your way to include him in lessons and to praise the little progress he makes. Other teachers say he is very withdrawn in their lessons.

4. Danielle is in your top set Year 8 maths class. She is very able and confident in maths and likes to show that she has got to the answer first. She is quite happy to show her disdain for the slower members of the class, which makes it particularly difficult for you to manage the wide range of abilities in this class. To make matters worse, there is a small group of pupils in the class with very challenging behaviour. You have to spend a lot of time keeping them occupied, which makes it difficult to pay much attention to the pupils who finish first. Danielle is usually one of them. On the occasions when you do ask her to do some extension work she usually does not do it, especially if it is homework.

Thinking about these individual cases will, we hope, have helped you to develop some general principles for successful communication at consultation meetings. Some of the points you may have considered are as follows.

Preparation. You need to be prepared in advance by having ready access to the pupils' grades on class work and homework, to information about their homework completion and to examples of their work. This would be very useful in, for example, telling Danielle's parents about the problem you have had in getting her to engage with extension work or for showing Amir's parents the quality of his work compared with the rest of the members of the class. It may also be useful to have prepared what you want to say and some advice on the next stage for each pupil.

Positive start. Some parents will be arriving unhappy with some aspect of their child's experience at school, and others will be nervous about speaking to teachers, possibly because of a poor school experience themselves. In either case, it is important to start by saying something positive about the pupil. This should have the effect of calming an aggressive parent or reassuring a nervous one.

Targets for future action. The interview will feel – and be – more purposeful if you can identify a target for future action resulting from it. This is especially effective if the pupil is present, but parents will also want to work out how they can help. For example, Carl's parents might be able to encourage him to read at home, and Brenda's parents will want to have a look at her coursework schedule with her.

Give parents a chance to talk. Parents' meetings can be a really good opportunity to find out about your pupils' home influences, their interests, motivations and aspirations. You might, for instance, find out about Amir's interest in astronomy. You also need to give parents a chance to ask questions and express their worries.

Be informative without using jargon. Many parents find assessment schemes, public exams and the National Curriculum (NC) bewildering. You will need to be aware of parents' needs in this area and sensitive to their degree of expertise. Some of the parents that you talk to will be teachers themselves, of course.

Make a good first impression and keep to time. You need to look as though you have made an effort to look presentable, which can be a particular challenge at 4 p.m. after a day's teaching. Another aspect of showing your concern for your visitors is to keep to your appointment times. This can be very difficult as well, but it can be done if you do not 'fill time' unnecessarily and are firm about ending each interview on time, offering to find another time to speak to the parents if necessary.

7.4　Written reports for parents

The school's governing body is responsible for ensuring that a curricular record is kept for every pupil and that it is updated at least once a year. As well as detailing academic achievements, the record should include information about the pupil's skills and abilities and about his or her progress in the school and any special educational needs requirements. If a pupil transfers to another school, the record should be forwarded to the receiving school. Parents may request to see a copy of this record. This, of course, is a more detailed document than the written report which schools must, by law, prepare on their pupils at least once a year and is the document to which you, as a subject or form tutor, will be required to contribute. The report, at Key Stage 3/4 must include:

- comments on progress, highlighting strengths and development needs;
- general review of progress in all areas of the curriculum;
- information on absence;
- arrangements for the parents and/or pupil to discuss the report with teachers;
- in Year 9: in addition, NC levels;
- in Year 10: in addition, target grades for GCSE.

Schools increasingly involve pupils in commenting on their reports before they are sent to parents, often as part of the academic tutoring system. Reports, then, are part of a cycle of assessment that involves pupils in self-assessment and target-setting. Chapters 9 and 10 have more to say on these subjects.

Task 7.3

Schools use a wide variety of formats for written reporting, some of which involve information and communications technology (ICT) and comment banks. Make a note of three reasons why the use of comment banks might be advantageous, and three ways in which they might have a negative impact.

Below is an example of a report produced using an ICT-based 'writing frame'. Some parts of the report are the same for every member of the class, some phrases are chosen from comment banks and some are composed particularly for this pupil.

Name: Ruth Bridge
Tutor Group 9SQ
French

Students follow the 'Route Nationale' course and are assessed on their ability to listen to, speak, read and write the foreign language. In French, 'higher' levels of attainment mean National Curriculum Level 4 and above.

Subject-specific comments:

In French, Ruth participates enthusiastically in oral work. She communicates with fluency and she can understand most things. In written work she conveys the meaning well with grammatical accuracy. She learns new vocabulary and language skills efficiently.

General subject comments:

Ruth consistently achieves higher levels of attainment;
– she works well and is self-motivated;
– she is always well mannered and behaves in a responsible way;
– she is always punctual;
– she is always prepared for lessons;
– she can always organize her work effectively;
– she works well individually and within a group or team;
– she always completes homework properly.

The excellent progress Ruth has made this year will be maintained by:

– continuing the level of effort shown throughout the year;
– checking spellings thoroughly on completion;
– correcting mistakes to avoid repeating them;
– wider reading in the subject.

Imagine yourself as Ruth's parent or carer. How would you respond to this report? How would it make you feel? Are there parts of it that are more informative than others?

What questions does it leave you with? Are your comments about ICT and comment banks, both positive and negative, borne out by this report?

Your thinking about Ruth's parents' viewpoint may have led you to some general principles about good report writing. Perhaps the three most important things to remember are:

- *Audience*: avoid jargon and think about whether parents will easily understand the language you are using.
- *Accuracy*: draw on evidence and examples so that your points are made more convincingly and with more clarity.
- *Acclaim*: praise and build on the positive, always including a suggestion as to how the pupil can make progress.

There is an expectation that reporting pupils' progress to parents will move increasingly to an online process, thus allowing parents access to information concerning their children's progress, behaviour, and attendance at points throughout the year. It is not intended that this will replace face-to-face dialogue with parents, or the annual written report, but that it will encourage parents' support of, and commitment to, their child and to the school.

7.5   Other contact with parents

Contact with parents can range from a chance meeting in the supermarket, through an informal exchange at a school drama production, to an individual meeting set up in school to discuss a particular problem. Take advantage of these opportunities as much as you can to make contact and to find out about your pupils' home backgrounds. This will help you to understand what motivates, interests and affects them. It is nearly always an advantage for pupils to feel that their teachers and parents know each other. Negative and positive messages from teacher to parent or vice versa are made more meaningful by personal knowledge.

As a subject teacher, your regular opportunities to communicate with parents are often limited. That means that any contact you do make is likely to have an impact. A note written home, or a phone call, is an effective way of amplifying praise. Some teachers keep a stock of pro forma letters or postcards in their mark book so that in the lesson, or as they are marking work, they can add a few words that explain the reason for the letter and hand it over to the pupil there and then. Contact with home may also be appropriate for reinforcing a reprimand. This sort of contact needs to be treated with caution as it can result, at two extremes, in the parent responding aggressively to the teacher or over-reacting in their punishment of the pupil. It is not unknown for the same parent to make both of these responses. As a student teacher or newly qualified teacher (NQT), in all cases you must familiarize yourself with the school's policy on contacting parents before acting independently.

7.6   Other adults in the classroom

The Training and Development Agency (TDA) website indicates that the number of staff supporting teaching and learning in schools has risen steadily from 25 per cent of the total school workforce in 1997 to 43.37 per cent in 2009. It predicts that numbers will continue to rise (Learning and Skills Improvement Service 2011). Thus, today's secondary school teachers are much more likely than in the past to be working with other adults in the classroom. Who are these assistants? What sort of work do they do? How will they expect you to behave to them? To get most benefit from the provision of assistants for yourself and your pupils, you will need to understand the roles and skills of these other adults and how you can best interact with them as a teacher.

Changes in policy on inclusion have meant that an increased number of sources of funding became available to schools to enable them to provide in-class support for pupils with special educational needs (SEN) and with English as an additional language (EAL) (see Chapters 21 and 22), although some of this has now been scaled back as a result of government cuts. The Remodelling Agreement signed by government and teachers' unions in 2003 resulted in changes to what teachers could be asked to do as part of their work. The agreement was followed in 2005 by a requirement on all schools to redesign their staffing structure to take changed roles into account. At the same time, the remit of the TDA was widened to include the professional development of support staff. Details about the qualifications framework and training opportunities for different categories of support staff are given on the DfE website at http://www.education.gov.uk/. The increase in numbers and importance of support staff were consolidated by each of these changes.

Many different terms are used to refer to adults other than qualified teachers who work in secondary schools. The following glossary includes the main ones.

Support staff. This term is used officially to refer to all staff in schools who are not qualified teachers. So, for example, it includes welfare/pupil support and administrative staff, librarians, cleaning and catering staff, school finance officers and technicians, as well as staff who support the learning of individual pupils.

Teaching assistants (TAs). This is the official term for staff who directly support teachers in their work in classrooms. The type of activities they undertake in the classroom include, among other things, preparing the classroom for lessons and helping pupils who need support to complete tasks/activities. They are always supervised by the class teacher.

Higher level teaching assistants (HLTAs). In 2003, the government began to encourage the creation of posts in schools that would involve more responsibility than had hitherto been the case. Alongside the new name came a qualification and a set of 'standards' for HLTAs. This was part of the process of improving the career structure for TAs. Higher level teaching assistants work across the curriculum and may provide support for a special subject area, or work within a particular department. They are likely to be involved in the planning of lessons and in the production of resources.

Learning support assistants. Learning support assistants (LSAs) are usually employed to support the learning of a particular individual pupil or group of pupils who have been identified as having SEN. They usually work under the direction of the school's special educational needs coordinator (SENCo). In secondary schools in particular, they form a large subset of those individuals commonly referred to as TAs.

Classroom assistants. This term is not used very much in official circles. It was used to describe the role of staff, usually in primary schools, who provided all kinds of practical support for teachers, from mounting display work to clearing up after art. Some consider it an undignified label.

Learning mentors. The role has something in common with that of TA, but a learning mentor is generally much more involved in the pupil's development outside school. Their work focuses upon supporting, motivating and challenging those pupils who are deemed, for whatever reason, to be under-achieving. They seek to identify 'the barriers to learning' experienced by pupils and to support them and their families in overcoming them. Their work includes, among other things, working outside the classroom on a one-to-one basis with pupils, perhaps developing literacy or numeracy skills, or supporting confidence-building. Learning mentors usually involve pupils in target-setting and action planning. They liaise with teachers as well as with other professionals, for example social workers, who may be working with the pupil and his or her family.

You will have realized from scanning the glossary that TAs have many, varied roles. They fulfil a vital role in schools and yet they are often overlooked in terms of staff development and school management. In fact, some TAs report that teachers do not know their names or have any idea what they do. A survey of its members conducted by the National Union of Teachers in December 2002 concluded that:

- Only one in seven teachers had received any training for working with TAs, and the proportion was less for secondary teachers; fewer than 2 per cent had received any training as part of their initial teacher training (ITT).

- Most secondary teachers spend less than one hour a week planning and preparing work with TAs, who often plan their own work independently and take no part in assessment and recording.

- More than three-quarters of the respondents (and a higher proportion of secondary teachers) thought that the most important benefit of working with TAs was the additional support provided for individual pupils or groups of pupils.

Since this survey was carried out, working with TAs has become part of every ITT programme and the Remodelling project (see above) has offered a lot of support to schools in re-thinking the way in which they deploy and support teaching assistants. A report by Ofsted (2010c: 5) on the impact of the workforce reform programme conducted between 2003 and 2009 concluded that:

> Collaborative planning between teachers and support staff, a shared understanding of what constituted good learning, and the direct involvement of support staff in assessing and recording pupils' progress led to more effective classroom support and intervention.

Nevertheless, it is easy to overlook the importance for you as a class teacher of working effectively with TAs. According to the National Strategy document *Leading on Inclusion*: 'There is evidence that suggests schools need to think carefully about **how** and with **whom** teaching assistants work' (DfES 2005d: 244). This is the result of findings reported in a 'Summary of research on commonly used interventions', which include the use of TAs in the classroom. Some of these findings are pertinent to all teachers who need to plan how to use TA support in a lesson. For instance:

> The presence of a teaching assistant prevents the class teacher from considering their own role in adapting the curriculum to ensure their pupils access and participation.
>
> (DfES 2006d: 2)

> TA support in class appears to increase the amount of time children spend on task, but this does not result in an increased rate of learning, perhaps because it does not help pupils to construct their identity as learners, and may actually hinder this process.
>
> (DCSF 2006d: 2)

Therefore, it can be seen that the teacher has a responsibility to plan to make effective use of support in the classroom. For instance, it is not a given that a SEN pupil will be supported by a TA sitting next to the pupil for the whole lesson. Teaching assistants often run intervention programmes for SEN pupils and gain qualifications in counselling or testing for exam concessions, as these are areas where support can be particularly effective and make the most difference to the progress of specific pupils.

Task 7.4

The following list identifies the principles adopted in one school to facilitate effective working relationships between teachers and TAs. Once you have read the list, reflect upon the issues you would raise at an initial meeting with a TA who works with individuals in a class for which you are about to assume responsibility.

PRINCIPLES FOR TEACHERS WORKING WITH TAs
1. Having mutual respect for each other in terms of working together for the benefit of pupils despite the pervasive attitude in society that helpers are inferior to those in charge.
2. Setting aside enough time to plan and evaluate together.
3. Recognizing that TAs are a vital resource in the classroom to be deployed in a flexible way.
4. Believing that SEN children are not the sole concern of the TA but as much the teacher's responsibility as other children in the class.
5. Aiming jointly to create an effective learning environment where all children are encouraged to work as independently as possible.
6. Helping all personnel to feel part of the departmental approach to teaching and learning and fostering inclusion.

7. Creating a definite role in the classroom for TAs to avoid them feeling like a 'spare part'.
8. Including all members of staff in meetings and ensuring that attendance is paid for.
9. Valuing the expertise each individual brings to any classroom and providing opportunities to realize potential to maximize everyone's contribution to learning and make the most of each other's abilities.
10. Promoting a team spirit to demonstrate positive role models for pupils, foster their self-esteem and present a united front where discipline is involved.

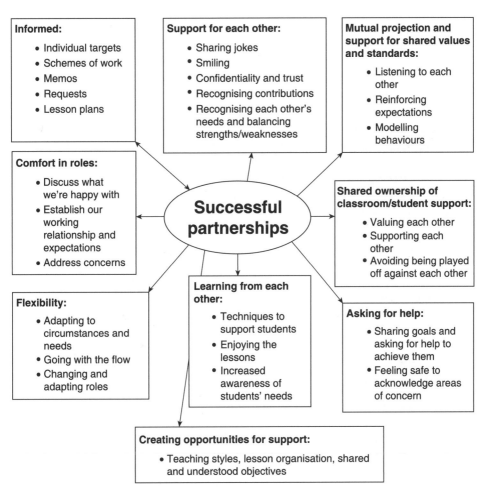

Figure 7.1 Successful partnerships (devised by colleagues in a school to foster successful partnerships between teachers and teaching assistants)

In many secondary schools, the work of TAs is organized by the SENCo who decides how to deploy the expertise and time of the TAs to best meet the requirements of the pupils identified as having SEN. This results in many different patterns of work for TAs. Three TAs described a typical working week as follows:

> In the course of the week I work with five different pupils. Most of them need my help because they have behaviour problems. I will often be with them for two or three periods in the day so I know them very well and know what has been happening for them earlier in the day.

> Over the week I support between 40 and 50 pupils both in the mainstream and in the special unit. I see most of them only once or twice a week. During six periods a week I am on 'rapid response' for one pupil. That means that if he gets into trouble in a lesson, I have to stop what I am doing to go and take him out to the unit.

> I am the LSA for the maths department and I support whichever maths class most needs my help. I get to know the teachers and the curriculum very well, and have a lot of contact with some of the pupils as well. I take a major role in identifying which pupils need support and in differentiating work for them. I feel I am really involved in supporting the teachers as well as the pupils.

Task 7.5

How would you expect the skills and abilities of these three TAs to differ? What does that mean about how you could work with them most effectively?

The same three TAs explained what they liked most about their work:

> I get most satisfaction out of struggling with kids who don't want to be in school. If we can get to the end of a lesson and they say they've enjoyed it, that's really great. I can think that I've helped get them through a difficult day, because every day at school is difficult for them.

> The thing I have enjoyed most recently was when I was working with a PGCE student with a mixed ability Year 7 class. She planned the lesson and she'd done a differentiated worksheet for the lowest ability pupils. I sat with them through the lesson and enjoyed the responsibility of teaching that group.

> You get lots back from the pupils. I'm really pleased when they manage to achieve something. Of course, it's not always like that. You give a lot of yourself and that can be hurtful when it goes badly.

The same TAs were also asked to describe what teachers did to help them to work more effectively. Here are their replies:

Involve me. Communicate. Not just about what the lesson is going to be but also where it fits in the scheme of work. It's usually done over a cup of coffee in the staff room. I like to get to department meetings. When I can get involved in the planning as well, I feel necessary and appreciated.

The most helpful teachers find time to give me a briefing before the lesson. Just a couple of minutes about what the lesson is going to be about. Giving me a copy of the worksheets at the start is really helpful. Otherwise I am turning up to the lesson not knowing what on earth is going to happen. Of course it's like that for the pupils. But it can make you feel really stupid and small.

The teachers who talk to you are the best. Otherwise you don't know whether they think you are helping. Everybody is different and has different strengths and preferences and if you don't talk, then you never find out what they are.

Communication is obviously a key issue. Plans for the lesson in which the TA is supporting your class need to be available to them in some form, but they will not have time to take in all the details of your lesson plan.

Task 7.6

Having read the preceding sections, how far do you agree with Ofsted's (2010d) conclusion that: 'Schools should ensure that teachers and members of the wider workforce plan collaboratively, agree intended outcomes for pupils, adopt a consistent approach to managing behaviour and agree procedures to assess and record pupils' progress'?

Take a lesson plan that you have used recently and decide what would be the minimum information that you could pass on to a TA about the lesson so that they are able to operate usefully within it.

7.7 Support from other agencies

You will have realized from the previous section that a number of agencies and organizations are involved with schools on a day-to-day basis. Often teachers will be unaware of just how many individuals and agencies visit the school and of the potential for some of their activities to overlap, and for confusion to arise. For example, the charity that comes in to run an enterprise education event with Year 10 may never meet the work-related learning coordinator, or the business studies teacher. Personal, Social, Health and Economic Education (PSHEE) tutors may not have an opportunity to accompany their pupils to a careers fair. In the best managed schools, of course, these activities will form part of a coherent programme and there will be dialogue between different teachers, form tutors and subject heads about what is happening. All this should be supported by strong leadership from the senior management team and, of course, from governors.

The importance of robust, and trusting, communication cannot be over-emphasized, particularly when dealing with young people whose needs are complex and whose backgrounds are likely to have a substantial impact on the ways in which they perform, achieve and behave in school. The recent Green Paper (DfE 2011a) has outlined proposals for a new single assessment process to replace the current multiple assessment procedures, which are sometimes protracted and frustrating. It is proposed that by 2014 all pupils who currently have a statement of SEN or learning difficulty would undergo a single assessment to identify their learning and support needs and would be provided with an Education, Health and Care Plan (DfE 2011a: 7). For a fuller discussion of these proposals, see Chapter 21.

7.8 Conclusion

In this chapter we have looked at the relationships that you as a classroom teacher will have with a variety of other adults who have a legitimate interest in the pupils you teach. The keys to success in each of these relationships are communication and partnership. The time you spend considering and listening to the other partner's point of view will be the factor that makes the relationship work for the benefit of the pupil whose progress is everybody's concern.

7.9 Recommendations for further reading and webliography

Campbell, A. and Fairbairn, G. (eds.) (2005) *Working with Support in the Classroom*. London: Paul Chapman.

Department for Education (DfE) (2011) *Support and Aspiration: A New Approach to Special Educational Needs and Disability: A Consultation*, Cm. 8027 (Green Paper). London: HMSO.

Lee, B. (2002) *Teaching Assistants in Schools: The Current State of Play*. Slough: NFER.

O'Brien, T. and Garner, P. (eds.) (2001) *Untold Stories: Learning Support Assistants and Their Work*. Stoke-on-Trent: Trentham Books.

Ofsted (2010) *Workforce Reform in Schools: Has it made a Difference? An Evaluation of Changes Made to the School Workforce 2003–2010*. London: Ofsted.

Rudney, G.L. (2005) *Every Teacher's Guide to Working With Parents*. Thousand Oaks, CA: Corwin Press.

Website
http://www.education.gov.uk

8

Communication in the classroom
Paul Elliott

8.1 Introduction

> Communication and the teacher–pupil relationship lie at the heart of teaching.
>
> (MacGrath 1998: 62)

The ability to communicate successfully with your pupils is central to your role as a teacher. Communication skills are very complex, but your success as a teacher depends upon them. We will consider the ways in which non-verbal communication occurs in the classroom, the features of verbal communication and, finally, take a detailed look at the art of questioning.

By the end of this chapter you should:

- appreciate that your ability to communicate effectively with pupils will play a major part in determining how successfully they learn;
- be aware of your scope for non-verbal communication in the classroom;
- be aware of the power of questioning as a teaching tool;
- be able to identify features of good practice in questioning technique.

If you communicate effectively with your pupils they will respond positively, but it is important to remember that communication is a two-way process. This means that when you are planning lessons you need to consider not only what you intend to communicate to pupils, but what you expect them to communicate to you, how they are going to do this, and how you might respond.

Consider the following questions:

How do pupils know . . .

. . . the objectives/intended learning outcomes of your lesson?
. . . how they will meet them?
. . . whether they are on target to meet them?

. . . when they have met them?

. . . what they need to do to progress?

And:

How do you know what your pupils know?

How can you promote deep learning?

You cannot answer these questions without a dialogue taking place. If communication involved one-way traffic from teacher to pupils, then teaching would be easy. Unfortunately, this ancient strategy of *filling empty vessels with knowledge* has proved ineffective.

To be a successful teacher, you need to plan what you are going to communicate, how you are going to communicate it, and how you are going to promote communication between your pupils and yourself and between pupils. A common mistake that student teachers make is to talk too much. If you do this, pupils will start to turn off from what you are saying and may miss the main messages. Successful teachers can facilitate quality learning with a minimum of words, but careful planning is essential if you are to achieve this.

8.2 Communication and power

Everyday conversation between people is characterized by particular features. Try listening to a conversation between two of your friends while thinking about how their conversation is structured. Their conversation will probably be punctuated by hesitations, interruptions, incomplete sentences that fade away, and lots of facial interaction (even when one or both parties are blind). This is very different from many verbal classroom interactions involving teachers. Typically, teachers tell pupils: when to talk, when to stop talking, what to talk about, and how well they have done it. In this traditional scenario, much of the talk is centred on one individual pupil at a time and the teacher demands that the class pays full attention to what is being said. Either the teacher is talking or a pupil is responding to the teacher. This means that the teacher is in a very powerful position; there is a 'strong asymmetry of power in interactions between teachers and children' (Wood, quoted in Norman 1992: 207).

By using the power of your position appropriately, you can build good relationships with pupils. When pupils trust you, you are in a good position to help them learn. To build such trust, you need to communicate with:

- clarity, keeping sentences short, simple, and focused;
- appropriate vocabulary, in terms of complexity and degree of formality;
- the aim of building pupils' confidence and willingness to participate;
- honest and useful feedback.

If your communication lacks any of these features, your pupils will either fail to understand what it is you are trying to communicate or, worse, will feel threatened by it. Remember that you are in a position of power in the classroom; you are the person who possesses most knowledge and you therefore have the responsibility to communicate effectively. Sometimes teachers tell pupils they have not listened properly when, in fact, it is the teacher who has not explained properly.

A growing number of educationalists argue that there is great value in promoting classroom dialogue in ways that challenge the traditional power relationship between teacher and pupil. Wells (1999) believes that dialogic inquiry, where teachers and pupils collaborate in a search for answers, is a process that leads to a much richer learning outcome.

8.3   Non-verbal communication

When you think of communication in a classroom, what form does it take? The first thing that probably comes to mind is verbal communication by the teacher. Classrooms throughout the land are full of teachers talking to pupils: explaining, questioning, instructing, praising, chastising, advising, and so on. This verbal communication is central to your work as a teacher and most of this chapter relates to this skill, but there are other forms of communication between teacher and pupils and their importance should not be under-estimated.

Simply by your presence in a classroom you are communicating with your pupils. In so many ways we send subtle signals to our pupils about:

- how we feel about ourselves;
- how we feel about them;
- how we feel about the subject matter of the lesson;
- how confident we are;
- how well organized we are;
- how competent we are likely to be at helping them learn.

These subtle messages are transmitted as a complex medley of signs and signals.

Compare the following two sets of signs and signals that exemplify positive and negative messages:

Positive	*Negative*
Neat/tidy/stylish dress	Untidy/disheveled/wildly eccentric or old-fashioned dress
Well-organized paperwork	Papers spilling out of bag, falling on floor
In the classroom before pupils arrive	Arrives after pupils
Cheerful, pleased to see pupils	Ignores pupils or scowls at them
Pleased to be there	Moaning about it being Monday morning
Calm, confident	Flustered, tense

Think carefully about how others are likely to perceive you. For a student teacher it can be helpful to try and conform to pupils' expectations of what a competent teacher should be like. Teaching is a profession where there is room for individuality and it is important that teachers provide a diversity of role models, but in practice there are limits beyond which you may struggle to function effectively. You should not expect to simply be yourself in the classroom. Observe experienced and successful teachers at work and then follow them into the staffroom after the lesson. As the staffroom door closes behind them, you will see that they metamorphose from the classroom version of who they are, their 'teacher self', into their 'real self'. The two personae will not be unrelated, but they are unlikely to be identical!

Part of the communication between you and your pupils will be in the form of body language. This is a very complex language, but one in which it is well worth developing fluency. As with other forms of communication, it is about teachers' and pupils' behaviour. Neill and Caswell (1993) explore the subject in more detail. As a teacher, there are some simple guidelines that will help you:

- Stand or sit confidently.
- Keep still! Shifting about distracts pupils and is taken as a sure sign of nerves.
- Control your hands! However nervous you are feeling inside, try to avoid fidgeting with them.
- Try to show the pupils the palms of your hands and make confident, slow gestures with them while you talk.
- Try to be positive and expressive with your face: smile and nod regularly when pupils say or do anything positive.
- Have the confidence to approach pupils for an intimate discussion of their work, but avoid invading their personal space.
- With smaller pupils in particular, it is much better to get down to their level rather than lean over them when having a one-to-one interaction.

The way that you use your body will not only influence the way that you are perceived, but also the way that you feel. If you can act with confidence, even when feeling nervous, you are likely to end up feeling more confident.

8.4   The teacher's territory

The confidence with which you use the teaching space will also send a message to your pupils. A mouse that is feeling vulnerable tries to hide. If it has to be somewhere in the open, it will look for cover or stay close to walls at the edges of open spaces. As a new teacher, you may sometimes feel like using the same strategy in the classroom. Do you feel safest behind the teacher's desk? Would you prefer to avoid going anywhere near the back row? It is natural to feel this way when you start teaching, but it is behaviour to avoid if you are to communicate the right message to your pupils. However nervous you feel inside, there should be no 'no-go' zones in your teaching room.

Just as it is important to get your body language right, it is important to get your use of classroom space right: cower at the front and pupils will sense your fear. Here are some general guidelines that are worth remembering:

- Moving confidently around a classroom 'marks' it as your territory.
- Using posters, pictures, and display work to personalize classrooms not only creates a more stimulating working environment but marks it as part of your territory.
- Addressing a class from different places in a room (this can be difficult in some small rooms) shows them that you are confident and at ease in the space.
- Talking to a class from the back of the room 'turns the tables' on those pupils hoping for a quiet life at the back.
- Moving among pupils to check their progress is important. It should be done soon after the start of a task to check that pupils have understood what they have to do.
- Whatever the layout of the room, you should make sure that all pupils are looking at you while you are addressing the class; this may mean that some or all will have to move around in their seat.

Some habits are best avoided:

- Moving around the room as you speak. This means the point of the pupils' focus is changing and will distract them from what you are saying.
- Turning your back on pupils for very long. If you stop to speak to one pupil, make sure that you scan the room regularly to check that everyone else is on task.
- Obscuring pupils' views of information on boards, overhead projector screens or interactive whiteboards. You do not want to become the excuse for pupils stopping work!

Task 8.1

Draw a sketch map of a room that you have taught in or are going to teach in. Think about how you could use the teaching space effectively and confidently. Mark on the map all of the places that you could stand or sit while addressing the class. These need to be places where you can scan the room easily and make eye contact with pupils. Think also about suitable places in the room to place resources, to carry out demonstrations or to get pupils to engage in role play or other activities.

8.5   Types of teacher talk

Teachers need to talk to pupils for a variety of reasons. Their talk falls into three general categories: cognitive, procedural, and managerial. Cognitive teacher talk concerns the content of the curriculum and includes the majority of the dialogue, questioning, and elucidation engaged in by the teacher. Procedural talk concerns how the work in the lesson is to be done; so it is about the nature of tasks, the teams in which pupils are to carry out the tasks, and the timing of the work. Managerial talk is that which relates to behaviour management, the giving of notices unrelated to the curriculum and so on. All of these categories of teacher talk are essential, yet much attention has been drawn to the need to shift the balance from procedural and managerial towards more cognitive talk. It has been suggested that two-thirds of lessons are talk, two-thirds of that talk is teacher talk, and two-thirds of teacher talk is about management and procedure rather than content (Norman 1992). As a new teacher you may well find yourself talking too much. Many new teachers are guilty of spending too long introducing content and explaining tasks, to the extent that pupils become bored and lose track of what is being said.

8.6   Pupil talk

Meaningful dialogue between pupils is crucial if you are to establish a learning community in your classroom. There is a range of pedagogical techniques that promote productive talk between pupils (see Chapter 16). These include techniques such as Think–Pair–Share, Jigsaw, and Envoys. The pupil-to-pupil talk encouraged by these techniques and initiatives is valuable for a number of reasons:

- It gives pupils a chance to learn from and teach each other.
- It builds pupils' confidence by giving them the chance to verbalize their ideas about the work in hand and a chance to practise using the subject vocabulary.
- It is less daunting than talking to the teacher, especially in front of the rest of the class and when one's ideas are still being formulated.
- It allows pupils to test ideas in an intimate setting before going public with them.
- It helps pupils to build social skills.
- It helps pupils to develop the ability to express themselves coherently and persuasively.

8.7   Your voice as a tool

You need to use your voice with precision and care if you are to get the best out of it. It also has to last you a long time, so it is important that you use it in a way that will avoid damage. Your voice is the main tool of your trade; think of it as a scalpel rather than as a sledgehammer!

Your voice has unique characteristics that make it distinct from anyone else's and you also have the ability to vary the way in which you speak. It is desirable to practise varying the way in which you use your voice to achieve different effects and emphases. Some people have voices that are easier to listen to than others, but there is a lot that everyone can do to maximize the potential of their voice. Volume, speed, pitch, projection, and expressiveness are examples of the features of your voice that you can try to vary to achieve maximum impact.

There will be times when you need to get a class's attention. Some teachers achieve this very effectively without using the voice, for example by giving a visual cue, such as raising their hand, or using a signal, such as a bell or gong. If you do raise your voice, once you have gained attention, you can dramatically reduce its volume. If you continue to talk to a class with the volume of your voice raised, you will provide pupils with the cover they need to start their own conversations. If you speak at a volume that pupils at the far side of the room can only hear clearly by concentrating on what you are saying, it becomes hard for them to start an illicit conversation.

You should certainly avoid shouting. Pupils *hate* teachers who shout and you will end up with noisy classes and a sore throat. Loud teachers create loud class-rooms. You need to be able to make yourself heard on the far side of a classroom, but you should aim to do this by *projecting* your voice, not by shouting. It is possible to learn to project your voice effectively. Before you speak, take a deep breath, be clear in your mind what you need to say, and then say it with clarity and conviction. Think about the tone of your voice as you speak so that you sound as if you are in authority rather than someone who is pleading with a class. A common mistake of new teachers is to talk too fast. If you do this, pupils may find it difficult to follow your explanations or instructions and sooner or later they will give up trying. Speak clearly and try using pauses to emphasize key points and to allow pupils to digest what you have said.

On becoming leader of the Conservative Party, Margaret Thatcher was given voice lessons. The main aim of this was to teach her to lower the pitch of her voice and give her more gravitas. Her advisers knew that voices with a lower pitch tend to carry more authority and sound more confident. Speaking at a higher pitch can make pro-jection in the classroom more difficult and, when you are under stress, the pitch will tend to rise further, making the situation worse. If you have a relatively high-pitched voice, you can try to practise using the lower end of your natural range and your train-ing institution may also be able to arrange coaching to help you do this. The Voice Care Network is also a useful source of advice (see www.voicecare.org.uk/).

8.8   Less is more

Teacher talk is very important but it is the quality of what a teacher says, rather than the quantity that matters. A lesson that is dominated by the sound of the teacher's voice is seldom a successful lesson. A lesson where the teacher says the minimum that is needed to interest pupils in the subject and explain the nature of a well-planned task or series of tasks that will engage their interest, can provide a powerful learning expe-rience. Take the time to plan what you are going to say, make sure that it is clear, unambiguous, and at a level appropriate to the listeners. Avoid unnecessary detail and repetition, check pupils' understanding, and allow them the chance to check that they have understood you. Then let pupils get on with the task. Once pupils are on task, you can circulate to talk to individuals or small groups. It is during these more intimate exchanges when you engage in dialogue with your pupils that much of the highest quality learning takes place and you will be able to build effective working relationships.

Task 8.2

The next time you plan a lesson, think carefully about what you need to say. Try scripting part of what you are going to say and then edit the script down to the minimum that is needed to communicate clearly the cognitive, procedural, and managerial aspects of the lesson. Aim to deliver the lesson with the minimum spoken input possible. Then record the lesson and evaluate how successful you have been.

8.9   The art of questioning

It is a little ironic that teachers spend so much of the time asking questions. It makes more sense for pupils to ask most of the questions, since it is teachers who have the knowledge and expertise. However, there are very good reasons why teachers should ask questions, most of which can come under the umbrella of 'assessment for learning' (see Chapter 9), for example:

* to establish what pupils already know about a topic or what skills they already have;
* to promote pupils' cognitive engagement with a topic;
* to check what pupils have learnt;
* to check the effectiveness of their own teaching.

There should also be opportunities for pupils to ask questions and engage in a dialogue with the teacher. While they need to be able to ask the teacher questions, pupils can also benefit from asking each other questions. The ability to ask effective questions is a skill that needs to be nurtured in pupils. There are various strategies we can use to help pupils to identify, phrase, and ask appropriate questions. The following are some ideas that you could try in the classroom:

* Get pupils to work individually, in pairs or in groups of three to devise questions relevant to the topic for the teacher to answer. Make the process anonymous to encourage pupils to pose questions they might otherwise feel too embarrassed or lacking in confidence to ask and then either: (i) have them place their questions in a box during one lesson for answering in the next; or (ii) tell pupils to fold up their questions and put them into a cardboard box. You can then draw out a selection to answer on the spot.

- Create a climate of enquiry by encouraging pupils to ask questions and speculate during the lesson; for example, chunk lessons, providing opportunities for pupils to raise questions at the end of each phase.
- Give pupils 'answers' and ask them to suggest what the questions were.
- Use the 'hot-seat' technique. This is where pupils, rather than the teacher, take turns at fielding questions from classmates.

8.10 Types of questioning

There are various categories of question that you can ask. They place very different demands on pupils and achieve different things, so you need to develop an awareness of how you are using questions. Certain questions can be considered 'low-order', meaning that the cognitive response they elicit is relatively undemanding. Some questions merely require the pupil to *recall* something and so test existing knowledge or observations, for example:

In which parts of Brazil is coffee grown?

This sort of question is often used at the start of a lesson to assess existing knowledge, but used too extensively it can bore or patronize pupils. It is important to develop a wider-ranging repertoire of questions that require higher-order thinking. Slightly more demanding is the *comprehension* question:

Why is Brazil a good place to grow coffee?

and the *application* question, which requires pupils to apply their knowledge to a different situation:

What other parts of the world might have conditions suitable for growing coffee?'

High-order questions make greater cognitive demands and require pupils to analyse, synthesize, and make evaluations. An *analysis* question might be:

Why is Brasilia the capital of Brazil?

A *synthesis* question demands that the respondent makes use of several pieces of knowledge to produce an answer:

What would happen to Brazilia if Rio was made the capital of Brazil?

An *evaluation* question requires the respondent to synthesize various pieces of information to make a judgement of some kind:

Would Rio make a better capital city than Brasilia?

These different types of question have been categorized according to Bloom and colleagues' (1956) Taxonomy of Educational Objectives (see Section 5.3).

Task 8.3

Choose a specific topic from your own subject area and devise six questions representing the categories exemplified above.

You will probably have heard of *open* and *closed* questions. Low-order questions tend to be closed questions; that is, there is only a limited number of correct responses and often only one. High-order questions tend to be open ones; that is, pupils can make a wide variety of appropriate responses. Open and closed, high- and low-order questions should have a place in your repertoire because they all have a part to play in effective questioning. However, pay particular attention to asking open questions that require elaborated answers in which pupils have to explain their thinking (Gipps 1994).

8.11   Planning questions

As with all aspects of teaching, it is best to plan your questioning strategy in advance. It should be linked to the objectives for the lesson and should be designed to achieve specific things. For instance, you may want to use questions to establish what is already known, to stimulate thought or to set up the major themes of the lesson. You should also use questions to check learning and to reinforce learning that has taken place. By planning questions in advance, you can think about the way that you are going to ask them and take account of a range of options:

- *The sequence in which you will ask them.* It may be important to ask questions in a logical sequence. In most situations, it is wise to start with lower-order questions and build up to asking higher-order ones.
- *The language you will use.* Avoid ambiguity and try to get the level of vocabulary right for the class you are teaching.
- *Designing questions for particular pupils or groups of pupils.* It is important to involve all pupils in questioning, not just the most able. Try to differentiate your questions so that some are suitable for all.

Good planning will make you feel more confident during the lesson and better able to ask questions effectively, to think on your feet, ask supplementary questions, and engage in effective dialogue with your pupils.

8.12   Asking questions

Having planned your questioning strategy for the lesson, it is important to think about how you are going to ask them. Whether you are asking questions of a whole class, a small group or just one individual, there are some basic principles of good practice to bear in mind. As with other forms of communication with pupils, you need to remember that their use of language is almost certainly going to be less sophisticated than your own, so questions need to be clear. The younger the pupils and the less sophisticated their language skills, the truer this will be.

Having asked your question, it is vital to allow pupils thinking or 'wait' time. It is very common for a new teacher to fail to do this because they are anxious to get the 'right' answer so that they can move on. You must avoid this trap. Think how you would feel if someone was firing questions at you and failing to give you time to consider your response. By giving several seconds of thinking time, you provide pupils with a better opportunity to make a positive contribution to the lesson and thereby raise their self-esteem, making them feel good about being in your lesson. If you do not get a response, try repeating the question because this will give them a little longer to think about it and allows those who were not concentrating the first time a chance to re-focus. You may also need to offer some prompts or clues to encourage pupils to have a go. There is also a danger that some pupils feel they have not had time to think or contribute because the teacher habitually accepts answers from those who raise their hands quickest or shout the answers out. Some teachers avoid this by operating a 'no hands' policy, giving children thinking time and then expecting everyone to answer if called upon (Black et al. 2002).

In a whole-class setting, you need to decide which questions to target at individuals or small groups and which to broadcast for anyone to attempt. If all of your questions are broadcast, you may only get responses from the most confident pupils. While such pupils can be useful in helping to roll out your structured lesson, if you neglect to involve other pupils this will leave them feeling isolated and you may miss the fact that the majority have lost the thread of the lesson. It is vital, therefore, to get in the habit of using both strategies to ensure that some of your questions are targeted at individuals and small groups. It is much easier to do this once you have learned pupils' names, but in the meantime you can employ other techniques, including:

- asking questions in sequence around the class;
- asking for a response from one of a group, for example 'Can anyone on the back left table tell me. . .';
- asking pupils to remind you of their name before they answer, so turning the session into an opportunity to learn more names.

What you must avoid is asking only those pupils who are keen to answer, who are sitting immediately in front of you, who need to be kept occupied or whose names you can remember.

Pupils sometimes need longer to think about certain higher-order questions, especially those that require them to reflect on issues or consider their own opinions. You can help pupils to get the greatest benefit from these types of question by giving them the opportunity to discuss their answers before replying. A useful approach is to first ask them to consider their response privately for a short time, then to ask them to discuss their ideas in groups of two to four, and finally to ask a spokesperson from each group to share their ideas with the whole group. This is sometimes known as Think–Pair–Share or the Private–Intimate–Public approach and it is an excellent way of involving all pupils in responding to a question.

Questioning is an important assessment technique, but how do you know whether a whole class knows the correct answer to your question? Rather than getting pupils to respond verbally, you can get them to respond visually to very good effect. If individual pupils or small groups each have a small dry-wipe board, you can ask them to write answers on the boards and hold them up for you to see. You can also create a class set of true/false, yes/no cards or traffic light cards (red = no, green = yes, orange = unsure) and get pupils to indicate their response to statements that you make. Even simpler is to ask them to put 'thumbs up' to represent 'yes', 'thumbs down' for 'no', and 'thumbs horizontal' for 'not sure'. All of these techniques allow you to scan the classroom and get an impression of how confident the class is with the material and whether there are individuals that may need extra help with the work.

8.13   Receiving answers

It's not only how you ask questions that is important, but also how you receive pupils' responses. It is best to avoid answering your own questions (and it is surprising how often novice teachers do this!). Answering your own question has the effect of:

- frustrating those pupils who simply needed more thinking time before responding;
- suggesting that you did not expect anyone to be able to answer;
- denying pupils the opportunity to test their own understanding and develop their own communication skills.

After asking a question, it is very tempting to take the first appropriate answer and move on, but this can be a mistake in some situations. By allowing more than one pupil to answer your question before you respond, you can get more ideas into the public arena and get a better feel for the understanding of the whole class. It is also good practice to invite pupils to evaluate each other's answers. This encourages greater pupil participation and active listening while allowing the teacher to spend more time listening, gaining a fuller picture of understanding within the group.

There are other choices to be made when responding to pupils' answers. First, you must decide whether to make a verbal response to a pupil's contribution. Generally, of course, you should, but there may be circumstances when it is best not to, for instance, when a clearly facetious response has been made. Sometimes an answer may be anticipating something that you wish to come to later and you may be unable or unwilling to adjust your plans to accommodate a change in sequence, in which case it is best to acknowledge the contribution and note that you will come back to it later. It can be very useful to repeat the answer or the key element of it because this allows other pupils to keep up and gives them a second chance to listen to the answer or, indeed, to hear it for the first time if the respondent has a quiet voice. You may wish to re-phrase an answer to make the point more clearly or concisely. It is certainly a good idea to praise contributions. If pupils receive praise for answers, they will be encouraged to make future contributions.

There will be occasions when the answers that you receive are factually errone-ous. In such cases you will generally need to correct the pupil, but this needs sensitive handling or you may demoralize them and put them off making future contributions: 'Thanks for that, it's a really good suggestion, but it's not quite right . . .' is much better than 'No, that's not what I'm looking for . . .'. In most cases, it is a mistake to allow factual errors to pass because it may be assumed you are endorsing them as correct. Wrong answers can be just as useful to you as correct answers in providing clues to pupils' thought processes, so you need to listen carefully to them.

Some pupils will give you responses that are part-way to answering the question and in these cases it can be worth taking the time to gently probe them and encourage a fuller answer:

That's an interesting idea, could you say a bit more about it?

That's an interesting answer, can you say more about what you have in mind?

By giving such opportunities you may discover that the pupil was not on the right track after all, but this would be a valuable thing to establish.

As you can appreciate, all of these different ways of responding to pupils' answers require you to be alert, sensitive, and aware of what you are doing.

8.14 Encouraging dialogue

Teachers who want to free themselves from the constraints of the traditional power relationship in the classroom need to think about how they are going to promote a dialogue with their pupils. At the heart of this approach is the idea of the teacher less as an authority figure and more as a fellow learner, facilitator, and expert witness. It entails being willing to give more control to pupils, with lessons driven by their questions, ideas, and enthusiasms. This approach can create and nurture a learning community and has the potential to produce much deeper learning.

Alexander (2005) identified the key features of dialogic teaching. First, it involves collective activity where the teacher and pupils work together on tasks. Second, it involves a reciprocal arrangement whereby the teacher and pupils share and listen to each other's ideas and views and consider alternatives. The teacher must support pupils by engaging in the sorts of good practice when asking questions and receiving answers described in Sections 8.12 and 8.13. The learning that results should accu-mulate into a coherent line of thought and enquiry, planned by the teacher to purposefully address specific objectives.

8.15 Avoiding questioning pitfalls

Questioning is a very powerful tool for promoting learning. A successful question-and-answer session can feel exhilarating and serve effectively to consolidate learning or move it forward. There are some common mistakes, in addition to those discussed above, that can cause such sessions to stall or lead to management problems. In general, it is best to avoid:

- asking questions requiring yes/no answers, unless the whole class is required to respond with visual signals such as YES/NO cards;
- asking questions with several valid answers, unless you are anticipating this;
- asking questions in a way that may encourage calling out. Good examples of these are questions that begin with the phrases 'Who can tell me . . .' and 'Does anyone know . . .'. If you think about such questions, you will see that the logical responses are not ones that you would want. It is much better to turn the question into an instruction: 'Put up your hand if you can tell me . . .'.
- over-use of 'response-seeking' (Black and Wiliam 1998a), an approach that entails fishing for a desired response, ignoring or rejecting unwanted answers, and then moving on as soon as the desired response is obtained. This promotes a surface approach to learning, encouraging guessing and the unthinking regurgitation of information that is poorly understood. It is also unhelpful to teachers because it fails to detect whether meaningful learning has taken place.

8.16 Theory into practice

You should now appreciate the importance of planning for effective communication with your pupils. Remember that it is about more than just what you say, but how you say it, as well as how you use your body and the space in which you teach. You should also realize that questioning is a powerful tool, but that you have to develop awareness of its finer points if you are to build successful relationships and promote learning.

8.17 Recommendations for further reading and webliography

Alexander, R. (2005) *Towards Dialogic Teaching: Rethinking Classroom Talk*, 2nd edn. Cambridge: Dialogos.

Department for Education and Skills (DfES) (2004) *Strengthening Teaching and Learning in Science Through Using Different Pedagogies. Unit 1: Using Group Talk and Argument*. London: DfES.

Mercer, N. and Hodgkinson, S. (2008) *Exploring Talk in Schools*. London: Sage.

Neill, S. and Caswell, C. (1993) *Body Language for Competent Teachers*. London: Routledge.

Norman, K. (ed.) (1992) *Thinking Voices: The Work of the National Oracy Project*. London: Hodder & Stoughton.

Wells, G. (1999) *Dialogic Inquiry: Towards a Sociocultural Practice and Theory of Education*. Cambridge: Cambridge University Press.

Wragg, E.C. and Brown, G. (2001) *Questioning in the Secondary School*. London: RoutledgeFalmer.

Website
www.voicecare.org.uk/ (The Voice Care Network)

9

Using assessment for formative purposes
Val Brooks

9.1 Introduction

What image does the word 'assessment' conjure in your mind? A piece of work after it has been corrected and assigned a mark? A silent hall filled with serried rows of examination candidates? School 'league tables' splashed across newspapers following the publication of examination results? A teacher questioning a class and attending carefully to responses? The diverse images that spring to mind remind us that assessment is a multi-faceted activity. This chapter focuses on arguably the most important purpose of assessment – the use of formative assessment to enhance teaching and learning.

The organization of this chapter reflects the stages in a school placement: induction; obtaining information about prospective teaching groups; planning a scheme of work (SoW); planning, teaching, and evaluating lessons. It suggests ways in which assessment can enhance these activities.

By the end of this chapter, you should:

- understand the concept of formative assessment;
- know why formative assessment is important;
- understand some of the ways in which assessment can be deployed to improve planning, teaching and evaluation;
- understand why and how to involve pupils in assessment.

9.2 Formative and summative assessment

Traditionally, *formative* assessment has been a neglected and poorly understood aspect of teachers' work (Black and Wiliam 1998a). Task 9.1 illustrates widely held assumptions that can hamper a teacher's ability to make effective use of assessment.

Task 9.1

Consider the following examples taken from visits to student teachers during school placement.

1. Student teacher A had written an *aide-memoire* across the top of his lesson plan in bold print.

(i) Tell them what they're going to learn.
(ii) Teach it to them.
(iii) Tell them what they've learnt.

Why is this approach flawed?

2. Discussion with student teacher B focused on planning a SoW. She had used the National Curriculum Programmes of Study to clarify learning purposes. Then she had planned for a variety of learning activities to cater for individual needs and the variations in learning style preference within the group. As her account made no mention of assessment, student B was asked how it would contribute. She pointed to a written assignment that pupils would complete at the end, explaining that it would be used to check what pupils had learnt.

How does student B view the role of assessment in her teaching? How else might she use it?

One of the problems with student A's approach is that he assumes that his pupils will learn exactly what he teaches them in exactly the way he intends them to learn. However, research, especially in conceptually difficult subjects like science, has found that it is not uncommon for pupils to understand a topic less well after teaching than they did before! The reasons for this are complex. For instance, pupils may start out with misconceptions that are incompatible with what is being taught. If teaching fails to address these misconceptions, confusion may be compounded when pupils try to assimilate new learning with pre-existing misconceptions. If teachers do not attempt to find out what pupils already understand about a topic, they cannot help pupils to link the ideas in the current lesson to knowledge that they already have, sometimes at an intuitive level. This means that the two sets of ideas remain separate and may be accessed by the pupil separately according to context. The relationship between what teachers teach and what pupils actually learn is not straightforward. Therefore, you cannot, as student A did, tell pupils what they have learnt during a lesson. The only reliable way of finding out what pupils have actually learnt is to assess them. For student B, assessment is a terminal activity that takes place once teaching has been completed. It offers a final check on what has been achieved before moving on. This is a traditional, and very limited, view of the contribution that assessment can make to teaching and learning.

Following a paradigm shift, it is now recognized that assessment is most helpful when it is an ongoing and integral part of teaching and learning so that feedback can be used at each stage in the planning/teaching/evaluation cycle. To be formative, assessment must have a 'feedback' and a 'feedforward' function. This means that feedback from one stage should be used at the next stage to improve subsequent teaching and learning. Consequently, assessment could, and should, occur at any stage – even before anything has been taught! There are three aspects of this paradigm shift that represent a radical departure from traditional practice:

- the idea that assessment could come first, rather than last, in the sequence of events;
- the idea that it should be used continuously to monitor progress and adjust approaches to teaching and learning;
- the idea that to maximize effectiveness, pupils must understand, and be fully involved with, assessment.

Summative assessment provides a systematic summing up of attainment through, for example, an end-of-topic test or a piece of homework. Typically, it results in a grade or level and signifies the end of something such as a unit of work or a Key Stage. Formative assessment is more like a thread weaving its way through the planning/teaching/evaluation cycle, binding the different elements and tailoring them to pupils' needs.

There are some common misconceptions about what distinguishes formative from summative assessment (see Newton 2007). One is that they involve different types of assessment. Summative assessment is often equated with external tests, whereas formative assessment is identified with what teachers do inside classrooms. However, test results can be used formatively and classroom assessment can be summative. For instance, a department that analyses end-of-Key-Stage test results to identify strengths and weaknesses in pupils' performances, and then uses the feedback to alter the teaching of certain topics, is using test results formatively. In contrast, teachers whose assessment is confined to giving ticks and crosses and to recording marks in mark books exemplify a summative approach, and their pupils will inevitably treat the marks as a means of comparing themselves with classmates. Neither party uses the assessment to obtain information that can be used to improve future performance. Although not all experts agree (see, for example, Newton 2007), there is a broad consensus that the real distinction rests on the *purpose* of the assessment. Only if there is an attempt to use feedback to improve teaching and/or learning is assessment formative. To be formative, assessment has to lead to action – doing something differently as a result of what has been learnt from the feedback. For instance, a teacher may use a written exercise to check pupils' understanding of a new topic and discover that a number of them are unable to complete the task because they are making the same basic error. Instead of pressing on with the final phase of the lesson as planned, she or he decides to use the remaining time to work through examples from pupils' work to illustrate and correct the problem. One way to check your own underlying purpose in carrying out an assessment is to ask yourself: 'Is this assessment FOR learning (formative) or assessment OF learning (summative)?'

A research team from King's College (Black and Wiliam 1998a, 1998b; Black et al. 2002) alerted the educational community to the capacity of formative assessment to improve teaching, learning and motivation, raising educational standards for pupils across the ability spectrum. Their 1998 study suggested that:

- the learning gains associated with formative assessment exceed those produced by most other educational interventions designed to raise attainment;
- formative assessment helps all pupils but is especially beneficial for low-attaining pupils whom it helps more than the rest;
- formative assessment reduces the spread of attainment while raising it overall.

Summative assessment, on the other hand, is often associated with 'high stakes'. Assessment is said to be high stakes when the results are regarded as having important consequences by those affected (for instance, a community might judge a local school by its examination results and the offer of a university place usually rests on results at Advanced [A] level). In contrast to formative assessment, high stakes summative assessment has been found to:

- narrow the curriculum and encourage transmission teaching and rote learning;
- widen the gap between high and low achievers;
- promote high anxiety among pupils and erode the self-esteem of low attainers (Harlen and Deakin Crick 2002).

These findings provide powerful reasons for making the development of formative assessment a priority during training.

9.3 School induction

Useful first steps at the start of a placement include identifying a school's assessment coordinator and obtaining a copy of the assessment policy. The policy should specify preferred approaches to target-setting, monitoring progress and providing feedback to pupils. Your department may have produced its own subject-specific guidance, so check whether there is also a departmental policy. In secondary schools, where pupils may be taught by ten or more teachers, a consistent approach is important to avoid confusion, so use these policies to ensure that your own practice is consistent with requirements.

When I trained as a teacher, conventional wisdom held that pupils should be allowed to make a fresh start with a new teacher who should avoid preconceptions about their capabilities. Although this principle was meant to apply to behaviour, one consequence was that student teachers possessed very little information about pupils' attainments and needs when they assumed responsibility for their learning. Nowadays, serving teachers can expect to receive a wealth of assessment data on teaching groups at the beginning of an academic year (see Chapter 10). Transferring data from one teacher to another has many advantages. It provides a smoother transition between years, helping teachers to pitch work appropriately from the outset.

Knowing what children should be capable of saves time that would otherwise be wasted rediscovering information that is already known. Similar principles apply to teaching placements, so familiarize yourself with assessment data held on groups you will be teaching. The following information is likely to be available:

- test and coursework results;
- the most recent assessment of pupils' current working levels and target grades/levels;
- assessments of attributes like organization and whether coursework is up to date;
- reading ages;
- details of children included on any special registers, such as for those identified as gifted and talented or those with special educational needs (SEN).

These prior assessments will help with differentiation (see Chapter 6) and pitching work at an appropriate level. There is also a case for undertaking your own assessment before finalizing teaching plans.

9.4 Assessment for planning

Traditionally, assessment played no part in the planning stage of the teaching cycle.
    The difficulties to which this can lead are illustrated by the following case study.

Case Study 9.1

Student teacher C taught a science lesson in which pupils investigated the factors affecting the strength of an electromagnet. To undertake the experiment, pupils needed to be able to construct a line graph to plot and interpret their results. When he marked pupils' accounts of the experiment, student teacher C realized that the point of the investigation would have been clearer if he had reinforced previous work on lines of best fit and their use in identifying trends and making predictions *beforehand*. He decided to go over the work again in the following lesson to address this shortcoming and to reinforce learning objectives that had been only partially achieved.

Student teacher C obtained feedback from pupils *after* he had taught them, whereas this feedback would have been most useful to him *before* he finalized his plan. It would have helped him to appreciate the prior learning that would play a key part in making the lesson meaningful and thus he could have avoided having to repeat the lesson.
    Is there any hard evidence to support this way of working? A large-scale American study is interesting in this respect (Black and Wiliam 1998a). It involved a

fresh intake of kindergarten children, most of whom came from disadvantaged home backgrounds. Socio-economic background and academic attainment are known to correlate closely, with more advantaged backgrounds correlating positively with educational attainment, whereas the opposite is true of educational attainment and disadvantaged backgrounds. Each year, many of these children were identified as having SEN at an early stage in their schooling. The purpose of the research was to determine whether a different approach to teaching could reduce the incidence of special needs referrals.

The research involved splitting the intake into two groups. One group was treated as a control group and taught as normal. The other group was placed on an eight-week experimental programme. Their teachers were trained to carry out baseline assessments before they did any teaching so that teaching could be matched to children's needs from the outset. After two weeks, pupils' progress was reviewed and teaching plans were modified in response to the feedback. There was a further review after four weeks when teaching plans were adjusted yet again. Thus, over the course of the programme, children were assessed three times: baseline assessment plus reviews after weeks 2 and 4 and, on each occasion, teaching plans were adapted in the light of the feedback.

To determine whether the experimental approach made a difference, both groups were given pre-tests in reading, maths, and science to establish a baseline for them. At the end of the programme, outcome tests in the same skills were used to measure whether there were any differences in their progress. The results showed that children's baseline scores provided a good indication of how well they would do in the final tests; that is, those who did best in the baseline tests were also likely to do best in the outcome tests. Nevertheless, the experimental group made significantly greater learning gains than the control group on all three subject tests. However, the key research question was whether the experimental approach had made a difference to the incidence of SEN referrals. Over a quarter of the children in the control group (1 in 3.7) were identified as having special needs. Did the experimental approach improve the performance of the other group? And if so, how big a difference did it make to special needs referrals? Make your own prediction and then turn to Note 1 (see p. 131).

Research such as this provides compelling evidence that pupils learn more effectively if teachers fine-tune their plans to learners' needs. Ausubel (1968: 36) explained this phenomenon thus: 'The most important single factor influencing learning is what the learner already knows; ascertain this and teach him [her] accordingly'. Assessment is the only reliable way of obtaining this information. It also helps teachers to develop a clearer understanding of how the learning jigsaw fits together and which pieces of prior knowledge (or skills) need to be in place before a new topic is introduced. Prior learning is particularly important in 'hierarchical' subjects where progressing to the next level is dependent on the acquisition of a hierarchy of knowledge, skills, and concepts (e.g. science, modern foreign languages, music and mathematics). However, it is a fundamental educational principle that learning should start from the point where the learner is. Therefore, assessment for planning is a critical component of formative assessment in all subjects.

Task 9.2

Identify some strategies for implementing assessment for planning. Two examples are given as a starting point.

1. Consider whether an end-of-topic test is suitable (or can be adapted) for use as a pre-test. A well designed pre-test can identify commonly held misconceptions and gaps in learning. It also provides a useful indication of progress when pupils are re-tested at the end.

2. Analyse a topic to identify necessary prior learning and knowledge, skills, and concepts to be taught. Using pupil-friendly language, produce a checklist of key learning points for pupils to 'traffic light'.

Note: Traffic lights involve using the colours red, amber, and green. They can be used in many ways; for example, they provide a highly visual record-keeping system and pupils can use them to self-assess work prior to submission. Here, their purpose is as a self-assessment tool, helping to identify those pupils whose knowledge and understanding are secure making them ready to move on (green), those who need to repeat work (red), and those whose learning is not yet secure so they would benefit from consolidation (amber).

Information gained from assessment for planning can be used to:

- identify prior learning that need only be revised, rather than wasting time repeating what pupils already know or can do;
- identify strengths that can be used as a foundation for building new knowledge and skills;
- reorient a SoW to pay particular attention to gaps in knowledge and misconceptions that are widely shared;
- differentiate to meet the particular needs of individuals;
- identify concepts and skills that will be required which are not subject-specific (e.g. the literacy and numeracy demands of a topic).

9.5 Building assessment into schemes of work

It is known that:

- effective teachers monitor pupils' progress closely (Harris 1998);
- pupils benefit from receiving rapid, regular feedback (Black and Wiliam 1998a).

These research findings suggest that assessment needs to be carefully considered during medium-term planning so that it can be properly integrated into the SoW. Close monitoring and rapid feedback are particularly important when new material is being introduced or when the subject matter is conceptually difficult or involves demanding skills. Opportunities for both should be identified in the SoW. Formative assessment requires teachers to view their medium-term plans as flexible working documents that can be adjusted in the light of feedback. If assessment is treated as a bolt-on extra, there is likely to be insufficient time to do justice to it and insufficient flexibility in the scheme to respond to feedback. This approach invariably raises concerns about the deployment of time. Under pressure to cover programmes of study in a limited amount of time, teachers worry about 'wasting' valuable teaching time on assessment. However, as Case Study 9.1 showed, assessment can make teaching and learning more efficient, reducing the amount of reinforcement and repetition involved so it does not necessarily require more time. Moreover, if it makes teaching and learning more effective, it should not be dispensed with on the grounds of wasting time!

Planning a SoW is also an opportunity to take an overview of the role of assessment. The principles of variety and match are as important in planning for assessment as they are in planning for learning. Therefore, the assessment demands that will be made of pupils, and the opportunities they will be offered, should be considered. Just as pupils have different learning style preferences, so do they favour different approaches to assessment. Indeed, some assessment techniques have been shown to display a gender bias. For instance, girls do better on extended writing tasks and boys on multiple-choice tests (Gipps and Murphy 1994). Similarly, some pupils perform better in one medium than another. A written medium favours those with well-developed literacy skills. Others may understand something just as well but would benefit from being able to demonstrate competence in a different medium, for example an oral or a practical task, or by using computer software.

Task 9.3

Take a SoW (preferably your own). If assessment has been considered, analyse the assessment demands and opportunities.

- Have points where progress should be monitored and pupils should receive feedback been identified?
- Are approaches varied or is there over-reliance on particular strategies (e.g. testing) or one performance medium (e.g. writing)?
- Are there opportunities for pupils to become involved in assessment?

If assessment has been overlooked, how could it be used to improve the scheme?

9.6   Assessment at the teaching stage: questioning

Questioning is, perhaps, the most useful and versatile assessment technique available. Because understanding can falter at any stage in the learning process, teachers need to be able to monitor progress continuously so that they can intervene promptly if problems arise. Questioning is easy to use and provides immediate feedback, making it very effective for monitoring progress. Unlike other commonly used assessment techniques, such as tests and homework, questioning does not require elaborate preparation or forewarning pupils about its use. It can be used as and when needed, providing instant feedback and allowing teachers to make on-the-spot decisions about how to proceed. Questioning also gives teachers access to the processes as well as the products of learning. When a teacher assesses a finished product (e.g. written work), although errors may be apparent, the reasons behind them may be hidden. Questioning has a diagnostic function, allowing teachers to probe pupils' reasoning and gain insight into thought processes that are causing difficulties. Skilful questioning has been described as: 'the single most important factor in students' achievements of high standards, where questions were used to assess students' knowledge and challenge their thinking' (Ofsted 1996a: 23). Therefore, questioning ranks among the top priorities for development by student teachers.

Chapter 8 includes an extensive section on questioning. Some of the points made there are particularly relevant to questioning as a means of assessment. For example:

- using open questions to elicit elaborated answers;
- allowing wait time;
- avoiding response-seeking;
- obtaining feedback from all members of the class;
- listening carefully to right and – perhaps especially – to wrong answers;
- providing honest feedback to pupils;
- providing opportunities for pupils to evaluate each others' answers;
- encouraging pupils to ask questions about what they are learning.

Task 9.4

Research suggests that teachers devote insufficient attention to developing high-quality questions that challenge or extend pupils' ideas, promoting higher-order thinking (Black and Wiliam 1998a).

Select a topic from your own subject and identify aspects that children are likely to find demanding. Devise questions that will help pupils to engage with the demands in a thought-provoking way.

Consider ways in which questions could be tackled (e.g. orally in pairs) and responses shared (e.g. 'hot-seating').

9.7 Peer- and self-assessment

Formative assessment only achieves its full potential when pupils become engaged with the process through self-assessment. Pupils who become skilled in self-assessment make impressive learning gains. For instance, in a study in which pupils were trained to make regular, usually daily, use of self-assessment in mathematics, over a twenty-week period the group made almost double the progress of a control group that did not practise self-assessment (Black and Wiliam 1998a). Findings such as this led Black and Wiliam to conclude that self-assessment is 'essential' rather than 'a luxury' (1998b: 19). However, self-assessment is a difficult undertaking beset with misunderstandings. For instance, teachers who claim to use self-assessment sometimes confuse it with a process better described as 'self-marking' (Ofsted 1998), where pupils mark their own work against a pre-determined mark scheme (Freeman and Lewis 1998). Some teachers worry about allowing pupils to allocate grades, believing them to be incapable of marking their own work reliably or honestly. Again, this represents a misunderstanding of the purpose of self-assessment, which is not about transferring the grading function from teachers to pupils. The real purposes of self-assessment are to equip pupils with:

- insight into the assessment criteria that will be used to judge their work;
- realistic notions of quality so that they can recognize 'excellent', 'good' and 'satisfactory' work;
- awareness of the gap between standards embodied in the assessment criteria and their own attainments;
- heightened awareness of learning and of themselves as learners, including their 'own cognitive resources; factors influencing performance; the demands of the task in hand; the range of possible learning strategies and when and how to use them' (Brooks and Fancourt, 2012).

Equipped with these understandings, pupils are able to regulate their own performance and tackle the attainment gap. Unfortunately, pupils also find self-assessment difficult and may take a long time to learn to use it effectively (Black 1998). Black and Wiliam have concluded that self-assessment is probably too difficult for pupils to attempt without first honing their skills through peer assessment. See Figure 9.1.

9.8 Written feedback

Constructive feedback is vital in helping pupils to progress. Nevertheless, one review of the literature on feedback found that two out of every five feedback effects were negative (Black and Wiliam 1998a). Given that feedback has both negative and positive potential, a key question concerns the types of feedback that are most likely to be helpful. Black and Wiliam (1998a) investigated the impact of three common feedback

---

- Share assessment criteria with pupils before they embark on a task;

- Make assessment criteria accessible by converting official language into a pupil-friendly idiom. Simplify criteria by using concise checklists or questions against which pupils can assess their performance;

- Use exemplification material to take the mystery out of assessment by providing concrete examples of what success looks like;

- Ensure that standards are well illustrated by providing examples of pupils meeting criteria with varying degrees of success (sources of exemplification material include the National Curriculum in Action website [www.ncaction.org.uk] and model scripts with examiners' commentaries produced by awarding bodies (Assessment and Qualifications Alliance [www.aqa.org.uk], Educational Excellence [www.edexcel.org.uk] and Oxford, Cambridge and RSA [www.ocr.org.uk]));

- Model assessment processes for pupils by sharing peer-assessment exercises with them;

- Introduce self-assessment once pupils have become competent peer assessors;

- Use peer- and self-assessment *during* a unit of work so that pupils have an opportunity to reflect on work while it is in progress and put what they learn into practice while it is *still* relevant.

Figure 9.1 Developing peer- and self-assessment skills

types on pupils' progress and motivation. They also explored whether the effects were influenced by ability. The experiment entailed a large sample of high-attaining and low-attaining 11-year-olds selected from a number of schools. For the purposes of the experiment, pupils were assigned to one of three groups that were mixed by school and ability:

- one group received individually composed comments on the level of match between their work and the assessment criteria that were described to all beforehand;
- the second group were given grades only;
- the final group received a grade and a comment.

The children's performance and motivation were then monitored over a series of tasks to determine which feedback type was most beneficial. Which group made most progress and were best motivated? Make predictions before turning to Note 2 for the results (see p. 131).

Providing constructive feedback is a sophisticated skill. Figure 9.2 identifies approaches that have been shown to be effective and those likely to have deleterious effects.

Target-setting is another means of converting feedback into feedforward.

Constructive	Counterproductive
✓ **Prompt feedback** The ideal is immediate feedback provided during performance so that pupils have an opportunity to implement what they have learnt before the work is complete.	✗ **Delayed feedback** Most likely to be ignored if pupils have already moved on to a new topic.
✓ **Written comments** When used to provide a clear explanation of ways in which work is successful and how future performance could be improved.	✗ **Marks and grades** A powerful form of feedback which 'overrides' comments. Encourages complacency in the able and despondency in the less able.
✓ **Task-involving feedback** Focuses on the knowledge, skills and concepts relevant to succeeding with a task.	✗ **Ego-involving feedback** Encourages pupils to focus on themselves, how well they are performing and comparing themselves with others.
✓ **Criterion-referenced assessment** Assessment is linked to explicit criteria which are clarified before pupils embark on a task.	✗ **Criterion-weak assessment** Criteria are muddled (Ofsted 1998) or tacit.
✓ **Scaffolded feedback** Creates a 'state of mindfulness' (Black and Wiliam 1998a: 51) with regard to the feedback, giving pupils as much help as they need to progress but no more.	✗ **Corrective feedback** Least helpful where teachers correct every error so that pupils are not encouraged to think about or apply the feedback.
✓ **Balanced feedback** Strengths and achievements are set against areas for improvement without dwelling unduly on either.	✗ **Unbalanced feedback** Dwells on the positive or the negative without properly acknowledging the other dimension.
✓ **Positive tone** Can be created by acknowledging achievements first and treating weaknesses as targets for development.	✗ **Negative tone** Can be created by drawing attention to what is wrong with work first or offering critical comments with no indication of how to improve.
✓ **Feedforward** Can be achieved by providing time for pupils to read and respond to feedback and by following up on previous feedback next time.	✗ **Feedforward absent** Where teachers neglect the links between feedback and future performance, pupils are encouraged to do likewise.

Figure 9.2 Providing feedback

9.9   Feedforward through target-setting

Setting targets for the end of a Key Stage or course is considered in the next chapter. Although endpoint targets are a natural focus for attention, they can only be achieved by identifying the sequence of smaller steps children must take to achieve their long-term goals. Therefore, it is individual learning targets, set on a day-to-day basis, that play a critical role in raising attainment (see Figure 9.3). These targets are important for the following reasons:

- Having a general aim to improve is almost as unhelpful as having no aim at all (Black and Wiliam 1998a).
- Ofsted (1998) warned that teachers find it difficult to provide feedback that combines honesty about the shortcomings in pupils' work with a positive tone. Instead, they avoid comments that might appear negative, producing feedback that is over-generous and misleading in its appraisal of the quality of pupils' work.
- Pupils often ignore feedback, failing to act on its suggestions for improvement.

Target-setting can address these difficulties. By taking a weakness, and converting it into a target, the need for explicit criticism is obviated. Instead of dwelling on difficulties, target-setting looks to the future, offering guidance on how to improve. It has been found to increase pupils' motivation and sense of purpose and accelerate rates of progress (Black and Wiliam 1998a).

Effective targets:

- are few in number;
- offer precise, measurable guidance on what pupils need to do to improve (compare 'Improve your presentation' with 'Improve the layout of your work by providing a margin, starting each new line next to the margin and using a sub-heading [underlined] for each section');
- are realistic and achievable in the short term, to maintain motivation;
- are task-related, focusing on knowledge, skills and concepts necessary to complete a task;
- are accompanied by regular opportunities for review;
- are those which pupils have been involved in selecting so they feel some ownership;
- are used as a reference point (e.g. pupils are reminded of them before embarking on a task and then offered feedback on their success in achieving them);
- involve pupils in deciding when targets have been met so that they become self-regulating.

Figure 9.3 Effective targets

9.10 Feedforward through lesson evaluation

Student teachers frequently fail to make the link between assessment and evaluation. Evaluations are often written before assessments have been completed. Even where assessment data is available, evaluation is completed without reference to it. Lesson evaluation is often impressionistic, based on students' personal perceptions of how well lessons went. Assessment offers a valuable source of evidence of the extent to which objectives have been achieved. It can add rigour to evaluation, either corroborating or refuting personal impressions.

Assessment also plays a part in evaluating teaching over longer periods of time. Patterns and trends can be detected in large bodies of data (e.g. the information for a year group over a full year) that are not apparent in small amounts of information. The analysis of large-scale pupil performance data is dealt with in the next chapter. It is mentioned here to indicate that evaluation at the microcosmic level fits into a bigger picture. The analysis that takes place at departmental, whole-school and national level is an extension of the scrutiny to which class teachers should subject their groups' progress and their teaching methods. At both levels, the key questions are:

- To what extent are all pupils achieving their full potential?
- How could teaching and learning be improved?

9.11 Looking ahead

The first decade of the twenty-first century witnessed a flourishing of interest in formative assessment among teachers and researchers. The term 'formative assessment' is used interchangeably with 'assessment for learning' in many publications, and a consensus on the extent to which these terms denote the same or different approaches to assessment has yet to be established. Assessment for learning is the favoured term in most government publications. Assessment for learning also became established at the heart of education policy, firing the interest that was initially sparked by Black and Wiliam's (1998a, 1998b) research. For instance, the Gilbert Review (DfES 2007a) identified assessment for learning as a priority for *all* schools and the following year assessment for learning became a National Strategy backed with £150 million of funding. Assessing Pupil Progress (APP), a related, government-sponsored initiative, developed in conjunction with the National Strategies.

Changes in government almost always lead to shifts in policy, and assessment for learning is no longer the national priority that it was for the Labour administration (1997–2010). The National Strategy materials have been archived and APP has been accorded voluntary status enabling schools to decide whether or not they wish to use it. Both measures are part of the Coalition government's commitment to reduce bureaucracy and free schools to decide what works best for them. Whatever happens at policy level, the thesis of this chapter is that there is sufficient evidence that formative assessment plays a pivotal role in enhancing the quality of what goes on in classrooms to justify all new teachers continuing to view it as a priority for their own professional development.

9.11   Recommendations for further reading and webliography

Black, P., Harrison, C., Lee, C., Marshall, B. and Wiliam, D. (2003) *Assessment for Learning: Putting it into Practice*. Buckingham: Open University Press.

Brooks, V. (2002) *Assessment in Secondary Schools: The New Teacher's Guide to Monitoring, Assessment, Recording, Reporting and Accountability*. Buckingham: Open University Press.

Centre for Educational Research and Innovation (2005) *Formative Assessment: Improving Learning in Secondary Classrooms*. Paris: Organization for Economic Cooperation and Development (OECD).

Clarke, S. (2005) *Formative Assessment in the Secondary Classroom*. London: Hodder Murray.

Ofsted (2003) *Good Assessment in Secondary Schools*, Reference HM1 462. London: Ofsted. Available at: www.ofsted.gov.uk/publications.

Websites

http://www.aaia.org.uk/ (website of the Association for Achievement and Improvement through Assessment)

http://www.school-portal.co.uk/GroupHomePage.asp?GroupId=162371 (website of the Suffolk Learning Hub – go to the assessment page)

http://webarchive.nationalarchives.gov.uk/20110202093118/

http://nationalstrategies.standards.dcsf.gov.uk/secondary/assessment (assessment materials from the former government's National Strategies, which have been archived)

Note 1

Only 1 in 17 children from the experimental group were identified as having SEN. This reduction was achieved by using assessment to inform planning. The study provides evidence of the learning gains made possible by tailoring planning to meet children's needs.

Note 2

Group	Performance	Motivation
Comments only	Raised and the improvement was sustained over the series of tasks	Followed a broadly similar pattern to performance but was also influenced by ability. • High achievers maintained a high level of interest irrespective of feedback type • Low achievers who received grades quickly lost interest
Grades + comments	Steady decline across the series of tasks	
Grades only	Initial improvement that was not sustained	

Note: Both feedback types that used grades were associated with a deterioration in performance and motivation.

10

Using assessment data to support pupil achievement
Chris Husbands

10.1 Introduction

Task 10.1

It is approaching the beginning of the autumn term. You are preparing your teaching for a Year 8 group. You have received data on the reading ages of pupils in the group. How might this information support your planning and teaching?

Table 10.1 Reading ages for a Year 8 class

Adam 10.1	Irma 11.1	Lauren 13.8	Sirinan 9.3
Aysha 14.6	James 9.8	Manisha 12.4	Syrha 11.1
Craig 11.1	Jimmy 11.5	Miranda 13.4	Tara 9.1
Georgina 12.1	Jo 12.0	Richard 9.5	Toby 8.1
Ian 11.4	Kimberley 11.7	Samantha 11.5	Vikki 7.9
Inderjit 10.7	Laura 12.2	Sarah 11.9	Yasin 7.8

Several features of the group are worth noting:

- all but three of the pupils (Aysha, Lauren and Miranda) have reading ages below their chronological age;
- three pupils (Yasin, Vikki and Toby) have reading ages that are more than three years below their chronological age;
- across this group, girls have higher reading ages than boys;
- two girls (Aysha and Lauren) have reading ages that are much higher than the rest of the class.

The reading age data here is an example – a relatively simple and crude example – of information that will help you to consider appropriate teaching methods, reading materials and writing activities for the group. It will also help you to consider other issues that could support your teaching: seating and grouping arrangements and individual learning plans for pupils in the group. It should help you to refine learning and outcome targets for pupils. In short, this sort of data should help you to plan learning more effectively. By using data in this way, you are beginning to make active use of attainment information to support planning for pupil achievement.

This chapter explores ways in which teachers can use data to support achievement. In particular, it sets out to introduce:

- the range of data that is available to teachers;
- the ways in which schools use that data;
- the target-setting process.

10.2 The range of data available

In the example above, reading ages were used to make some initial judgements about teaching and learning. Although reading age data is valuable, and helps teachers to think about the sort of curriculum materials that learners can access, it is also rather crude. Schools do not depend only on reading age material to help them plan. Reading age data measures only one aspect of learners' attainments, and quickly becomes outdated. There is evidence that some groups of children perform less well on reading tests than others: pupils whose first language is not English, for example, may underperform on a reading test given their cognitive attainment. Different curriculum areas use language, and written materials, in different ways: reading age data may be relatively unhelpful in supporting mathematics, science and music or art teachers. Moreover, in the last decade, the range, quantity and quality of data available to teachers has expanded enormously. They now have access to comprehensive data on pupil performance, progress and achievement, and they are able to make use of this to track pupil progress and identify appropriate targets for learning outcomes. Schools have in place sophisticated tracking strategies that draw together a range of attainment data and allow teachers to map their strategies against a range of data, as well as to track the extent to which learners are making expected progress.

New teachers face particular challenges in making best use of the range of data available. They need to find ways of making judgements about the reliability of information available and about methods of deploying information to support good teaching and learning, and they need to work out how to integrate data, and schools' strategies for using it, with their routine planning activities. This has become more pressing as schools have personalized teaching and learning (see Chapter 6), since effective personalization depends on the availability and use of reliable data about pupils' attainment.

Since the introduction of National Curriculum (NC) tests in the 1990s, schools have been able to access a vastly increased quantity and quality of information on pupil attainment, and to compare the performance of both individual pupils and groups of pupils in school against other groups within the school, previous performance, and national performance patterns. Primary schools are required to report formally on pupil attainment against the 8-level national scale at the end of Key Stage 2 (KS2) (at age 11). At KS3, pupils are also assessed against the 8-level scale. In English, mathematics, science and modern languages, schools are required to report on pupils' attainment against each attainment target; in the other foundation subjects, they are required to provide an overall subject level. These results are derived from school-based assessment, supplemented in the case of English, mathematics and science by optional tests. By the end of KS2, the majority of pupils are expected to achieve level 4 in English, mathematics and science, so that a pupil who achieves level 4 is said to be performing 'at expected level', while a pupil working at levels 1, 2 or 3 is performing 'below expected level'. Because KS2 assessment data covers the whole of the National Curriculum, and is supported by both test and teacher assessment data, it provides secondary teachers with a range of assessment information that can inform decisions about teaching and learning at KS3. All this means that in addition to reading age data, a school will have available NC performance data on the pupils in your Year 8 teaching group. And it will have been able to use that data during Year 7 to make judgements about the ways in which these pupils can access the secondary curriculum. Table 10.2 sets out an assessment data profile that a secondary school might receive on two pupils.

This is clearly a wider variety of data than that provided by reading scores alone, and it begins to point up some issues for teaching. Mayuresh, for example, appears to be working at or above the expected level in core subjects, but his reading score, at level 3 on both test and teacher assessment, suggests that there are potential difficulties in reading. Kirsty is working below the expected level and there appears to be a particular difficulty about writing. Multiplied across cohorts of learners, this data on entry to secondary school is a potentially rich source of information. During Year 7, it will be confirmed or revised by continuing teacher assessment. Schools may also wish to calculate a 'fine' level that is more nuanced than the overall subject level, by averaging the pupil's scores across the subject; Kirsty's fine test score in English, for example, is $(3 + 2 + 2 = 7)/3$, or 2.33 – as we will see later, this enables some finer analysis.

The use of KS2 assessment data is not straightforward. Persistent doubts have been expressed about its reliability, particularly near the boundaries of levels, and about the relationship between test results and teacher assessments; as the examples in Table 10.2 suggest, there can be discrepancies between test and teacher assessments. Given the extent to which primary schools are held accountable on the basis of their pupils' performance in KS2 tests, considerable effort is expended in Year 6 on boosting pupil performance, as a result of which many secondary schools treat the results with some caution. Finally, the data are rather crude – there are eight levels, but 90 per cent of pupils entering secondary school are assessed at level 3, 4 or 5, so test results provide little discrimination between pupils. As a result, schools have become adept at looking below 'headline levels' at the ways in which levels are made up, at discrepancies between test and teacher assessment, and at patterns across subject areas, in attempts to make NC test data more usable.

Table 10.2 Key Stage 2 attainment profiles

	Mayuresh		Kirsty	
	Test assessment	Teacher assessment	Test assessment	Teacher assessment
Overall subject level: English	4	3	2	3
AT1: Speaking and listening	5	4		3
AT2: Reading	3	3	3	2
AT3: Writing, including spelling and handwriting*	4	4	2	2
Overall subject level: Mathematics	5	4	2	3
AT1: Using and applying mathematics	5	4	2	3
AT2: Number and algebra	5	4	2	3
AT3: Shape, space and measures	4	4	2	2
AT4: Handling data	4	4	2	2
Science	4	4	3	3
Design and technology		4		4
Information and communication		4		3
Technology		4		2
History		3		2
Geography		4		2
Music		3		3
Art and design		5		4
Physical education		4		3

* At the time of writing, a formal review of the KS2 curriculum has just been completed. A key change arising from this review is that the English writing test will be replaced by teacher assessment of writing composition from 2013 but a test will be retained for more technical aspects of writing (spelling, grammar, punctuation and vocabulary). The new test will also be implemented in 2013.

Task 10.2

Look at Table 10.2. What implications do the data have for planning work in the first term of Year 7 for Mayuresh and Kirsty?

Given the difficulties of reading ages and NC scores, schools have turned to other assessment devices to provide more robust data on pupils. There is now an exceptionally wide range of such data available. The most widely used sources of datasets that can support schools' uses of attainment evidence are those provided by the National Foundation for Educational Research (NFER) (http://www.nfer.ac.uk), the Curriculum, Evaluation and Management (CEM) Centre at the University of Durham (http://www.cemcentre.org/), and the Fischer Family Trust (FFT) (www.fischertrust. org). NFER and CEM both provide standardized testing materials that schools can purchase, and a calibration/benchmarking service that enables schools to compare individual pupil and cohort characteristics with those of pupils nationally. NFER Cognitive Abilities Tests (CAT) and CEM Year Eleven Information System (YELLIS) and Middle Years Information System (MidYIS) are essentially cognitive reasoning tests that are not content- or syllabus-dependent. Administered across ranges of schools, they provide comparative data for schools of pupils' attainments, allowing schools to compare an individual's performance with that of a large sample of pupils, or to understand in more detail the make-up of their intake compared with overall performance patterns. Both NFER and CEM present learners' profiles in cognitive domains: MidYIS tests permit assessment of Vocabulary, Maths, Non-verbal and Skills. MidYIS, which is used in over 1500 schools, standardizes results nationally with 100 representing the average score. Pupils are sorted into four equally sized bands from A (the highest) to D (the lowest). This analysis allows schools to examine their own cohort in relation to the national cohort and, drawing on previous years' MidYIS, KS3 and GCSE data, to make predictions about pupils' KS3 and GCSE outcomes. Information is confidential to the school, and not used for publication. Pioneering work to develop predictive datasets was done with the A Level Information System (ALIS), which was the precursor of MidYIS and YELLIS. Schools submitted pupil-level examination data at 16+ (GCSE), and then the A level performance of the same pupils two years later. These data were used to explore patterns of pupil performance and, over a number of years, to track with some degree of certainty the A level outcomes for learners with a given level of GCSE performance. Over a number of years, and over a large number of sites, this developed into a robust data set that allowed schools to explore the performance of their pupils as a whole or as subgroups (e.g. boys, girls, those studying mathematics, those studying English, etc.) against the performance of a large cohort. ALIS enabled schools to explore extremely good performance and patterns of under-performance and to feed the results of this analysis into their planning. YELLIS and MidYIS applied the principles of ALIS earlier in pupils' careers, using very large datasets to predict GCSE outcomes for pupils with given YELLIS profiles.

The Fischer Family Trust data works in a slightly different way, since no additional testing is involved. Although, like CEM and NFER, Fischer data are based on using pupil progress data to predict likely performance in subsequent tests, the Fischer datasets are derived from NC and GCSE performance. The Fischer approach is based on the premise that there is a strong association between pupils' attainments at KS2 and the same pupils' attainments in Year 9, and strong associations between KS2 attainment and pupils' attainments on NFER CAT or CEM MidYIS tests taken in Year 7. Based on these starting points, the Trust's researchers explored the

performance of different *groups* of pupils in KS3 assessment, examining the influence of gender, entitlement to free school meals and those for whom English is an
additional language, and looking in detail at pupils whose performance was much
higher or much lower than expectation. From this, the Trust has developed data systems that allow local authorities, schools and teachers to explore pupil performance
against expectation based on looking at all pupils nationally, pupils in similar schools
and pupils in higher performing schools. The Fischer Family Trust profiles are widely
used in school self-evaluation and, in conjunction with other data, provide a powerful
tool for mapping pupil progress.

Task 10.3

Table 10.3 summarizes the range of entry data for some of the pupils in the
Year 8 group we began by looking at. Study it to determine what more you can
surmise about these learners' capabilities than was apparent from reading age
data alone. How might you use this information to inform your planning and
teaching of these pupils? What difficulties and pitfalls do you see?

Table 10.3 Year 7 entry data

Pupil	Reading age	NC English	NC Maths	NC Science	Vocabulary	Mathematics	Non-verbal	Skills
		National Curriculum			MidYIS			
Ian	10.04	3	4	3	101	108	100	104
Inderjit	9.7	3	3	2	97	92	103	101
Samantha	10.05	3	3	3	95	94	95	96
Lauren	13.8	5	4	4	116	105	110	112

Taken together, NC, CEM or NFER and Fischer Family Trust analyses put in the
hands of schools powerful resources that can be used to map and analyse pupil performance, exploring the experiences of particular classes or groups within the school.
Schools have available to them datasets that permit the analysis of pupil performance
in fine detail. Used together, such data allow schools to establish assessment management systems that track performance in relation to expectation and to challenge
teachers and pupils to try to exceed expectation. As pupils move through their secondary career, the school will be able to flesh out data profiles in increasing detail,
adding further information to track performance, and to use this to intervene to support pupils. Although we are looking here at the patterns exhibited by individuals,
schools will want to identify patterns among year groups to help direct support and
resources. This range of data across a cohort or class allows schools to make initial

judgements about grouping strategies or teaching needs of groups of pupils. Schools will rapidly supplement this data with their own within-KS data to build up an increasingly sophisticated pattern of information, which will allow them to track pupils' progress.

The data we have reviewed so far is based on deriving a set of expectations for schools and learners from national data: everything so far has been based on national norms. In practice, no school itself conforms to national norms, so schools deploy a variety of evidence and data – including FFT, YELLIS and MidYIS – to explore patterns of performance of individuals and groups of learners. Consider the data in Figure 10.1, which presents a simple version of an input/output attainment diagram for a school. The school has compared pupils' performance on a test at entry to the school with their performance on tests at the end of their school career. Each data point represents the performance of a single pupil, showing their performance on the exit test against their performance on the input test. A best-fit line has been applied to the data. This line shows the overall trend and the expected outcome for a pupil at each level of input performance. Each pupil below the line has performed *below* expectation for their level of input performance, and each pupil above the line has performed *above* expectation. What the school will wish to do is to analyse at group and individual level those pupils who performed *substantially* above or below expectation, and to look for any common characteristics among these pupils. For example, it may explore the difference between expected and actual performance separately for girls and boys, and discover that girls were disproportionately represented among those under performing. It may also analyse the performance of different ethnic and language groups within the school. It could analyse the outcome based on different

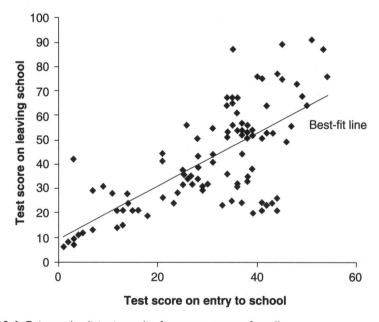

Figure 10.1 Entry and exit test results for a year group of pupils

teaching groups, and discover that pupils in groups taught by one teacher did particularly well: the school would then want to identify and disseminate that teacher's good practice. The school may also analyse the outcome based on individual factors. In particular cases – such as pupils whose performance was disappointing given their starting point – it may wish to call on the specialized knowledge of their tutors. It may discover that their performance was the result of traumatic events, such as the experience of family breakdown. Schools will also expect staff to examine the performance of pupils with moderate or severe learning difficulties in their classes and ensure that their progress is as good as possible. Local authorities carry out area analyses of performance, looking at the experience of individual schools with particular groups of pupils to inform overall thinking about performance within the authority, and its improvement. These analyses are an essential part of school life, but there are real dangers in over-interpreting data which may be based on small cohort sizes or which are not sensitive to pupil characteristics. Predictive data do not always take account of the moderating effect of special educational needs or pupils with English as an additional language (EAL), for instance. Pupils may enter secondary school with poor KS2 results and leave with far higher GCSEs than would have been predicted because they have radically improved their command of English along the way.

The real power of data for schools is not simply analytic, but also *predictive*. The key underlying premise that drives this is that prior attainment is the principal driver of subsequent attainment. As Figure 10.2 demonstrates, the higher a pupil's KS2 attainment score, the greater the likelihood of them securing high grades at GCSE. Essentially, the data underpinning Figure 10.2 enable schools to identify levels of

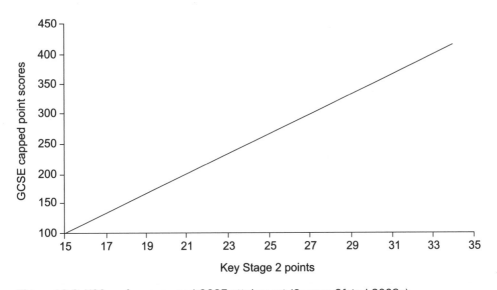

Figure 10.2 KS2 performance and GCSE attainment (*Source:* Ofsted 2008a)

Note: GCSE score derived from the points score to a maximum of eight subjects per pupil and scoring A* = 58 points, A = 52 points, etc.; KS2 performance based on levels × 6 (i.e. the graph is derived by multiplying the level score for each child by 6)

Table 10.4 Jesson bands and outcome probabilities

Average KS2 points	<22.5	22.55–25.54	25.55–28.54	28.55–30.54	>30.55
Jesson band	1	2	3	4	5
Likelihood of securing 5 A*–C grades at GCSE, including English and mathematics	2%	13%	43%	73%	92%

floor expectation for pupil performance, and to be clearer about overall expectations. To make this more readily understandable, many schools now make use of David Jesson's work (Ofsted 2008a). The Jesson tool uses KS2 data to divide pupils into five bands, based on their KS2 scores (see Table 10.4). These figures enable a school to predict pupil outcomes *if the school performs clearly to national norms.*

Table 10.5 provides two examples to demonstrate this. The two schools in Table 10.5 each have 200 pupils in a year group. In School A, pupils are evenly divided across the five KS2 bands. Such a school might expect 2 per cent of the 40 pupils in Band 1 to secure five A*–C grades at GCSE, including English and mathematics – that is, one pupil – but 92 per cent (or 37) of the pupils in the top band. The intake of School B is distributed differently, but the same principles apply, so that in School A we would expect 45 per cent of pupils to secure 5 A*–C grades at GCSE including English and mathematics, and 23 per cent of pupils in School B. These are, of course, crude data but they can be translated in a number of ways to identify expected performance levels for pupils in examinations (e.g. Figure 10.3).

Table 10.5 Two examples of the application of Jesson bands

	Jesson band					
	1	2	3	4	5	Total
Likelihood of securing 5 A*–C grades at GCSE, including English and mathematics	2%	13%	43%	73%	92%	
School A						
Number of pupils in each band	40	40	40	40	40	
Number of pupils expected to secure 5 A*–C grades at GCSE, including English and mathematics	1	5	17	29	37	89 (44.5%)
School B						
Number of pupils in each band	60	80	40	10	10	
Number of pupils expected to secure 5 A*–C grades at GCSE, including English and mathematics	1	10	17	7	9	45 (22.7%)

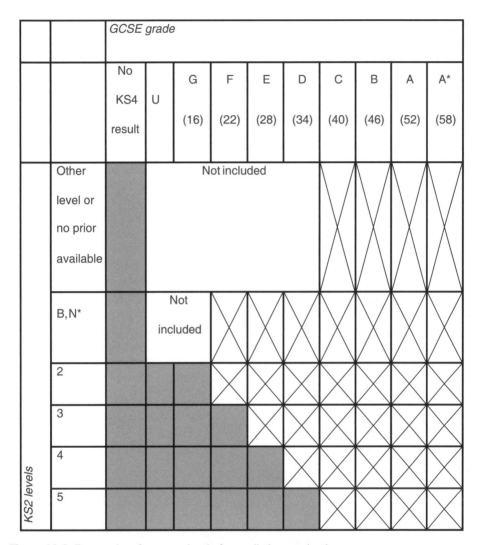

Figure 10.3 Expected performance levels for pupils in examinations
(*Source:* http://www.raiseonline.org.uk/)

Note: Contains public sector information licensed under the Open Government Licence v1.
*Pupils Below level 2 are Not assessed

Armed with this information, schools are in a potentially powerful position. For example, they are able to define realistic and challenging expectations for individual pupils. School B, in the example above, is a school performing below the 'national floor expectation' (35 per cent of pupils achieving 5 A*–C grades GCSE, including English and mathematics). The school needs to explore the data it has available, but also its curriculum and its pedagogy to design interventions that will enable it to meet or exceed the floor expectations: the Jesson bands, after all, deal with the likelihood of scoring patterns of outcome grades based on national norms – they are not, and should not, be limiting for individual learners. In the decade before 2010, considerable effort was spent trying to develop performance measures for schools that set the value-added in school into context – contextual value-added (CVA) sought to map out for schools their overall performance based on a series of assumptions about pupil prior attainment, gender, special educational needs (SEN), first language, ethnicity, measures of deprivation, measures of pupil mobility, age distribution and the number of 'looked after' children in the school. Since 2010, CVA has been abandoned, partly because it was difficult to use but also because it was perceived as giving schools some legitimacy to allow disadvantaged pupils to under-achieve. The emphasis now is on challenging all pupils to add at least two levels of performance per key stage, although some will of course do better. New value-added measures, focused on progress over time, are planned: one will measure achievement from KS2 to KS4 and another will focus on progress in the English Baccalaureate subject areas (see Chapter 13).

We have now looked at the basic technical and conceptual tools for data analysis and target-setting in school and, before considering how they might be used, it would be sensible to review them. First, schools have an array of different sorts of evidence available to them that can be supplemented by internally generated data. Sorting and using these data effectively presents schools and teachers with a significant challenge. Second, data exist that allow schools and teachers to make initial judgements about the needs of individuals and groups of learners. Third, national datasets also exist that allow schools to make predictions about pupil learning outcomes based on very large datasets and thus to set realistic targets for pupil outcomes based on national expectation and local knowledge.

Task 10.4

When you are on school placement, find out how the assessment manager in your school draws together assessment data and find out the cycle for using such data to map pupil progress in Years 7 and 8.

What steps are taken to challenge pupils who are not performing at least to expected levels of performance and to extend those who are exceeding expectations?

10.3   Using data to support achievement

The challenge for schools is to turn data into a dynamic driver for improvement that supports interventions in learning and teaching. All that we have seen so far is that data can be used descriptively to analyse pupil needs and patterns of attainment and to identify patterns of over- and under-attainment rather than to support achievement. There are two challenges here: interpreting and analysing data in ways that are helpful to teachers and learners and developing frameworks for target-setting.

Target-setting deploys a set of techniques that turn essentially static performance data into a dynamic process involving negotiation between teacher and learner. It uses the data available to schools to make realistic but challenging judgements about what individual learners can achieve. This, of course, does not follow from analysing data in itself. The use of national datasets could easily promote a fatalistic approach about what might or might not be possible: a pupil with a particular input score might easily be written off given the predictions about what pupils with that input score might expect to attain by the end of their schooling. The challenge is to use data to demonstrate to learners that if the majority of pupils with a given profile end up with a particular outcome, then application, commitment, effort and good teaching can help them to do better than that. Schools have approached this in a variety of ways. Some have thought about targets in the 'comfort' and 'challenge' zones; others have considered 'minimum targets' and 'extended targets'; still others have used national data to demonstrate what some pupils, whatever their level of entry performance, can potentially achieve. The effectiveness of target-setting depends on teachers' ability to translate the data available into short-and medium-term targets that learners are motivated to achieve. This, in turn, depends on skilled teaching and active mentoring: identifying with learners what their potential is and then working to identify the barriers to achieving this potential. In most schools, responsibility for using data to promote achievement is shared between subject teachers and pastoral staff. The challenge is to take the data and, having made them comprehensible and usable, to deploy them to define challenging targets that encourage learners to aspire to succeed. Too many targets, or over-ambitious targets, de-motivate learners just as much as inadequately challenging targets. Once data have been used to identify potential success, the task passes back to teachers to deploy all their professional skills and abilities in motivating and supporting pupils, removing barriers to learning, making material accessible and defining tasks in ways that help pupils meet, and if possible exceed, their targets (see Chapters 6 and 9).

In conclusion, this chapter has explored the increasingly sophisticated ways in which schools and teachers can make use of a huge range of data in support of effective teaching and improved learning. The range of data available and the number of techniques deployed to make best use of it have increased enormously over the last decade, and schools will become even more sophisticated in using new techniques over the next decade. There are obvious dangers in an over-reliance on quantitative data, and your responses to the tasks will have alerted you to some of these. Data can help to map outcomes and trajectories but normally, at best, can only diagnose areas for further investigation and analysis. It will suggest areas on which teachers and pupils can work productively; it will not in itself tell you or your pupils what to do. The important thing in using data, as in all other areas of school life, is to focus on supporting pupil achievement, raising pupil expectations and maximizing potential.

10.4   Recommendations for further reading and webliography

Goldstein, H. (2001) *Using Pupil Performance Data for Judging Schools and Teachers: Scope and Limitations.* Available at: http://www.bristol.ac.uk/cmm/team/hg/using-pupil-performance-data-for-judging-schools-and-teachers.pdf [accessed 31 August 2011].

Gray, J., Hopkins, D., Reynolds, D. and Farrell, S. (1999) *Improving Schools: Performance and Potential*. Buckingham: Open University Press.

Hedger, K. and Jesson, D. (1998) *The Numbers Game: Using Data in the Secondary School*. Shrewsbury: Shropshire County Council.

Ofsted (2008) *Using Data, Improving Schools*. London: Ofsted.

Websites

http://www.cemcentre.org (The Curriculum, Evaluation and Measurement Centre at Durham University manages MidYIS, YELLIS, and ALIS.)

www.raiseonline.org (The Ofsted link for the RAISE online project, which replaces PANDAs and Pupil Assessment Trackers.)

www.nfer.ac.uk (The NFER website provides information and guidance on Cognitive Ability Tests.)

Note

I am grateful to Ian James, at Mulberry School for Girls, Tower Hamlets, for his help in the preparation of this version of this chapter.

11

Positive approaches to supporting pupil behaviour

Lynn Reynolds

11.1 Introduction

Promoting positive behaviour in the classroom and supporting teachers with this task is high on the agenda of educational reform (DfE 2010). All teachers need to be able to understand and manage behaviour in the classroom effectively to promote learning and the well-being of learners. Naturally this is an area of concern for many student teachers at the start of their teaching career, as well as for experienced teachers, given the fact that there is an expectation that schools will provide a safe, orderly environment and that teachers are accountable for pupils' academic achievement (Rosas and West 2009). Most student teachers are looking for 'practical things that will work in the short term as one of their main objectives is understandably to get order in order to teach' (McNally *et al.* 2005: 180), possibly leading to a neglect of the central principles that should guide practice. Effective classroom management is underpinned by good professional practice and entails:

- high expectations of all pupils;
- the delivery of well-prepared lessons appropriately informed by the use of formative assessment and thus matched to pupils' learning needs;
- opportunities for pupils to succeed and to have both academic and social successes recognized;
- teachers who offer good role models and whose behaviour promotes mutual respect;
- systems that support the individual teacher.

The teacher's role is to promote positive learning behaviour and to respond effectively to incidents of undesirable behaviour. Teachers develop a tool kit – strategies that they employ almost automatically with some doing this more effectively than others – and this resource is constantly replenished from the experiences they have every day. Successful teachers continue to develop their understanding of behaviour management and the associated skills throughout their career, regularly reflecting on their own practice.

This chapter will enable you to:

- take a critical look at policy and theory supported by research findings;
- develop an understanding of the characteristics of learning behaviour and how to promote this;
- consider a range of strategies for positive classroom management.

The focus in this chapter is on proactive planning to nurture a positive learning environment and thus on prevention, rather than reaction and punitive responses. Newly qualified teachers (NQTs) need to have constructive relationships with learners based on high expectations, awareness of relevant legislation, respect for diversity, and commitment to achievement. Self-awareness, adaptability, identification of professional needs, and commitment to professional development are key attributes for teachers entering the profession. Student teachers have their own beliefs, drawing on their experience as learners, from the workplace, and family contexts. These beliefs will shift during training and beyond as each individual builds their own tool kit and finds ways to align beliefs with practice (Roehrig *et al.* 2009).

For most children, part of the process of growing up involves challenging, or at least renegotiating, relationships with parents and teachers who have been authority figures. In addition to the difficulties of adolescence, some young people bring 'baggage' into school from difficult lives. Teachers need to be sensitive to pupils' experience and see their behaviours in context, rather than 'labelling' them as disruptive. The ways in which we categorize pupil behaviour are notoriously imprecise and subjective and the behaviour that one teacher finds infuriating may be seen by a colleague as good fun.

Task 11.1

Remember some of the things you or your friends did at school – good and bad! List five things that you would now consider to be 'good behaviour' and five things that you would consider 'bad behaviour'. Now, write beside each of these how this action affected your learning. Is good behaviour always linked to a useful learning experience? Similarly, is bad behaviour always linked to a poor learning experience? Now, list five characteristics of the learning behavior that you would like to promote in your classroom.

Now read the following quotations:

We tightened a pupil's head in a vice.

We locked a teacher in a store cupboard.

> We climbed through the loft hatch and banged on the ceiling of the classroom below.
>
> We coated the drawer handle of the teacher's desk with syrup.
>
> I organized a pupil rebellion in which we refused to attend lessons.
>
> Who do you think were these miscreants?
> (Two head teachers, two university lecturers, and one chief education officer)

11.2   Behaviour policy

Consideration of how government policy has developed is important, as it reflects shifting perceptions of what constitutes 'good' behaviour and the link between behaviour and learning. Major developments such as the National Curriculum (NC), league tables, and testing have served to reconfigure the expectations of pupils and teachers alike. As education has become increasingly politicized, behaviour has come to the fore, triggering government reports (DES 1989; DfES 2005d). The Elton Report (DES 1989) focused on addressing standards of behaviour that were perceived to be declining. As well as acknowledging the impact of pupils' background on behaviour, there was clear reference to the role of the school and 'the quality of its leadership, classroom management, behaviour policy, curriculum, pastoral care, buildings and physical environment, organisation and timetable and relations with parents' (DES 1989: 89–90). The term 'classroom management' has steadily replaced 'behaviour management' to acknowledge a teacher's role in planning engaging lessons, pitched at the right level and delivered well.

Following this, the Behaviour and Attendance strand of the National Strategies aimed to support teachers with behaviour and attendance training and materials that forged a link with teaching and learning, thus strengthening the understanding that pedagogy and practice underpin improved behaviour. Although the National Strategies have since come to an end, the materials are still useful, and widely used in schools, with programmes such as SEAL (social and emotional aspects of learning) giving explicit guidance on how to encourage behaviours such as group work to support positive learning behaviour (DfES 2005d).

Alongside these changes, New Labour expressed a commitment to the inclusion of all learners (in mainstream if possible) with the document *Excellence for all Children* (DfEE 1997d), which created a potential source of tension for pupils and teachers. *Every Child Matters* (DfES 2003e) strengthened the move towards working with the individual child to meet their needs: 'We all share a duty to do everything we can to ensure that every child has the chance to fulfil their potential' (DfES 2003e: 6), thus paving the way for 'personalized learning' (DfES 2004a). An increasing expectation that schools and teachers would be responsive to individuals, rather than expecting individuals to fit in, was developing. This was underpinned by an expectation that the teacher would have a 'heightened awareness of how individuals achieve best and be prepared to change practice based on this' (Ellis and Todd 2009: 27).

Media interest resulted in another review focusing on behaviour in 2005, the Steer Report (DfES 2005a), which resulted in *Higher Standards, Better Schools for All* (DfES 2005e). The key findings highlight the importance of:

- a consistent approach to behaviour management;
- effective school leadership;
- strong classroom management, learning, and teaching;
- transparent rewards and sanctions;
- appropriate behaviour strategies and the teaching of good behaviour;
- planned staff development and support;
- effective pupil support systems;
- collaborative liaison with parents and other agencies;
- well-managed pupil transitions;
- appropriate organization and facilities.

There is little here that is different from the earlier Elton Report (DES 1989) with research findings supporting these points (Watkins and Wagner 2000). However, it marks a definite move towards a more secure link between behaviour, teaching, and learning, perhaps reflecting the impact of the National Strategies in strengthening pedagogy.

More recently, the need for guidance on the discipline of pupils has been addressed by the Education and Inspections Act 2006, which gave official guidance on the 'rights and responsibilities' of those involved. The Coalition government have made their commitment to addressing behaviour concerns very clear with *The Importance of Teaching* (DfE 2010). There is a different emphasis here, focusing on 'discipline and respect' and giving schools more freedom to exclude difficult pupils and increasing the rights of teachers to search pupils and issue detentions – behaviour is linked to pupil safety rather than learning. Ofsted will inspect and guide schools as to effective and ineffective practice particularly with respect to bullying. There is little mention of learning and a clear message that the government will be less prescriptive about how this is managed in the classroom.

Task 11.2

Read and contrast the final recommendations of the Steer Report (DfES 2005a) and *The Importance of Teaching (DfE 2010)*.

Note the areas that both documents address and also note the differences in emphasis and language.

11.3 Background theories

Approaches to addressing the complex issues involved in managing classroom behaviours are informed by a wide range of theories about what causes pupil misbehaviour, how to assess behaviour, and what interventions are effective.

This section will look briefly at three fundamental underpinning approaches to the issue of pupil behaviour. As space is limited, you are recommended to follow this up with further reading (see, for example, Ayers *et al.* 2000; Porter 2000; Roffey 2011). Theories link to different stances about the social world and human behaviour and you will be able to make links between your own belief systems and some of these ideas.

Most teachers make flexible and eclectic use of strategies that derive from each of these approaches, but have a strong preference for strategies that fit with their own philosophical ideas.

Behavioural approaches

The behavioural model addresses the observed behaviour rather than seeking explanations in cognitive or psychological causes. You can read more about behaviourism as a theory of learning in Chapter 4. Behaviour is influenced by the antecedents – the environment in which the behaviour occurs – and is reinforced by the response it gets. The model uses an ABC formulation:

- A for Antecedent
- B for Behaviour
- C for Consequences

Changing behaviour may involve changing the antecedents (e.g. reorganizing seating arrangements), observing precisely the frequency and context of the behaviour and looking at what reinforces it. To increase the incidence of good behaviour, the teacher needs to notice and respond to this, while unwanted behaviours should be dealt with by use of sanctions but not rewarded by lots of attention.

Whole-school approaches such as Assertive Discipline or Discipline for Learning seek to enable teachers to respond consistently to behaviours with a clear tariff of responses. Within the classroom, a discipline plan allows for clear rules that are taught to the pupils, positive recognition of pupils for following the rules, and a system of consequences for not following the rules. Much effective behaviour change has been achieved by these approaches, not least because they are accompanied by training of all the teaching and support staff, the development of a coherent policy, and consistency in application of the approach.

There are some concerns that arise with this approach – do the pupils internalize the better behaviour or is it bound to the context? For some it works well. Better behaviour may enable better learning; thus, better educational achievement and consequent improvement in self-esteem will enable some pupils to pass through difficult periods. Others, especially those who are having a difficult time outside school, may need approaches that give them more space to look at feelings, and programmes such as SEAL can be very useful in this instance. It is important to note also that behavioural engagement is just one aspect of being engaged in the lesson. Emotional and cognitive engagement is also essential for effective learning to take place (Fredricks *et al.* 2004)

Cognitive approaches

A further set of theories attaches importance to the child's experience and to understanding its impact on behaviour. Cognitivists believe that young people's perceptions, their understanding of a situation, their emotional state, the stage of their development and the context all affect their behaviour. Interventions are targeted at helping them think through irrational, distorted or impulsive responses. Pupils with behavioural problems may not have the cognitive skills they need for appropriate interactions with their peers or with teachers and other staff. Problem-solving training and social learning approaches can help pupils develop new behaviours.

How people feel about themselves determines their self-esteem and this plays a significant part in the ability of pupils to be effective learners, as pupils with low self-esteem are vulnerable to failure and to criticism. A young person with high self-esteem can take risks in their learning and in their relationships. Low self-esteem means playing it safe and avoiding trying out new things. There are ways in which teachers can help protect and develop the self-esteem of vulnerable pupils:

- learn pupils' names and use them;
- use praise – specific and personal;
- reprimand the behaviour, not the person;
- repair the relationship;
- apologize if you are wrong;
- look after your own self-esteem;
- develop sensitive practices – for example, let pupils choose whether they read aloud;
- don't show pupils up by making comparisons and/or mocking them.

The ecosystemic model

The ecosystemic model is based on systems theory, which sees the school as part of interconnected systems, each part influenced by change in the other parts. Porter (2000) characterizes this as one of the 'democratic' theories. These look at young people and teachers as equal actors in the teaching and learning enterprise and as each having rights to have their needs met, albeit in different roles. Relationships lie at the heart of these theories, and the emotional needs of participants in learning are included in the framework. That different people have different understandings of the same events is central to the ecosystemic model. Any event may be subject to various interpretations, with some more likely than other to enable progress.

To change the situation, we need to look at where it is stuck and seek ways of understanding it that will encourage change. Teacher and pupils can get locked in a negative cycle: this theory would encourage the teacher to look at the situation from the pupils' perspectives and seek ways to cooperate with them. The assumption is that there are different interpretations of a situation, each equally valid, and the behaviour of teachers and pupils draws on those interpretations. The technique for thinking about a problem from a different perspective is called 'reframing' and requires the teacher to think of alternative explanations for the behaviour and ways in which they might respond differently. Teachers who took part in research by Tyler and Jones (2002) found that, in spite of initial resistance and scepticism, there was an improvement in dealing with entrenched problem behaviours and that they were more relaxed and so were their classes.

Pupil participation has received considerable interest in recent years as part of the growing understanding of the potential power of consultation with pupils or pupil voice to reduce barriers to learning (Flutter and Rudduck 2004). For this to be successful, pupils' ideas need to be encouraged and, importantly, listened to. Pupils want a learning environment that fosters a sense of agency and ownership, as well as collaborative learning within social contexts (McIntyre *et al.* 2005). This study mapped the success of teachers who 'listened' and adapted, and the continuing frustration for those that failed to engage with pupils' ideas.

11.4 Strategies for classroom management

Task 11.3

As you read the next section, try to link strategies with the theoretical frameworks outlined above. Note where they fit neatly and where there is a lot of crossover.

Think about your own beliefs and how well these approaches suit the sort of teacher you want to be.

Teachers need strategies to enable them to plan for positive behaviour, to prevent the onset of poor behaviour, and to respond effectively when such incidents occur. Although most young people want to learn and resent their learning being impeded by other pupils' disruptive behaviour, the same pupils are able and may be willing to take advantage of a chance to reduce a lesson to chaos.

The Elton Report (DES 1989: 69–70) states that: 'teachers' group management skills are probably the single most important factor in achieving good standards of classroom behaviour' and that 'those skills can be taught and learned'. This is still highly relevant. Skills and strategies are essential and can be learned through 'the right kinds of training, experience and support'. Applying them depends on a pragmatic assessment of the context and it is not the purpose of this chapter to offer strategies as blueprints. You need to consider them, try them out, add those that work for you to your tool kit, and pursue further skills through reading and observation of experienced colleagues. There are excellent resources to draw on in pursuing the development of your skills. Behaviour4learning is a website supported by the Training and Development Agency (TDA), which seeks to enhance the development of skills and understanding in trainee teachers.

Task 11.4

Think of someone you thought was a good teacher from your own school days:

- Make a list of the key features that you think made them memorable.
- Identify how many of those features were linked to lesson content, to classroom management skills, and to personality. What other categories?
- What qualities or skills of that teacher do you share?
- What qualities or skills would you like to develop?

The interactions between a teacher and the pupils in any particular classroom are determined by key features that you as a classroom teacher can influence, a number of which will be considered in the following sections. The books by Sue Roffey (2011) and Bill Rogers (2011) provide a fuller overview of these.

Whole-school policy

The Behaviour and Attendance strand of the National Strategy sought to strengthen and develop whole-school approaches to behaviour, requiring all schools to review their policies about behaviour and attendance and identify areas for improvement. As well as including specific support for schools in particularly challenging circumstances, the Strategy focuses on whole-school perspectives, identifying and sharing best practice in order to develop consistent and effective policy to secure positive behaviour and attendance.

Whole-school behaviour policies also address the school's response to issues of bullying, including racial and sexual harassment. *Learning Behaviour: Lessons Learned* (DCSF 2009a) offers a comprehensive review of the Steer Report with a strong focus on how behaviour and learning policy should be developed within schools along with the identification of good practice. Consistency, pupil participation, and consultation with parents were just some of the points that emerged from this useful document. Consistency and clarity are particularly relevant for boys (Ofsted 2005c). The Coalition government has indicated its commitment to ensuring that schools have a policy to deal with inappropriate behaviour, with much more mention of exclusions, detentions, and reasonable force than in previous documents – 'We will support head teachers to maintain a culture of discipline and respect' (DfE 2010: 34) – and less mention of learning.

Policies underpin school rules or codes of conduct, which are usually expressed positively, signalling what is required, rather than a list of 'don'ts'. Thus, 'Walk in the corridors' is seen as more positive in promoting desired behaviour than 'Don't run', which focuses on the negative. In many schools, you will see a written 'code of conduct' displayed in strategic locations that provides a shared framework for promoting good behaviour.

All teachers and trainee teachers must be familiar with their school policy on behaviour and attendance and use it in a consistent fashion to encourage a whole-school understanding of good behaviour.

High expectations

Teachers' expectations have an impact on pupils' behaviour and on their learning. High, but realistic, expectations should inform your approach and you need to signal this in the way you address pupils both as a group and individually.

The negative impact of 'labelling' is seen as a key influence on negative outcomes for some pupils, particularly the most vulnerable – and remember that the 'acting-out' or 'acting-up' pupil may be vulnerable, although it may not feel like that to you. Labelling links to the idea of positive and negative expectations and also of a self-fulfilling prophecy.

Think about the following scenario:

- The teacher expects Jaz to behave badly, probably because he has been warned in the staffroom.
- Every time Jaz steps out of line, the teacher notices because it confirms negative expectations, even though Jaz is no worse than other pupils.
- By the end of the lesson, the teacher is convinced that Jaz is a troublesome pupil, thus confirming the original expectations.
- At the same time, Jaz feels that she can do no right even though she knows her behaviour has been no different from anyone else's.

The sibling phenomenon is associated with labelling theory. Pupils may arrive in secondary school already labelled by their association with their older siblings, again, often in the staffroom. There is a difficult balance to strike between the information that it is useful to know about your pupils as a new teacher and the labelling effect that staffroom talk may encourage. Your own professionalism and judgement is critical. Of course, pupils have expectations too. The research into pupil voice has added to our understanding of what pupils expect from teachers – and their views are well worth listening to (Haydn 2007). When asked about teacher characteristics, pupils rated subject knowledge, the ability to explain things well, being friendly, and talking normally as most important. Other factors included teachers being polite, not being absent, marking homework, and having a sense of humour.

Positive relationships

Gaining respect from pupils and establishing authority happen within the context of the relationships built by the teacher. These relationships need to be based on confidence that you have the right to manage the class. Genuine liking for and interest in young people is important and pupils will be aware of this at once. Listening to pupils carefully, using names, and learning about pupils' personalities and enthusiasms is very important in showing an interest in pupils – and planning lessons that will engage them.

How you present yourself is important. A calm sense of determination that you are in control of the lesson and expecting the best from your pupils will contribute to a positive outcome. You do need to *look* like a teacher, rather than like a student or a fellow-pupil, and for some this can be difficult. It is important to create an identity that signals 'grown-up in charge' both to pupils and to yourself. As noted in Chapter 8, body language and voice are also important tools in managing a class effectively. Video recording the lesson and reviewing with a colleague is an invaluable tool in helping you determine what you 'look like' as a teacher. It also helps you to identify what 'learning' looks like in your classroom and whether your classroom management techniques are encouraging the type of learning that you had hoped for.

The teacher's self-conviction is an important signal to pupils while the opposite, self-doubt, is an open invitation to create trouble. The conviction underlying this chapter is that warmth and genuine engagement with pupils are important qualities and valuable tools. However, student teachers often find that a natural desire to be chummy with pupils, particularly at the outset during initial visit days, sets up relationships that are hard to shake off when they become responsible for managing the class. While the old adage 'don't smile till Christmas' seems grim these days, it is prudent to adopt a teacher persona from the outset, even when it feels awkward.

Rogers (2011) carefully considers and suggests ways in which positive relationships can be developed. The right verbal cues must be used and there are some simple rules that can make a significant difference such as using the word 'thanks' rather than 'please'. 'Everyone looking this way, thanks' carries an expectation of what is directed rather than a request. Another useful tactic is to focus on the expected or required behaviour. 'Jack, facing this way, thanks' communicates the required behaviour concisely. Non-verbal prompts are often used to strengthen the verbal cue and may also be used instead of a verbal prompt. Non-verbal prompts can help avoid unnecessary tension; however, the success of this rests on the pupils understanding the prompt, and thus the consistency with which the teacher has used this previously.

Planning for classroom management

Planning for classroom management is as much a part of lesson planning as subject content. There are some key questions that you need to ask yourself (Haydn 2007: 74): How much or what type of control do you want during the lesson? How will this shift throughout the lesson? Kaufman and Moss (2010) have shown that trainee teachers often struggle with the difference between organizing the lesson and managing the learning, both of which have an impact on behaviour. Organization includes understanding the physical environment and factors such as pupil movement. Using technology effectively is a particular area that requires both careful organization and a consideration of the desired learning.

Most effective teachers anticipate and prevent disruption by careful planning for key stages of the lesson:

Beginnings of lessons
- Try always to be there first, properly prepared, with everything you need.
- Control the entry to the classroom by standing at the doorway to greet pupils, remind them of the rules (e.g. coats off, bags at the back).
- Have an initial activity ready for them to get on with, already projected on the whiteboard or on the desk, so that they are occupied while you settle everyone and get the main lesson started.

Transitions between activities
- Make sure every pupil stops what they are doing to listen to your instructions; do not talk over them.
- Give clear instructions; check they have understood.
- Make sure you give clear guidance about how much time they have – try using one of the online stop clocks that are freely available.

Handing out resources and equipment
- Use reliable pupils to hand out books and equipment, otherwise it holds up the flow of the lesson.
- Find the time to speak to the teaching assistant (TA) before the lesson to discuss the potential for any organizational support.

Dealing with interruptions by minimizing their disruptive impact
- Politely ask someone who comes in to wait while you get to a point where you can talk to them.
- Plan how you will respond to requests to leave the room (check whether there is guidance on this in the school behaviour policy).
- Respond to disruptive behaviour by talking quietly to the pupil individually, avoid public showdowns, and if necessary ask them to see you after the lesson.
- Use the language of choice: 'If you cannot work quietly here, then you will have to work elsewhere'. The important feature of this is that there are no free choices; all choice has got to be within what is expected in your classroom.

Ending lessons
- Anticipate so there is plenty of time left for reviewing learning, setting homework, and clearing up.
- Warn the group that they will go when you tell them, not when the bell rings.
- Make sure that pupils leave chairs tidy and pick up litter.
- Provide positive feedback on the learning, progress, and behaviour, if appropriate, that has occurred in the lesson.
- Let pupils go in groups or rows, when they have tidied up and are ready and quiet.

Routines and rules

Bill Rogers has a user-friendly approach to setting up rules, routines, and responsibilities and it is well worth looking at his books or DVDs (see p. 160). Rogers makes the important point that you are establishing routines right from the beginning. If pupils carry on talking when you are talking, then you are establishing that it is acceptable. While Rogers' work includes dealing with very difficult behaviour, his emphasis on routines, on clarity, on reinforcing desired behaviour, and on dealing with problems in the least intrusive way is useful for most situations.

Rogers (2011: 44) suggests several rules to encourage desired behaviour involving:

- treatment of others in class (peers as well as adults);
- communication (this includes systems such as hands-up, but also how people speak to each other in class);
- learning behaviour (including cooperation and support, accessing support from the teacher);
- movement about the class (entry and exit, respecting others' space);
- problem-solving (including settling disputes).

Establishing these rules in discussion with the class provides a sense of ownership that can be further strengthened by careful use of inclusive language: 'In our classroom, we . . .'. Posting them on the classroom wall provides a point of reference and allows for an early preventive reminder ('Rosie, remember our rule about . . .').

Task 11.5

Write a list of classroom rules, no more than five in total, to cover the key features of: entry to the classroom and readiness for the lesson; movement within the classroom; getting teacher's attention; teacher's cues for whole class to attend; responses to and behaviour with other pupils; closure systems for ending a lesson.

The rules should be easy to understand and suitable for putting up on the classroom wall. Make sure they are expressed positively. What are your expectations across the age range? Will all pupils adhere to the same rules?

Planning to meet the needs of all pupils

This is a challenge and an opportunity for teachers in the current climate of inclusion (see Chapter 21). Inclusion embraces the idea that the school community should be representative of and include all the community members of school age: thus, teaching approaches and management strategies need to be based on the individual learning needs of pupils. Differentiation and the planned and effective use of classroom support are key elements in preventing disruption. Work pitched at too low a level will bore pupils and at too high a level will make some defensive and anxious. Key to achievement is participation, as pupils have an active role to play in their own learning, closely linked to pupil voice, which was discussed earlier.

Rewards and sanctions

You should notice pupils being good and respond to desirable behaviours as well as to academic achievements. Use praise generously and specifically, so that the pupil (and any others in earshot) knows what was praiseworthy. However, do not devalue praise by giving it where it is not deserved. As pupils get older it is more appropriate for praise to be more private, as public praise may have a negative effect.

Praise is rewarding, as is positive written feedback on work or in homework books. Some teachers write letters home to acknowledge good behaviour. Giving pupils responsibility can be used to reward good behaviour. Some schools have whole-school or year systems that can be used to acknowledge merit for positive behaviour as well as for good work.

You should recognize 'baggage', although no matter how carefully you plan a lesson, you cannot control the baggage that a pupil may bring with them from home, from an earlier lesson or from relationships with peers that may make them disruptive. As well as establishing routines and rules, teachers need to be ready to respond when disruptive behaviour occurs.

Teachers need to relate to whole-school policy and responses to poor behaviour need to take into account the whole-school policy. Serious problems will invoke the school systems, which probably include referral to year head or senior management, time out, detentions, letters home and, as a last resort, exclusion. There should be clear lines of support for students and new teachers in a school that spell out how to get help to deal with major difficulties. Find out at an early stage what the back-up systems are and how to access them.

You should respond early and lightly, as most disruption can be dealt with within the classroom by the teacher. Your first reaction to the early signs of disruptive activity should be very low on a tariff of responses. Many behavioural problems can be spotted early and deflected effectively with small interventions. A suggested tariff of interventions is as follows:

- The 'look';
- Proximity control (moving closer to the disruptive pupil);
- Praise to person adjacent who is on-task;
- Private word (this is less confrontational if delivered from the same height, thus crouching rather than towering over);
- Re-statement of task;

- Rule reminder: 'remember our rule about . . .';
- Direct questions: 'What are you doing?' 'What should you be doing?' (avoid 'Why are you doing that?' questions);
- Offer choices: 'If you do not put the mobile phone away, I will have to ask you to stay at break'.

When low tariff interventions have not succeeded in dealing with problem behaviour and tensions rise, teachers need to employ strategies to remain calm. Angry or exasperated responses can easily exacerbate tense situations and shouting will not help. Instead:

- Take a few deep breaths to calm yourself.
- Own what you are feeling: 'I am angry because . . .'.
- Use assertive language: 'I don't swear at you. That language is unacceptable here'.
- Lower your voice as soon as possible.
- Allow cool-off time for both parties: 'We will follow this up tomorrow morning'.
- At a meeting with the pupil, explain what made you angry at the time, listen to the pupil's perceptions, refer to relevant rules, discuss how to make reparations, or deal with a similar incident next time.
- Repair and rebuild the relationship (Rogers 2011).

Support for the teacher

You need to ensure that you have systems of support in place as a student or a new teacher. Some or all of the following will be useful to you:

- A member of the senior management team usually has responsibility for pastoral and discipline matters.
- The special educational needs coordinator (SENCo) or, in some schools, behaviour support specialist teacher, will have particular knowledge about pupils with behavioural difficulties and their needs.
- School mentors can offer advice, demonstrate skills, and point you in the direction of other skilled teachers.
- Peers can offer excellent support, including peer observation as a basis for discussion about your approach.
- Reading, making use of websites, watching DVDs, and trying out new ideas can all be helpful.
- Use stress-busting techniques such as exercise, relaxation, playing in a band, and talking to friends!

Task 11.6

1. Think about the following situation and how you would react:

You are teaching in your first week of school placement when Ryan, a pupil you have not met before, comes in and walks deliberately and slowly across the front of the room between yourself and the pupils you are addressing.

2. Consider how your reaction to the situation would be affected if you knew that:

- Ryan is a regular troublemaker who frequently tries to 'needle' teachers.
- Ryan has been asked to take a message around the school by his head of year.
- Ryan is six feet tall.
- Ryan is small for his age and his mother says he is very nervous – often too frightened to come to school.
- Ryan has Asperger's syndrome (a form of autism).
- It is a science lesson and you are demonstrating a potentially dangerous experiment.
- The mentor has warned you not to stand any nonsense from this group and especially not from Ryan, who rarely comes to school.
- The class laughs uproariously.
- The class falls silent.

Underlying teachers' responses to pupils are sets of assumptions and pre-suppositions that can get in the way of responding to pupils' needs and building positive relationships. If you, as a teacher, strive to avoid jumping to conclusions, are sensitive to pupils' needs, and *listen carefully* to what they have to say, you stand a good chance of promoting positive behaviour and avoiding disruption and conflict.

11.5   Conclusion

This chapter has introduced you to some ideas about managing pupil behaviour in a positive and planned way. The central resource in this process is you, the individual teacher and your skills, working within a framework of the school community, its ethos and its policy on behaviour, which is in turn informed by government policy. Your skills will take time to build up and you will learn most from reading about and observing a range of practices and selecting approaches that fit the sort of teacher you are becoming.

Good teachers reflect constantly on their own practice and seek ways to develop new approaches that fit with their value system and suit their personal style. Bromfield (2005) points out that recognizing your concerns is a prerequisite for finding solutions. It is tempting, and easy, to blame the pupils when a lesson goes wrong. The trouble is that this does not help you to make the sorts of changes that might improve things. A teacher can change the lesson plan, vary seating arrangements, alter the order or content of the lesson, or vary the activities or the pace to meet the needs of a particular group or a group at a particular time. Flexibility to respond to the context is an important part of the teacher's skill, and preparation for a range of eventualities is invaluable for beginning teachers.

11.6 Recommendations for further reading, viewing and webliography

Bromfield, C. (2005) PGCE secondary trainee teachers and effective behaviour management: an evaluation and commentary. *Support for Learning*, 21(4): 188–93.

Haydn, T. (2007) *Managing Pupil Behaviour: Key Issues in Teaching and Learning*. London: Routledge.

Kaufman, D. and Moss, D. (2010) A new look at preservice teachers' conceptions of classroom management and organization: unconvering complexity and dissonance. *The Teacher Educator*, 45: 118–36.

Roffey, S. (2011) *The New Teacher's Survival Guide to Behaviour*, 2nd edn. London: Sage.

Rogers, B. (2011) *Classroom Behaviour: A Practical Guide to Effective Teaching, Behaviour Management and Colleague Support*, 3rd edn. London: Paul Chapman. Very useful practical approach to effective behaviour management, looking at setting up systems with a new class, dealing with challenging pupils, managing anger – pupils' and our own – and strategies for when things get difficult.

DVDs

Rogers, B. (2000) *Cracking the Challenging Class*, DVD set. Expensive, but useful and set in the UK context – one to look for in libraries or teachers' centres.

Websites

www.alfiekohn.org/index.php (Alfie Kohn writes and speaks on human behaviour and education. Although based in America, his website has a large range of articles to encourage you to reflect and question the strategies that we use. 'Discipline is the problem, not the solution' (1995) is a particularly interesting read.)

www.behaviour4learning.ac.uk (a major resource, established by the TDA to support student teachers and teachers; has useful links to up-to-date articles, reports, research, and lots of practical help). Available at: http://webarchive.nationalarchives. gov.uk/20101021152907/ http:/www.behaviour4learning.ac.uk [accessed 13 October 2011].

http://www.education.gov.uk/schools/pupilsupport/behaviour/behaviourpolicies (This website will keep you informed about recent government initiatives and guide you towards resources and support.)

http://www.education.gov.uk/schools/toolsandinitiatives/teacherstv (Teachers TV has a wealth of resources and a separate section on behaviour. This will allow you to watch some of the strategies that have been mentioned in this chapter. There is also a series of short videos tackling common issues by Sue Cowley, which are particularly useful).

http://webarchive.nationalarchives.gov.uk/20110809091832/

http://www.teachingandlearningresources.org.uk (There are a number of resources on this website regarding behaviour and learning. These are mostly aimed at practicing teachers but still worth a browse.)

http://www.ofsted.gov.uk/Ofsted-home/Publications-and-research/Browse-all-by/Education/ Inclusion/Behaviour (There are a number of very useful and very accessible publications on the Ofsted website concerning behaviour. Two in particular that are well worth a look are *Improving behaviour and attendance in secondary schools* (2008) and *Managing challenging behaviour* (2005).)

12

Using ICT to support learning
Mick Hammond

12.1 Issues in using ICT in school

This chapter addresses the use of information and communications technology (ICT) in teaching your subject. I present three case studies of student teachers using ICT followed by a discussion of planning to use ICT in your teaching. Finally, I point you to further sources of information.

By the end of this chapter, you should be:

- aware of different motives for using ICT in school;
- able to assess the contribution of ICT to teaching and learning;
- able to plan for using ICT in your own teaching.

12.2 Different motives for using ICT

I will consider three examples of student teachers using ICT in their placement schools. These examples illustrate a range of ICT applications as well as different levels of planning. I will use them to consider the planning, implementation, and evaluation of ICT in teaching, and how classroom experience can be used to inform future planning. These examples or 'case studies' are necessarily rooted in the teaching of particular subjects but they raise general issues, so please do not skip them even if the subject context is unfamiliar.

Task 12.1

Before reading the commentary that comes after each case study, ask yourself:

- What is ICT contributing to pupils' learning?
- What are the strengths and weaknesses of the teacher's approach?

Case Study 12.1

Anthony, a student teacher of English, was worried about several aspects of his teaching and fretful about his relationships with pupils, which were often confrontational. He freely admitted to becoming interested in the use of ICT as something that might get the pupils working in class and, in his own words, 'bring them over to my side'. He booked an ICT room and planned a lesson based on pupils' understanding of *Romeo and Juliet*, the play they had been reading. Pupils would be asked to prepare a 'pitch' trying to persuade a production company to make a film of the play. Pupils would use presentation software. He had used the software many times before and felt confident of being able to demonstrate its use and deal with any problems pupils had. He asked a colleague, a student teacher of ICT in the same school, to give him a short demonstration of how to log on and save work on the school network. This colleague volunteered to be on hand to deal with any technical hiccups that might arise during the lesson.

Anthony prepared his presentation to explain the aims of the lesson. He set pupils to work in pairs at their machines. He monitored their work and tried to prompt them into recalling the key events of the play and move them away from investigating Clip Art and other images, and embellishing text. At the end of the lesson he asked for volunteers to talk through the work they had done in front of the rest of the class. His evaluation of the lesson was not extensive or formal. However, he felt the lesson had been a great success as the pupils seemed much more positive and his relationship with the pupils had been far less stressful. Nevertheless, although the pupils had been 'on-task', he was not quite sure what they understood the task to be. They had spent a lot of time 'playing on the computer' rather than addressing his learning goals. He could see that the pupils would need more time to finish the presentation, something he had not predicted, and decided to try to book the room next lesson.

Commentary

This case study does not represent an ideal model of introducing ICT into your teaching but it is consistent with the haphazard way in which many teachers get started with ICT. It is worth remembering that computers and computer programs are rarely produced with schools in mind – teachers adapt widely available tools for their own use and settings. This may sound like an indictment of Anthony, and of schools in general, but it is not meant to be. Anthony faced a challenge in the classroom so he looked around and used what was available to try to address the issue. Having said that, his planning of the lesson was rudimentary. He took pupils' skills for granted. Fortunately, he chose a software application that had a 'low entry threshold' (one that pupils could start using without long and detailed explanation) and one with which they were, in fact, familiar. Again he was fortunate in having a colleague to support the technical side of the activity – he would have found any hitches very difficult to address himself. He was unsure of the learning goals of his lesson and hence did not set out his objectives very clearly. He could have structured his introduction more clearly and provided a 'mock-up' of the kind of presentation he was looking for. He could, for example, have explained that he wanted to see a synopsis of the plot and a statement about why the play would still be relevant to audiences today. He could have encouraged pupils to focus on specific scenes or on how language was being used to persuade. On the positive side, he asked pupils to work in pairs. This had one advantage of reducing the number of pupils asking for technical assistance, as they were encouraged to help each other. More importantly, however, it would prompt pupils to discuss their ideas together and their understanding of characters and themes in the play. Pupils were asked to present their work using bullet points so there was not a lot of waiting while one entered text and the other watched.

Anthony believed the lesson to be successful as the pupils had been on-task, or at least they had not disrupted his lesson or his teaching. He was preoccupied with his own role as a teacher and relied on his own 'gut' feelings to evaluate the lesson. Of course, the introduction of ICT is not a guarantee of increased motivation but it is a common observation, and a commonly reported finding, that many pupils do enjoy using ICT. Why this is the case is not always clear; pupils often find their enjoyment of ICT difficult to articulate. However, they do seem to take satisfaction from making decisions and seeing the consequences of those decisions on screen. For example, in Anthony's lesson pupils could add and delete text, insert images, and introduce sound and animation quickly and easily. The use of the computer provided opportunities not available when using pen and paper. ICT has an expressive quality that seems to motivate pupils. Many, though by no means all, young people feel at home with digital gadgetry and Anthony wanted to show that his world as a teacher was not as far removed from that of his pupils as they might have thought.

It was doubtful whether Anthony's subject teaching aims in the lesson had been fully met or even properly articulated. Pupils were as much focused on format as content. He learnt valuable lessons from this class. In doing this kind of work again, he would need to focus pupils' attention on the content of their work. Next time he would stress the need for a simple, uncluttered, and consistent background and work to a series of writing 'frames' to help pupils plan their presentation. He would need to think about timings, to make pupils aware of the timescale to which they were work-ing, and to book the room over two lessons not one. As time at the computer was limited, he might provide a template and a bank of images and film clips for pupils to work from. He realized that he was fortunate to have ICT support but in the future he would need to prepare in more detail. He also needed a contingency in case the network broke down – this was something he had only thought about once pupils had told him of its unstable performance. At a later point he might also expand the range of ICT tools that he used and the kinds of activities he could ask pupils to carry out. For example, pupils could be asked to provide a short news report of an event in the play for a local radio in the form of a podcast or to role-play and film a particular incident from the play. These could be uploaded to a school virtual learning environ-ment (VLE) or learning platform for pupils to share.

Case Study 12.2

Baljit, a student science teacher, had a specific focus on her pupils' subject learning in her use of ICT. She was aware that pupils had spent a long time collecting data manually in their laboratory work and were not sufficiently focused on drawing conclusions from experiments. She felt it was important that pupils could 'tell stories about data' if they were going to develop their information handling skills. She planned two lessons based on software with which she was familiar from training events she had attended. In the first, she introduced data-logging software to help pupils explore the many variables involved in determining the speed of a vehicle rolling down a ramp. Trolleys and ramps were set up in the laboratory with light gates to measure the speed of the trolley as it reached the end of the ramp. Pupils released the trolley from different points on the ramp and measurements were taken and entered on a spreadsheet. Graphs of the results were displayed. To support pupils, Baljit gave a short demonstration on using the software and provided a brief help guide. Each group of pupils was asked to discuss their results and to provide an explanation of why the speed of the vehicle changed with the distance it had travelled. As an extension, pupils could look at the relationship between speed and other variables, such as the height of the ramp or distance travelled on leaving the ramp.

A follow-up lesson gave pupils an opportunity to extend their work on interpretation of data. Baljit set up a circus of activities using temperature sensors. The first investigated the effect of surface area on cooling. Here temperature sensors recorded the temperature of two hot potatoes – one large, one small – every five seconds. A second experiment involved wrapping a temperature sensor in cotton wool and comparing the cooling effect of different liquids, including alcohol and water. A third investigation examined the insulating properties of different materials by recording the temperature of water inside containers insulated with cotton wool, paper, and other materials chosen by pupils.

Pupils were asked to focus on the key variables in each experiment, to describe the relationship between these variables, and provide an explanation to account for any relationships they had identified. In fact, each experiment raised challenging scientific concepts that Baljit would need to develop later. For now, she was concerned that pupils generated and justified their own hypotheses about the events they were investigating.

Baljit believed the two lessons to have been successful, as she had uncovered many misconceptions about interpreting data that she was able to address in whole-class discussion and in one-to-one work. Pupils had supported each other in using the software. The area that worried her most was the social dynamic within groups and dealing with whole-class discussion at the end of the activity. Not all pupils had contributed to the discussion and she had not left enough time to develop her response to pupils' ideas.

Commentary

Unlike Anthony, Baljit had planned her use of ICT in detail and had a clear idea of how it could contribute to pupils' learning about science. In this case, the automatic features of the program gave pupils opportunities to capture data over very short periods, something they could not do accurately by hand and eye. The software took away the repetitive graph-drawing work and allowed pupils to focus on higher-order skills of interpretation. The use of the technology was nicely staged so that all pupils could obtain experience of using the data-logging software before the circus of activities. The software had a relatively low entry threshold and any difficulties were addressed through help sheets, peer support or occasional teacher intervention. The case study illustrates how a very simple and long-established approach to computer-based data collection can work really well to support the teaching of higher-order skills. Pupils are unlikely to take advantage of opportunities for reflection and discussion without teacher intervention. Although Baljit had built discussion into her planning, she would need to fine tune her approach during her placement, for example, developing ideas for plenary sessions.

Case Study 12.3

Carlton, a student teacher of geography, was enjoying his school placement and receiving good feedback on his teaching. His major area of concern was how much time he seemed to spend setting, chasing up, and marking homework. The results seemed disproportionate to the effort he was putting in. He worked in a school that was highly committed to ICT and had attended an after-school session that had introduced him to the learning resources on the school's VLE or 'learning platform'. Already one department had built up a substantial set of presentations, forums, and links to outside sites. He wondered if he could build a similar site for his pupils to support them in their homework or what he now wanted to call 'learning tasks'. Perhaps he could even produce simple quizzes that could automatically mark work and send finely tuned feedback?

After much discussion with the ICT coordinator, he scaled down his plans. He would focus on one topic, population growth, which he was covering with a GCSE class. He would post his presentations to the VLE, provide links to BBC and Geography Association resources, many of which contained images and short video clips, and create a closed discussion forum that he would monitor. He would try to guide pupils to and through the material by setting weekly tasks which they would report back to him and their peers via the discussion forum. These tasks were mini investigations that required pupils to access and draw relevant conclusions from online resources. He would encourage pupils to email each other or email him at any time if they needed help.

The innovation met with mixed results. One good thing was that using the learning platform turned out to be easier than he had imagined, as he had a model from which to work and ICT support from within the school. The key point in his preparation was to include his classroom presentations but to avoid hours writing online material when there were so many external sites that pupils could access. Looking at his records, he found that more pupils were completing their homework than had previously done so and he felt less stress in cajoling pupils, not least because no-one could say they had lost their handouts or could not contact him to find out what to do. However, much of the work pupils submitted was cursory and, where extended, there seemed to be a lot of copying and pasting of text from the sites he had provided. The discussion forum had not taken off, although some pupils had posted and responded to messages about a recently reported decline in birth rates in India and two pupils had emailed him to ask for clarification about one of the resources that might have enabled them to complete the task. At the end of the placement, Carlton sought more formal feedback from the pupils and designed and carried out a questionnaire survey. He discovered that web access was not a problem for most pupils – they could access his site at home or through school machines during lunch or at the end of the day. He gained a better idea of pupils' widespread use of networked environments and how they juggled access to the learning platform with participation in their preferred social networking sites. Pupils were positive about the innovation, they liked the idea of text communication and the greater access to pictures and moving images. However, many did not actively take part in discussion and when it came to websites, they frequently found the text too difficult to understand, something he had not fully considered.

Commentary

Like Anthony, Carlton was attempting to use ICT tools to motivate his pupils as much as to address specific subject learning objectives. Carlton had latched on to the idea of developing online support through work he had seen in another subject. Nonetheless, the potential contribution of ICT to his subject teaching was considerable. It would provide pupils with 'anywhere, any time' access to a much wider range of learning material and access to discussion beyond the classroom.

There were limitations in his planning. First, he had not thought in advance how those without access to the internet would fare – in the event, this did not appear to be a serious difficulty but it might have been. He had not communicated to pupils what was involved in the shift from setting homework to providing 'learning tasks'. The latter he associated with pupils making choices about the resources they accessed and working through them at their own pace. However, he had not modelled how this would happen and had not been precise in what he wanted pupils to do with the resources once they had been located. Here, there was a major difficulty with pupils' information handling skills. He assumed that pupils were advanced information handlers because they appeared to be confident using networked environments in their everyday lives. In fact, they lacked the knowledge and skills to analyse the information they accessed. They could not identify key points within a text or transform information for another audience. The discussion forum was another challenge. It had been helpful for some pupils but he had not made his expectations clear to them, such as: explaining to them the value of exchanging ideas; the number of posts they should, as a minimum, contribute; the need to respond positively to each other and avoid personal asides. The innovation left him with more questions than answers but Carlton decided to pursue his investigation further, as there were both practical and pedagogic positives to come out of the innovation that he could build on.

12.3 Planning your use of ICT

These case studies show some of the starting points teachers had for using ICT and some of their experiences. They are summarized in Table 12.1. I will draw together some of the lessons learnt from the case studies in the form of key questions to ask yourself in planning your use of ICT within a lesson or series of lessons.

Table 12.1 Summary of issues in the use of ICT in three case studies

Case study	Problem/ opportunity	Planning	ICT knowledge and skills	Contribution of the technology	Implementation	Evaluation methods
Anthony	Address motivation of pupils	Minimal	Familiar with software; assumed pupils would know how to use it	Expressive of relevance; provisional nature of text (easy to alter)	Computer room; pair work; some whole-class teaching	Monitoring; teacher-focused
Baljit	Focus pupils on interpreting data	Extended; learning goals explicit	Familiar with software; demonstrated use to pupils	Automatic data collection and display	Laboratory; group work; whole-class starters and plenaries	Scanning class; use of question and answer, plenary; pupil writing
Carlton	Develop out-of-lesson learning	Broad, but learning goals not made clear	Taught how to use the software; assumed pupils would know how to use it	Storage of multimedia resources; interactivity through electronic communications	Machines accessed in school and at home; pupils have high level of control over what resources to access and when	Monitoring; questionnaire survey

What does ICT contribute to teaching my subject?

First and foremost, consider what you are expecting the use of ICT to contribute to your teaching. For example, ICT may enable:

- storage of information (in particular, 'anywhere, any time' multimedia material);
- automatic functions (e.g. logging data, recalculating within spreadsheets);
- interactivity between user and software (e.g. an interactive quiz at the interactive whiteboard) or between users (e.g. discussion forums);
- provisionality (e.g. rapid deletion and reformatting of text).

A further feature of ICT is the speed at which functions are carried out, so that it allows the user to do things that would be very difficult to do otherwise. ICT also has an expressive quality so that it is, at least initially, seen as new and potentially exciting.

A key issue is what these attributes of ICT can help you to do in your teaching. Anthony wanted to use the storage and interactivity of ICT to engage pupils in his lessons but instead focused on pupil motivation and his own discomfort with the group. In a similar way, a student teacher who feels under constant pressure when carrying out whole-class teaching might look to create multimedia presentations for the interactive whiteboard (IWB) to better engage pupils' attention. Of course, in both these cases, the use of ICT will open up new opportunities that may not have been anticipated. For example, Anthony found it natural to use pair work around the computer, something he was normally more resistant to doing. Similarly, users of IWBs often get pupils in front of the class to demonstrate to their peers in a way they would not consider when using a conventional whiteboard. In the second example, Baljit was much clearer in her mind about the cognitive contribution of ICT and how it could contribute to re-focusing pupils' learning on higher-order skills.

The conclusion from the case studies is that, as you plan your use of ICT, you need to think carefully about how ICT supports learning. Often student teachers focus on the behavioural or affective contribution of learning. This is rightly so – try learning to teach without paying attention to pupil engagement! However, this is not paying full attention to what technology can offer or indeed what teaching is about. As you plan your lesson with ICT, consider how you expect technology to contribute to pupil understanding of a topic and how you are going to convey your expectations of learning outcomes to pupils. You will probably not get it right first time, so learn from the feedback of your pupils and adapt accordingly.

Are pupils supported in crossing the ICT skills threshold?

You will want to ensure that pupils have easy access to ICT. This means that they have the necessary knowledge and skills to use the software. If not, provide simple demonstrations and help sheets in support. Use peer support in the classroom rather than running around trouble-shooting at the computer. Think carefully if you are planning to use software that has a high entry threshold. For example, creating a web page, using photo manipulation software or other less used progams will be a challenge for most pupils. Avoid the assumption that pupils are confident and skilled with technology simply because they use social networking sites.

Are you confident in your ICT knowledge and skills?

Enthusiasm, learning by trial and error, and a willingness to admit to lack of knowledge go a long way in working successfully with ICT. But the lesson from the case studies is to make sure you know how to use the appropriate software – you can become unstuck if the school is using an earlier version or later version of a program you are familiar with. Remember, too, that saving material on school networks is not always intuitive. Ensure that you have technical support for your first attempts in working with pupils.

How and when will pupils have access to machines?

All three teachers had to plan around access to machines. Carlton assumed pupils had out-of-school access; you will need to check this for yourself. If you intend using the internet, make sure you are familiar with any school policies. In school you will need to book a computer room or organize access to portable machines or to departmental resources. What do you see as the pros and cons of each approach? If you have a limited number of machines, the pupils will need to work in pairs or groups. Is this desirable in the lesson you are planning or is it a constraint?

Have you planned work away from the machines?

The same rules apply to using ICT as in any other lesson. If you think whole-class starters and plenaries are a good idea, then use them when the lesson involves ICT.

Move pupils away from machines so you have their full attention.

Have you planned a contingency?

Have you got contingency materials if the network fails? Can you quickly adapt if getting started takes much longer than you thought (for example, the network is slow, pupils have forgotten passwords, their skills are not as you imagined)? Can you use the computers for a follow-up lesson if you need to?

How are you going to monitor and evaluate pupils' use of ICT?

The case studies showed that question-and-answer, intervention with groups, and plenaries were all good monitoring tools. How can you use your monitoring and evaluation of pupils' work to inform future planning? Would a short questionnaire survey on pupils' use of ICT be appropriate?

Task 12.2

Plan for the use of ICT in a lesson in school. Address all the questions in the above section.

12.4　Where can I find out more about using ICT in my teaching?

All of the issues discussed above are covered in depth in a range of academic and practitioner reporting. One of the key issues highlighted earlier with respect to ICT use is the focus on behavioural and affective engagement. Our own work in this area is covered in Hammond *et al.* (2011). This paper reports on how and why a cohort of student teachers used ICT. It also looked at the constraints on ICT use and concluded that student teachers in many schools need to be resourceful and proactive in using ICT even when there is a strong expectation to do so.

The discussion of the contribution of ICT draws on the idea of 'technological, pedagogical and content knowledge' (TPaCK) put forward by Mishra and Koehler (2006). Put very simply, the idea is that an effective teacher is likely to have a good understanding of his or her subject (content knowledge) plus good understanding of how to teach the subject and the kind of problems pupils will have (pedagogical knowledge). A teacher making effective use of ICT has, in addition, a good understanding of both how to use technology (technological content knowledge) and its contribution to teaching and learning (technological pedagogical knowledge). Thus TPaCK is a mix of knowledge of your subject and knowledge of technology. In the examples, only Baljit could be said to have effectively developed TPaCK.

There is, of course, a wide range of software and ideas for teaching with ICT that are specific to your subject and you will find your subject association a good source of advice here. There has been a lot of recent interest, however, in two applications of ICT across all subjects. These are IWBs and learning platforms. Interactive whiteboards are now widely available in schools and are often the ICT resource that student teachers use most frequently. Research in this area suggests that IWBs help teachers improve the pace of lessons and engagement of pupils. They may also assist with inclusion, for example, enlarging text for pupils with sight impairment, illustrating concepts with visual images, and recording and sharing pupils' ideas. Often student teachers say they like using IWBs as they can prepare lessons more fully in advance and create more 'lively' resources. Many appreciate the opportunity to talk through a presentation while facing the class rather than turning their back to write at a traditional whiteboard. On the flip side, the idea of dialogic teaching with the IWB is not widely understood and there is a suggestion that teachers may be providing overly long presentations when using presentation slides inflexibly. For further information, see Rudd (2007) and Higgins *et al.* (2007).

Learning platforms generally refer to a mix of software to support, in the context of teaching and learning, online access to resources, collaboration areas such as wikis and discussion forums and blogs, and to multiple-choice assessment or interactive quizzes. They are an attempt to network learners, teachers, and material while controlling and monitoring access. Often a learning platform is in practice a VLE, but some schools provide a mix and match of software rather than one integrated package. Schools have struggled to integrate learning platforms in their teaching but innovative uses have been developed with schools showcasing work to parents and other audiences and having pupils routinely discuss work together (see Jewitt *et al.* 2010). The use, in particular, of discussion forums raises the issue of e-safety and while schools will have their own polices, you should also know about the wider issues (thinkuknow.co.uk offers advice for teachers and pupils here).

You will almost certainly have been directed to online and paper-based reading on the use of ICT in your subject. To explore more general issues, you may want to look further afield, for example Leask (2001) is still relevant though dated in parts. To get a more contemporary perspective on the use of ICT, look at Futurelab reports (www.futurelab.org.uk). Here you can find overviews in the form of literature reviews on several topics, including ICT and creativity, mobile learning, digital video games, and learning and e-assessment.

The issue of curriculum change with ICT is debated at length by academics, many of whom are asking why (at least from their perspective) ICT seems to have had so little impact on teaching and learning (e.g. Gouseti 2010). There are different ways of looking at this but a recurring theme is that, in spite of investment, there are still difficulties with: accessing machines in classrooms – and in particular fully maintained machines with support on site; 'inertia' – for example, few teacher training partnerships have yet to get round to providing detailed modelling of online discussion with pupils; and a mismatch between the opportunities that ICT offers and high stakes assessment. The constraints felt by teachers in their use of ICT are covered by Somekh (2008), and Lewin and colleagues' (2003) study remains relevant regarding the limits of out-of-school learning.

The British Educational Communications and Technology Agency (Becta) supported ICT Test Bed project (Somekh *et al.* 2006) provided an account of special circumstances, i.e. schools with high access and high support. ICT was seen as making a positive contribution to learning outcomes and there was some evidence that teachers made most use of applications such as IWBs, which they could most easily incorporate into their everyday teaching routines. Studies such as this provide credible evidence that the use of technology can have a positive impact on learning achievement but so much depends on context and what is being measured. A side issue here is the suggestion that younger people (including many student teachers) have been so exposed to technology in their formative years that they are 'digital natives' or 'netizens' – the web is their resource of choice, they prefer multimedia to books, are constantly online, and can multitask. I would question many of the assumptions here but nonetheless ask why much of teaching has stayed the same when the world outside has changed so much.

12.5   Recommendations for further reading and webliography

Hammond, M., Ingram, J. and Reynolds, L. (2011) How and why do student teachers use ICT? *Journal of Computer Assisted Learning*, 27(3): 191–203.

Higgins, S., Beauchamp, G. and Miller, D. (2007) Reviewing the literature on interactive whiteboards. *Learning, Media and Technology*, 32(3): 213–25.

Leask, M. (ed.) (2001) *Issues in Teaching Using ICT*. London: RoutledgeFalmer.

Rudd, T. (2007) *Do Whiteboards have a Future in the UK Classroom?* Bristol: Futurelab. Available at: http://www.futurelab.org.uk/events/listing/whiteboards/report.

Website

http://www.futurelab.org.uk/events/listing/whiteboards/report

SECTION 3

Secondary schools and
the curriculum

13

What should we teach?
Understanding the secondary curriculum

Chris Husbands

13.1 Introduction

The curriculum is one of the most obvious aspects of schools. Not only does the curriculum describe what pupils learn, but the daily routines of secondary schools are marked by the division of the curriculum into subjects for study: English, mathematics, science, PSHEE (personal, social, health and economic education), music, art, humanities and so on. Their staffs are organized into curriculum teams, either through conventionally described school subjects ('the biology department', 'the English department') or through broader curriculum areas ('the humanities faculty', 'the language area'). Student teachers themselves are trained, above all, to teach a secondary school subject, normally defined in terms of their own degree specialism or closely related to it. The curriculum, in many ways, defines what school is about. 'What did you do at school today?' is one of the most routinely asked – and routinely avoided – questions of a child's life! We all know what goes on in school: pupils learn and teachers teach. What they learn, and what they teach, is defined by the curriculum. As we shall see, however, the curriculum is far from straightforward, and in many ways is one of the most complex and least obvious aspects of school life. Understanding the curriculum involves far more than understanding the list of subjects that goes to make up the school timetable. It involves exploring questions about what is taught, how it is taught and organized, about the relationship between knowledge, skills and attitudes, and, more controversially, why the things that are taught in schools have been selected as being significant and worth teaching to young people. These questions are difficult enough in themselves, but they derive from two more fundamental questions, about which there is always considerable disagreement between teachers, within schools and throughout society: what should children learn in school, and how should they learn it? These are difficult and complex questions not just because there is always more material that could be taught than there is time available to teach, but because they raise fundamental questions about the purposes of education itself.

After reading this chapter, you should have:

- developed a clear understanding of different ways of thinking about and organizing the curriculum;

- formed ideas about what the school curriculum is for;
- begun to explore how the curriculum is changing.

13.2   Curriculum debates and disputes

Before exploring the organization and structure of the school curriculum in England in detail, it is useful to identify some of the underlying debates about the curriculum which shape policy at national and school levels and which are resulting in pressures on the curriculum. Three are of particular importance. They are to do with the purposes of the curriculum, with learners' entitlement and with who should decide what is in the school curriculum.

Perhaps the most fundamental issue in discussions about the curriculum relates to debate about its purposes. The school curriculum is one of the main ways in which a society socializes its young into knowledge and ways of thinking. Any curriculum is a selection from all the things that might be taught, and the way in which a curriculum is developed will depend on ideas about its purposes. Because this is in itself controversial, disagreements about the purposes of the curriculum are often ferocious. Children learn different sorts of things in schools: they build up knowledge, they develop skills and they acquire attitudes. There are those who regard the primary purpose of education as the acquisition of certain types of knowledge. Some emphasize the importance of the school in inducting children into a cultural heritage, emphasizing the significance of making great literature, music or art accessible to the next generation. The American cultural critic, E.D. Hirsch (1996), argues strongly that 'cultural literacy' – providing access to a common-core, knowledge-rich curriculum – is a central mission of schooling. There are those who see the primary purpose of education as being the acquisition of transferable 'skills for work', which will prepare young people for the demands of the workplace. There are those who stress the significance of education in developing learners' sense of their own capacities and abilities. Of course, a simple response to these debates is to argue that the curriculum must serve several purposes: it must transmit usable knowledge, develop practical skills and produce rounded individuals. However, the balance we give to these different goals will shape both the organization of the curriculum and the teaching of individual subjects. For example, we might debate both the place of music in the school curriculum, and the extent to which the subject should be concerned with talent-spotting musical giftedness, developing the skills of concentration and collaboration, and offering all young people opportunities to enjoy the capacity to make music.

A second issue relates to learners' entitlement. Most of us have views, even if we cannot articulate them clearly, about the basic entitlement that should shape learners' experience in school: those minimal things that we expect schools to teach every learner. Politicians often talk about the importance of the 'basics'. By this, they normally mean that they expect every child to be taught to read, to write and to attain basic numeracy. In the nineteenth century, this conception of entitlement led to the idea that schools were fundamentally about the 'three Rs': reading, (w)riting, and (a)rithmetic. Although this sense of 'the basics' is still prevalent – for example, in the emphasis on synthetic phonics in early literacy teaching – few would now regard this as an adequate account of the basic curriculum entitlement in a complex, advanced society. Most teachers and educationalists would extend the list.

Task 13.1

What did you not learn at school that you wish you had? What did you learn at school for which you have since found no use?

What would you include as compulsory elements in a curriculum for children who will be adults in the middle of the twenty-first century?

Your own list might include some or all of the following. You might have included facility with information and communications technology (ICT) as a basic entitle-ment – an addition to the entitlement that could not have been foreseen by Victorian advocates of the three Rs. You might have considered that schools have an obligation to prepare pupils for the world of work by teaching them a range of transferable skills, including the abilities to work collaboratively in groups, to apply knowledge to the real world and to take responsibility for their own learning. In a society in which many adults will change employment frequently, you might consider that an essential com-ponent of the curriculum is to lay the foundations for lifelong learning. Looking at other areas, you might consider that schools have failed their pupils if they have not prepared them for independence in adult life: this might include the teaching of basic cookery skills, or the rudiments that will enable them to understand their cars. Given the notorious difficulties that parents have in exploring issues relating to sex educa-tion or drug and substance abuse with their own children, your entitlement curricu-lum might include the expectation that all schools will offer PSHEE. You may have taken the view that in a complex, multicultural and diverse society, schools have an obligation to undertake some political or citizenship education. You may well feel that the ability to make sense of the modern world through an understanding of history, geography, sociology or economics is an essential component of the curriculum.

This list of potential entitlements is, by now, long. It is difficult, in the absence of hard cases or agreed criteria, to argue that any of these areas is not essential. For exam-ple, are you content with school leavers who have no understanding of how our democ-racy works, or how to boil an egg, or of strategies to prevent sexually transmitted diseases? But it is also apparent that the list of entitlements has become almost impos-sibly large. In building curricula, choices have to be made. If the entitlement is too great, then there is no room for choice, and some pupils will become disaffected by having to learn things that do not connect with their own lives. If the entitlement is too small, then schools run the risk of premature specialization – that is, ruling out of the entitlement for pupils important elements that will enable them to make informed choices later on. There is also the risk of the emergence of different curricula for children labelled as 'academically successful' or 'academically unsuccessful'. The debate about entitlement is a long one. The 1944 Education Act, which made provision for a free secondary education for all children, introduced different types of school providing different types of entitlement curriculum to supposedly different types of children. 'Grammar' schools offered an academic curriculum to the supposedly most able 15–25 per cent, technical schools offered an applied curriculum to those deemed at 11 years of age to be technologically oriented and secondary modern schools offered a 'practical' and 'vocational' curriculum to the rest. One of the main impetuses for the reform that introduced comprehensive schools was recognition that this sort of divisiveness from the age of 11 was inadequate, ineffective and unfair. Despite the widespread promotion of curriculum specialism for secondary schools – specialisms now include technology, science, mathematics and computing, performing arts and humanities – the principle of selection by ability or aptitude has not re-established itself in the secondary system.

Debates about entitlement intersect with debates about the *purposes* of the curriculum. We might argue, for example, that all young people have a shared entitlement to a broad, balanced curriculum throughout their schooling. At the other extreme, we might argue that the entitlement curriculum might differ for different groups at different stages of their schooling dependent on interest, attainment and motivation. There is currently an extended debate about the 14–16 curriculum following the Coalition government's decision in 2010 to define an 'English Baccalaureate' based on pupils securing examination success at age 16 in English, mathematics, science, a modern or classical language, and history or geography. Introducing the English Baccalaureate, the Secretary of State for Education – perhaps implicitly echoing the views of Hirsch – argued that these subjects encapsulated an irreducible academic core for learners; his critics argued that it was backward looking to define a modern qualification in which success at history and Latin secured success, but success in IT and engineering did not. The debate about the English Baccalaureate is a case study in disagreement over the purposes of the curriculum, about what counts as 'worthwhile' knowledge and about who should define the content and structure of the curriculum. Mathematics is a part of the compulsory curriculum for learners from age 5 through to 16 and, at the time of writing, there are tentative proposals to develop entitlement to mathematics as part of the 14–19 curriculum. Nonetheless, some mathematics educators have argued that the subject is not well served by its 'privileged' status, and that learners should be given choice as they mature about whether to learn mathematics. Once we have decided which subjects should be taught and when, there are similar debates about purposes that often translate into bitter disputes about particular issues within school subjects: whether in a multicultural society the balance of school history should focus on British history or global history, whether and how Shakespeare should be a compulsory element in the English curriculum, and so on. There is no 'right' answer to questions like these, which depend on different views about the purposes of the curriculum. You will encounter these debates in the teaching of your own subjects.

Behind these disputes lies a third area of disagreement – that is, *who should decide* the content of the curriculum. It could be argued that teachers should decide the content of the curriculum: they, after all, have professional expertise in the management of pupil learning. This, indeed, was the belief that underpinned curriculum policy-making in England between about 1944 and 1988. David Eccles, Conservative minister for education in the early 1960s, spoke of the 'secret garden of the curriculum, into which ministers wandered at their peril', and government largely devolved curriculum management to the Schools Council, which had a majority of teacher professional association representatives. Alternatively, it could be argued that parents should be able to control the content of the curriculum: we might argue that it is parents who know best about their own children's needs. In the Netherlands, considerable curriculum authority is devolved to parents, who can attract state support to set up schools, and the Coalition government has extended similar rights to parent groups who wish to set up so-called 'free' schools. There is debate about the extent to which parents should exercise influence, or even control, over the curriculum. Schools are required to consult parents over the content of sex education provision, and parents can exercise the right to withdraw their children from religious education and sex education in school. We might regard other groups as having an important part to play in decision-making regarding the curriculum: religious and community groups, universities or employers – who, after all, employ pupils after they leave school – or, perhaps most radically of all, pupils themselves. There is, of course, another key influence on the curriculum: the government. At different times, and in different ways, government has claimed to represent the views of parents or of employers, or of other social groups in its planning for the curriculum, and a number of studies have explored the ways in which government reflects different influences in its curriculum policy (Graham 1993; Elliott 1997; Chitty 2002).

13.3   The National Curriculum

In retrospect, however, what seems most surprising is how slow government was to take direct control of the curriculum in English schools. Only in the 1988 Education Reform Act did government assume power to establish a National Curriculum (NC). Established between 1988 and 1991, the NC has been substantially revised on three occasions. The first was in 1994, in response to widespread teacher protests about what was seen as an unworkable initial specification. Subsequent revisions in 2000 and 2006–2007 were part of scheduled reviews. At the time of writing, the NC is subject to an extensive review of its structure, format and organization, designed to define with greater precision an irreducible 'core' and to allow schools greater freedom to develop their own curriculum. Thus, further substantial change is scheduled for phased implementation, starting in 2014.

Currently, the NC provides a basic curriculum structure for schools, although, as we shall see, it has become more complex as waves of reform and implementation have overtaken it. Tim Oates (2010) has recently argued that the NC in England lacks the stability of some other national curricula. As we explore the NC, you might want to consider the balances it strikes between entitlement and choice, between different purposes and between the differences in influence of power groups in the education system. The basic structure of the NC is set out in Table 13.1. Compulsory schooling is divided into five Key Stages (KS), from Foundation (introduced in 2000) to KS4. At each stage, curriculum requirements set out targets for pupil attainment in a range of subjects. However, the review that is taking place at the time of writing may lead to a new structure based on years rather than Key Stages.

Learning to teach the NC is a demanding task for new teachers. There is content to master and issues of planning to overcome. The formal requirements of the NC must not only be addressed through well-focused teaching, they must be addressed in ways that engage and support the learning of all pupils. However, the NC does not describe the full range of the school curriculum. The NC is itself a part of the wider school curriculum and many elements of the school lie outside its formal requirements. Religious education (RE), although a compulsory element of the school curriculum for all pupils in school from 5 to 19 since the 1944 Education Act, is not a part of the NC. Before 1988, ironically, RE was the only subject schools were required to teach and in 1988 it was felt to be too controversial for the government to prescribe the content of RE. Schools are also at liberty to add subjects to the curriculum. For example, some secondary schools add Latin to the KS3 curriculum, others add Mandarin, and yet others business studies; these decisions reflect different assumptions about the most effective way to enhance or develop the curriculum. More radically, schools may decide to restructure the curriculum around organizing themes, intersecting with the requirements of the NC.

At KS4, much of the provision is outside the NC, which requires only the teaching of an Extended Core (see Table 13.1). Thus, history, geography, art and music are elements of the NC at KS3 but not at KS4, while vocational elements of

Table 13.1 An overview of the National Curriculum

Stage	Age	School year
Primary education		
Foundation Stage	3–5 years	
Key Stage 1	5–7 years	Years 1 and 2
Key Stage 2	7–11 years	Years 3–6
Secondary education		
Key Stage 3	11–14 years	Years 7–9
Core subjects (English, mathematics, science)		
Foundation subjects (ICT, history, geography, citizenship, art and design, music, PE, design and technology, modern languages)		
Plus RE, careers education and sex education (statutory but outside the NC)		
Key Stage 4	14–16 years	Years 10–11
Statutory subjects (English, mathematics, science, ICT, citizenship, PE, work-related learning, RE and sex education)*		
Entitlement areas (which must be made available to students who wish to study them): arts, design technology, humanities, modern languages		
Diplomas (Level 1 and Level 2), various BTEC qualifications, OCR Nationals (see Chapter 19)		

*GCSE success at Grade C or above in English, mathematics, two sciences, history or geography, and a modern or ancient language makes up the English Baccalaureate. AS levels taken in the relevant subject before the end of KS4 also count.

Table 13.2 Post-16 education

Stage	Age	School year
Post-16 (sometimes referred to as KS5)	16–19 years	Years 12 and 13
4 or 5 AS levels (2 or 3 units each) in Year 12		
3 A2 levels (2 or 3 units each) in Year 13		
2 or 3 AS units + 2 or 3 A2 units combine for 1 A Level (other qualifications include the International Baccalaureate, the European Baccalaureate, Diplomas (Level 3), various BTEC qualifications, OCR Nationals, and a variety of workplace-based training and education programmes)		

the curriculum, such as work experience or vocationally related courses, are likely to feature at KS4 for some learners. The post-16 curriculum (see Table 13.2) lies entirely outside the NC (save for the legal requirement, in practice often ignored, for post-16 pupils in schools to study RE). At the time of writing, the government is also reforming the 14–19 curriculum in an attempt to develop a more coherent phase of learning, with a clearer articulation of pupil entitlement, which maps progression routes through a variety of learning provision, including a stronger vocational offer (see Chapter 19).

Task 13.2

Read the NC Order for your own subject. (If you are training to teach a non-NC subject, read a GCSE or other examination syllabus in your subject.)

How does this document reflect wider ideas about the content and purpose of the curriculum?

13.4   Beyond the National Curriculum

The NC can thus be seen as nesting within the school curriculum, and schools are increasingly encouraged to use curriculum freedoms to give a distinctive flavour to the curriculum that reflects the ethos of the school, for example, reflecting specialist status as a language college or a business and enterprise college, or responding to particular features of the school's location or intake. Schools are asked to articulate the basis for their curriculum planning and to take responsibility for developing distinctive elements to the curriculum. The school's *planned* curriculum is a tool for combining their responsibilities to deliver statutory elements of the curriculum – the NC, RE and PSHEE – with the non-statutory elements that it wishes to emphasize.

The planned curriculum will need to be much more than a list of content. It will need to clarify the aims of the school's curriculum and to identify mechanisms for translating those aims into practice, defining knowledge, skills and concepts. It will also need to identify an 'organizational' framework for achieving these aims, as well as a set of assessment and evaluation arrangements for establishing the effectiveness of the curriculum. At present, for example, some schools are looking beyond AS/A2 assessment and making use of the International Baccalaureate as an assessment device post-16. The planned curriculum adapts the national and whole curriculum to resources, learners and school ethos. However, the *planned* curriculum typically differs from the *delivered* curriculum. No school ever quite teaches what it plans to teach in its curriculum statements. There are a number of reasons for this, some of them quite accidental and unpredictable. Changes in staffing, long-term staff absences, unexpected opportunities to become involved in curriculum development projects, local and national initiatives, and circumstances may all affect the delivery of the planned curriculum. Finally, the curriculum *experienced* by individual learners may differ markedly from the curriculum experienced by other learners. Again, this can happen for a variety of reasons, perhaps due to the school's decision to differentiate provision for different groups, or due to learners' decisions to take different routes through the school's planned curriculum.

Task 13.3

Find out about the range of possible curricula that different learners at KS4 might follow at www.aqa.org.uk, www.edexcel.org.uk, and www.ocr.org.uk.

Why do you think schools are so strongly committed to choice in curriculum for pupils post-14? What dangers might lie in a wide choice?

We have seen that the school curriculum is a complex construction, comprising the whole curriculum, the NC, the planned curriculum, the delivered curriculum and the experienced curriculum. However, to understand learners' experiences in school, one further concept needs to be considered: *the hidden curriculum*. The hidden curriculum is the term generally used to describe the implicit, often unintended and often very subtle, messages schools convey about learning, knowledge and achievement. The hidden curriculum is very powerful, but often difficult to pin down. It consists of the assumptions about how learning is to be conducted that schools convey unconsciously through, for example, the way classrooms are organized and work is presented. Messages about the sorts of achievements that are worthy of praise are communicated through notices and honours boards that can be seen around schools and in the kinds of achievements that are praised in newsletters. There are often hidden messages about an implied hierarchy of subjects. For instance, school reports are normally presented loose leaf, with English, science and mathematics at the front and art and music at the back. Underlying messages can also be detected in the organization of staff handbooks and in how well equipped different subjects are. Some commentators have argued that this is not just about a hierarchy of subjects and achievement in schools, but something more fundamental about schooling, conveying messages about what counts as knowledge in our society, and how that knowledge is organized and presented. Critics of the English Baccalaureate have argued that it reflects deeply traditional assumptions about the worth of subjects: and some of its advocates have accepted, and indeed rejoiced, in the criticism.

Task 13.4

What other ways might there be in which schools communicate a 'hidden curriculum' to learners? How can schools and teachers become more aware of the 'hidden curriculum'?

At the time of writing this chapter, there are enormous pressures for change on the curriculum; this is partly a result of curriculum review, but it also reflects serious questioning in and beyond schools about how best to prepare young people for a rapidly changing world. Some argue that schools should be resolutely traditional in the curriculum they offer, that established subjects, with their well-defined approaches to the construction of knowledge, provide a basis for sound education at any time. Others argue that subjects constrain thinking, and that the challenges of the modern workplace and the contemporary world call for the application of complex knowledge to new problems, requiring a thematic or problem-based approach to the curriculum. Increasingly, policy-makers and schools are under pressure to develop curriculum solutions to what are seen as pressing educational difficulties, such as the deep disaffection from schooling found among working-class boys or the persistent differences in attainment among different ethnic and social groups. There are pressures for more 'relevance' to the world of work in what is taught, the way it is taught and its assessment. There are pressures to use the curriculum as one tool for combating social exclusion and poor health through the effective provision of personal and social, drugs and sex education, and developing links with out-of-school agencies. There are pressures on all curriculum areas to make increased use of new technologies for learning as part of a strategy for preparing pupils for a changing world. There are pressures to improve standards of educational performance, which involve schools in making adjustments to the curriculum to improve the performance of individuals and groups of pupils so that learners can achieve the best possible outcomes. These pressures translate into specific curriculum innovations, some of them discussed in detail elsewhere in this book. Schools are certainly becoming more distinctive in the curricula they offer, but those curricula reflect the sorts of choices about content, organization and structure that have been discussed here. As your career develops, these and other issues will be matters for lively discussion and decision-making. The ways in which they are resolved in the schools in which you work will depend on a number of things. They will, of course, depend on patterns of national policy and local provision. However, they will also depend on the answers you and the teachers you work with give to questions about what should be taught, what pupils' entitlement should be, what the curriculum is for and who has the power and authority to develop it.

13.5   Recommendations for further reading and webliography

Hircsh, E.D. (1996) *The Schools We Need and Why We Don't Have Them*. New York: Anchor Books.

Oates, T. (2010) *Could do Better: Using International Comparisons to Refine the National Curriculum in England*. Cambridge: Cambridge Assessment.

White, J. (ed.) (2003) *Rethinking the School Curriculum: Values, Aims and Purposes*. London: Routledge.

Young, M. (2009) *Bringing Knowledge Back In*. London: Routledge.

Website

Information about the curriculum review is available at:

http://www.education.gov.uk/schools/teachingandlearning/curriculum

14

Spiritual, moral and cultural development
Judith Everington

14.1 Introduction

The curriculum should reflect values in our society that promote personal development, equality of opportunity, economic well being, a healthy and just democracy, and a sustainable future. These values should relate to:

- ourselves, as individuals capable of spiritual, moral, social, intellectual and physical growth and development;
- our relationships, as fundamental to the development and fulfillment of happy and healthy lives, and to the good of the community;
- our society, which is shaped by the contributions of a diverse range of people, cultures and heritages;
- our environment, as the basis of life and a source of wonder and inspiration that needs to be protected.

(National Curriculum 2007)

This chapter will focus on spiritual, moral and cultural development. By the end of the chapter, you should:

- understand what is meant by spiritual, moral and cultural development in the context of the secular secondary school;
- know the legal and professional requirements relating to spiritual, moral and cultural development;
- understand how spiritual, moral and cultural development can be promoted in teaching and pastoral work;
- know how to obtain guidance on and ideas for promoting spiritual, moral and cultural development.

14.2 Spiritual, moral and cultural development – what's all that then?

'That's RE isn't it, and assemblies?'

'Moral development sounds like something to do with cold baths and keeping idle fingers busy!'

'Spiritual development is surely a very private thing and I'm worried about interfering in it.'

'I'm interested in the idea of cultural development but my subject isn't "arty".'

Task 14.1

What do you associate with each of the terms spiritual, moral and cultural development? Write a list of immediate thoughts and feelings. Are they negative or positive? Where have they come from?

In this chapter, you will find 'official' definitions of the terms. However, when approaching these complex and sensitive dimensions of teaching and learning for the first time, it is important to be aware of the understandings that you have already formed and the feelings that are associated with these. For example, some students' experience of school and higher education may have convinced them that they have little or nothing to contribute to one or more of the areas of development. Others will have attended faith-based (e.g. Islamic, Roman Catholic, Church of England, Jewish) schools and may have understandings that are different from those that are current in secular secondary schools. Through recognition of preconceptions and existing attitudes, it is possible to set these aside to develop a critical openness to new definitions and possibilities.

Whatever your responses to the task above, you may have been inclined to skip over this chapter. Research indicates that student teachers tend to be most interested in those aspects of their training course that have to do with teaching their subject effectively, controlling their classes, and forming good relationships with pupils. They take less interest in matters that fall outside these concerns. However, in this chapter you will be asked to consider the view that a teacher's ability to teach, manage, and relate to pupils effectively is greatly enhanced by her or his ability to take account of and draw upon pupils' spiritual, moral, and cultural lives, and provide opportunities for development.

14.3 Requirements and responsibilities

The quotation at the beginning of this chapter is from the introduction to a previous version of the National Curriculum (NC), which re-states the 1988 Education

Reform Act requirement for the school curriculum to promote pupils' spiritual, moral, and cultural development (SMCD). Schools document their provision for SMCD and Ofsted inspects this provision and its outcomes. In the 2011 proposals to revise the Ofsted inspection framework, it is made clear that inspectors will 'consider' how well the school promotes pupils' SMCD in their judgement of the overall effectiveness of the school and that inspectors will refer to this in their reports (Ofsted 2011c: 5–8). The importance of SMCD is indicated in the statement, 'What matters most is how well schools ensure achievement, learning and behaviour for their pupils, as well as contributing to their spiritual, moral, social and cultural development. These aspects will be the guiding principles for the new school inspection framework' (p. 8). The proposals outlined above indicate an intention to continue viewing SMCD as something that permeates the whole of school life and should be reflected in every aspect of teachers' work, including their relationships with pupils and with other people who work in the school. At present, this whole-school perspective is outlined in statements about the school's ethos that appear in its prospectus and policy documents and it seems that this practice will continue. Student teachers have been expected to demonstrate that they can contribute to SMCD in their work with pupils and although the current national standards for qualified teacher status (QTS) do not make specific reference to SMCD, a number clearly refer to spiritual, moral, and cultural matters (DfE 2011c).

14.4   Defining spiritual, moral, and cultural development

To what does the term 'spiritual' refer?

In one definition it is said to refer to 'a dimension of human existence which applies to all pupils' and as 'something fundamental in the human condition which is not necessarily experienced through the physical senses and/or expressed in everyday language' (SCAA 1995: 3). Other definitions refer to an inner life or self; our non-tangible personality or our self-awareness (Bigger and Brown 1999: 6).

Spiritual development

Of the three areas considered in this chapter, spiritual development is the most difficult to define. There is a vast body of literature devoted to exploring such slippery questions as: 'Is there such a thing as a human spirit?', but what matters for most teachers is having a definition that is clearly related to the context in which they are working.

Some student teachers will undertake one or more of their school placements in faith-based schools and some will eventually take up posts in such schools. In faith schools, guidance related to spiritual development will reflect the religious beliefs and values associated with the origin of the school and this guidance will need to be consulted. In this chapter, the context considered is the secular school, which is responsible for the development of young people from a wide range of backgrounds and with a wide range of attitudes to religion – from fervent atheism, via mild curiosity, to profound commitment to a religious faith. Mindful of the need to provide guidance that is inclusive, those who have offered definitions appropriate for the secular school stress that spiritual development should not be viewed as synonymous with religious development. At the same time, it must include pupils who will view spiritual development in relation to their religious development. The Standards for QTS (DfE 2011c) indicate that teachers need to know something of the backgrounds, personal beliefs, and attitudes of pupils if they are to recognize and deal sensitively with individual needs.

In what aspects of their lives do or can young people develop spiritually?

It has been suggested that young people develop spiritually in and through their:

- *beliefs and values*: as they develop personal (for some, religious) beliefs and values, but also begin to understand the beliefs of others and how individual and shared beliefs shape people's lives and identities and lead to decisions and actions;
- *feelings, emotions, and inner experiences*: for example, the sense of being moved by beauty or kindness or angered by injustice; a sense of awe, wonder, and mystery – in response to the natural world or to a sense of a reality beyond the material world and the limitations of human understanding;
- *search for meaning and purpose*: for example, asking 'why' when reflecting on hardship and suffering or on the origins and purpose of life, or responding to the challenging experiences of life such as death or loss of love and security;
- *self-knowledge*: an awareness of oneself in terms of thoughts, emotions, and experiences and a growing understanding of one's own identity as a unique individual, but also as a member of groups and communities;
- *relationships*: recognizing and valuing the worth of each individual; building trustful relationships with others and developing a sense of the responsibilities that trust entails;
- *creativity*: exploring and expressing innermost thoughts and feelings through art, music or creative writing and using the imagination, inspiration, intuition, and insight.

(based on SCAA 1995: 3–4)

Like most definitions of spiritual development, those above have been arrived at by adult professionals. However, research undertaken in a range of comprehensive schools found that Year 9 pupils' own understandings of 'spiritual' and 'spiritual development' were 'uncannily similar' to the kind of adult definitions provided above. It was also found that, even when pupils struggled to find words, they 'communicated a great depth of understanding and feeling' in their responses to questions about spiritual matters (Wintersgill 2002: 8).

Moral development

Like spiritual development, moral development is not easy to define, is the subject of much controversy and debate and, in faith schools, will reflect the religious beliefs and values associated with the origin of the school. However, in the context of the secular school, the guidance offered by government and other authorities has suggested two major strands of pupils' moral development:

- knowledge, understanding, and, at least implicitly, acceptance of the moral values and codes and conventions of conduct which are promoted within the school and which reflect those promoted in society;
- knowledge and understanding of criteria for making moral judgements and the ability to employ these in making their own judgements, in relation to personal behaviour and moral issues.

Between the first and second strands there is a tension and potential for conflict. This reflects one of the most fundamental and enduring tensions within education and within the teacher's role – the tension between 'training' young people to become 'good citizens' and providing them with the tools to think for themselves and make their own judgements and decisions.

At school level, the extent to which there is tension or conflict between moral 'training' and 'empowering' will depend on many factors, including the ways in which moral values and development are presented in school ethos statements and are inter-preted by school managers and other members of staff. However, in any school it is difficult to avoid the fact that there will be times when teachers will be enforcing the school's moral values and code, and other times when they will be encouraging pupils to look critically at the moral arguments put forward by adults and develop confi-dence in making their own moral judgements.

This difficulty is illustrated in the definitions of moral development drawn up by Ofsted, with reference to the role of schools and to pupil characteristics. The school-related definitions begin with a statement that leans strongly in the direction of the 'training' view of moral development. So, schools that are encouraging pupils' moral development are likely to be 'providing a clear moral code as a basis for behaviour which is promoted consistently through all aspects of the school' (Ofsted 2004a: 18). In the list of characteristics of pupils who are becoming 'morally aware', the emphasis is much more on independent thinking and the individual's will to act in accordance with moral principles. So, pupils will be developing:

- an ability to distinguish right from wrong, based on a knowledge of the moral codes of their own and other cultures;
- a confidence to act consistently in accordance with their own principles;
- a commitment to personal values in areas which are considered right by some and wrong by others;
- a willingness to express their views on ethical issues and personal values;
- an ability to make responsible and reasoned judgements on moral dilemmas;
- an understanding of the need to review and reassess their values, codes and principles in the light of experience.

(Ofsted 2004a: 17)

Leaving aside the issue of consistency, the characteristics above reflect an emphasis on the empowerment of pupils, which, as we shall see, plays an important role in citizenship and personal, social, health and economic education (PSHEE) (see Chapters 18 and 25).

Cultural development

The term 'culture' is used and understood in different ways, in different contexts. In everyday speech, to refer to someone as 'cultured' often implies that they are well educated in and appreciative of the Arts. Another common usage of the term is in 'multicultural', although this is being replaced by the more flexible term, 'cultural diversity'. In sociological debate, the term 'culture' is fiercely contested, but there is some agreement that it refers to the expression of the fundamental concepts and values of a community, and that these are subject to continuous development and change.

Attempts to define cultural development in an educational context have drawn upon these differing understandings of 'culture/cultural'. The report of the National Advisory Committee on Creative and Cultural Education (1999), *All Our Futures*, has been an influential work in this area. The report identifies four central roles for education in the cultural development of young people. In their guidance, Ofsted (2004a: 23–6) provides a commentary on each of these and outlines their view of the characteristics of pupils who are becoming 'culturally aware'. These are summarized below.

1. *To enable young people to recognize, explore, and understand their own cultural assumptions and values.* Pupils need to understand their own culture. This gives them a sense of identity and a language with which to communicate, receive, and modify the shared values of the culture. Such language embraces customs, icons and images, artefacts, music, painting and sculpture, dance and technology, as well as verbal and literary forms. There will also be agreed norms of behaviour and opportunities to participate in celebrations that mark key ideals or events. Pupils who are becoming culturally aware will be developing an ability to understand the meaning and significance of, and to use, the various forms of cultural 'language', and a willingness to participate in and respond to artistic and cultural enterprises.

2. *To enable young people to embrace and understand cultural diversity by bringing them into contact with attitudes, values, and traditions of other cultures.* Within any culture, there will be sub-cultures and the dominant culture of any one group of people is only one among many in the world. With improvements in communication, we are also beginning to recognize a 'world culture' that people need to understand and feel comfortable with. Pupils who are becoming culturally aware will be developing an ability to appreciate cultural diversity and to accord dignity to other people's values and beliefs, thereby challenging racism. They will be developing an openness to new ideas and a willingness to modify cultural values in the light of experience, and a sense of personal enrichment through encounter with cultural media and traditions from a range of cultures.

3. *To encourage a historical perspective by relating contemporary values to the processes and events that have shaped them.*

4. *To enable young people to understand the evolutionary nature of culture and the processes and potential for change.* Cultures are always changing and growing. Pupils who are becoming culturally aware will be developing an understanding of the processes of cultural development and change and an appreciation of the inter-dependence of different cultures. This will involve understanding the influences that have shaped their own cultural heritage, and facing the prejudices that lead to dismissing or marginalizing unfamiliar traditions.

The emphasis on cultural diversity in the summary above may seem daunting to student teachers whose lives and educational experiences have provided little opportunity to learn about a range of cultures. At the end of this chapter, you will find references to websites that provide material on a wide range of religious and cultural matters and practical guidance on cultural development. During your training, you should be given opportunities to learn about cultural diversity. You may also be able to gain knowledge and understanding through a placement in a school in which a range of cultures is represented.

During your school placements, you may wish to consider the extent to which the schools actively promote the kind of cultural development described above. However, as we have seen, the current national standards for QTS (DfE 2011c) require all student teachers to gain sufficient knowledge and understanding to take account of cultural diversity in their teaching.

Task 14.2

Look back at your initial responses to the terms spiritual, moral and cultural development. How do they compare to the descriptions above?

Which of the aspects of SMCD above do you feel most and least comfortable with, and equipped to deal with? Make a note of the things that you will need to find out about before and during your training course.

Make a quick-fire response to the question, how could your specialist subject promote spiritual, moral and cultural development?

14.5   What does it all mean in practice?

In this section, we will look briefly at the relationship between SMCD and the *Every Child Matters* agenda (DfES 2003e). We will then consider the four overlapping areas of a teacher's work in which there are opportunities for pupils' SMCD: subject teaching; citizenship and PSHEE; pastoral work; and assemblies/collective worship. Each area will be considered in a separate section, but in 'real life' there is no clear separation between these, and the opportunity or need to contribute to pupils' SMCD can crop up at any point in a teacher's day. In 'real life', too, the distinction between spiritual, moral, and cultural development breaks down. The following example, 'Spiritual, moral and cultural development in a teacher's day', is intended to illustrate these points.

Case Study 14.1

Stuart arrives at school to find a fight brewing between two girls in his tutor group. One is accusing the other of spreading rumours about her 'sex life'. Stuart intervenes and reminds both about the importance of respect for others and self-respect.

At the staff briefing, all Year 7 teachers are asked to support the sponsored 'Silly Hair Day' organized by the pupils in aid of 'Children in Need'.

At the Year 9 assembly and act of collective worship, some of Stuart's tutor group read out their own poems on 'Being on the Outside'. The Head of Year follows her short talk with a minute's silent reflection on how it feels to be an outsider, and what each of us can do to break down barriers and enable everyone to feel included.

During the second lesson, a Year 10 pupil asks Stuart why they need to spend 'so much time looking at the situation in other countries'. Stuart reminds the whole group that to be at the cutting edge these days, it is crucial to have a global perspective.

At lunchtime, Stuart attends a meeting to discuss plans for the cross-curricular field trip to Stonehenge.

In the afternoon, his Year 8 pupils are put into groups to explore and come up with solutions to a conflict between three families who live in adjoining flats, but have very different lifestyles and needs.

In the evening, Stuart downloads the lyrics of a song that is well known to his Year 11 groups and that he will use to help them explore the idea that the effects of a single action go far beyond the intentions of the actor.

As a student teacher, you will not have to cope with all the situations described above. However, you will encounter many like them and you will be expected to demonstrate that you can contribute to SMCD in your work with pupils, as outlined below.

Every Child Matters

Chapter 20 provides an account of the government initiative referred to as *Every Child Matters* (DfES 2003e) and of the five intended 'outcomes' for children and young people: that they enjoy and achieve; achieve economic well-being; stay safe; be healthy; and make a positive contribution. The key point to be made here is that the ideals and aspirations reflected in these outcomes and those of SMCD are the same. Ofsted have been inspecting spiritual, moral, social, emotional, and cultural development in the context of schools' performance in promoting pupils' enjoyment and achievement and enabling them to make a positive contribution (Ofsted 2005d). The case study above provides some examples of what this might mean in the daily life of a teacher. However, commentators have been quick to point out that all of the *Every Child Matters* outcomes involve pupils' SMCD. For example, to enable pupils to 'stay safe' and 'be healthy', schools will need to provide opportunities for them to develop their self-esteem, to reflect on what is meant by and contributes to a 'healthy mind', and to consider the consequences of drug and alcohol abuse for themselves, others, and society. If pupils are to be encouraged to achieve 'economic well-being', they will need to develop a belief in their own value and potential but also explore the factors that contribute to inequalities and how these might be addressed at a societal and global as well as a personal level.

Subject teaching

The extent to which subject departments and teachers actively promote SMCD in their planning and teaching will vary from one school to another. However, at present Ofsted inspectors are reporting on SMCD in subject teaching and some local authorities encourage departments to refer to these matters in their scheme of work (SoW). Awarding bodies are required to make explicit reference to the ways in which their GCSE and GCE courses contribute to SMCD.

Leaving aside external pressures, there is some evidence that planning SMCD into SoW and lessons can improve the quality and outcomes of learning. A research project, undertaken by secondary school teachers in Bristol, found that when SMCD were planned into lesson objectives, and teaching and learning strategies were geared to achieving these, pupils' discussion and critical thinking skills developed and they became more engaged and motivated in their learning (Midgley *et al.* 1999: 3).

How can all subjects contribute to SMCD?

The arts and humanities are often viewed as the natural subjects to promote SMCD. However (and despite teaching that has disguised the fact), there is a long tradition of exploring such matters in maths and the sciences. In subjects that straddle these categories, opportunities for SMCD have been recognized and developed, and support is provided on a number of SMCD-related websites. Adult perceptions of 'SMCD-friendly' subjects may also be challenged by those of pupils. For example, there is research evidence to suggest that some pupils view PE and sport as important in their spiritual development (Wintersgill 2002: 6).

Whatever the subject, there are two main ways in which SMCD can be promoted: through the topics that are taught and through the teaching and learning methods used.

Topics at Key Stage 3

At KS3, teachers of most subjects will be covering topics dictated by the NC programmes of study. Opportunities for SMCD are more obvious in some of these than in others, but can be identified in the process of interpreting the programmes of study to produce units of work and lesson plans. When the teachers involved in the Bristol-based research set out to plan SMCD into lessons, they found no difficulty in identifying opportunities for development in the content of existing SoW and/or in the application of content (Midgley et al. 1999: 2).

Table 14.1 indicates the kind of topics or aspects of topics that can provide opportunities for SMCD, in their content or application of content.

Table 14.1 Opportunities for SMCD

	Spiritual development	*Moral development*	*Cultural development*
Maths	Mathematical principles behind natural forms and patterns	Calculation of amount of paper used in the lesson related to the number of trees needed	Analysis/presentation of numerical data on family expenditure in different cultures
Science	Role of scientific discoveries in changing people's lives and thinking	Why sustainable development is important	Relationship between culture and nature of scientific exploration
Art and design	Exploring ideas and feelings in creative work	The role of A&D in political propaganda	Cultural variations in the representation of universal themes
Design and technology	Aesthetics in the design of a product	Environmental impact of products	Analysis of cultural influences on design
Physical education	Developing pride in skills and an ability to cope with losing	Exploring/developing values of cooperation and inclusion in sport	Performing dances from differing cultures
Modern foreign languages	Expressing personal feelings and opinions in the target language	Reading/responding to 'problem page' letters in the target language	Learning about the culture of the target-language country
Geography	Human responses to environmental hazards	Reasons for changes in the distribution of economic activities	Population distribution and change – why, how, and the consequences
History	The power of religious beliefs in people's lives and deaths	'Myths of racial superiority' in events past and present	The development of 'multicultural' Britain

	Spiritual development	Moral development	Cultural development
Religious education	Religious/non-religious views of what happens at death	Differing perspectives on the development of 'cloning' techniques	Cultural variations in the interpretation of religious texts
English and drama	Expressing a personal 'vision for the future' in creative writing	Creating dramas that explore conflict between the values of family members	Exploring the content and style of poems from differing cultures

Topics at GCSE and AS/A level

At this level, the topics taught are determined by national criteria and by the examination specification (syllabus) that the department has chosen. At present, awarding bodies must ensure that specifications include the identification of opportunities for spiritual, moral, ethical, social, and cultural issues if appropriate to the subject. At the time of writing, a survey of GCSE and AS/Alevel specifications indicates that it is common practice to refer to such opportunities in all subjects.

The kinds of SMCD-related topics indicated in Table 14.1 are indicative of those that appear in KS4/5 specifications, but you can further your understanding of SMCD in your specialist subject by reading the relevant sections of the specifications that appear on exam board websites. For example, in GCSE information and communications technology (ICT) pupils might explore issues related to privacy and the confidentiality of data, and use the technology to obtain, analyse, and report on data related to the distribution of wealth. In business studies, they might consider non-financial reasons why people work in organizations, ethical stances of those who control or try to influence businesses, and the workings of multinationals across cultural divides.

Task 14.3

What do you think of the suggestions for your specialist subject in the section above? How do they compare with the ideas that you suggested in response to Task 14.2?

What advantages and disadvantages might there be in focusing on SMCD in subject teaching?

Teaching and learning methods

Although the content of some subjects is more obviously related to SMCD than that of others, teachers of all subjects can and do promote development through their teaching methods. These methods need to be of the kind that encourage pupils to think for themselves. Opportunities to work with others are important, but activities that enable pupils to reflect 'privately' are also needed. Examples of both kinds of activity are:

- expressing opinions and listening to those of others;
- exploring and discussing issues from a range of perspectives;
- simulations, for instance, role-plays;
- working collaboratively, for instance, to solve problems;
- reflecting privately on issues, experiences, and feelings;
- sharing experiences and feelings in 'safety', for example, in friendship pairs.

In all cases, teachers need to create a learning environment in which pupils feel sufficiently secure and confident to express and explore their views, feelings and experiences.

Citizenship and PSHEE are explored in Chapters 18 and 25, but they are considered here because both play an important role in promoting SMCD.

Citizenship

Citizenship became a statutory subject in secondary schools in 2002. The programmes of study and non-statutory SoW for the subject reflect the three interrelated strands of citizenship: Social and Moral Responsibility, Community Involvement, and Political Literacy. Spiritual, moral, and cultural matters are so deeply embedded in these strands that it would be difficult for teachers to contribute to citizenship effectively without promoting SMCD. Some of the following key concepts from the KS3 programmes of study illustrate the intertwining of citizenship and SMCD:

Weighing up what is fair and unfair in different situations.

Considering how democracy, justice, diversity, toleration, respect and freedom are valued by people with different beliefs, backgrounds and traditions within a changing democratic society.

Exploring the diverse national, regional, ethnic and religious cultures, groups and communities in the UK and the connections between them.

(QCDA 2007a: 29)

These concepts can be explored through subjects, but schools are encouraged to deliver citizenship in a variety of ways. During your school placements, you might be asked to support your tutor group in their 'democratic decision-making'. You might be involved in a cross-curricular project, such as creating a 'peace garden' in the school grounds. You might also be able to teach or observe a dedicated citizenship lesson on an SMCD-related topic such as 'human rights'.

Personal, social, health and economic education

Personal, social, health and economic education has been part of the NC for secondary schools since 2000 and in its current form it is encompassed in two non-statutory programmes of study: 'Economic wellbeing and financial capability' and 'Personal wellbeing'. In the former, SMCD is not strongly represented, although the rationale for the programme of study includes the claim that it will expand pupils' horizons for action 'by challenging stereotyping, discrimination and other cultural and social barriers to choice' (QCDA 2007b: 227). Moral development is clearly envisaged in the recommendation that pupils should explore 'social and moral dilemmas about the use of money' (QCDA 2007b: 231). In the 'Personal wellbeing' programme of study, opportunities for SMCD are very evident. There is an emphasis on the exploration of values and moral issues; the importance of developing an awareness of the similarities and differences between people of differing race, religion, and culture; and the need to challenge prejudice and discrimination. A statement from the programme of study rationale sums up these concerns:

> As they (pupils) explore similarities and differences between people and discuss social and moral dilemmas, they learn to deal with challenges and accommodate diversity in all its forms. The world is full of complex and conflicting values. Personal wellbeing helps pupils explore this complexity and reflect on and clarify their own values and attitudes.
>
> (QCDA 2007a: 243)

Schools deliver the PSHEE curriculum in a number of ways: through dedicated lessons and PSHEE events; through other subjects; and through the pastoral system and assemblies. These latter opportunities will be considered in the final sections of this chapter.

Pastoral care and guidance

Pastoral matters are examined in Chapter 24, and this section will focus on one aspect only: 'pastoral casework'. 'Pastoral casework' covers work with individual pupils on any aspect that affects their development and attainment. It includes supporting pupils when they have personal problems, are in need of encouragement, or want to talk about experiences, feelings or issues that they are grappling with. In many schools, it is expected that teachers who act as pastoral tutors will be a 'first port of call' for pupils in their tutor group who want to talk. However, any teacher may be sought out by a pupil in need.

As a student teacher you will not be given sole responsibility for a tutor group, and all tutors should hand over serious problems (such as suspected child or drug abuse) to senior pastoral staff. Nevertheless, you may find that pupils choose to speak to you about personal matters. You should find guidance on managing these situations in the school's staff handbook, but an awareness of the spiritual, moral, and cultural dimensions of young people's experience and development will be important in enabling you to respond to pupils with sensitivity. For example, we have seen that adolescents can be interested in, or even deeply concerned about, spiritual matters. In the spiritual development research referred to above, a number of the pupils who offered lengthy and very thoughtful accounts of their spiritual feelings and experiences made it clear that they would not feel able to share these with other pupils. An awareness of this may help teachers to recognize and encourage pupils who need or would benefit from opportunities to talk about spiritual matters.

Young people from religious backgrounds may hide their beliefs, practices, and special events from their peers, but may need or just want to talk to someone about these. A teacher who has some knowledge and understanding of pupils' backgrounds, and of religious and cultural beliefs, practices, and sensitivities will be in a position to respond sensitively to these matters.

Moral development issues raised by pupils can be difficult for teachers caught between their 'training' and 'empowerment' roles. However, an awareness of the tension can be helpful, especially when pupils are not in trouble, but want to explore issues with a teacher. A PGCE student found herself drawn into an informal discussion with Year 12 pupils about 'soft drugs'. She recognized the pupils' right to hold their own views and to discuss such matters openly. At the same time, she was able to raise questions about the 'down-side' of getting involved with such drugs and to keep her own pro-legalization views to herself!

Assemblies and acts of collective worship

The assembly is a traditional part of school life and, at one time, was synonymous with the act of worship. Now, however, a distinction is drawn between the two. Schools can provide 'secular assemblies' whenever they wish, but are required by law to provide a daily act of collective worship.

Large-group (for instance, year-group) assemblies are an important means of bringing pupils together to share an 'inspirational' experience and a sense of belonging to the school community. They are also a useful means of covering aspects of citizenship and PSHEE. Careful planning and good speakers can produce genuinely 'moving' assemblies. However, the involvement of pupils as presenters or even as organizers and leaders of assemblies has the advantage of encouraging pupils to view the assembly as 'their time', rather than as an opportunity for senior staff to rant about the state of the school site!

Assemblies may include an act of collective worship, although in secular schools it is rarely possible to have more than one large group assembly a week and this leads to difficulties in meeting the requirement for a daily act of worship. However, the law allows for flexibility in the timing of, and grouping for, collective worship, and one option is for tutors to set aside a few moments during the daily registration or tutor period for quiet reflection/worship. In practice, many schools have simply failed to meet the requirement, and this is one reason why head teachers have called for changes in the law and guidance relating to collective worship. Other reasons, shared by many in and outside the teaching profession, have to do with opposition to the very idea that pupils in a secular school should be required to attend an act of worship.

Parents have the right to withdraw their children from collective worship and teachers have the right to withdraw on 'grounds of conscience'. In practice, very few parents exercise their right. The reasons for this are complex, but a major factor has probably been the creative way in which schools have interpreted the requirements. Few would accept the idea that young people who have no belief in God should be forced to worship or pray to God. However, all pupils are capable of reflecting on spiritual and moral matters, if these are of a kind that have meaning for them and are presented in ways to which they can relate. An inclusive act of worship will allow for a spiritual response from some pupils, and a worshipful response from others. This may mean that pupils will begin by listening to a presentation on a spiritual/moral theme. They will then be invited either to reflect quietly on what they have heard (or on a related thought or question) or to offer their own prayer. The benefits to pupils of this opportunity for a moment's stillness, reflection or prayer make it likely that even if the law is changed, many schools will continue to build some 'private time' into assemblies.

Task 14.4

How do you feel about those aspects of a teacher's work that involve guiding pupils in and through matters that are very personal to them?

Do you have any concerns about how you will be able to remain true to your personal beliefs, values and attitudes and promote the spiritual, moral and cultural development of your pupils?

Note down your responses to these questions so that you can give more thought to these and perhaps share some in your training sessions.

At the beginning of this chapter, you were asked to consider the view that 'the teacher's ability to teach, manage, and relate to pupils effectively is greatly enhanced by her or his ability to take account of and draw upon pupils' spiritual, moral, and cultural lives and provide opportunities for development'. What do you think now?

14.6 Recommendations for further reading and webliography

Bailey, R (ed.) (2000) *Teaching Values and Citizenship Across the Curriculum*. London: Kogan Page.

Bigger, S. and Brown, E. (eds.) (1999) *Spiritual, Moral, Social and Cultural Education: Exploring Values in the Curriculum*. London: David Fulton.

West-Burnham, J. and Huws Jones, V. (2008) *Spiritual and Moral Development in Schools*. London: Continuum.

Websites

SMSC Online at www.smsc.org.uk (aimed at teachers and includes guidance on all spiritual, moral, social and cultural matters, including examples of good practice)

RE-Net at www.re-net.ac.uk (a one-stop web portal for teacher educators and trainee teachers that will provide links to a number of sites that deal with SMCD matters)

Two valuable websites have been closed down following withdrawal of government funding but useful material from these can be found in the government archives at: webarchive.nationalarchives.gov.uk:

Multiverse (provides teacher educators and trainee teachers with a comprehensive range of resources focusing on the educational achievement of pupils from diverse backgrounds)

Respect for all: valuing diversity and challenging racism through the curriculum (includes policy documents, guidance for teachers (including subject guidance) and examples of good practice)

15

Raising attainment

Sean Hayes

15.1 Introduction

Ensuring that young people fulfil their potential at school should be at the heart of their whole teaching and learning experience. In secondary school, this will largely be determined by the progress they make at Key Stages 3 and 4 – and at Key Stage 5, if they stay on at school or college post-16. This chapter complements Chapter 10, identifying factors known to affect performance and setting out ways in which teachers can analyse pupil performance data and use this analysis to inform and implement improvement strategies.

By the end of this chapter, you should:

- understand the key factors behind variations in pupil performance;
- know how to analyse the range of data that is available to teachers;
- understand the data analysis tools at your disposal and how to use them;
- be able to identify under-achieving and high-achieving pupil groups;
- have gained an overview of the strategies that have been developed to help maximize attainment for all pupils.

Analysing attainment data involves knowing your pupils and getting behind the raw data on performance, as indicated in a Department for Children Schools and Families (DCSF) paper, *Smoking out Underachievement*:

> Successful schools [and teachers] understand how to use their data to make practical changes in the classroom. They peel away the overall school figures to identify pockets of underachievement within their school and identify the pupils at risk of underachievement in the future.
>
> (DCSF 2010c: 1)

15.2 Caveats and health warnings

Teachers should be aware of some important caveats when analysing data on pupil performance. The same groups of pupils rarely under-perform consistently either over time or across the Key Stages. The target groups identified nationally and locally as being at risk of under-performance will not necessarily be the target groups in your school or even in your class. In the same way, the profile of your gifted and talented pupils will not necessarily be the same as that in another school. You should exercise caution when analysing and targeting groups with small numbers of pupils, as it can be difficult to conclude that something is either statistically or educationally significant when referring to a small group. Sometimes it can be a single pupil who is under-performing and it might be unrelated to him or her being part of a particular group. It may be due to factors in their particular teaching and learning experience or to external events largely beyond your control. Improvement is not always linear or upwards, as Gray observed about the lack of consistent year-on-year improvement in many schools, in his foreword to the book *Forging Links* (Sammons *et al.* 1997): 'in the majority of cases schools' 'effectiveness' fluctuates from one year to the next'.

One should remember that data alone will not determine everything about the performance of a school or its pupils. At best, the analysis of data opens up questions and lines of enquiry. You should use the findings from data analysis to provide evidence that tests your interpretation and hypotheses. You will need to use your professional judgement to decide what the data mean and what, if anything, should be done as a result. Quantitative analysis is a valuable approach to use in identifying under-performance and in helping teachers decide how to address it, but it must also be understood that education is a social process and not everything can be explained or resolved by the results of data analysis.

15.3   Raising standards in secondary schools: the challenge

Since the introduction of the National Curriculum (NC), the English education system has become one of the most data rich in the world. Central government now collects performance data at individual pupil level at every Key Stage and is able to match those data, using Unique Pupil Numbers, from one Key Stage to the next, creating large datasets that enable a comprehensive level of analysis of both pupil outcomes and progress. Within a school you will encounter several types of attainment data (see Chapter 10). All of these will tell you something about a pupil's level of attainment.

As stated above, the effectiveness of schools fluctuates from year to year; however, the national pattern of performance at GCSE has been one of year-on-year improvement and within the English education system there is an expectation of continuous improvement. Figure 15.1, which shows GCSE results from 2001 to 2010 for the percentage of pupils achieving five or more A★–C grades and five or more A★–C grades including English and mathematics, is a clear illustration that performance at GCSE has improved on both measures over this decade. This upward trend in performance, and the political expectation that it will continue to improve in the future, is also an indication of the aspiration that has been set for the nation's young people. The same expectation will be reflected in individual schools, where the aspiration to raise standards of attainment will be at the heart of everything that teachers are expected to do.

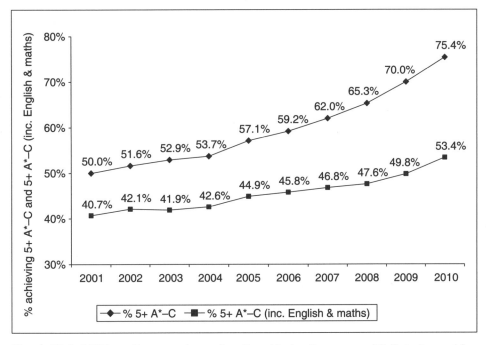

Figure 15.1 GCSE results: percentage of pupils achieving five or more A*–C grades and five or more A*–C grades (including English and mathematics), 2001–2010

You are likely to have been aware of an annual debate, as the GCSE results are announced, as to whether standards are genuinely rising or not. The evidence seems to be compelling for the percentage achieving five or more A★–C grades. Although the percentage achieving five or more A★–C grades including English and mathematics is improving, it is at a slower rate and the gap between the two measures is widening. In practice, it is not a matter of whether standards are rising or not, but whether they are rising fast enough – and for all pupils. Still too many from specific groups in our society under-achieve; too many fail to reach their full potential – with all of the consequent problems that this causes for both individuals and society as a whole.

Task 15.1

Log on to the DfE website, then locate the School and College Performance Tables web page (www.education.gov.uk/performancetables/index.shtml) and find the latest GCSE performance tables for your school and local authority.

What do these tables tell you about the performance of your school in relation to other schools in your area and in relation to local authority and national averages?

There are many factors relating to pupils that are known to correlate with attainment. These include prior attainment, level of attendance, the impact of individual teachers, the pupil's intrinsic motivation, including their self-esteem, self-regulation and personal resilience, and in some cases, external factors such as a disrupted or chaotic home background or other major life event. All of these factors may help to explain variations in an individual pupil's performance, and in some cases, these factors may explain why under-performance has occurred. For example, a pupil might have a prior attainment profile from Key Stage 2 (KS2) that is the expected level (Level 4) in English, mathematics, and science, and they might be motivated to learn and be resilient but a major life event might have disrupted their learning. This could be the death of a parent or close family member, which reduces their resilience and could impact adversely on their progress, leading to under-performance at the end of KS3 or in their GCSE examinations. Situations like this will largely be unforeseen and outside the control of the class teacher and will require the effective use of pastoral support to help get the pupil back on track, alongside a programme of work that affords the pupil the chance to catch up with their peers. The impact of circumstances beyond the school was observed by Kerr and West (2010: 25), who recognized that: 'children's academic performance cannot be divorced from what happens to them outside school – in their families, communities and neighbourhoods'.

Other factors, such as the pupil's attendance record or the role played by an individual teacher, could impact positively on a pupil's progress and attainment. While good attendance at secondary school does not guarantee success, research shows that there is a high correlation between attendance and performance and that pupils with an attendance record between 95% and 100% are several times more likely to achieve five or more A*–C GCSE grades including English and mathematics than those pupils with low attendance. The majority of pupils will perform broadly in line with their ability, their own expectations, and the expectations of their teachers. However, there will be some pupils who over-perform and exceed expectations, and there will be others who under-perform, achieving less than they should have. Identifying potential under-performance or performance that is better than expected is the challenge of knowing your pupils and being able to analyse their performance. National data on performance show some of the specific patterns of inequality of outcomes and the pupils and groups of pupils who are most likely to be over-represented as low or high achievers. The following list has been adapted from Kerr and West (2010):

- on average, White British pupils (both boys and girls) are more likely than other ethnic groups to demonstrate sustained under-achievement;
- of the minority ethnic groups, Chinese and Indian pupils are generally the most successful and Black Caribbean pupils the least successful, although this pattern is far from consistent across the country;
- poverty, as indicated by the pupils being eligible for free school meals, is strongly associated with low attainment and more so for White British pupils than for other ethnic groups;
- children from homes with single and/or unemployed parents and parents who have few educational qualifications themselves often do less well at school;

- children with special educational needs (SEN) and children in care (often called 'looked after' children) are among the most vulnerable in the education system and are more likely to have outcomes below those of their peers.

These patterns are echoed in the findings from major educational research studies over recent years. However, the list is by no means exclusive or exhaustive, as teachers may find that the groups of pupils who are over- or under-performing in their school are not on this list. Although the research studies identify broad patterns, the different factors often interact to compound a pupil's advantage or disadvantage. For example, the under-performing group may not just be White British children but White British boys who are eligible for free school meals, or it might be Black Caribbean girls who are also persistent absentees who all live in the same housing estate. This potential interaction of factors opens up the idea that some pupils are likely to experience multiple disadvantage or advantage, which suggests that the level of analysis that is required might involve a degree of complexity. All of these factors, whether personal to the pupil, external to the pupil or pertaining to groups of pupils and, singularly or in combination, can help explain variations in performance. The data in Table 15.1 show the performance of some of the main contextual pupil groups at

Table 15.1 Percentage of pupils in contextual groups achieving five or more A*–C grades (including English and mathematics) with percentage points gaps

	2006/07	2007/08	2008/09	2009/10
Gender				
Girls	49.9%	52.3%	54.4%	58.6%
Boys	41.7%	44.2%	47.1%	51.1%
Percentage points gap	8.2%	8.1%	7.3%	7.5%
First language				
English	46.0%	48.5%	51.1%	55.2%
Other than English	43.5%	45.1%	47.7%	52.0%
Percentage points gap	2.5%	3.4%	3.4%	3.2%
Free school meals				
Non-free school meals	49.4%	51.7%	54.3%	58.5%
Free school meals	21.4%	23.8%	26.6%	30.9%
Percentage points gap	28.0%	27.9%	27.7%	27.6%
SEN provision				
No identified SEN	53.4%	57.8%	61.3%	66.2%
All SEN pupils	10.3%	13.2%	16.5%	20.0%
Percentage points gap	43.1%	44.6%	44.8%	46.2%

Source: DfE Statistical First Release 37/2010

GCSE in England from 2006/07 to 2009/10. Performance is based on the percentage of pupils in each group achieving five or more A*–C grades including English and mathematics alongside the gap in percentage points between each group in each category.

Although we have seen in Figure 15.1 that GCSE performance has been improving steadily over many years, most of the contextual attainment gaps have remained broadly at the same level over the four years in Table 15.1. These national data provide a useful reference point when analysing the results in your school but you should note that what happened nationally might not be replicated within your school and the challenge within schools should be to close these gaps, wherever they are encountered.

The next section considers how to identify the contextual and other factors that are correlated with performance, while helping you to carry out your own data analysis, to measure their impact on attainment.

15.4 Analysing attainment data

Teachers need to have good assessment data to ensure that they can:

- plan and deliver a relevant curriculum and appropriate lessons;
- set realistic yet stretching targets based on evidence;
- know that learners make the appropriate amount of progress; and
- identify variations in pupil performance.

To make intelligent use of data, teachers need to understand what is available and get behind the figures to explore the strengths and weaknesses in pupil performance. Secondary school teachers should have prior attainment data on their pupils from KS2, baseline assessment data from any tests that the school administers to pupils on entry (e.g. Cognitive Ability Tests, CATs), and also marking schemes for homework and coursework and on-going assessments that may be part of a pupil tracking system. Then, at the end of KS3, teachers will have NC levels and a range of assessment data across KS4 culminating in their actual GCSE grades at the end of Year 11.

First and foremost, teachers must know where to get the data from, particularly the data on entry to a school. As a newly qualified secondary school teacher, knowing the key personnel in the school will be important when it comes to accessing the relevant assessment data. This will vary from school to school but these are likely to include: the office manager for contextual data on your pupils; the assessment coordinator or data manager for baseline assessment information and advice on whole-school marking schemes, target-setting, and pupil tracking; and the special needs coordinator (SENCo) for information on specific pupils, including the more vulnerable young people and the gifted and talented. Some of these personnel are also likely to be the ones who can give you usernames and passwords for external data analysis tools, such as RAISEonline and Fischer Family Trust (FFT).

The prior attainment data from KS2 and results of any tests that the school administers on entry have been explained in Chapter 10, in terms of how the information can help teachers make judgements about the ways in which pupils can access the secondary curriculum. These purposes can be described as follows:

- to provide diagnostic information on pupils' cognitive strengths and weaknesses and learning styles and preferences;
- to inform any policies that the school has regarding pupil grouping, streaming and/or setting;
- to establish a baseline for setting targets and measuring pupils' progress to KS3 and KS4.

The information can also form the starting point for your on-going analysis of pupil performance and can help you to identify pupils at risk of under-performance and to track your high-achieving pupils. These purposes can be summarized as follows:

- to support pupils who start secondary education already struggling with basic literacy and numeracy;
- to maintain momentum for those at risk of slowing in the progress they make;
- to ensure that all those who are already achieving at a high level continue to be challenged.

For new teachers, the first opportunity to do some data analysis is to build a picture of your class's ability on entry. You can do this by taking their KS2 levels from the end of primary school and creating an ability profile of the pupils; this can be augmented by the pupils' entry test scores (Strand 2006). This combination should provide a broader picture of ability and, if you have entry test scores from non-verbal reasoning tests, these can be very helpful in providing a picture of underlying academic potential, particularly for pupils with English as an additional language (EAL). Assessment data also have predictive value and can be used to inform and support pupil and whole-school target-setting. In relation to target-setting, research demonstrates that: 'a combination of reasoning [tests] and Key Stage 2 tests together provides the most reliable basis for predicting future performance' (Strand 2006: 223).

   Target-setting at national, local authority, school, and pupil level has been a feature of government policy for the last two decades. The change of government in 2010 has seen a subtle shift in the use of target-setting as a lever to drive up standards. The pre-existing statutory requirements on schools and local authorities to set targets have effectively been removed; the shift has been more towards giving schools greater control over the targets they might set and a reduction in the number of targets and the element of prescription. This does not mean that target-setting no longer has a role to play. For classroom teachers there will still be value in setting long-term targets for individual pupils within their subject, which will usually be expressed as a NC level for the end of KS3 and a grade for GCSE. English and mathematics teachers will contribute to the percentage of pupils making three or more levels' progress between KS2 and KS4 in their respective subjects, and all GCSE subject teachers will contribute to the percentage of pupils achieving five or more A*–C grades including English and mathematics. Table 15.2 shows the national performance for

Table 15.2 Percentage of pupils making three or more levels of progress between KS2 and GCSE from 2007 to 2010

Subject	2007	2008	2009	2010
English	61.2%	63.5%	64.7%	69.3%
Mathematics	54.6%	56.3%	57.9%	62.0%

Source: DfE Statistical First Release 10/2011

the percentage of pupils making three or more levels of progress between KS2 and GCSE from 2007 to 2010, in English and in mathematics. The underlying trend on this measure is an improving one, which mirrors the improving trend for the two 5+ A*–C GCSE measures in Figure 15.1.

Task 15.2

This task is about analysing performance at GCSE. By completing this task, you will have achieved two objectives:

- Analysing data in several ways: over time, by context (gender and prior attainment), against national benchmarks and estimates.
- Writing about your analysis in a clear and consistent way.

Table 15.3 provides information on results of ten pupils (five girls and five boys) in a GCSE subject in 2011. The table also shows the pupils' average KS2 level on entry to the school in Year 7, their FFT GCSE grade estimates and the percentage chances of that grade being achieved.

Table 15.3 Results of ten pupils in a GCSE subject in 2011

Pupil	Gender	GCSE subject grade achieved in 2011	KS2 level on entry	FFT estimated grade and % chances of achieving that grade	
Anna	Girl	B	4	B	40%
Dee	Girl	A*	5	A	38%
Salma	Girl	C	5	A	44%
Mary	Girl	A	4	B	33%
Farzana	Girl	E	3	F	41%
Barry	Boy	C	4	C	45%
Kevin	Boy	A	5	B	33%

Pupil	Gender	GCSE subject grade achieved in 2011	KS2 level on entry	FFT estimated grade and % chances of achieving that grade	
Javier	Boy	D	4	C	38%
Kofi	Boy	E	3	E	42%
Tom	Boy	B	4	C	37%

Calculate the percentage of A*–C grades achieved by girls, boys, and both sexes combined in 2011 and write these percentages into the blank cells in Table 15.4.

Table 15.4 The percentage of A*–C grades achieved

GCSE indicator	2009	2010	2011	2011 National	2011 FFT Model D estimate
Girls % A*–C	66%	70%	—	70%	64%
Boys % A*–C	58%	64%	—	60%	56%
Overall % A*–C	62%	66%	—	65%	60%

Now fill in the gaps in the following narrative based on the GCSE performance information in Tables 15.3 and 15.4. The narrative describes the pupils' performance in this GCSE subject in 2011.

The overall performance in this subject in 2011 has _____ compared with 2010 by _____% points. The performance of girls has _____ by _____% points and the performance of boys has _____ by _____% points.

The underlying trend in overall performance since 2009 is _____. The underlying trend in girls' performance since 2009 is _____ and that of boys is _____.

The overall performance in this subject is _____ than that nationally by _____% points. The performance of girls compared with girls nationally is _____. The performance of boys compared with boys nationally is _____.

The overall performance in this subject is _____ than the FFT estimate by _____% points. The performance of girls compared with the FFT estimate for girls is _____. The performance of boys compared with the FFT estimate for boys is _____.

The pupil who demonstrated the most marked under-performance in this subject, based on their prior attainment and estimated grade, was _____.

The predictive value of FFT data is explained in Chapter 10 and teachers should be aware that FFT estimates are frequently used by schools to inform their target-setting process. Remember, however, that estimates are not in themselves targets and they are subject to wide margins of error, as evidenced by FFT estimates being set alongside the percentage chance of them being achieved. A function of the FFT package is to provide estimates for the end of KS3 and KS4. Schools can choose the level of challenge they want from FFT estimates and many schools use estimates based on the top performing 25 per cent of schools in England or even the top performing 10 per cent of schools, which builds in challenge and aspiration to the targets and helps drive school improvement. The other main function of FFT is to enable schools to analyse their actual performance at the end of KS3 and KS4, using the FFT models of value-added and contextual value-added (CVA). The FFT approach to CVA is very similar to the approach used in RAISEonline, which is explained below.

In 2006, the DCSF and Ofsted jointly developed and commissioned one of the most powerful tools available to teaching staff for analysing patterns of performance in schools. The RAISEonline program (Reporting and Analysis for Improvement through School self-Evaluation) is web-based and interactive (www.raiseonline.org). It provides a common set of interactive, online analyses to schools and local authority officers, as well as being used by Ofsted inspectors to raise questions and hypotheses to explore during a school's inspection. Teachers can access RAISEonline with a user-name and password. RAISEonline for secondary schools contains analysis of GCSE outcomes and it offers two types of functionality: a set of fixed format PDF reports and an interactive capability.

The majority of the outputs from RAISEonline are based on value-added and CVA. At the time of writing, it has been confirmed that the focus of analysis will shift away from CVA back to value added. However, it is still useful to understand CVA and how it differs from value-added, as it has been used for several years in both RAISEonline and the FFT analysis. CVA models take account not just of pupils' prior attainment but also a range of contextual factors, known to affect attainment, including the pupil's gender, SEN, first language, and ethnicity; together with measures of deprivation, such as the pupil's free school meal status, measures of pupil mobility, age distribution of the cohort, and the number of children 'looked after' in the school. CVA creates a sophisticated model that produces estimates of performance that are based on how pupils with every possible contextual profile performed nationally in the previous year. It is the very large size of the national cohort each year, over 500,000 pupils, which gives this model its high degree of validity and reliability. Table 15.5 shows an example of the RAISEonline output for a school in GCSE English covering three years.

The 'Cohort for CVA' in Table 15.5 is the number of pupils in the school who had matched prior attainment data from KS2 and the 'Coverage' tells you what percentage of the whole cohort that was; remember, only pupils with prior attainment can be included in any type of value-added analysis. The 'CVA school score' is centred on a score of 1000 and indicates how pupils in the school performed compared with similar pupils in similar schools nationally. A score above 1000 means that the pupils have achieved positive value-added and below 1000 means negative value-added. The '95% confidence limit ±' should be added to and subtracted from the

Table 15.5 Contextual value-added performance in English, 2008 to 2010

GCSE English	2008	2009	2010
Cohort for CVA	254	224	236
CVA school score	1005.1	997.4 ↓	1003.0 ↑
95% confidence interval ±	0.9	0.9	1.0
Significance	Sig+	Sig–	Sig+
Percentile rank	1	70	7
Coverage	95%	94%	100%

Source: Ofsted RAISEonline (adaptation)

CVA score and this indicates that you can be 95% sure that the true score lies between the two values obtained. In Table 15.5, the CVA score in 2010 is 1003, so you can be 95% sure that the true score lies between 1002 and 1004. If the lower end of the range is above 1000, the performance is positive and statistically significant, hence 'Sig+', and if the upper end is below 1000, it is negative and statistically significant, hence 'Sig–', as it was in this example in 2009. In the live system, a significantly positive CVA score is shaded green and a significantly negative score is shaded blue, while a non-shaded entry in the 'significance' row denotes that performance is not significantly different from average. The 'Percentile rank' tells you where the school is placed in a rank of all secondary schools nationally, so in 2010 this school was ranked at the 7th percentile for English, which means that only 6 per cent of schools had a better CVA score. If the CVA score changes significantly from year to year, you will see an upwards or downwards arrow next to your school's score.

In relation to the identification and analysis of low- and high-achieving pupil groups, RAISEonline becomes most useful when it is used interactively. In the interactive version, you should log on, select your own school, and go to the section called 'Reports and Analysis'. From there you should select 'Click here to view all analyses available', which will take you to a file structure that lists all of the available analyses in the system, then go to 'KS2–4 Expected vs. Actual Scatterplot (Sec 6)'. This takes you to the Scatterplot on which the majority of the CVA analysis in RAISEonline is based (see Figure 15.2).

The main difference between CVA and value-added is that CVA creates an expected outcome (see x-axis in Figure 15.2), whereas value-added uses prior attainment as the input measure (see Chapter 10, Figures 10.1 and 10.2). At KS4, an expected score is constructed from a pupil's prior attainment at KS2 and all of their contextual information that goes into the model, each of which is given a coefficient, and then calculating what similar pupils in similar schools achieved in the previous year. In Figure 15.2, each of the markers in the graph represents one pupil and pupils above the black line ('Zero CVA Line') have positive value-added and those below have negative value-added. The lines either side of the black line represent the interquartile cut-offs, so pupils plotted below the lower dotted line are in the bottom quartile nationally and pupils above the upper doted line are in the top quartile. The outer lines represent the 10th and 90th percentiles and pupils plotted above the 90th

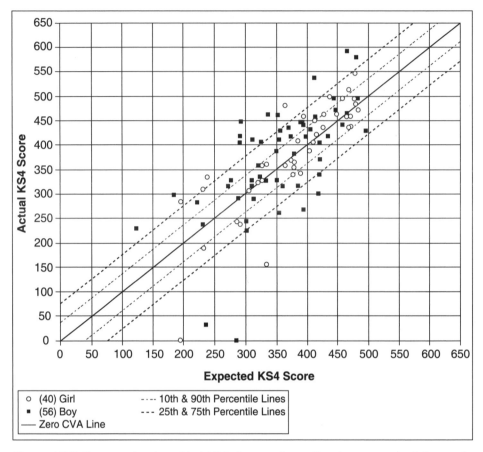

Figure 15.2 Contextual value-added KS2–4: overall, predicted versus actual for pupils (*Source:* Ofsted RAISEonline Training materials)

Note: Contains public sector information licensed under the Open Government Licence v1

percentile can be considered to have significantly out-performed compared with their estimate, whereas those plotted below the 10th percentile can be considered to have significantly under-performed in relation to their estimate. The black squares represent boys and the circles represent girls.

Within your own school, you can double click on each of these markers and that will take you to the pupil's individual performance data, which will show you how they performed in relation to their estimates. This provides useful information that can help you to identify and target under-performing pupils. In addition, you can export the pupil level data into another format (e.g. EXCEL), which will allow you to carry out further analysis. Within RAISEonline, once you have selected this scatter-plot, you can apply 'Groups' and 'Filters'. You can use the group function to compare one or more different groups (e.g. boys and girls). Alternatively, you can use the filter function to look at just one group, such as boys or White British pupils with SEN who are eligible for free school meals, or a specific ethnic group or selection of ethnic groups. Groups and filters are the most appropriate functions to help teachers to identify variations in pupil performance, or to test hypotheses about which groups of pupils might be over- or under-performing.

It is envisaged that a very similar range of functionalities will be available when RAISEonline reverts back to using value-added, which will still enable teachers to analyse the data using groups and filters to identify over- and under-performance.

Task 15.3

What factors would you consider and what measures would you take if the estimates for pupil performance from the statistical models, such as FFT and RAISEonline, were noticeably different from your predictions of the pupils' future performance?

To engage with this task you might want to consider some of the following:

- Are external factors involved, e.g. are some pupils recently arrived from abroad with English as an additional language (EAL) or are they experiencing instability in their home lives?
- Did they make very good progress in primary school but their progress has appeared to stall in secondary school?
- What do other teachers say about how they have managed this in the past and what are their predictions for these pupils?
- Speak to the pupils and their parents about their own expectations to find out how they feel about the targets that you have set.

The next section considers some of the strategies that you might employ to address over- and under-performance.

15.5   Strategies for responding to variations in performance

Strategies for maximizing pupil performance have evolved over many years and the challenge for you as a teacher, once you have identified groups of pupils who have over- or under-performed, is to decide what, if any, strategies you need to put in place to get under-performing pupils back on track and what you need to do to stretch your high-achieving pupils. Some of the strategies that you might employ will be directly related to teaching and learning and the curriculum, and these have been covered in other chapters, including Chapters 6, 9, 10 and 13.

One of the apparently unusual features of educational outcomes within the English education system is that some pupils appear to make no progress between one Key Stage and the next. In secondary schools, this has been particularly evident between KS2 and KS3, where data over many years shows that between 10 and 20 per cent of pupils stand still or even regress by one NC level in at least one of the three core subjects of English, mathematics, and science. Where a teacher encounters this through on-going pupil tracking of performance and in the end-of-KS3 teacher assessments, one is drawn to evidence of potential under-performance. Sometimes there are valid educational reasons for this, including: the pupil was already struggling with literacy and numeracy at the start of secondary education; the pupil was struggling with the transition from primary to secondary school; the pupil lost momentum and their progress began to slow down. This phenomenon is often referred to as the 'Year 7 dip', which is not so problematic if the pupil gets back on track in Years 8 and 9 but is a major concern if there is no demonstrable evidence of improvement and progress across the whole of KS3. Educational strategies to avoid pupils making limited or no progress at all include intensive support for literacy and numeracy, regular pupil tracking and assessment, effective use of the *Making Good Progress* materials (DfES 2007b), personalized learning, and in some cases one-to-one tuition. However, research (Hayes and Clay 2007) has shown that this level of sustained under-performance can sometimes be the result of factors other than academic progress and attainment. Earlier in this chapter, I referred to the potential negative impact of external events on a pupil's attainment. These could include the pupil being part of a peer group culture that does not value education, through to major life events such as family breakdown, which could result in the pupil having low motivation and self-esteem, leading to low resilience and a reduced capacity for being self-regulating in their learning. Cassen *et al.* (2009), who studied the link between educational outcomes and adversity and resilience, defined resilience in learners as follows:

> Resilience is . . . positive adaptation in the face of adversity. It is a process that explains the way in which some individuals achieve good outcomes despite the fact that they are at high risk for poor outcomes. Risk factors are those variables that signal an increased chance of poor outcomes.
>
> (Cassen *et al.* 2009: 1)

In this chapter, we have addressed many variables that could lead to poor outcomes, and while some of them may be ameliorated by effective teaching and learning and appropriate educational interventions, personal factors such as resilience cannot necessarily be taught. In the secondary school context, resilience has to be nurtured and developed, partly through whole-school policies and also by individual teachers and other staff involved in delivering the personal, social, health, and economic education (PSHEE) curriculum and pastoral care. For example, schools that manage the transition well from primary to secondary will enhance children's resilience by taking a whole-school focus at this key time in young people's lives. However, how can individual teachers help young people build resilience once they have identified that they are at risk of poor outcomes? Cassen *et al.* (2009: 10) take the following view: 'Interventions through families and schools can reduce disadvantage and promote resilience among children'.

One response that a school can make for its pupils, whose potential for low performance might also lead to reduced resilience, is to set up a programme of peer mentoring. Peer mentoring is a form of mentorship that takes place in learning environments such as schools, usually between an older, more experienced pupil and a younger pupil. However, it is important that such a programme is not solely rooted in under-achievement or that it is seen as being done only for ethnic minority pupils or just for one gender. Mentoring should be initiated as a whole-school intervention and pupils should be offered it for a wide range of reasons, so that it is not only seen as a response to one issue. Cross-age mentoring is generally considered to be more appropriate and beneficial than same-age mentoring in the secondary school context.

It was mentioned earlier that low-performing pupils might be part of a peer group culture that does not value education, so another strategy for teachers would be to encourage and support pupils to change their friendship groups. This would not only get them into a more academically minded group, it would also demonstrate that they were building personal resilience. In research into the reasons cited by pupils from deprived backgrounds as helping them achieve above their estimates at GCSE, several pupils said that changing their friendship group was an important factor (Hayes *et al.* 2009). What the successful students in this research managed to do was to build, through their own resilience, a strong academic self-concept and positive peer support. Alongside changing friendship groups, teachers should work on helping students to be more self-regulatory in their learning, which will benefit, in particular, low-performing pupils who have started to become demoralized and demotivated.

Parents often provide support for their children's learning and this can be either emotional or academic support or both. Parents continue to be important to their children's education after early childhood, not only in home activities but in their relationship with their children's schools. One research survey found this relationship to be exceptionally significant and encouragement of the relationship by schools should be an important part of their policy interventions: 'Parental involvement in a child's schooling is a more powerful force than any other family background indicator such as social class or family size . . . and contributes to 10% or more of variation in educational achievement' (Desforges and Abouchaar 2003: 106).

Chapter 7 covers the range of ways that schools can work effectively with parents and other adults and, in relation to raising attainment, an area where parental involvement can be particularly beneficial is in the target-setting process. Teachers should not only share targets, including curricular targets, target minimum grades and stretch targets, with pupils but should also share them with their parents. This helps parents to know what is expected of their children and enables them to play a role in supporting their children to meet the targets. Effective parental involvement that supports teachers to raise their pupils' outcomes by as much as 10 per cent could be the difference between success and failure for some pupils.

This chapter has also covered the identification of pupils who might be considered to have over-performed, often referred to as high achievers or the gifted and talented. As well as addressing issues of under-performance, it is also important that teachers stretch their more able pupils so that the gifted and talented fulfil their potential. The first task for you as a teacher is to know who your gifted and talented pupils are, and as a new teacher you may be supported in this by a gifted and talented coordinator in the school. Guidance from the DCSF (2009b) on managing the education of gifted and talented youngsters recommends a sharp focus on the identification, support, and development of such pupils, which will bring the energy and aspiration to unlock their potential. An effective approach to this can demonstrate a school's determination to do the best for every child, providing rich opportunities for engagement with parents and enabling children to reflect on and improve their own learning. The development of gifted and talented pupils also provides a challenge for schools to take stock of children currently identified as gifted and talented learners and to consider whether disadvantaged pupils and minority groups are properly represented, challenging preconceptions and embedding inclusive approaches. Work in this area consequently enables schools to take action to narrow attainment gaps and take steps to accelerate the progress of more able pupils. A DCSF publication, *Breaking the Link: Everyone's Business* (2009c), highlighted how the accurate identification of gifted and talented pupils is to ensure that pupils from disadvantaged backgrounds are not under-represented: 'Of the roughly ten per cent of pupils identified by schools as gifted and talented, there is a significant under-representation of those from disadvantaged backgrounds . . . great potential is currently going unrecognized, and perhaps undeveloped'.

15.6 What does this mean for me?

As a newly qualified teacher (NQT), you will be entering school and the classroom at a time when the educational system is as data rich as it has ever been. You will be expected to engage with data to help you and the school identify both under- and over-performance and to use those data to put strategies in place to remove under-performance and to stretch the high achievers, so that all pupils fulfil their potential. Hopefully you can achieve this while playing a part in building a school ethos that recognizes pupils as individuals and celebrates effort and improvement as well as attainment.

The main implications for your practice should be to:

- find out practical information on the context of your pupils and administrative information such as usernames and passwords for the relevant data tools and websites that you will be expected to use;
- understand and use the whole-school systems that are in place for marking, assessment, and pupil tracking;
- understand achievement and attainment data and how to use the tools at your disposal to interpret such data;
- recognize under-performance and how to implement the range of strategies for addressing it;
- be able to identify your more able pupils and know how to stretch them academically;
- take responsibility for your own continuing professional development (CPD) and learn from best practice within your school and elsewhere.

15.7   Recommendations for further reading and webliography

Hayes, S.G., Shaw, H., McGrath, G. and Bonel, F. (2009) *Using RAISEonline as a Research Tool to Analyse the Link between Attainment, Social Class and Ethnicity.* British Education Index Reference184218. London: Information, Research and Statistics Team, Greenwich Children's Service.

Kerr, K. and West, M. (eds.) (2010) *Social Inequality: Can Schools Narrow the Gap?* London: British Educational Research Association.

Sammons, P., Thomas, S. and Mortimore, P. (1997) *Forging Links: Effective Schools and Effective Departments.* London: Paul Chapman.

Strand, S. (2003) Getting *the Best from CAT: A Practical Guide for Secondary Schools.* London: NfER Nelson.

Websites

www.education.gov.uk/rsgateway/index.shtml (Department for Education – Research and Statistics Gateway web address)

www.education.gov.uk/performancetables/index.shtml (Department for Education – School Performance Tables web address)

www.raiseonline.org (Ofsted – RAISEonline web address)

16

Literacy across the curriculum
John Gordon

16.1 Introduction

Spend any amount of time wandering around a school, down corridors or into classrooms, and the chances are you will encounter some physical manifestation of what is often termed 'literacy across the curriculum' (LAC). You may see examples of pupils' writing in display cabinets; you may notice laminated cards of subject-specific vocabulary decorating the walls; and you may spot phrases that help pupils structure their writing arranged carefully in sequence on various whiteboards. This chapter concerns schools as environments rich in language, and asks you to consider the contribution to literacy development you might make in your own subject discipline.

In this chapter, you will:

- reflect on what is meant by both 'literacy' and 'literacy across the curriculum';
- learn about whole-school literacy initiatives over the past decade;
- be introduced to current issues and priorities of policy relevant to literacy;
- consider literacy in relation to your own subject;
- learn about some current thinking concerning key approaches to reading, writing, speaking and listening that may be helpful to teaching in your subject.

16.2 What is meant by literacy across the curriculum?

You have just read a description of a school environment demonstrating cross-curricular literacy practices in action. What thinking lies behind these signs of LAC? Surely it can't be the case that attention to standards of reading, writing and oral communication in schools is a new idea?

Lewis and Wray (2000) assert that contemporary interest in the development of literacy across the secondary school has to be seen as part of a cycle that follows from the report *A Language for Life*, otherwise known as the Bullock Report (DES 1975), although just prior to that books such as *Language, the Learner and the School* (Barnes *et al.* 1969) had considered whole-school language policies. The Bullock Report itself begins with some contextualizing historical detail, citing the Newbolt Report's (Board of Education 1921) findings that employers were disappointed to find young employees 'hopelessly deficient in their command of English' and that they considered the teaching of English in schools of the day to produce 'a very limited command of the English language'. Reflecting on the school's role in the same period, in the report *English for the English*, George Sampson (1921: 25) stated 'all teachers are teachers of English because every teacher is a teacher in English. That sentence should be written in letters of gold over every school doorway'. Whole-school literacy was as important then as it is today, its purposes contested and its effectiveness alternately criticized or vigorously defended just as they are now.

If pupils' aptitude and facility with language – their literacy skills – have been often debated in terms of the national economy and state of the workforce, discussion has also extended into other concerns. The 1921 quotation describing 'deficient' levels of skill could paraphrase more recent statements concerning adult literacy: 'in 2006 a government-sponsored review into basic skills, the *Leitch Review*, found that more than five million adults lack functional literacy, the level needed to get by in life and at work' (Jama and Dugdale 2010: 5). In this instance it becomes evident that literacy is not just about employability, it is about functioning on a day-to-day basis. Some commentators take the scope of literacy still further, to contend that literacy is about so much more than basic skills. Richard Hoggart, for example, presents a view of literacy as inseparable from social justice, democracy and true citizenship (Cox 1998). More recently, similar ideas have been espoused in discussions of 'new literacies' (Cope and Kalantzis 2003), developed in the context of globalization and the new forms of communication that arise from developing technologies.

The most recent Ofsted survey on the matter, *Removing Barriers to Literacy* (Ofsted 2011a), makes it difficult to conceive of whole-school literacy as anything other than a priority. It highlights particular pupil groups that make markedly less progress in literacy than others, describes inadequate use of assessment data to support progress and recognizes that many secondary teachers simply do not have the benefit of training in fundamental aspects of literacy education that could make a significant difference to pupils' progress. It confirms literacy as a whole-school issue relevant to every teacher no matter their discipline.

Have all of these points in mind as you read this chapter. Thinking about what the word 'literacy' can mean is essential to developing your ability to support pupils in the way they engage with and respond to your own subject area, and to contributing to 'literacy across the curriculum' in a manner that will be enriching both to your pupils and to your school. In addition, you will be playing your part in removing potential barriers to literacy, contributing to an inclusive and holistic ethos of secondary education.

Task 16.1

Before you read any further, attempt the following activities:

- Consider and write down your own definition of literacy.
- Identify three activities, common in your subject, which you believe develop pupils' literacy skills likely to be applied (a) elsewhere in school and (b) in contexts beyond school.

16.3   Literacy across the curriculum – official guidance since 2000

In 2001, a framework of recommendations for LAC was disseminated to schools (DfEE 2001b) through documentation covering several dimensions of literacy teaching in the secondary phase. The influence of that document is still strong (there has been nothing on a comparable scale since), although the more recent survey by Ofsted (2011a) makes clear, ten years on, that though the initiative supported important advances in literacy provision, difficulties still remain.

The 2001 strategy identified different areas of literacy encompassing spoken language as well as more conventional associations with the page or screen. Literacy was presented as integral to teachers' assessment practice, to inclusive education (e.g. 'support for EAL learners'), and to pupils' thinking skills. The overt treatment of non-fiction and the role of the school library signalled connections across subject specialisms, and the possibility of common approaches to texts and resources. These connections were more fully outlined in the collection of Literacy Progress Units (DfES 2001c) first issued in the same year. These described precise programmes of intervention and support for pupils considered to be working below expectations of average attainment in reading and writing at Key Stage 3 (KS3), providing material on phonics, writing organization, information retrieval, reading between the lines, spelling and sentences.

Removing Barriers to Literacy (Ofsted 2011a) maintains attention to these items and reiterates the importance of continued intervention informed by a whole-school perspective. It stresses the continued gap in literacy attainment between some groups and the rest of the population. Those making less progress in the secondary phase include Black Caribbean boys, children from low-income families and looked-after children. In addition, one in five children leaving primary school does not reach the expected standard in reading and writing with implications for their progress in the secondary phase. More positively, the report indicates there are instances of schools where these difficulties are addressed. Practices that support improved progress include teachers holding generally high expectations of pupils' achievement, an emphasis on speaking and listening from an early age, a rigorous approach following a planned sequence of guidance, rigorous assessment practice and attention to individual needs. One item to bear in mind for your early practice in this area is that even colleagues working in the most successful schools believed there was no 'eureka' moment – meaning that they adopted no unusual or especially novel approach, rather they worked through a process of 'painstaking adjustments' as they monitored the impact of strategies used. They recognized, too, that variations in pupil achievement persisted and that the work was an on-going process. Several specific actions are identified in the survey that you can incorporate in your own teaching. It reports that 'where staff had included an objective for literacy in all the lessons, senior managers noted an improvement in outcomes across all subjects, as well as in English' (Ofsted 2011a: 7). In addition, literacy skills were taught in contexts where language demands and use were 'relevant and meaningful' to learners, indicating attention to real purposes (The National Strategies 2009). At the point of planning there was 'outstanding use of national test and assessment data to raise the expectations of staff and to set sufficiently challenging targets'. Do you know the reading or spelling ages of the pupils you teach? How does this influence the texts you choose to share with them, or the support you offer for vocabulary development and writing?

Other items relate to the role of an individual teacher within the whole school. Of particular relevance is access to and use of data relating to pupils' transition between KS2 and KS3. Where these data are not shared or acted upon, Ofsted notes that pupils' progress into KS4 may be limited. Ofsted (2011a: 6) recommends schools designate 'at least one senior member of staff with an excellent knowledge of literacy and its pedagogy' who can advise on the stages of language development and how and when to provide additional support. They may also coordinate the work of 'learning mentors' who contribute to programmes of intervention in addition to the core time-table for pupils. Although Ofsted saw few instances of systematic phonics teaching in the secondary schools, leading on this may also become part of the secondary phase remit given the continued difficulties many pupils have with decoding (for example, manifest in stilted reading aloud, even before comprehension is taken into account) and encoding (for instance, rendering words on a page with correct spelling). At the very least, there is scope in the secondary phase for a wider appreciation of how to consider these difficulties diagnostically in support of further progress.

16.4   Thinking about literacy in your own subject

When you begin to think about how pupils use words in your own subject, think also of what they need to do in your subject that they perhaps don't do in any other area of school life. What type of writing are they asked to do? Are there specific *genres* of writing that they must use, such as reports, instructions or diaries? Are there very specific *purposes* for which they write: to explain, to persuade, to describe or to speculate? In what contexts do they usually write: with a computer, in books, on worksheets? The same principles apply to reading. What sort of texts do they commonly encounter? Are these electronic or paper-based? Do these combine words with images, with pictures, maps or diagrams? Again, the concepts of *genre* and *purpose* become relevant: it may be that pupils look at particular forms of text to find equally distinctive types of information. Speaking and listening activity is no different: do pupils talk to hypothesize, to predict or to recount? Do they need to develop skills of negotiation or collaboration? In each arena of literacy you will ask pupils to do things pertinent to your subject and perhaps *only* to your subject within the whole-school setting. By recognizing your role as a teacher of literacy, you will begin to respond to the urgent issues outlined in *Removing Barriers to Literacy*. A step further is to recognize what literacy means in your subject, to develop expertise in 'literacy for history' or 'literacy for art', for example. Perhaps we should begin to think instead of *literacies* across the curriculum, given that each area makes unique demands of pupils.

Of course literacy in your subject is not just about what you ask pupils to do. It is also about the attitudes you foster towards language use and the general atmosphere of your lessons. How do you use display space? If you display key vocabulary on classroom walls, do you ever refer to it as you teach, or ask pupils to interact with the information? How do you introduce pupils to pages in books or details in worksheets? Do they have time to scan for information? Do you give helpful directions, for example, guiding the group to the third paragraph down? Do you make good use of presentational resources, of an overhead- or data-projector, to display the text that pupils may have in front of them on their desks? Do you take care with your own handwriting on the board or in books? How do pupils feel in your lessons about asking about spellings? How do you respond to inaccuracies of pupil spelling that occur when they attempt to use unfamiliar or ambitious vocabulary in their writing? How do you organize pupil talk? Do they share ideas prior to writing, have thinking time before putting pen to paper or finger to keyboard?

Each question here deserves careful reflection. The ways in which you respond, and what you actually do as a teacher, culminate to affect how pupils communicate with each other and with you. To some extent, you determine the value they attach to words and activity with language, with a bearing too on their propensity and facility to communicate in environments not only beyond your lessons but also beyond the world of school.

16.5 Key words in your subject

A good place to begin in your consideration of subject-specific literacy is at the level of individual words. The important words, often the jargon of subjects, have come to be known as 'key words', and it is often these that you see presented around the school environment, in specially demarcated areas of a whiteboard or across classroom walls. How do pupils come to understand the concepts conveyed by the words, and how do they begin to use them in context, in their own talk and in their own writing?

In her book about the language needs of EAL (English as an additional language) learners, author Norah McWilliam (1998) details an excellent and versatile strategy that has merits across subjects and for all learners. She calls it 'rich scripting', a process that involves pupils bringing their existing knowledge of language to bear on words they encounter in subject-specific settings. Sometimes these words may be familiar to them in other contexts, but can have very precise meanings and uses within a specialism. McWilliam provides the example of 'peak' in geography, which pupils may already know through everyday idioms such as 'peak performance' or 'career peak'. Other examples might include 'scale', used differently across maths, music and art, possibly known to pupils beyond school as a concrete noun (e.g. as in bathroom scales, dragon scales) or as a verb ('to scale the rock face'). McWilliam's strategy is about making explicit the associations and resonances of any given word, so pupils can understand better its distinct meaning in the subject context, but also so that in heard speech they can distinguish it from homophones – words that sound the same – so that they fully understand its use in the immediate context (returning to an earlier example, a peak in geography is not the same as 'a peek'). Addressing such subtleties can be helpful in support of EAL learners, but also valuable in making all pupils alert and sensitive to the nuances of words, in creating language-rich classrooms.

If you use key words on displays to enrich the environment, use them to aid your teaching and to assist pupils. Quick reference to a word in print to support spoken use can be of help to pupils who benefit from visual learning strategies. The connection may help them to assimilate the spelling of the word by seeing its letters and remembering its shape. You may also wish to present different classes of word on different coloured paper, for instance yellow for nouns ('bunsen burner', 'test tube', 'tripod') and green for verbs ('react', 'liquefy', 'combust'). If pupils are to be helped to learn about these different classes, a common colour code is probably best adopted consistently across a school.

No doubt you will wish to support pupils in accurate spelling of key vocabulary. Ensure you appraise yourself of the various ways in which individuals learn spellings: some prefer to see words written down, some need them sounded out, others have to know how it feels to write the word themselves, while others remember through mnemonics or word games (e.g. to get the commonly misspelt 'necessary' right, remember 'one collar, two sleeves'). At the same time, try to understand the reasons why words are misspelt. Does the pupil make a guess based, perhaps reasonably, on how the word sounds? Has the word been confused with a commonly used homophone? Does the pupil regularly forget to double consonants where they should?

16.6 Supporting pupils with reading in your subject

It is likely that a significant amount of the information with which pupils are asked to engage in your subject is encountered through the verbal mode in print or on screen. Often written text will be combined with other visual items such as photographs, flow charts or illustrations. Even within written text, graphic elements such as typography, headings and spacing influence how the text is read and sometimes dictate how it should be approached.

If we come to such material as experts well versed in our specialisms and familiar with their text types, it can be easy to assume that pupils also know how to approach them. However, we should appreciate that pupils may not understand what we take for granted. Many textbooks, for instance, are not designed to be read across the page and down from the top-left corner, line by line, every word being taken in. Instead, they often comprise columns and figures, between which the reader's gaze may move back and forth, and it may be the case that different parts of the page can be rapidly scanned while others require close reading. Such approaches to reading need to be made explicit to pupils, and ideally demonstrated (or 'modelled') so that all have equal opportunity to access curricular content. For this very reason one of the initial Literacy Progress Units (DfES 2001c) focused on 'information retrieval' and contained a section on the reading skills of scanning and skimming, with geography and science textbook extracts for consideration. With this in mind, it is worth reflecting too on the demands of internet reading, where texts incorporate moving images and sound, and which are organized in complex, non-linear arrangements. Some commentators reflect on such reading in the context of 'multi-literacies' (Kress 2003) or 'new literacies' (Cope and Kalantzis 2003), stressing that it is rare for contemporary texts to isolate the verbal mode. It thus becomes important to understand how readers approach and make meaning from a non-verbal item such as a diagram, just as it is useful to consider how it is understood in relation to any accompanying verbal text. Unsworth (2001) is especially pertinent in this respect, offering detailed analyses of specialized school textbooks and identifying distinct grammars of design for each.

Having reflected on how you can help pupils orient themselves to the texts relevant to your subject, it is probable that you will want them to read for specific purposes and for particular information. But how do you prevent reading becoming a relatively passive activity, where, even though eyes glance over a page, detail may not be assimilated? 'Directed activities for reading and thinking' (DARTs; see Guppy and Hughes 1999) is a term used to describe strategies that marry literacy skills with thinking skills, requiring pupils to engage deliberately and often interrogatively with the texts before them, usually in pairs or groups rather than in silent, individual reading. Examples of DARTs include:

- providing pupils with a prose text that has been disrupted, perhaps with paragraphs presented out of sequence, which pupils must restore to chronological order;

- asking pupils to shape a given number of questions about a text, possibly requiring some that relate to factual or literal details within the text (reading the lines), some that respond to bias or inferred meanings (reading between the lines), and some that consider the text in context, for instance how it came to be written or how it might be used (reading beyond the lines);

- summarizing the text in a given number of words (necessitating selection of detail), or representing it in a different form (e.g. transforming a series of instructions into a flow chart).

All require careful attention to the detail of texts, invite discussion and promote higher-order cognition (according to Bloom's Taxonomy: Bloom *et al.* 1956; see Chapter 5), and most approaches can be applied to a variety of texts across many subject disciplines. They are all likely to influence pupils' engagement with your subject.

Task 16.2

Identify five genres of text encountered by pupils in your subject. For each, try to articulate the reading strategies employed by readers when approaching that genre.

16.7 Supporting pupils with writing in your subject

Pupils write differently in different subjects. In some areas, they are frequently asked to write quite lengthy extended prose; in some, short answers of only a couple of sentences, even one or two words, may be legitimate. Elsewhere pupils may be asked to write poems, letters, create newspaper articles, make posters. Expectations of how their work will be presented will also vary. In some instances, much of their writing will be considered 'draft', not intended for public viewing or 'best' formal presentation. At other times, they may be writing for display on the classroom wall, or for sharing on a school website or in a discussion forum. Behind each purpose for writing and mode of presentation lie numerous decisions, assumptions and skills: as with reading skills these need addressing overtly with a class.

Research into the written responses of pupils in examinations (Ofsted 2003a), and more general consideration of their writing across several genres (Lewis and Wray 1998), has suggested that pupils are not always familiar with the conventions of the types of writing they are asked to do in school. Furthermore, if they have at least some success with any given genre, they often have difficulty sustaining the quality of their writing across a whole piece, with concluding sections often relatively weak. It also seems that facility with different genres can relate to gender. Generalized findings suggest that boys, through their reading, may be relatively comfortable with quite a range of non-fiction forms, and that girls tend to be more at ease with a broader repertoire of fiction and 'literary' forms.

The strategy for LAC offers a range of responses to this background. To ensure pupils are familiar with the conventions of, say, fieldwork report writing in geography or match report writing in PE, it is recommended that teachers provide pupils with 'models' for these types of writing. These are examples of successful writing in the chosen genre, which the teacher can use to illustrate important conventions essential to the text type. This might involve looking closely at the organization of the text, noting the focus of each paragraph and common phrases that contribute to the clarity of the piece, perhaps drawing attention to a sequence ('First . . .', 'Second . . .', 'In summary . . .') or to the juxtaposition of statements ('On the one hand . . .', 'Conversely . . .', 'In contrast with . . .'). Each genre will have its own distinct phrases. In the jargon of LAC, these are frequently termed *connectives*, and are considered essential to a pupil's ability to present and develop ideas in writing, and to their likelihood of writing successfully within the conventions of the genre at hand.

Not only can teachers present 'models' so that pupils have a sense of how their finished writing might look, they are also advised to model the *process* of writing in the given genre. This can involve demonstrating the writing process via a whiteboard, overhead projector or interactive board, shaping sentences in front of pupils, and articulating the decisions you make as a writer. What thinking lies behind the sentence you have just written? Why is the next sentence important in developing the idea? Why have you decided on those particular areas of focus for the six paragraphs that make up the main body of the writing?

A complementary approach to the writing process is the use of 'writing frames', formats that provide a scaffold for pupils' own attempts at writing in a given genre. Generally, these identify the key organizational elements of a text, usually through boxes arranged on a worksheet, and include conventional phrases, often connectives, which act as a prompt for a pupil's writing. Such frames can provide a means of differentiating support for writing in your lessons, and can be designed to include varying degrees of detail. It is important, however, that the frames do not become inhibitive. If not carefully presented they can restrict pupils' responses as discussed in a paper by Fones (2001) which describes a process of developing writing frames to support able writers within English without limiting their thinking.

Task 16.3

Choose one genre in which pupils are likely to write in your subject. Create a writing frame to support them in recognizing the structural features and connectives relevant to the genre.

16.8 Supporting pupils' speaking and listening in your subject

Like writing, the talk-based activity you ask pupils to do can be considered along the lines of genre. In what types of talk do you ask pupils to participate? Do they give talks to an audience, perhaps with presentational devices such as posters, flipcharts or PowerPoint? Are they asked to work through formal debates, opposing teams thrashing out an issue? Do you want them to take part in role-plays, for example as members of a community debating an issue at a council meeting? Do they solve problems in groups? Once more, the types of talk they engage in have specific demands, particular organizational features and distinct turns of phrase, and may also require a certain register of speech (some may necessitate Standard English, in others a colloquial idiom will be apt).

The same principles of 'modelling' apply. In the case of a formal debate, maybe pupils should see an extract of a debate in the Commons, noting conventions of address ('With respect to the Honourable gentleman/lady . . .', 'Mr. Speaker . . .', 'Objection!'); in the case of a presentation to other members of the class, perhaps give a short talk yourself, use examples from video, or invite another pupil (a sixth-former perhaps) to demonstrate. If you are using a complex group work activity, be sure that at the first attempt the process is highly structured and regard it as a model for future work: it will take time for pupils to understand and be comfortable with the procedure. In each case you may find it helps to give pupils prompt sheets of the key phrases that support discussion, especially in group situations. Do pupils know how to signal polite disagreement with one another or how to put an opposing view without offence or aggression? Can they build on the comments of others ('Just like Mary said, I think . . .'), or open the floor for peers ('Is there anything you'd like to add . . .')? Prompts like these can contribute to pupil talk becoming self-sustaining, with less need for teacher intervention, just as writing frames support individual responses on the page.

Bear in mind the relationship between talking in groups and thinking skills. In this respect, the work of Vygotsky (1986) is relevant (see Chapter 4). Especially important is the idea that talk acts as a means of rehearsing, clarifying and refining ideas, and these processes support the assimilation of those ideas in the mind of the individual ('intramentally'), aiding understanding and recall. The way in which you organize groups will be significant, and factors to consider include the propensity of pupils to share ideas or, conversely, to refrain from involvement; potential clashes of personality; the ability of pupils to manage and sustain their own conversation; and the knowledge and confidence of individuals in relation to the topic in hand. You are unlikely to leave the selection of groups to chance: the decisions you make cannot be separated from principles of behaviour management, differentiation or inclusive education.

Task 16.4

Identify a talk-based task in your subject that could be conducted through group work.

What ground rules do you need to establish for the task?

List phrases that are likely to help pupils organize the discussion, for beginning their contributions and for inviting others to speak.

Try to identify the thinking skills developed as part of the task, with particular attention to those developed through pupils' dialogue that would be unlikely to occur in individual writing activities based on the same topic or idea.

16.9   Conclusion

Whether or not cross-curricular literacy has a profile in individual schools or government thinking, literacy is always an issue for a teacher, whatever their specialism. Moreover, as *Removing Barriers to Literacy* (Ofsted 2011a) describes, not only is literacy an urgent matter for many pupils in terms of their immediate engagement in school, it will also have a profound impact on their life opportunities beyond. Literacy is intimately connected with their enjoyment of and success in a subject, and in turn with their self-esteem. Literacy skills are at the heart of every pupil's ability to find a way into subjects, to access curriculum content; and often too they are central to a pupil's ability to succeed in assessments, especially formal and summative assessments, in a system where responses written on paper in silent exam conditions predominate. Ultimately literacy is about communication, and because communication is about our relationship with others, it is about identity and participation. Literacy is an issue for education in the broadest sense, part of the 'hidden curriculum' as much as the overt curriculum, always there.

16.10   Recommendations for further reading and webliography

Klein, C. and Millar, R.R. (1990) *Unscrambling Spelling*. London: Hodder & Stoughton.

Lewis, M. and Wray, D. (eds.) (2000) *Literacy in the Secondary School*. London: David Fulton.

McWilliam, N. (1998) *What's in a Word?* London: Trentham Books.

Mercer, N. and Hodgkinson, S. (eds.) (2008) *Exploring Talk in School*. London: Sage.

The National Strategies (Secondary) (2009) *Key leaflet: reading for real, purposeful and relevant contexts*. 01102-2009PDF-EN-04

Unsworth, L. (2001) *Teaching Multiliteracies across the Curriculum*. Maidenhead: Open University Press.

Websites

www.warwick.ac.uk/sta./D.J.Wray/index.html (David Wray's website)

http://www.literacytrust.org.uk/ (The National Literacy Trust website)

17

Numeracy across the curriculum
Fay Baldry, Jenni Ingram and Andrea Pitt

17.1 Introduction

Developing numeracy may appear to be more relevant in some curriculum subjects than others. However, all teachers have a role in supporting pupils to develop both the skills and the habits of mind required to be numerate. Around 20 per cent of young people still enter the workplace without the numeracy skills they need (Ofsted 2011b) and the implications for society are broad:

> People who reach adulthood with poor numeracy skills are more than twice as likely to be unemployed, and are far less likely to receive work-related training, get a promotion or receive a raise. Adults with poor numeracy are also more than twice as likely to have become a parent during their teenage years, to have long standing illnesses or disabilities and are far more likely to have experienced depression.
>
> (NIACE 2011: 4)

Although it is dangerous to jump to conclusions about the causes of these disadvantages, there is an accumulation of evidence suggesting that, as well as having adverse implications for public finances, poor numeracy affects an individual's wellbeing.

We begin this chapter by exploring the importance of numeracy and a range of definitions and interpretations of the term. We then examine both where numeracy can be found in a range of curriculum subjects and how a range of curriculum subjects can support the development of pupils' numeracy. We end by outlining some common calculation strategies pupils use, and offering suggestions for how you can support the development of numeracy in your own teaching.

By the end of this chapter, you should:

- understand the various ways numeracy has been defined and the implications these might have for teaching and learning;
- be ready to consider the numeracy opportunities and demands in your own subject area;

- be familiar with some of the approaches to mental and written calculation often taught in primary schools.

17.2 The importance of numeracy

Technological developments continue to contribute to substantial changes in the nature of employment, with widespread use of information technology transforming the type rather than the quantity of numerical skills needed. A knowledge-based economy, involving more complex communication and cognitive loads, is likely to demand that numerical skills are embedded in analytical problem-solving, justification of decisions, and cross-disciplinary working. To compete in a global economy, employers have highlighted the need for an increasing number of numerically literate people to work *at all levels* within business organizations (Smith 2004). The issues facing the world today are not confined to particular subjects. For example, the problems arising from population growth, sustainability, and depletion of resources all draw upon possible solutions from a range of disciplines, including mathematics. In an increasingly complex, interdependent and interrelated world, all levels of working will require non-routine thinking and communication situated in interdisciplinary environments.

By developing pupils' numeracy across the curriculum, we are supporting them to both understand and begin to improve these interdisciplinary ways of working. Embedding numeracy across subjects can impact on teaching effectiveness, pupils' motivation, and development of alternative ways of working. Other subjects can offer authentic situations that genuinely require numerical approaches to solve problems, thereby highlighting the real value of numeracy. Pupils may be more motivated to learn numeracy skills when the context is relevant and they see a real purpose for developing them (Ainley 2008). A report summarizing recent research supports the link between effective learning and learning based in context (Bell *et al.* 2008), so the opportunity to work in an interdisciplinary manner can increase confidence and competence as pupils widen their experience of using mathematics in context.

Teachers have a role to play in challenging the widely held view that it is acceptable to have poor standards of numeracy: 'we need a cultural shift in our attitude to maths and numeracy' (NIACE 2011: 4). Numeracy is more than a 'tool kit' of numerical approaches that pupils can select from to perform calculations; at its most effective it involves a way of thinking that is interwoven with problem-solving, critical analysis and other higher-level cognitive skills. Cross-curricular numeracy can provide authentic contexts that enable effective learning, support the development of pupils' numeracy, and extend the range of approaches they can take to understand other curriculum areas. Thus, we all share the responsibility of raising pupils' understanding of the importance of numeracy as well as its relevance for their personal proficiency.

17.3 What is numeracy?

There is no common definition of numeracy and what it might mean to be numerate. The definition of numeracy is important, however, because it influences policies and practices in schools and employment. In this section, we explore a variety of definitions and the implications these might have for teaching and learning.

Task 17.1

How would you define numeracy?

What concepts and skills do you think are needed for an adult to be considered numerate?

What do you think is the relationship between numeracy and mathematics?

The term numeracy was introduced in the Crowther Report (1959) to represent the mirror image of the word 'literacy'. The Cockcroft Report used the term to imply:

> . . . the possession of two attributes. The first of these is an 'at-homeness' with numbers and an ability to make use of mathematical skills which enables an individual to cope with the practical mathematical demands of his everyday life. The second is an ability to have some appreciation of information which is presented in mathematical terms, for instance in graphs, charts or tables or by reference to percentage increase or decrease. Taken together, these imply that a numerate person should be expected to be able to appreciate and understand some of the ways in which mathematics can be used as a means of communication.
>
> (Cockcroft 1982: para. 39)

However, at the time of writing of the Cockcroft Report, many people saw numeracy as the ability to perform numerical calculations and little more. Even today, many people perceive numeracy as restricted to numerical calculations.

With the introduction of the National Numeracy Strategy, further refinements of the meaning of numeracy developed. The definition given in the National Numeracy Strategy was 'a proficiency which involves confidence and competence with numbers and measures . . . and an inclination and ability to solve number problems in a variety of contexts' (DfEE 1999: 4). The evaluations of the impact of the strategy on the teaching and learning of numeracy or mathematics in primary schools describe it as 'the ability to process, communicate and interpret numerical information in a variety of contexts' (Askew *et al.* 1997: 10).

The developments in definitions emphasize the need for pupils to make connections between different mathematical ideas and to be able to select and use strategies that are both efficient and effective. Being numerate involves more than possessing the mathematical knowledge, skills, and techniques needed to solve problems within a context. It includes contextual knowledge such as awareness of the relationship between the context and the choice of skills and techniques needed and the confidence and disposition to interpret and find sufficient information to make decisions and judgements.

The term 'mathematical literacy' is used across the world in a similar way to numeracy. The OECD (2003) defines mathematical literacy as:

> . . . an individual's capacity to identify and understand the role that mathematics plays in the world, to make well-founded judgements and to use and engage with mathematics in ways that meet the needs of that individual's life as a constructive, concerned and reflective citizen.

This relates to the description of functional skills in the National Curriculum (NC), described as 'the skills and abilities [children] need to operate confidently, effectively and independently in life, their communities and work' (QCDA 2007b: 'Functional skills' section), yet with an emphasis on the roles or responsibilities associated with being a numerate citizen.

The *Numeracy Counts* report (NIACE 2011) shifted from numeracy being about skills to focus more on mathematical thinking, confidence, and comfortableness when working with numbers. This includes decisions about whether to use mathematics in a particular situation, what mathematics it is appropriate to use, and how to use the mathematical result within the context in which you are working. This shift in focus reflects the growing need to see and interpret mathematics in a variety of contexts rather than simply performing accurate calculations. Most people today carry a calculator in the form of a mobile phone, which can perform accurate calculations when required, but responsibility for knowing which calculations to perform, what the results should look like, and what to do with the result still lies with the individual.

Task 17.2

Revisit your answers to Task 17.1.

How would you alter or adapt your responses in light of what you have just read?

17.4 Recent government initiatives relating to numeracy

The National Numeracy Strategy (NNS) developed out of a pilot project in 1996 and was first implemented nationally in primary schools in 1999. The focus of the NNS was on mental strategies for calculation and the role of whole-class interactive teaching. While emphasis was placed on mental and oral strategies, the NNS included all aspects of the mathematics NC, such as geometrical reasoning, handling data, and problem-solving. In 2001, the strategy was extended to Key Stage 3 (KS3), but was referred to as the Framework for Teaching Mathematics or the Mathematics Strategy. Neither the NNS nor the Framework for Teaching Mathematics was statutory but they were widely adopted by schools, often functioning as a scheme of work (SoW), because they offered detailed learning objectives, medium-term plans, examples and ideas for teaching particular topics.

Also in 2001, the DfES launched a 'Numeracy Across the Curriculum' initiative where schools with KS3 pupils were expected to run whole-school initiatives and training to encourage subject departments to collaborate to raise standards in numeracy (DfES 2001c). The aims of this initiative were to encourage schools to explore opportunities for collaborative planning and teaching of mathematical topics, and to discuss situations where the teaching of mathematics could be enhanced by using examples from other subjects. In 2011, the strategies ended and resources and materials were archived. However, other initiatives, such as functional skills, continue to emphasize the broader role of numeracy across the curriculum. Ongoing initiatives relating to the assessment system and curriculum development mean that the role of numeracy across the curriculum continues to evolve.

17.5   Numeracy within curriculum subjects

In this section, we focus on numeracy as it occurs in different subject areas. Numeracy is often considered to be most relevant to science and information and communications technology (ICT), yet aspects of numeracy occur in all curriculum subjects. For example, there is a multitude of contexts within design and technology where numeracy skills, such as accuracy and the interpretation of errors in measurement, play a key role. The design and creation of any mechanical model requires accurate construction and an appreciation of the impact of different ranges of tolerances at each stage to ensure that the model works. Alternatively, area, surface area, and volume are all key aspects that need to be considered in the design of packaging.

Although in geography, numeracy is perhaps most visible in the use of graphs and charts, the geography curriculum also requires pupils to explain interactions in and between physical and human processes, which could include analysis and interpretation of numerical data. For example, within human geography pupils study themes such as urban change, migration, and sustainable development where manipulation of large numbers, trends, given in both graphical and percentage forms, and comparisons between countries of different size are but three of many situations where numeracy plays a part.

Science is probably the most obvious subject in which numeracy makes a regular appearance, most notably in the use of tables and graphs to record and interpret data from experiments. These processes involve pupils in selecting methods to collect adequate data for the task, measuring with precision, and manipulating numerical data to make valid comparisons and draw valid conclusions. However, some concepts and terminology differ between science and mathematics. For example, 4.2×10^{32}, would be described as 'scientific notation' in a science lesson but as 'standard form' in a maths lesson, although the underlying issues of handling and interpreting very large and very small numbers is common to both. Of all the sciences, physics is probably the one most closely associated with numerical approaches, with elements such as manipulation and use of formulae, relationships involving ratio and compound measures coming readily to mind. It is prudent to note, however, that when summarizing recent research, Uhden *et al.* (2011: 2) reported one of the common strategies employed by pupils to solve quantitative problems as 'blindly plugging quantities into physics equations and churning out numeric answers without understanding the physical meaning of their calculations', so pupils may need a dual approach, from both the subject and numeracy perspectives, to develop understanding.

When ICT and mathematics are mentioned together, most would not be surprised to find spreadsheets following shortly after, with their use often involving the storage, manipulation, and generation of data with the possibility of taking both numerical and symbolic approaches. However, the interconnections between numeracy and ICT extend beyond spreadsheets. For example, one of the many ICT processes in the NC that resonates with numeracy is 'test predictions and discover patterns and relationships, exploring, evaluating and developing models by changing their rules and values' (QCDA 2007b). Because of the capacity of ICT systems to perform many calculations, process data in a variety of ways and generate results, all without judgement, ICT will only be an effective tool for pupils if they 'consider the assumptions made and the appropriateness and accuracy of results and conclusions' (QCDA 2007b). These considerations are part of what it means to be numerate.

The next section explores some of the more generic skills within numeracy and mathematics, such as problem-solving and communicating effectively, which also feature in other subjects.

17.6 Supporting numeracy through other curriculum subjects

Numeracy is more than a set of mathematical tools that can be used and applied in other subjects. Numeracy is also about reasoning and problem-solving, which includes: pattern spotting; modelling, representing, and interpreting situations; and communicating effectively. These processes are equally fundamental in other curriculum areas. Probably one of the most important issues, though, is pupils' confidence and comfortableness in using and interpreting mathematical representations, such as numbers, graphs, and tables. A wide range of sources, including numerical representations of situations, could potentially be discarded or misinterpreted in the analysis of issues because of uncertainty over the meaning of the numerical representations.

The humanities subjects often explore how ideas, experiences, and values are portrayed and constructed in various sources. While these sources are often textual, there is a wealth of quantitative material that can be used to supplement these sources. Pupils need to be able to analyse critically both qualitative and quantitative sources and see the strengths and weaknesses of the models used to represent different perspectives.

Many of the creative arts subjects involve the use of patterns, sequences, and ratios; most obviously, the symmetry of many artistic works or dances, rhythmic patterns in music and dance, and ratio and proportion in art. Graphical representations of the structures of plays can be used to compare and contrast different genres. Many will recognize the works of M.C. Escher, appearing frequently in art and mathematics lessons, providing vivid and unusual access to the worlds of transformations, isometries and topology.

In science, while pupils are exposed to a variety of quantitative measures and approaches, there are nevertheless similarities between working mathematically and working scientifically. Thus, links between these subjects can move beyond common procedural activities towards common behaviour and ways of thinking.

17.7   Calculations

One of the key features of the NNS and the Framework for Teaching Mathematics involved teaching pupils a wide range of formal and informal, mental and written strategies for calculating. Pupils were then encouraged to choose appropriate strategies for themselves, taking into consideration the efficiency and effectiveness of the chosen strategies. A wide variety of strategies are available to pupils and the limited space here means we cannot introduce you to them all; instead, we focus on those strategies that are likely to be less familiar to you.

Task 17.3

Think about the method you would use to calculate the following:

69 + 24
74 – 38
12 × 15
73 × 58
849 ÷ 23

Now think of a different way of calculating them.
And another way . . .
How many different ways can you think of performing each calculation?

Mental strategies were emphasized in the NNS (QCA 1999a) and pupils were encouraged to develop a wide range of strategies and choose flexibly between these when faced with a calculation they could not instinctively answer. The empty number line can be used for a variety of calculations and individual students may partition the numbers in different ways when representing them on the empty number line. For example, the number lines in Figure 17.1 show two different ways of using a number line to calculate 56 + 27. The first example partitions 27 into 20 + 4 + 3, while the second partitions 27 into 4 + 23. Each of the partitions enables the pupils to use the tens boundaries in different ways. In the first example, the 7 is partitioned into a 4, bridging through 80, before adding the 3. In the second example, the 4 is used first to take it to 60 before adding the remaining 23. These are two possible examples, but there are others such as a pupil adding on 30 and compensating by then subtracting 3. The words 'partitioning' and 'compensating' are used extensively in mental calculations for the four main arithmetic operations in primary schools.

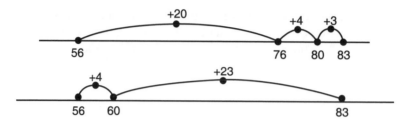

Figure 17.1 Using an empty number line for addition calculations

Mental strategies focus on recognizing and using patterns within numbers to make other calculations easier, for example, recognizing that multiplying by 4 is the same as doubling and then doubling again, a form of partitioning.

Written strategies are also varied and pupils are again encouraged to choose an appropriate one (QCA 1999b). Some of the earlier written strategies such as the 'area' method or the 'grid' method for multiplication emphasize the place value of the numbers, where if you are multiplying 46 by 57, the partitioning of 46 into 40 + 6 retains the value of 40. The more compact version, which is often considered to be the standard method of multiplication, is often calculated ignoring the place value of the individual digits. The 'area' or 'grid' methods are also useful for multiplying algebraic expressions because of the emphasis the partitioning places on the underlying mathematical structure (see Figure 17.2).

The 'area' method		
	40	6
50	2000	300
7	280	42

The 'grid' method		
×	40	6
50	2000	300
7	280	42

48 × 57 = 2622

May become:

Expanded version

$$
\begin{array}{r}
4\ 6 \\
5\ 7\ \times \\
\end{array}
$$

6 × 7	4 2
40 × 7	2 8 0
6 × 50	3 0 0
40 × 50	2 0 0 0
	2 6 2 2

Compact version

$$
\begin{array}{r}
4\ 6 \\
5\ 7\ \times \\
\end{array}
$$

46 × 7	3 2 2
46 × 50	2 3 0 0
	2 6 2 2

Figure 17.2 Progression in written multiplication methods

Expanded version using chunking

```
        587
       −170   10 × 17
        417
       −170   10 × 17
        247
       −170   10 × 17
         77
        −68    4 × 17
          9
so 587 ÷ 17 = 34 remainder 9
```

Compact version

```
        34 r 9
17) 587
    510
     77
     68
      9
```

Figure 17.3 Progression in written division

Pupils often find division the most challenging calculation to perform. One standard written strategy for division is based on the idea of 'chunking', where division can be approached as a process of repeated subtraction. So when calculating $578 \div 17$, pupils subtract 'chunks' of 17 that they are confident using, such as 10×17 (see Figure 17.3).

In Figure 17.3, the pupil chose to take away three chunks of 10 followed by a chunk of 4. Another pupil may have chosen to take away a chunk of 20, followed by a chunk of 10, and then two chunks of 2. Pupils choose the chunks that they are comfortable working with but are encouraged to choose accurate and efficient chunks. This is true not only of the chunking method for division; pupils are encouraged to consider and move towards accurate and efficient methods for performing a wide variety of calculations.

One of the key skills that pupils need to develop is deciding the appropriate method of calculation. For some, calculations can be performed quickly and accurately using purely mental skills; others will require some form of written strategy. However, a third option is using a calculator or a computer to perform calculations. Pupils need to be able to decide when it is appropriate to use a calculator. However, while a calculator can perform accurate calculations, pupils still need to choose which calculation to perform, check the reasonableness of the result and interpret this within the context.

Task 17.4

Think about the calculations that pupils may need to perform in your subject.

When is accuracy important?

When might a focus on accuracy hinder the understanding of the context?

17.8 Supporting pupils with numeracy in your lessons

When pupils encounter mathematical situations in your lesson, you can help them to gain confidence and develop their numeracy by:

- discussing the mathematical situation with pupils;
- building in opportunities that draw upon mathematics in an authentic way;
- asking questions, such as 'How did you get that answer?', 'How do you know?', 'What does it mean in this context?';
- encouraging pupils to share their ideas and discuss their thinking;
- encouraging explanation, reasoning, and justification;
- listening to pupils;
- supporting pupils' own methods of calculating or working, provided they are accurate and appropriate;
- focusing on the concepts within the mathematics rather than the procedures used to perform calculations;
- talking to the mathematics department in your school to develop coherent approaches to numeracy;
- incorporating genuine data that are often 'messy' rather than artificially contrived numbers.

17.9 Conclusion

Why have definitions of numeracy continued to evolve? Their prominence serves to highlight governments' and institutions' belief in the importance of numeracy, with reports repeatedly emphasizing its impact on both individuals and the wider community. Their continued evolution suggests that the broad, complex, and reflective nature of numeracy has yet to be fully embraced by all. We have argued that embedding numeracy across the curriculum allows pupils access to those authentic contexts that make numeracy relevant to them.

We have discussed how numeracy can enhance the learning of pupils in other subjects and is an integral part of the interdisciplinary approaches that are likely to feature in their future; we would be naïve, however, to believe that new ways of working will be restricted to our pupils. As technology develops, we may find ourselves modelling these very same interdisciplinary approaches, with knowledge-based subject boundaries becoming blurred by an increased demand for non-routine thinking skills. We conclude, therefore, that it is important for the economic wellbeing of the country and the life chances of individual pupils that all teachers strive to enhance the learning of numeracy in their subjects.

17.10 Recommendations for further reading

Ollerton, M. and Watson, A. (2001) *Inclusive Mathematics 11–18*. London: Continuum.
Ward-Penny, R. (2011). *Cross-curricular Teaching and Learning in the Secondary School: Mathematics*. London: Routledge.

18

Citizenship
Terry Haydn with Alison Kitson

18.1   Introduction: what does it mean to be 'a good citizen'?

By the end of this chapter, you will have:

- considered and reflected on what citizenship education in schools might entail;
- gained a more developed understanding about recent developments and current thinking about citizenship education in schools;
- gained an awareness of the different ways in which citizenship education is delivered by schools;
- developed an understanding of the ways in which citizenship education is relevant to all teachers, no matter what subject they teach;
- developed a fuller understanding of the range of ways in which you can contribute to the citizenship education of the pupils in your care.

Task 18.1

Think about what you understand by the term 'a good citizen'. Cover a sheet of A4 or A3 with as many characteristics of a 'good citizen' as you can think of.

Think of ways you might be able to group or categorize the characteristics you identified. The following are some possible categories to get you started:

- values;
- identity;
- participation;
- political/economic/social/religious;
- life skills.

You may wish to add more characteristics as you begin to categorize them.

There have been different ideas about the attributes required to be 'a good citizen'. Victorian and early twentieth-century pronouncements placed an emphasis on the ideal of the loyal and obedient citizen. At the beginning of the twentieth century, the Board of Education identified 'obedience, loyalty, courage, strenuous effort, service-ableness' as 'all the qualities which make for good citizenship' (Board of Education, 1905). Another strand of citizenship education has been the idea that schools should attempt to cultivate a sense of a shared or common identity, of being 'A British Citi-zen', which would help to secure a shared appreciation of, and common loyalty to the state, and contribute to 'community cohesion' (see, for example, Brown 2006).

A vision of education for citizenship that has emerged in more recent years is that of 'the critical and enabled citizen' (see, for example, Tosh 2008), which places great-er emphasis on the information literacy and intellectual autonomy of young people. Another facet of citizenship education about which there are differing views is the comparative 'weight' that might be accorded to 'the rights' of citizens, and their duties and responsibilities to the state.

It is generally acknowledged that the experience of schooling has an influence on the ideas, values, dispositions and competences of young people when they leave school (e.g. Gorard and Smith 2008). Given that the 1996 Education Act forbids 'the promotion of partisan political views in the teaching of any subject in the school', it is perhaps understandable that the territory of citizenship might induce a degree of trepidation or uncertainty in the minds of student teachers in terms of how to handle citizenship issues. Ofsted reports have pointed out that citizenship education places particular demands on teachers, especially if they are not subject specialists, 'many working far from their comfort zone both in subject knowledge and teaching approaches' (Ofsted 2006a: 1).

A clear warrant for teaching citizenship can be found in the curriculum pre-scribed by the most recent National Curriculum for Citizenship (QCDA 2007a) and the 'Aims, Values and Purposes' of the National Curriculum (QCDA 2007b), both of which, it should be noted, are currently under review. Both these documents provide what has been an 'officially sanctioned' statement of the attributes, values, and dispositions that education for citizenship should attempt to develop.

18.2 The recent development and current position of citizenship education in the UK

It is helpful to have some understanding of the ways in which citizenship education has evolved in the UK in recent years. Traditionally, citizenship education in Britain has not had a secure and substantial place in the school curriculum (Kerr 1999). However, in 1997, citizenship was placed firmly on the educational agenda. David Blunkett, then Secretary of State for Education, pledged to 'strengthen education for citizenship and the teaching of democracy in schools'. The Advisory Group on Edu-cation for Citizenship and the Teaching of Democracy in Schools was formed in 1997 under the chairmanship of Sir Bernard Crick. Its final report came out the following year and the Citizenship National Curriculum Orders, published in 1999, emerged out of this. Citizenship was introduced in primary schools in September 2001 as part of the non-statutory framework alongside personal, social and health (PSHE) education. A year later, in September 2002, it was introduced as a statutory foundation National Curriculum (NC) subject at Key Stage 3 (KS3).

The Final Report of the Advisory Group on Citizenship (commonly known as the Crick Report) was published in September 1998 (QCA 1998). In its introduction it outlined what it saw as the main aims of citizenship education. This document laid the foundations for the teaching of citizenship in schools. The following extract from the report provides an indication of the sort of citizenship education that was envisioned, and of the Group's ideas about 'the good citizen'.

> We aim at no less than a change in the political culture of this country both nationally and locally: for people to think of themselves as active citizens, willing, able and equipped to have an influence in public life and with the critical capacities to weigh evidence before speaking and acting; to build on and to extend radically to young people the best in existing traditions of community involvement and public service, and to make them individually confident in finding new forms of involvement and action among themselves. There are worrying levels of apathy, ignorance and cynicism about public life. These, unless tackled at every level, could well diminish the hoped-for benefits both of constitutional reform and of the changing nature of the welfare state. To quote from a speech by the Lord Chancellor earlier this year (on which we end this report): 'We should not, must not, *dare not*, be complacent about the health and future of British democracy. Unless we become a nation of engaged citizens, our democracy is not secure.
>
> (QCA 1998: 7)

The report went on to identify the crucial areas that should inform the citizenship curriculum. Borrowing from T.H. Marshall's definition (Marshall 1950), which highlighted three elements of citizenship (the civil, the political and the social), the report recommended that any citizenship curriculum should be based around:

- *Community involvement.* This is fairly self-explanatory. It was argued that pupils need to understand their place as a community member as well as an individual. This brings with it certain responsibilities or duties. The community might be the school or the local area.
- *Political literacy.* This is a broader term than simply 'political knowledge', although it does imply the teaching of some factual knowledge. In addition to knowing and understanding about our political systems and other areas – such as the justice system – pupils also need to develop the skills of debating, decision-making and critical thinking.
- *Social and moral responsibility.* At its most basic level, this is about the way we behave towards each other and our environment and, in particular, the *values* that underpin this behaviour. This might range from the way children interact in the playground to the attitudes young adults have about the law or about sustainability.

It will be clear that the Crick Report (QCA 1998) did not envisage a citizenship curriculum that was primarily about learning facts. The report put a strong emphasis on

This cube may help to reinforce the Inter-relationship of the essential elements and to confirm the need to approach them in a developmental and sequential way through the four Key Stages. This approach underpins the learning outcomes, as set out by Key Stage, that follow.

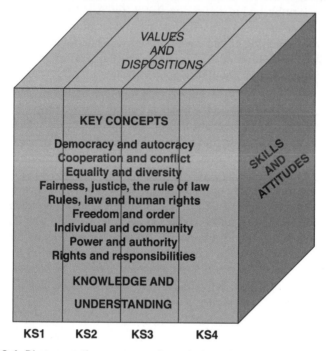

Figure 18.1 Diagrammatic representation of the relationship between elements of the citizenship curriculum (*Source: QCA 1998*)

education *for* citizenship (so that pupils *become* good citizens), rather than simply *about* citizenship (in which case, it might entail, say, teaching them about how Parliament works). Their definition was a more active one in which knowledge, understanding, skills, values and dispositions all had a part to play. Figure 18.1 illustrates how the essential elements are interrelated.

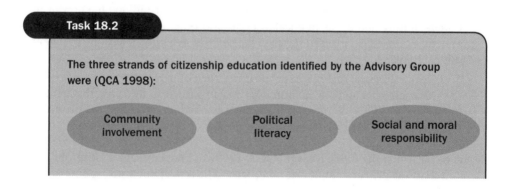

Task 18.2

The three strands of citizenship education identified by the Advisory Group were (QCA 1998):

Community involvement

Political literacy

Social and moral responsibility

1. What might each strand involve in terms of citizenship education? If you were to create a *curriculum* based on these strands, what sorts of things might you include? Create a spider diagram around each strand to record your ideas.

2. Begin to classify your ideas into:
- knowledge
- skills
- values.

3. Compare your ideas with the actual programmes of study for KS3 and KS4 in the Citizenship National Curriculum (http://www.nc.uk.net). You will see that the programmes of study are organized around three key concepts ('Democracy and justice', 'Rights and responsibilities' and 'Identities and diversity: living together in the UK') and three key processes ('Critical thinking and enquiry', Advocacy and representation' and 'Taking informed and responsible action').

As you study the NC Orders, think about how the programmes of study deal with issues of:

- *Rights and responsibilities*: where does the balance lie?
- *Identity*: how plural is it (i.e. how much account is taken of social diversity)? Is it a British/English/European/global identity?
- *Values*: what values underpin the whole document? How far do notions of democracy and democratic values infuse it?
- *Autonomy*: is citizenship education about producing compliant and conformist young people or critical and active citizens? To what extent can it be both?

4. Using *only* the programmes of study for KS3 and KS4, define what a good citizen is in one paragraph. Compare this with your original definition in Task 18.1. What are the similarities and differences? Can you explain them?

The Crick Report (QCA 1998) provided a basic structure for delivering citizenship education and a clear rationale and a mandate for teachers to work in these areas. It echoed the feeling in some quarters that societal change in the areas of the family, religion and employment paths pointed to an increasing need for teachers and schools to provide guidance to young people in how to live their social and civic lives post-school (Margo and Dixon 2006).

In the light of race-related disturbances in the north of England and the London bombings of 2005, the Ajegbo Report on *Diversity and Citizenship* (DfES 2007c) advocated that in addition to the three 'strands' of citizenship education suggested by the Crick Report (social and moral responsibility, community involvement and political literacy), the secondary curriculum for citizenship education should include a new element entitled 'Identity and diversity: living together in the UK'. This would mean that all pupils, as part of compulsory secondary citizenship education, would be taught about shared values and life in the UK. This was to be informed by an under-standing of contemporary issues and the relevant historical context that gave rise to them. Ajegbo added that this approach should be supported by a range of measures to ensure that all curriculum subjects adequately reflect the diversity of modern Britain, and that schools are appropriately supported in delivery of this education for diversity. Although not part of the original National Curriculum for Citizenship, this recommendation received the strong support of the Education Secretary, Alan Johnson, who announced that it would become compulsory for secondary school pupils up to the age of 16 to learn about shared values and life in the UK in their citizenship lessons. He said that youngsters would be encouraged to think critically about issues of race, ethnicity and religion, with 'an explicit link' to current political debates, the news and a sense of British values:

> More can be done to strengthen the curriculum so that pupils are taught more explicitly about why British values of tolerance and respect prevail in society and how our national, regional, religious and ethnic identities have developed over time ... I believe that schools can and should play a leading role in creating greater community cohesion. The values our children learn at school will shape the kind of country Britain becomes.
>
> (quoted in Brett 2007: 3)

In the 2007 revision of the Citizenship National Curriculum (QCDA 2007a), the third key concept – 'Identities and diversity: living together in the UK' – reflects the thrust of Ajegbo's report. Moreover, the focus of Ofsted inspection of schools was expanded to take into account the extent to which schools were promoting commu-nity cohesion. The fact that this facet of education was to be one of the criteria for inspection clearly put pressure on schools to respond.

In the light of these developments, citizenship education became an integral part of the school curriculum, with the subject constituting a compulsory part of the cur-riculum, an option at GCSE level and part of the framework for school inspection. The emergence of initial teacher education courses for teachers of citizenship as a discrete subject reflected these changes.

18.3 Implementing the citizenship curriculum

You should now have a clearer sense of the recent development of citizenship educa-tion and some of the concerns that shaped it. Creating a citizenship curriculum is only half of the story, however. Implementing it in schools is a different challenge altogether. You may be teaching in schools that approach the teaching of citizenship in radically different ways, and you should be prepared to work effectively within any of these differing approaches.

The following alternatives give an indication of some of the most prevalent models of citizenship education in UK schools:

- Discrete citizenship provision taught by a specialist in separate curriculum time.
- Citizenship taught as part of a timetabled personal, social, health and economic education (PSHEE) course by a specialist team.
- Citizenship taught within and through other subjects.
- Citizenship events and activities delivered as special one-day events that replace the standard timetable; for example, Global Citizenship or Human Rights Day, health week, school council election or mock political elections.
- Citizenship as part of a pastoral or tutorial group activity in tutorial time.
- Citizenship learnt through pupils' participation in the life of the school and wider community.

Task 18.3

Take these modes of delivery and consider what the advantages and disadvantages of each might be.

Figure 18.2 summarizes the advantages and disadvantages of each approach and you may wish to compare it with your own response to the task above. Most importantly, it is not intended that schools should adopt a single mode of delivery but rather that they will *combine* a number of approaches according to their own particular needs. For example, a school may adopt a model that looks something like this at KS3:

- two blocks of PSHE lessons of seven lessons each, in Years 8 and 9, devoted to specific citizenship elements;
- responsibility for delivering aspects of the citizenship curriculum located within the history, geography, religious education (RE) and English departments in Years 7, 8 and 9;
- a whole-day event for each year group, for example, Human Rights Day in Year 9;
- extended tutorial time every Friday in Years 8 and 9 to discuss and debate current affairs;
- increased status and influence of school council; pupils allowed to stand for election to join the school's governing body;
- community projects, including fund-raising by individual tutor groups and involvement in local recycling schemes.

As you can see, this model combines several of the modes of delivery contained in Figure 18.2. Thus, no two schools are likely to operate exactly the same model.

This chart is intended to help schools discuss and decide on ways of combining different modes of delivery for citizenship. *It is not intended that schools should select a single mode of delivery.*

Citizenship delivery	Advantages	Disadvantages	Implications
Discrete citizenship provision taught by a specialist in separate curriculum time	• Separate subject identity • Expert input • Aids progression • Effective monitoring and evaluation • Effective reporting to parents	• Citizenship seen as the responsibility of only one person • May discourage whole-school approach • Timetable pressures • Lacks strength of team approach	• Training needed for specialists • Expertise invested in only one person • Need for senior management support • Communication • Timetabled slot
Citizenship taught as part of a timetabled PSHEE course by a specialist team	• Expertise through team knowledge and experience • Team support • Specialist planning and development • Focused sessions on specific themes • Context of overall personal and social development	• Teachers may not know personal aspirations of pupils • Lessons may be seen as separate from other personal development activities • Competing timetable demands	• Timing of activities • Citizenship coordinator part of team • Time needed to do the subject justice • Range of specialist teachers needed
Citizenship taught within and through other subjects	• Context for citizenship learning within other areas of the curriculum • Integrated approach gives relevance for learning in the subject • Raises standards and enriches other subjects (see Key Stage 3 National Strategy)	• Different approach needed at Key Stage 4 • Danger of 'tokenism' • Possible lack of experience in active learning • Lack of consistency • Coordination across departments	• Training in knowledge and participatory approaches for all subject teachers • Lialson to provide informed support for subject specialists • Extra time needed to meet both citizenship and subject objectives
Citizenship events and activities delivered off timetable, e.g. Human Rights Day, health week, school council election, mock elections	• Focus on a specific element • High status event for the school • Pupil enjoyment • May be planned and taught by experts • Attracts high-quality speakers/visitors	• Timetable disruption • Difficult to develop analytical and critical abilities • Pupils may be absent • Citizenship may be seen as a series of isolated events	• Advance planning Cooperation of a wide staff/pupil group • Time needed to prepare and follow up • Incorporate into existing activity weeks or events

Figure 18.2 Different modes of delivery for citizenship (Source: QCA 2001, Appendix 2)

Citizenship as part of a pastoral or tutorial group activity in tutorial time	• Links to other areas of personal development • Opportunities for pupils to reflect on personal strengths and undertake target-setting • Builds relationship between tutor and pupils	• The tutor room may restrict teaching approaches • Teaching expertise likely to be limited for citizenship • Lack of time – possible dilution by other issues • Difficult to maintain consistency of teaching and learning	• Production of materials and delivery strategies • Training for NQTs • Ongoing training for tutors if they move through the Key Stage • Need to ensure consistent delivery
Citizenship learnt through pupils' participation in the life of the school and wider community	• Encourages whole school approach • Pupils learn from real-life activities • Pupils involved in decision making gives relevance to policies • Fosters good links between school and community	• Need to cover all requirements of programme of study • Difficult to ensure progression • Time needed to set up mechanisms where they do not exist	• Time needed for pupils to reflect on participation • Community links need to be identified • Need to encourage all pupils to participate

Figure 18.2 *(Continued)*

One of the biggest decisions a school must make with regard to implementing the citizenship curriculum is whether to deliver much of the content through separate citizenship lessons or through PSHE, or whether to integrate it into other subject areas. History was mentioned in the Crick Report as having particular relevance, as were geography and English, but, in fact, citizenship can inform the teaching of *all* subject areas. This was recognized in the QCA Official Schemes of Work, which include advice about maximizing opportunities for the delivery of citizenship in all the core and foundation subjects at KS3 (QCA 2001).

18.4 Understanding your subject's contribution to citizenship education

Much of the school curriculum is devoted to the study of particular subject disciplines. This is because it is felt that study of these disciplines offers a way for young people to make sense of, and thrive in, the society they will be part of when they leave school. It is important for subject teachers to think about the whole variety of benefits that the study of their subject can bestow on the pupils they teach. In different ways, all subjects help to prepare pupils to be active, participating citizens, explore ethical and moral values, and help them towards a critical understanding of a part of their world. Effective teachers not only possess a sophisticated understanding of the benefits that can accrue from study of their subject, they are able to transmit an understanding of these benefits to their pupils. Several recent studies, however, have shown that many pupils have a very limited grasp of why they are studying particular school subjects (Adey and Biddulph 2001; NASC 2002). It can be helpful for teachers to be explicit about *why* pupils are studying their subject, as well as possessing conceptual clarity in their own minds about the full range of benefits it offers, and the ways in which it will contribute to their ability to become fulfilled and successful citizens in their lives after school.

One of the problems arising out of the introduction of citizenship education in the UK was that some subjects appeared to have a stronger or more obvious role to play than others. History appeared to have a major role, for instance, in developing pupils' understanding of Britain's system of parliamentary democracy. Similarly, geography seemed to have an obvious link to environmental matters and ideas about 'global citizenship'. For other subjects, such as PE and mathematics, the links to citizenship seemed less apparent, and led to some teachers of those subjects being dismissive of the role that the subject might play in terms of its contribution to citizenship. Another criticism that has been made of the way in which citizenship education has been introduced in the UK is that insufficient attention was paid to making explicit subject connections with citizenship agendas. In the words of John White (2010: 32):

> The 2000 revision of the NC brought in extensive aims, most of them to do with fostering the personal qualities expected of a citizen in a liberal democracy, like 'autonomy, care for others, respect for the environment, critical thinking, work for the common good', however 'no attention at all was paid to how these were meant to mesh with aims within the subject'.

Because of these factors, it is all the more important that teachers of *all* subjects proactively explore ways in which their subject can contribute to citizenship education.

Task 18.4

What contribution do you think your own subject area could make to citizenship education at KS3, KS4 or both? Look at the programmes of study again (www.nc.uk.net), together with suggestions from some of the key citizenship web portals such as www.citized.org.uk. Does your subject lend itself to the development of any aspects of the four elements? Remember, it may be the case that you are better placed to develop the *skills* of citizenship more than the *knowledge* and *understanding*. Note down some of the ways your subject area might make a contribution.

18.5 Modelling citizenship in your classroom

As well as considering the contribution that your subject can make to citizenship education, you should remember that pupils are also influenced simply by spending time (in many cases, hundreds of hours) in your classroom. The classroom in itself is a community of citizens, albeit 'embryo' ones. What happens in your classroom, how things operate, how people are treated, what rules and conventions apply, will have an impact on the values, attributes and dispositions that pupils acquire, and will influence pupils' interactions with others as 'social human beings'. Even something as apparently trivial as the practice of leaving the classroom reasonably tidy for the next teaching group sends messages to pupils about respect and consideration for others. Cultivating and sustaining a classroom climate where aggressive and intimidating anti-social behaviour does not occur is another (and perhaps more important) aspect of modelling the sort of 'society' that pupils will learn to respect and appreciate. Research has indicated that pupils prefer teachers who are able to create a relaxed and cooperative working atmosphere in the classroom, and who are able to prevent some pupils interfering with the learning of others, in a calm, reasonable and understated way, rather than by stridency and threats – a democratic but ordered classroom as opposed to an autocratic or anarchic one (see, for example, Rogers 1998; NASC 2002).

One of the most graphic descriptions of the qualities that pupils should acquire to prepare them for citizenship and adult life can be found in the section of a previous version of the Citizenship National Curriculum, which defines its values, aims and purposes (DfEE/QCA 1999: 10–13). This can be a comparatively neglected component of the NC among trainee teachers, and yet it provides clear guidance, and a powerful mandate, for how teachers might run their classrooms to help develop 'the good citizen'.

Task 18.5 asks you to consider the extent to which your classroom provides opportunities for pupils to develop some of the qualities and attributes described in this section of the NC that will prepare them for adult life and make them 'good citizens'. Education is not a value-free zone. This section of the NC also states that education should 'reaffirm our commitment to the virtues of truth, justice, honesty, trust and a sense of duty' (DfEE/QCA 1999: 10). All the qualities and attributes described above can either flourish or wither in secondary classrooms, and the individual classroom teacher is a key factor in determining the extent to which these attributes and values will be developed. Gorard (2010) cites a number of research studies that suggest that *modelling* the qualities associated with good citizenship is one of the most powerful ways that teachers can transmit to their pupils the values and dispositions that are characteristic of 'good citizens'. Conversely, if teachers do not 'practise what they preach' in terms of respect and consideration for others, fairness, integrity and so on, these values will not resonate as powerfully.

Task 18.5

In your classroom, to what extent do pupils get the opportunity to develop the following qualities and attributes? (These are some, but not all, of the opportunities mentioned above.)

- to learn and work independently and collaboratively;
- to think creatively and critically;
- to solve problems and make a difference for the better;
- to become enterprising and capable of leadership;
- to develop integrity and autonomy;
- to challenge discrimination and stereotyping;
- to make informed judgements and independent decisions;
- to understand their rights and responsibilities;
- to form and maintain worthwhile and satisfying relationships based on respect for themselves and others;
- to develop the ability to relate to others and work for the common good.

18.6 Citizenship and school ethos

Citizenship education is not just about delivering the curriculum, however. In principle, at least, it should also have an impact on the whole *ethos* of a school. This was highlighted in the Crick Report:

> There is increasing recognition that the ethos, organisation, structures and daily practices of schools, including whole-school activities and assemblies have a significant impact on the effectiveness of citizenship education. Through such climate and practices schools provide implicit and explicit messages which can have a considerable influence, both positive and negative, on pupils' learning and development. Schools need to consider how far their ethos, organisation and daily practices are consistent with this aim and purpose of citizenship education and affirm and extend the development of pupils into active citizens. In particular, schools should make every effort to engage pupils in discussion and consultation about all aspects of school life on which pupils might reasonably be expected to have a view, and wherever possible to give pupils responsibility and experience in helping to run parts of the school. This might include school facilities, organisation, rules, relationships and matters relating to teaching and learning. Such engagement can be through both formal structures such as school and class councils and informal channels in pupils' daily encounters with aspects of school life. To create a feeling that it is 'our school' can increase pupil motivation to learn in all subjects.

> (QCA 1998: 36)

Some people argue that schools as institutions are antithetical to true citizenship. This is because schools have tended to be largely non-participatory in terms of structures and rules and characterized by pupils being told what to do rather than being invited to debate negotiate and 'own' the rules and conventions that operate in schools and classrooms. There are signs, however, that this is changing. School councils are now well established in most schools, and 'pupil voice' is taken into account more than in the past. In some schools, these changes are to a degree cosmetic, and exert little influence on the running of the school; in others, they have a significant role in interviews for staff, on decisions relating to uniform and rewards and sanctions, and on a range of issues that make a difference to how the school is run.

Gorard (2010: 58–9) makes the point that schools might be seen as 'mini-societies', and can provide all pupils with 'a decade or more of experience exemplifying how we might want society to be'.

18.7 Teaching approaches to citizenship education

We have already explored how citizenship can be modelled through day-to-day teaching and also how it can be integrated into your own subject teaching. But there may also be times when you teach citizenship more explicitly. Teaching elements of citizenship well – and in particular, controversial issues – requires particular approaches. The 2007 Citizenship National Curriculum states:

> Citizenship equips pupils with the knowledge and skills needed for effective and democratic participation. It helps pupils to become informed, critical, active citizens who have the confidence and conviction to work collaboratively, take action and try to make a difference in their communities and the wider world.
>
> (QCDA 2007a)

An essentially didactic, one-way style of teaching is clearly not appropriate here. Instead, a more active, participatory style that invites pupils to take responsibility for their own learning, to discuss and debate and to reach informed, independent judgements is encouraged. For many teachers, this is a style with which they are already familiar and, indeed, it may already characterize their typical teaching strategies. For others, however, it represents a departure from the norm and from strategies with which they feel comfortable. Certainly, the teaching of controversial and sensitive issues is an area with which many feel uncomfortable. How can they avoid accusations of bias? How can they avoid conflict breaking out in the classroom? How can issues be handled sensitively enough by both teachers and pupils? Teachers trained in the humanities are probably the most at ease with such topics, but there are certain questions that are helpful prompts in exploring such issues. For instance, the following questions, taken from QCA guidance, encourage pupils to think around citizenship issues:

- What are the rights and responsibilities in this situation? How might they conflict?
- Do you think that situation (or rule, behaviour, etc.) is fair? Why, why not?

- How could it be made fairer?
- How does this relate to your experience?
- What are the issues here (including the rights and wrongs of the situation)?
- What moral or legal rules are relevant here?
- What do you think would be the best (or fair) outcome for all concerned?
- Who do you empathize with (or feel sorry for)? How do you think they feel?
- What might be the consequences of that (for individuals or the group)?
- What should happen to the people who did that and why?
- What would happen if everyone behaved like that?
- What could you say to X to persuade them differently?
- Who had power and/or authority? How did they use it? Fairly? Wisely?
- Who should make that decision? An individual? The whole group?
- How far should these people be treated as equal or different and on what grounds?
- What personal qualities are needed for this role or task?
- What beliefs or ideas are commonly held about this type of situation?
- What kind of society do you want to live in?

Task 18.6

1. Imagine you have been asked to teach your tutor group about fertility treatment for women who have passed the menopause *or* about the wearing of religious symbols such as the cross or the veil. Which of the above questions might help you to tease out the key ideas?

2. Think of an issue, problem or area of debate that affects your classroom teaching or the subject you teach. How might you discuss this issue with your pupils while at the same time explaining to them that their views may not necessarily lead to the changes that they might like?

18.7 Assessing citizenship

The 2007 version of the National Curriculum for Citizenship (QCDA 2007a) brought in an eight-level assessment model for attainment in citizenship (plus an 'exceptional performance' level). These descriptions summarize what pupils will know/be able to do. Teachers are required to decide whether a pupil is achieving the expectation, working towards it or exceeding it. Ofsted reports suggest that the assessment of pupils' progress in citizenship has been one of the weaker elements of citizenship teaching, with many teachers having 'only a very tentative understanding of standards and progression in citizenship' (Ofsted 2006a: 39). However, both Ofsted and the Citizenship Foundation (www.citizenshipfoundation.org.uk) have suggested ways of assessing pupils' progress effectively, derived from visits to schools where they have encountered 'good practice' in citizenship assessment.

One of the underpinning principles behind more successful approaches to assessment is the acknowledgement that it should be broad and balanced, across the four main strands of citizenship, avoiding a narrow focus on what pupils know and understand, and taking account of the active and 'social' nature of the aims of the citizenship curriculum:

> The assessment of skills and application and participation are continuous and formative, often based on teachers' observation of process, as well as discussion with individuals and groups of pupils about success criteria and how far these have been met. But there is also sufficient emphasis on knowledge and understanding through assignments, the assessment of formal presentations, written tests and examinations and other evaluations.
>
> (Ofsted 2006a: 40)

In some schools, teachers have successfully used group, peer and self-assessment, with an emphasis on process as much as outcome. Assessment needs to take account of the full breadth of the citizenship curriculum, and encompass pupils' knowledge and understanding, skills and dispositions, and willingness to participate and 'make a positive contribution'. It is important to note that some schools were criticized for setting *too little* written work in citizenship – as with other subjects, there is a body of knowledge that pupils need to acquire, and written work is one way of testing for knowledge and understanding in this area.

The following list provides examples of aspects of pupils' performance where judgements might be made on pupil progress:

- How good is their substantive knowledge of the factual content of the course? (knowledge and understanding)
- How sophisticated is their understanding of key concepts and issues? (knowledge and understanding)
- How good are they at expressing and justifying a personal opinion, orally and in writing? (skills)
- How appropriately do they respond to the opinions of others? (social interaction/ dispositions)
- To what extent do they contribute appropriately to whole-class and small-group discussions? (participation)
- To what extent do they demonstrate an interest in social, moral and political issues? (dispositions/commitment)
- How well do they work cooperatively with others? (skills/dispositions)
- To what extent do they get involved in school or community affairs? (participation).

It should be added that the extent to which pupils involve themselves in school activities or groups outside school is to some extent a personal issue, and needs to be handled sensitively. There are pupils who are not 'joiner-inners' but who have an intelligent personal interest in and understanding of citizenship issues, and who are developing as mature and responsible citizens.

At the time of writing this chapter, pupils can also take citizenship as an examination subject. At KS4, there are several short-course GCSEs available in Citizenship Studies that deliver the KS4 citizenship curriculum and recognize the work completed by pupils by awarding a grade. Schools are not obliged to follow this route but it is interesting to note that there has been a rapid increase in the number of pupils taking GCSE short-course citizenship, up from 38,000 in 2005 to over 84,000 in 2008 (Ofsted 2009a).

18.8 Lessons learned and the future of citizenship education in schools

What can we learn from the first years of compulsory citizenship education in the UK?

Commitment

An evaluation of the implementation of citizenship education conducted by Ofsted (2006a) reported wide variations in the quality of citizenship education, with some schools providing inspirational and high-quality experiences for pupils, but over a quarter of provision being deemed 'inadequate'. Much of the variation is attributed to differing levels of commitment that schools, departments and teachers bring to citizenship education. Ofsted talked of some teachers being almost in denial about citizenship education, hoping that 'it will go away' (Ofsted 2006a: 1), and 'reluctance, resistance, scepticism' (Ofsted 2005b: 6). There appeared to be a tendency for some schools to adopt a 'we do it already' approach (in a vague, general and unspecified way).

More recent reports suggest 'encouraging progress', with over half of schools visited judged 'good' or 'outstanding' in their provision. However, it was also acknowledged that citizenship education is much better and stronger in some schools than others (Ofsted 2009b). In an evaluation of citizenship education published in 2009, Ofsted reported that best practice was likely to emerge from schools where the subject had 'dedicated and regular space on the timetable', rather than being a minor and occasional 'slot' within PHSE programmes, and where pupils have opportunities to take on leadership roles in their school community, through volunteering, community action or as part of a school council (Ofsted 2009b).

A more cautious or sceptical assessment was provided by White (2010), who pointed out that in terms of priorities, citizenship education fell some way below other considerations, most notably the pressure to cover subject curriculum content and maximize examination performance, particularly with regard to GCSE and A level grades: 'Subject teachers tended to skip over the section in the National Curriculum handbook about larger aims, and dwell on what was prescribed for them in their own discipline. The big aims became no more than mission statements, worthy, but ignorable' (White 2010: 302).

As in other facets of education, outcomes depend partly on the commitment of senior management teams and individual teachers. Much depends on what 'messages' are sent about citizenship education – by policy-makers, senior management teams and individual subject teachers.

The importance of active learning and pupil talk

Citizenship is in some ways distinct from other subjects in its overall objectives, with more emphasis on process issues. This requires teachers to develop skills in facilitating high-quality pupil talk, discussion and argument. Discussion needs to be:

> ... well planned and sequenced, with due attention to inclusion, and with pupils required to justify opinions, sustain their argument and make informed judgements on the issues being discussed. Additionally, there should be opportunities for reflection on their conclusions or the reasons for differences of opinion to reinforce learning and achievement.
>
> (Ofsted 2005b: 5)

The importance of initiative with resources

Another criticism of citizenship provision in some schools was poor preparation, and the lack of high-quality resources that would have an impact on pupil engagement in the subject. Teachers teaching 'out of field' are tempted sometimes to spend less time preparing lessons rather than more, or to be over-reliant on resources provided by others, without reading through materials carefully, and refining and adapting them so that they are used effectively. Given the development of citizenship resources, which are now freely available on the internet, there is no excuse for over-dependence on low-grade worksheets and tatty, dull handouts. As long as pupils are not left to browse purposelessly on the internet, ICT can be a way of building up what Walsh (2003) terms 'powerful learning packages'. The internet can be useful in finding 'impact' resources, which can be vividly imprinted on pupils' memories long after the lesson has ended. (See p. 257 for some examples of citizenship portals.)

Making citizenship relevant to the lives of young people

Ofsted (2005b: 4) reports that 'achievement is high where pupils understand the relevance of what they are studying'. Citizenship lends itself to the use of modern media, news, newspapers and the internet. Many schools adopt a flexible approach to the topics to be dealt with to maximize topicality and relevance, by incorporating 'stories of the day', and placing an emphasis on 'issues of the day and how we read them'. It can also be helpful to be explicit about the relevance of such issues to the lives pupils will lead when they leave school.

The challenges and opportunities for citizenship education are therefore manifold. It is clear from surveys conducted with pupils (e.g. Kerr *et al.* 2003; Kerr 2005) that their political and civic knowledge is extremely variable and is strongly linked with parental educational background. Pupils also appear to place significantly greater trust in their families and friends than they do in politicians and government-related institutions and, while most say they intend to vote in national and local elections, very few express a desire to join a political party or become involved in local politics. If one of the key (though not uncontested) aims of citizenship education in this country is to encourage greater participation in public life, then these findings suggest that there is a long way to go. Nevertheless, the very fact that citizenship education has had a statutory presence in the secondary school curriculum is a far cry from the rather more token gestures of previous years. Taking it further – ensuring that all pupils have access to high-quality citizenship education – will depend on the commitment and enthusiasm of well-informed and inspirational teachers who believe that citizenship education is an important entitlement for all young people. It will also depend on the outcomes of the current review of the school curriculum.

18.9   What next for citizenship education?

At the time of writing, the position of citizenship education for the forthcoming decade is uncertain. The Coalition government that assumed power in May 2010 has instigated a review of the NC, and there is no guarantee that citizenship will retain its current position and status within the curriculum. Current Secretary of State for Education, Michael Gove, has made a number of speeches advocating a return to 'traditional' school subjects and has been critical of the requirement for schools to teach citizenship (see, for example, Paton 2010). The Association for Citizenship Teachers (ACT) has expressed concern that, in the light of a number of statements by policy-makers, citizenship may lose its status as a compulsory element of secondary education (Shephard 2011). Moreover, the most recent White Paper on education outlines plans to 'streamline' school inspections, so there is no longer a requirement to report on areas such as equality and community cohesion (DfE 2010b).

Whatever the outcomes of the review of the NC, or changes to the Ofsted inspection framework, we would argue that anyone becoming a teacher still needs to think about the full range of ways in which their teaching will influence the citizens that will emerge from their experiences of school subjects, classrooms and schools as institutions. As former Chief Inspector of Schools, Christine Gilbert, has argued, schools have a duty to develop the 'social responsibility, community involvement and political understanding' of their pupils (quoted in Ofsted 2010b: 1).

18.10   What citizenship education means for you

Whatever the outcomes of the review of the school curriculum, it is likely that you will be involved in citizenship education in some form or another. Think again about the reasons you want to become a teacher. For most, the answer lies in making some kind of a difference. As a subject teacher, that difference mainly lies at an individual level – helping pupils achieve their best. As a teacher of citizenship, the difference can be about making a difference to individuals *and* society as a whole.

At a common-sense level, being a good citizen means being able to lead a happy, successful, ethically sound and socially responsible life in the society pupils will be part of when they leave school. Although considerable pressure has been put on schools in recent years to improve pupil attainment in school subjects, there is more to education than examination performance. Teachers must address the wellbeing of the child as a whole, and ensure that all pupils have the opportunity to fulfil their potential and are able to make a positive contribution to society when they leave school. Being a citizen means being 'a grown-up', with the civic and social responsibilities that that entails. It means being intellectually autonomous and socially responsible, being able to interact effectively and appropriately with other adults, and act within generally accepted codes of behaviour, while possessing the intellectual faculties to examine those codes critically, and an understanding of how one might reasonably act to 'change things for the better'. If you have spent time inside schools, you will know that there are many pupils who will need help in 'getting there' and developing these attributes by the time that they leave school.

18.11 Recommendations for further reading and webliography

Arthur, J. and Cremin, H. (eds.) (2011) *Debates in Citizenship Education*. London: Routledge.
Arthur, J. and Davies, I. (2008) *Citizenship Education*. London: Routledge.

Websites
www.citizenshipfoundation.org.uk (Citizenship Foundation website)
www.citized.org.uk (CitizED)

19

14–19 curriculum reform
Ian Abbott and Prue Huddleston

19.1 Introduction

There are currently around 2.5 million young people in England between the ages of 14 and 19 (DfE 2011b). Not all these young people are in full-time education and, of those who are, the majority are in colleges of further education, not in school. This may surprise those of you who have spent the years between 14 and 19 in a school, probably studying A levels. You may be unaware of the range of programmes available for this age range – general, vocational, occupational – and the range of institutions in which they are delivered. Since the early 1980s, there have been several attempts to reform and re-structure the 14–19 curriculum in England in an effort to address some long-standing and interrelated problems. The 14–19 curriculum was dominated by a narrow range of academic qualifications which were perceived to be insufficiently applied or practical. Furthermore, pupils were encouraged to specialize in a small number of subjects, often in related areas, at an early stage in their education. Vocational awards, on the other hand, were held in low esteem. This problem was compounded by the fact that vocational qualifications were developed on an ad hoc basis by different awarding organizations, leading to a proliferation of awards and no coherent framework to show how these different awards might relate to one another or to academic qualifications. Academic and vocational pathways remained separate, making it difficult for learners to combine elements from each or to change pathways. Perhaps the most serious consequence of these failings was that too many young people left education or training prematurely because available provision failed to meet their needs and aspirations.

Over the years, different reform initiatives have attempted to:

- achieve parity of esteem between academic and vocational qualifications;
- develop a flexible system that allows pupils to combine vocational and academic elements or switch pathways;
- develop a framework that incorporates the three pathways – general (academic), vocationally related and occupational – and show how they relate to one another;

- treat 14–19 as a unified phase rather than two separate phases, thereby opening up opportunities for pupils to progress at variable rates or to skip certain qualifications altogether;

- encourage more young people to stay in education and training for longer. From 2013, young people will be expected to participate in some form of education or training, though not necessarily full-time, until the age of 17, and from 2015 this expectation will extend to 18. These changes were set out in the Education and Skills Act (DCSF 2008).

By the end of this chapter, you should have developed:

- an understanding of the policy debate taking place within 14–19 education;
- a familiarity with proposed 14–19 curriculum reforms;
- an awareness of the range of 14–19 qualifications;
- an awareness of the new organizational structures being developed for 14–19 education.

The Coalition government is committed to significant reform of the education system for 14–19 year olds; this focus on the 14–19 age range is not new. A number of key policy initiatives illustrate the major changes that have taken place over the past decade. For instance, Curriculum 2000 (QCA 1999c) introduced the first major reform of A level since its inception in 1951 in an attempt to broaden the post-16 curriculum and raise the status of equivalent vocational programmes. This had a significant impact on post-16 teaching and learning strategies in all subject areas with, for example, revised subject content and much greater use of coursework. This change has now been reversed, with the emphasis once again shifting towards terminal examinations, and a consequent reduction in the permitted amount of coursework. In addition, in many cases at both GCSE and A level, coursework has been replaced by controlled assessment.

In September 2002, a range of applied GCSE courses was introduced in eight curriculum areas. Work-related learning has grown in importance and, in recent years, a large number of pupils in Years 10 and 11 have had aspects of the National Curriculum (NC) disapplied to allow them to spend part of their week studying vocational programmes at local further education (FE) colleges. Partly as a consequence of this type of development, different partnerships and collaborations have been developed between schools, colleges and other agencies. Many schools, especially in urban areas, have developed close links with FE colleges to broaden the curriculum available to their pupils across the full range of 14–19 provision. However, changes proposed in the Wolf Report (DfE 2011f) (see below) and formalized in the government's response are likely to have a profound effect on these partnerships, the nature and content of vocational qualifications offered to young people, and the prescription about what types of qualifications will qualify for school league table points.

There is a growing acceptance that the school system should move away from a focus on the age 16, with the completion of GCSEs, as a cut-off point. Instead, 14–19 provision should become more flexible and responsive to individual pupil needs with increased emphasis on personalized learning. A number of alternative, but equal, pathways could then be developed. Diversity of provision was a key feature of previous government policy. Schools specialized in certain areas, such as business and enterprise, sport, languages or technology. Greater diversity could lead to increased use of individualized learning programmes. Pupils could study a variety of programmes in different institutions with different learning outcomes. However, with the introduction of academies, university technical colleges and studio schools, this collaboration, while highly desirable, may diminish with institutions seeking to retain learners in their own establishments. Whatever the future brings, there is no doubt that the pattern of provision for 14–19 education has altered significantly since 2000 and, given the Wolf Report, further change is certain.

As a consequence of this debate and the various policy initiatives implemented by successive governments, 14–19 education and training is likely to remain a contested and shifting terrain. All the major components of the system will be subject to scrutiny and review, including: assessment; qualifications; funding; progression opportunities and routes; patterns of provision; and the organization of schooling itself. As you enter the teaching profession, you need to keep abreast of the broader policy debate taking place within 14–19 education and how this is affecting your subject and your pupils more generally.

Task 19.1

What are the strengths and weaknesses of the existing 14–19 curriculum?

For your subject area, list the changes you would like to see introduced to the 14–19 curriculum.

19.2   14–19: the current policy agenda

The Coalition government has professed a desire to design a 14–19 curriculum and qualifications system that meets the aspirations of all and encourages as many young people as possible to participate in education and training post-16. Compared with our major competitors, the post-16 staying-on rates have continued to lag behind. However, in 2010, 89.9 per cent of 17-year-olds were participating in some form of education or training; the equivalent figure for 18-year-olds was 67.5 per cent (DfE Statistical First Release SFR 15/2011). These figures mask substantial regional variations and do not include the impact of the current economic downturn: young people not in education, employment or training (NEET) approached one million in October 2011. The target for 16–19 participation in education and training has been set at 90 per cent, a figure comparable with the participation rate in the best performing countries, while the target for participation in higher education has been set at 50 per cent.

There are similarly ambitious targets for apprenticeships. The Leitch Report (2006) recommended a target of 500,000 a year by 2020. The current government has affirmed its commitment to apprenticeships as the main route for those not participating full-time in education. They involve a blend of work-based and theoretical learning with off- and on-the-job training elements. Apprentices have employed status and work up to 30 hours a week, with a minimum of 16 hours. The training element must be at least 280 guided learning hours per year. Apprenticeships can be offered at Intermediate (equivalent to five good GCSE passes), Advanced (equivalent to two A level passes) or Higher (NVQ 4) levels.

Taken together, these targets for post-16 participation, in whatever form, place a significant demand upon the system at Key Stage 4 (KS4) to provide a curriculum that is challenging and engaging, and that allows breadth and flexibility of opportunity sufficient to encourage young people to commit themselves to continued learning. The key drivers for reform continue to be the need to build a system that meets the needs of a diverse range of learners, that permits an appropriate choice of courses and qualifications, and that allows for flexibility across and between learning pathways, for example, schools, colleges and workplaces. Central to the vision is the desire to ensure that programmes of learning lead to clear destinations for learners, rather than the current 'snakes and ladders' arrangement whereby learners are often prevented from pursuing different pathways once they have embarked on a particular route.

At the same time, the Coalition government is committed to ensuring that the 'basics' are in place for all young people. Although school standards have improved since the mid-1990s, more than one in six young people leave school without being able to read and write, and add up properly (Leitch 2006). Thus, a target of Level 2 achievements in functional skills (English, mathematics and information and communications technology [ICT]) has been set as part of any learning pathway. The Wolf Report (DfE 2011f) recommends that young people not achieving at least a grade C in GCSE English and mathematics by the age of 16 should be supported in re-taking the examination post-16. There is considerable current debate as to the suitability of GCSEs in English and mathematics as indicators of basic functionality. These subject areas and qualifications are likely to undergo further review. In addition to the emphasis placed on the achievement of basic skills, the so-called 'soft skills', much lauded by employers, have been re-packaged as personal, learning and thinking skills. These include skills aimed at developing 'independent enquirers', 'creative thinkers', 'reflective learners', 'team workers', 'self managers' and 'effective participators'.

Although Curriculum 2000 was intended to broaden the range of academic and vocational qualifications that could be accessed by young people post-16, in reality this has not happened to any significant extent. Young people have tended to take additional qualifications within the same subject group and to continue to pursue a vocational or academic pathway, rather than a mixed diet. In addition, a number of 'perverse incentives' (DfE 2011f) have encouraged schools to enter pupils for large numbers of qualifications, irrespective of their currency in the labour market or for progression opportunities, so that the schools gain performance table points.

Underpinning the whole area of 14–19 reform is the recognition that any change needs to build on secure foundations not just at KS3 but during the primary years: 'the strongest predictor that can be identified of whether someone will drop out of school is the grades achieved at the end of primary school' (Evidence given to the House of Commons Select Committee: Education, Fourth Report, July 2011). The current reform of 14–19 education and training is intended to bring about long-term change throughout the whole system rather than attempt to tackle reforms in a piece-meal fashion.

The development of a 14–19 continuum of learning, rather than a system punc-tuated by a clear end-point at 16, as in the present arrangements, opens up the pos-sibility for increased flexibility in the place, pace and progression of learning. It has been argued that 16 is an arbitrary end-point for many young people. For instance, it might be appropriate for some pupils to skip GCSEs in certain subjects and progress immediately to AS level. Alternatively, significant numbers might benefit from rather more extended programmes that allow them to reach the 'Holy Grail' of five A⋆–C GCSE grades, or their equivalent, in three rather than two years (Huddleston 2002). Many of these pupils choose to continue their studies in FE colleges, often as a result of poor prior learning experiences. The courses that they select are often vocational in orientation.

Task 19.2

Pre-16 students can currently enrol in FE colleges and it is planned to make this option more widely available so that students can access high-quality vocational provision alongside their core KS4 curriculum.

What would you suggest as a minimum broad curriculum entitlement for young people embarking on a vocational qualification at age 14?

Should vocational qualifications be delivered in specialist establishments with industry-standard equipment by vocational experts, or can they be delivered within the context of a large secondary school?

19.3 The qualifications landscape

If you are starting to teach in a large comprehensive school, you might be struck by the range of programmes offered to 14–19 year olds. From your own educational experience, you may be far more familiar with programmes leading to qualifications such as GCSEs and A levels. However, many schools prepare students for qualifica-tions which can be described as general (e.g. GCSE and A levels), those which can be described as vocational or vocationally related (e.g. BTECs, OCR Nationals or Diplomas), and those which contribute to Foundation Learning (e.g. Entry level certificates, Functional Skills at Entry level).

Foundation Learning is the national suite of learning for 14–19 year old learners working predominantly at Entry level or Level 1 who require a more personalized learning programme and who are not yet ready to embark upon full Level 2 qualifications, such as GCSEs.

> Foundation learning is designed for low attaining 14- to 19-year olds (as well as 19- to 24-year olds with high-level special needs). It aims to increase participation, attainment and progression. There is no overarching qualification; young people work on a personalised programme that leads to a mix of small, flexible qualifications, as a basis for progression to further learning or employment. It can be delivered in schools and colleges, or by training providers.
>
> (DfE 2011e)

The sometimes bewildering array of qualifications, their relative status and equivalence has caused wide-scale debate for decades, which has attempted to focus attention on what type of curriculum offering and qualifications should be available for 14–19 year olds within the maintained schools sector. In addition, you should be aware that your school will not be the only institution offering programmes for 14–19 year olds within your locality. There will be other schools, sixth-form colleges, FE colleges, university technical colleges and training providers offering qualifications, or units of qualifications to learners. As a teacher in a secondary school, you may also be sharing the teaching of some of your pupils with colleagues in FE colleges. Your pupils may be spending some of their time each week with you in school and attending a local college for other parts of their programme,

The Raising of the Participation Age (RPA) to 17 by 2013 and to 18 by 2015, legislated in the Learning and Skills Act 2008, and confirmed in the White Paper, 'The Importance of Teaching' (DfE 2010), has brought these issues into sharper focus. The Act requires that all 16–19 year olds should continue to participate in some form of education and training by 2015. This does not mean that young people will be required to remain in full-time education, but it does require that a wide range of part-time education and training options be available to those who are described as not in education, employment or training, as well as those described as in a 'job without training'. At the same time, there is a policy commitment to increase the number of apprenticeships available to 16–19 year olds. In short, it is expected that all 16–19 year olds will be in one of three routes by 2015: full-time education at school or college; on an apprenticeship; or participating in part-time education or training if they are working or volunteering full-time.

The delivery of RPA will require all the actors within the education and training system, described above, to play a part and increasingly for those actors to work together rather than in competition. Ultimately, local authorities will have the responsibility to ensure that all 16–19 year olds have access to education and training opportunities suited to their needs and also the support that they require to enable them to participate. This support is likely to include pre-programme independent advice and guidance, as well as support during any education and training experience to ensure that young people remain on track and progress. Ultimately, the goal is to improve the skills of all young people by ensuring that they have access to qualification routes which provide progression to further education and training, employment or higher education, and which reduce levels of youth unemployment and potential exclusion.

This changing landscape requires a qualification system that is transparent and allows young people and other stakeholders, including employers, to navigate their way through it in order to understand what a particular qualification means in terms of its degree of difficulty, size, level and expected learning outcomes. While it is invidious to compare different types of qualifications, for example practical with academic, the education system has long been in the habit of doing so, and it is inevitable that the practice will continue, at least in the minds of most stakeholders. For this reason, over recent years, a National Qualifications Framework (NQF) has been developed, which has attempted to locate qualifications within a common framework with an indication of equivalences across three pathways: occupational, vocationally related and general (academic). All accredited qualifications are awarded an NQF level. If a qualification shares the same level as another qualification, for example NVQ2 and GCSE A*–C, it means that the demands on learners are roughly equivalent, although the content and duration of the two qualifications may differ. There has been an attempt to bring the majority of qualifications within the NQF, although a significant number, particularly vocational and occupational qualifications, remain outside it. Vocational and occupational qualifications are now being incorporated within a Qualifications and Credit Framework (QCF) (see below); it is the intention that general qualifications, such as GCSEs and A levels, should remain outside this framework.

Figures 19.1 and 19.2 illustrate the way in which the current structure is classified. You should note that at 14–19 the main focus is upon qualifications at Entry to Level 3. Qualifications at Level 4 and above are broadly comparable to those within

Level	Examples of NQF qualifications
Entry	Entry Level certificates
	English for Speakers of Other Languages (ESOL)
	Skills for Life
	Functional Skills at Entry Level (English, maths and ICT)
Level 1	GCSEs grades D–G
	BTEC Introductory Diplomas and Certificates
	OCR Nationals
	Functional Skills at Level 1
Level 2	GCSEs grades A*–C
	Functional Skills at Level 2
Level 3	A levels
	GCE in applied subjects
	International Baccalaureate

Figure 19.1 Examples of the National Qualifications Framework (adapted from and available at: http://ww.direct.goc.uk/en/EducationandLearning/QualificationsExplained)

Level	Examples of QCF qualifications
Entry	Awards, certificates and diplomas at Entry Level Foundation Learning at Entry Level Functional Skills at Entry Level
Level 1	BTEC Awards, Certificates and Diplomas at Level 1 NVQs at Level 1 Foundation Learning Tier pathways Functional Skills at Level 1
Level 2	BTEC Awards, Certificates and Diplomas at Level 2 OCR Nationals NVQs at Level 2
Level 3	BTEC Awards, Certificates and Diplomas at Level 3 BTEC Nationals OCR Nationals NVQs at Level 3

Figure 19.2 Examples of the Qualifications and Credit Framework (adapted from and available at: http://ww.direct.goc.uk/en/EducationandLearning/QualificationsExplained)

the Framework for Higher Education Qualifications (FHEQ), including Higher National Diplomas, undergraduate and postgraduate degrees and professional qualifications. The full Framework covers levels Entry to 7. Examples given above range from Entry level to Level 3, the levels with which you are most likely to have contact in school.

You will probably recognize immediately that attempts to incorporate all qualifications within a rigid framework and to assign equivalences across different pathways is something of a cosmetic exercise. These qualifications are so different in their content, structure and purposes that it is like trying to compare chalk and cheese. Nevertheless, this reform sought at least to ensure that, although qualifications may differ, there would be opportunities to move across and between them.

The current reform of 14–19 provision is considering ways in which vocational pathways and qualifications might be streamlined. A Qualifications and Credit Framework (QCF) (see Figure 19.2) is also under development that will attempt to bring vocational and occupational qualifications within a common framework, thus allowing credits to be built up in small steps, according to the needs of learners. A unit is the smallest element of learning for which credit can be awarded and credits for individual units can be accumulated to provide full qualifications. This will be significant in moving towards the full implementation of RPA, since young people may be unable to gain full qualifications through a single learning episode, but are more likely to be able to build up qualifications over time, unit by unit. Levels illustrated are Entry level to Level 3 although, as in the NQF, the QCF extends to Level 7.

Many young people in full-time education post-16 experience financial hardship, especially since the withdrawal of the education maintenance allowance (EMA) by the Coalition government in 2011, and depend upon income from a steady stream of part-time jobs. The retail, hospitality and catering sectors are highly dependent upon student labour to sustain their operations. Reforms are exploring ways in which this type of informal learning might be recognized within the proposed new structures. Whether or not young people would wish to have this type of experience recorded is another matter. The development of young people's employability skills has become a higher priority for the DfE both as part of the social inclusion agenda for getting young people into training and employment and as part of the drive to higher skills and economic competitiveness (DfES 2002b; Leitch 2006).

Proponents of frameworks, such as those described above, argue that there will be benefits for learners, learning providers and employers in these arrangements in that they will provide, among other things, flexibility, choice, opportunities to vary the pace of learning, and to build increasingly personalized programmes of study to meet individual learner and employer needs. Clearly, the infrastructure required to support the implementation of such a complex system, including unique learner numbers and electronic learner achievement records, is significant, not to mention the professional development needs of those who deliver such programmes.

The picture that emerges of the 14–19 landscape is one that is characterized by a range of provision in terms of qualifications on offer and range of providers. In schools, the provision is dominated by the general route, GCSEs and A levels, although increasingly schools have offered vocationally related options in conjunction with, or separate from, the general route, for example BTECs and A levels, or BTECs in place of GCSE. Foundation learning, at Entry Level and Level 1, accounts for a smaller proportion of learners, but is already well established. Further education colleges predominately offer vocational, or vocationally related, qualifications to this age group, although the total number of A level candidates in colleges exceeds those from schools (taking into account adult learners as well). For training providers, the main scheme on offer is apprenticeships, followed by Foundation Learning and provision, which aims at preparing young people for employment.

A range of factors has influenced this pattern of provision, perhaps most importantly the need for providers to generate qualification outcomes for all young people; after all, these are the metrics by which institutions are judged through performance league tables and ultimately through the funding that they receive. In many cases, this broadening of the curriculum offer has been prompted by Ofsted inspections and by area inspections with the aim of improving the chances of young people to gain a qualification, or at least units towards a qualification, to ensure that the system is inclusive and that all learners can access provision suited to their needs and abilities.

To achieve this, over the past ten years, new partnerships of providers have been established to widen the offer beyond single institutions, so that a young person might spend some time following a vocational programme in a college while accessing the core curriculum in school. In 2002, the Increased Flexibility Programme, for example, made provision for young people to attend college, or a training provider, for up to two days a week in order to follow a vocational programme, with the remaining three days spent in school. Young Apprenticeships, introduced in 2004, enabled 14–16 year olds to access high-quality training, leading to a vocational qualification, within a company or college, coupled with 50 days of work experience, together with their core curriculum entitlement delivered in school.

What emerges from this, albeit brief, overview is a 14–19 landscape characterized by a heterogeneous group of young people, a complex and fragmented system of qualifications delivered by a diverse range of institutions and providers. Perhaps most significantly, it is a landscape dominated by a particular view of the world, a world preoccupied with academic qualifications, with an end point of entry to higher education. Such a world has tended to under-value those qualifications that are not designed for entry to higher education, but could do so, but which are equally important in terms of achieving mass participation to age 19 and which will also contribute to developing the high-level skills much lauded by employers.

19.4   Review of vocational education – The Wolf Review

In 2010, the Coalition government commissioned Professor Alison Wolf to undertake an independent review into vocational education specifically focusing upon:

> . . . how vocational education for 14- to 19-year-olds can be improved in order to promote successful progression into the labour market and into higher level education and training routes . . . to provide practical recommendations to help inform future policy direction, taking into account current financial constraints.
>
> (DfE 2011f: 19)

From earlier sections in this chapter, you will have realized that the provision of high-quality vocational education has been a long-standing challenge for the nation. The Wolf Report suggests that while there is much good-quality provision, there is still work to be done to provide young people with good-quality vocational programmes that lead into the labour market or to further and higher education. Her specific criticisms highlight:

- The lack of high-quality vocational opportunities for 16–17 year olds, which results in young people moving in and out of short-term programmes and employment, described as 'churn', and being unable to either progress or to find suitable employment.
- The large number of low-level vocational qualifications available which do not allow progression and which hold little value in the labour market.
- The low levels of achievement in English and mathematics (the benchmark considered as GCSE A*–C) among this cohort. Wolf reports over 50 per cent of young people failing to achieve both these qualifications by the end of KS4; at 18 years of age the percentage is still below 50 per cent.

The RPA agenda (see above) brings these issues into sharper focus and requires a fundamental re-thinking of what is offered to young people who perforce are required to participate in some form of education or training to age 18. The type of educational experience they have between 14 and 16 will impact upon opportunities post-16; if young people engage in vocationally related programmes pre-16, as many already do, for example through BTECs, OCR Nationals or Diplomas, then these should provide secure foundations for progression. One of the chief concerns raised by Wolf is that too many young people are trapped in routes that do not permit such progression.

Wolf's review concludes with twenty-seven recommendations, all of which have subsequently been accepted by government. These recommendations focus upon a number of 'organizing principles' (DfE 2011f):

- Young people should not be tracked into 'dead end' routes that fail to allow progression either to further education and training at a higher level, or into the labour market.

- The centrality of high-quality independent information, advice and guidance for young people and their parents/carers about what is available and where it might lead.

- The need to simplify the existing system and thus reduce the proliferation of qualifications and awards.

You should look at Wolf's recommendations, and the government's response, in more detail; space does not permit a full discussion of all the recommendations, but some clear messages can be distilled that will have a bearing on your work as a teacher. For example, pupils will no longer be able to build up large numbers of qualifications to achieve a higher points score for the schools' league tables; key indicators must be drawn from a common core curriculum including English and mathematics. Emphasis must be placed upon encouraging those in the lowest quintile of achievement at KS4 to move towards Level 2 qualifications as soon after 16 as practically possible. Those pursuing vocational qualifications full-time post-16 should have the opportunity to access programmes that are broadly based, allow adequate contact time, include rigorous assessment, and include wider learning 'non-qualification' opportunities (often referred to as 'enrichment'). Work experience post-16 is seen as making a positive contribution to young people's learning and preparation for the labour market. Students who have not achieved English and mathematics GCSE A*–C by the age of 16 should be required to include these subjects in any further course that they follow. To this end, continuing professional development (CPD) for teachers of English and mathematics is to be strengthened.

Of particular importance for you, as beginning teachers, is that you may be working with colleagues from outside your school. In future, those teaching within FE colleges will have their qualifications recognized for teaching in schools. This has not been the case previously and while 'qualified teacher status' (QTS) was recognized for teaching in colleges, 'qualified teacher learning and skills' (QTLS) was not recognized for teaching in schools. This change is long overdue since many young people from 14 onwards attend both school and college to follow a particular programme.

The Report also makes recommendations concerning the role of professionals, other than teachers, in the delivery of vocational programmes. It is likely that you will have a view about this, but it is useful to reflect how extending an invitation to a professional business person, scientist, journalist or nurse, for example, might enhance the teaching of your subject.

Task 19.3

Bearing in mind what Wolf has said, and from your own observation in school:

- What do you understand as 'high-quality core education that equips (young people) to progress, whether immediately or later, to a very wide range of further study, training and employment'?
- What should such a core education include?
- At what age should young people decide to specialize?
- What do you understand the difference to be, if any, between taking a qualification and undertaking a programme of study?

The key messages outlined in the DfES (2005) *14–19 Education and Skills White Paper* were designed to:

- place a greater focus on the basics;
- offer learners a better curriculum choice;
- provide learners with more challenging options and activities;
- provide new ways to tackle disengagement.

Compare these aims with those set out in the Wolf Review. How far are they similar and in what ways do they differ?

Why do you think the provision of education and training for the 14–19 age group has proved such a challenge?

What are the barriers to the full implementation of such reforms? What are the drivers for reform?

19.5 Conclusion

As a teacher, you can be certain that the profession you have entered will change rapidly as your career unfolds. This is especially likely for those of you who spend most of your time teaching the 14–19 curriculum.

The drivers for reform are multiple, interrelated and complex. They reflect wider changes at a societal and, increasingly, global level. The reforms are being driven by the twin agendas of high standards and inclusion. These include the economic imperative to develop a highly qualified, skilled and flexible workforce to maintain the country's competitiveness in increasingly global markets, and the need to ensure that opportunities are available for all irrespective of the route they choose to follow. Earlier attempts to reform 14–19 education have resulted in a range of schemes and interventions, the majority of which failed to fulfil their early promise and did not achieve the hoped for parity of esteem between different pathways.

A key obstacle has been a market-, funding- and qualification-led reform process. Another has been a sectoral approach that has separated off various forms of provision, some of them overlapping, including school, FE, higher education and work-based learning. Although current reforms speak of the need for collaboration and cooperation between institutions, providers, government agencies and employers and of the importance of a demand-led approach to provision, without impartial information, advice and guidance, it is difficult for learners to make informed choices. The provision of high-quality information, advice and guidance will be crucial to the successful achievement of the RPA aims. What providers offer their learners will also be influenced by what competitor providers offer. Much remains to be done to put in place the recommendations outlined in the Wolf Report and in the White Paper 'The Importance of Teaching' (DfE 2010). The extent to which a genuine ladder of opportunity is offered to every young person, rather than a series of hurdles to weed people out of education and training, remains to be seen.

19.7 Recommendations for further reading and webliography

Department for Children Schools and Families (2008) *The Education and Skills Act 2008*. London: DCSF.

Department for Education (DfE) (2010) *The Importance of Teaching: The Schools White Paper 2010*, Cm 7980. London: DfE.

Department for Education (DfE) (2011) *Review of Vocational Education* (The Wolf Report), DFE-00031-2011. London: DfE.

Department for Education and Skills (DfES) (2005) *14–19 Education and Skills*. London: DfES.

Websites

http://www.direct.gov.uk/en/EducationAndLearning?QualificationsExplained/DG_10

http://www.1419.lancsngfl.ac.uk/getfile.php?src=1717/What_is_Foundation_Learning.pdf [accessed 11 August 2011]

http://www.excellencegateway.org.uk/media/Foundation%20Learning%20Tier%20Support%20Programme/A_guide_to_Foundation_Learning_DCSF.pdf

SECTION 4

Making schooling work for all: the inclusion agenda

20

Safeguarding and child protection
Chris Hallett

20.1 Introduction

All children deserve the opportunity to achieve their full potential. The Children Act 2004 specified five outcomes that are key to children's and young people's wellbeing:

- be healthy;
- stay safe;
- enjoy and achieve;
- make a positive contribution;
- achieve economic wellbeing.

This chapter deals with the concepts of keeping children safe and child protection within a school setting. The government defines safeguarding and promoting the welfare of children as follows:

- protecting children from maltreatment;
- preventing impairment of children's health or development;
- ensuring children are growing up in circumstances consistent with the provision of safe and effective care.

Child protection is considered part of safeguarding and promoting welfare. It refers to the activity that is undertaken to protect specific children who are suffering, or are likely to suffer, significant harm. Effective child protection is essential as part of wider work to safeguard and promote the welfare of children (DfE 2011c).

By the end of this chapter, you should understand:

- the context of safeguarding and child protection as important elements of schools' work;

- the regulatory framework and guidance relating to child protection and the obligations placed on schools;
- typical approaches to dealing with child protection in schools;
- the implications for teachers and student teachers in dealing with child protection cases.

20.2 Context

All teachers have a key role in child protection; they are the members of staff who spend most time with young people aside from their parents, families and carers. Teachers are able to observe young people over time and can identify changes in behaviour and appearance. They are also in a position to build up a trusting relationship with a young person, which should enable that young person to turn to them and share any worries or anxieties they might have about their care.

Schools also contribute via the curriculum by developing young people's awareness and resilience to keep themselves safe from harm through the framework for Personal, Social, Health and Economic Education (PSHEE) and the Healthy Schools Programme. These help young people to consider and manage risks.

Safeguarding and promoting the welfare of young people, and in particular protecting them from significant harm, depend on effective joint working between agencies and professionals who have different roles and expertise. Children who are most vulnerable, such as those in local authority care and those with special educational needs, are also at greater risk of harm and social exclusion and are in particular need of an effective, coordinated approach. The Department for Children, Schools and Families (now the Department for Education) published a key document in 2010 entitled *Working Together to Safeguard Children*. This document recommends that children in schools should be taught to:

- recognize and manage risks in different situations and then decide how to behave responsibly;
- judge what kind of physical contact is acceptable and unacceptable;
- recognize when pressure from others (including people they know) threatens their personal safety and wellbeing;
- develop effective ways to resist this pressure.

Safeguarding and promoting the welfare of young people require effective coordination. The Children Act 2004 required each local authority to establish a Local Safeguarding Children Board (LSCB). The LSCB is the key statutory mechanism for agreeing how the relevant organizations in a particular area will cooperate to safeguard and promote the welfare of young people in that locality and for ensuring the effectiveness of what they do. The schools working within a LSCB area are key in reporting child protection concerns for investigation. Teachers within schools have a key role in contributing information, knowledge and expertise within such an investigation and the assessment of potential abuse.

Working Together to Safeguard Children (DCSF 2010b) also sets out the remit of abuse and neglect that requires child protection, stating that abuse and neglect are forms of maltreatment of a young person. It identifies four categories of abuse that require child protection:

- physical abuse;
- emotional abuse;
- sexual abuse;
- and neglect.

It defines the content of these forms of child abuse as follows.

Physical abuse

Physical abuse may involve hitting, shaking, throwing, poisoning, scalding, burning, drowning, suffocating, or any other action that could cause harm to a young person. Physical harm may also be caused when a parent or carer fabricates symptoms or deliberately induces illness in a young person.

Emotional abuse

Emotional abuse is the persistent emotional maltreatment of a young person such as to cause severe or persistent adverse effects on the child's emotional development. Some level of emotional abuse is involved in all types of maltreatment of a young person, although it can occur in isolation. It can involve conveying to a young person that they are unloved or worthless, not valued, excessively ridiculed, denied opportunities to have a view or opinion to the extent that it prevents the young person from participating in normal social interaction. It could also involve witnessing or hearing the ill-treatment of another person, such as domestic abuse in the household. It can involve serious bullying, including cyberbullying, causing young people to feel frightened or in danger. It can also cover circumstances when young people are being exploited or corrupted into engaging in inappropriate actions with other people.

Sexual abuse

Sexual abuse involves forcing or enticing young people to take part in sexual activities whether or not the young person is aware of what is happening. The activities may involve inappropriate physical contact, assault by penetration such as rape or oral sex or non-penetrative acts such as masturbation, kissing, rubbing and touching the outside of clothing. It can also include non-contact activities such as involving young people in the production of sexual images, watching sexual activities, grooming a young person in preparation for abuse (including via the internet), or encouraging young people to behave in sexually inappropriate ways. It should be noted that both males and females can commit acts of sexual abuse, as can children on other children.

Neglect

Neglect is the persistent failure to meet a young person's physical and/or psychological needs, which is likely to result in the young person's health or development being impaired. Neglect can involve a parent or carer failing to provide adequate food, clothing and shelter (such as excluding the young person from home or abandoning them). It can involve failing to protect the young person from physical and emotional harm or danger. It also covers the need for parents to provide adequate care and supervision of the young person. Finally, parents have to ensure that the young person has access to appropriate medical care or treatment.

20.3 Regulatory framework for child protection in schools

Working Together to Safeguard Children (DCSF 2010b) states: 'Schools (including independent and non-maintained schools) and further education institutes have a duty to safeguard and promote the welfare of pupils under the Education Act 2002. They should create and maintain a safe learning environment for children and young people, and identify where there are child welfare concerns and take action to address them, in partnership with other organisations where appropriate'. Section 175 of the Education Act 2002 places this duty on schools – it is not a discretionary responsibility for schools. The Children Act 2004 (Sections 10 and 11) re-enforces this duty for schools and other statutory agencies by requiring local authorities to make arrangements to promote cooperation between partners in ensuring that children and young people are protected from harm and neglect. These obligations are facilitated thought local Children Trust arrangements but specifically in relation to child protection through the LSCB.

As mentioned above, the LSCB is the key statutory mechanism for agreeing how the relevant organizations in each local area will cooperate to safeguard and promote the welfare of young people in that locality, and for ensuring the effectiveness of what they do. The responsibilities of the LSCB include policies and procedures for dealing with child protection, including the thresholds for intervention and assessment on a robust multi-agency basis. Section 47 of the Children Act 1989 places a duty on the local authority children's services department to investigate any child's circumstances where it is determined that a child who lives, or is found, in their area, is suffering, or is likely to suffer, significant harm.

All statutory agencies working with children, including schools, have a duty to cooperate and share information in relation to child protection investigations. LSCBs must take all reasonable steps to ensure that schools are represented in their work. It would clearly be impractical for every school to attend the LSCB, so a robust and fair system of representation needs to be identified to enable each school to receive information and be in a position to carry out its obligations through the policies and procedures of the LSCB. Some LSCBs organize this responsibility through a sub-committee for representatives from schools to meet and be informed and involved in the work of the LSCB. LSCBs also organize multi-agency training and development courses for teachers and other educational staff to build up their knowledge base on child protection.

20.4 Approaches to dealing with child protection in schools

Schools are key to promoting the wellbeing of young people. Teachers spend so much time with young people, getting to know them intimately, that they are well-placed to notice if young people are showing signs that something is wrong. The bonds that develop between pupils and teachers mean that young people may choose to confide in a teacher when they have any concerns. Schools are thus in a position to help protect young people. Schools are no longer simply places of learning and are now expected to be able to respond to young people's emotional, physical and social needs as well as their academic needs. With an increased awareness of safeguarding and child protection, schools have become a valued resource and support within the safeguarding partnership with other agencies in a locality.

There is a range of ways that schools ensure that young people are safeguarded. The *Every Child Matters* agenda (DfES 2003e) emphasized all aspects of prevention and early intervention associated with protecting young people and, in addition, schools have many policies and procedures in place supporting young people with additional needs such as health and safety, positive handling and the common assessment framework (CAF). The CAF is a national framework and advice can be sought on how to instigate it through the local authority CAF coordinator. The advantage of a CAF is that it can mobilize help and support at an early stage and prevent a situation from escalating to a child protection investigation.

Child protection procedures are implemented in higher risk cases and to protect these young people, all schools should have a written child protection policy drawn from the LSCB guidance. Each school also designates a senior member of staff to respond to child protection concerns. This post often carries the title-designated teacher for child protection or designated child protection officer. This person will have received additional training in child protection and will be fully aware of local procedures should an incident be identified within the school. Their training should be updated at least every two years. Schools also implement safer recruitment procedures, which set out how allegations against any member of staff will be addressed.

A school's child protection policy and procedures for handling suspected cases of abuse of young people should outline how to:

- recognize different types of abuse;
- record concerns promptly, confidentially and securely – separate from the main pupil file;
- report concerns to the designated teacher for child protection;
- cooperate fully with other agencies and participate in child protection processes;
- report any unexplained absence of a young person subject to a child protection plan to social workers;
- refer to allegations policy;
- demonstrate a commitment to safer recruitment.

School governors and governing bodies also have responsibility for ensuring a school has an effective policy and procedures. A governor should be appointed to lead on child protection and should be able to provide advice and support. This governor should have received additional training to enable them to carry out this task effectively. However, the designated teacher for child protection should be the first point of contact for a teacher who has identified any concerns of potential or actual abuse of a young person.

The designated teacher is responsible for:

- making decisions about what action needs to take place;
- consulting with other agencies;
- making a child protection referral to children's social care;
- supporting other teachers in attending meetings concerned with the child protection process;
- sharing information appropriately and seeking support if necessary;
- monitoring staff training in the school on child protection;
- ensuring that teachers are appropriately trained and prepared in child protection to their level of responsibility and ensuring their training is regularly updated;
- keeping child protection policies in the school up to date;
- liaising with the head teacher to inform them of any issues and ongoing investigations within the school;
- ensuring that there is always adequate cover for this role in their absence.

20.4 Implications for teachers and student teachers

All staff, including non-teaching staff, should receive basic training in child protection and know how to report concerns to the designated teacher for child protection. It is essential that teachers take action where they have concerns about the welfare of a young person. Their first duty must be to the safety of the young person. The young person might disclose for the first time to a teacher that he or she is being abused physically, sexually or emotionally. In addition, a teacher might have observed that a young person is being neglected and there has been a failure on the part of a parent or carer to protect them. At this stage it is important that the teacher is aware of the limits of their role and the importance of following agreed procedures, as set out by their LSCB and the school's child protection policy. They should listen to the pupil carefully, provide support and record immediately what has been related to them. It is important to avoid leading questions that put words into the child's mouth or make assumptions about what may have taken place. Although it is not appropriate to question the child, as this is the role of social workers and the police, the teacher may ask a few open questions to clarify what is being said and to be able to make an informed referral to the local authority children's service office. It is important to stress that teachers do not themselves investigate cases of suspected abuse. Investigations are undertaken via multi-agency child protection systems with the police and social workers normally taking the lead. However, teachers have a clear role in contributing information and advice to this process.

Teachers should never promise a pupil confidentiality, as it needs to be explained that information will have to be passed on to other professionals to ensure that the child, plus other children possibly, remains safe from harm. If a young person is pouring out an account of abuse, it is not appropriate to stop them. Instead, teachers should listen carefully and record in detail what has been said. The teacher needs to know just enough to be able to make a referral against the threshold of 'reasonable cause to suspect actual or likely significant harm' (Section 47 of the Children Act 1989). At this stage, the teacher would need to consult with the designated teacher for child protection in the school who will be aware of the guidance for making referrals under child protection procedures.

Teachers do not need parental consent to make a child protection referral to children's services or the police. If there are sufficient grounds to suspect that a young person has suffered abuse, or is likely to suffer significant harm, a decision about when and what to tell the parents or carer will become part of the multi-agency child protection investigation decision-making process. The rationale for this is that to inform parents could expose the young person to further risk or affect the evidence-gathering process. A decision on how and who is to inform the parents is part of the strategy discussion or meeting with other agencies.

Following a referral, the teacher will be an important contributor to the multi-agency child protection investigation. Schools have a statutory duty to assist the local authority in carrying out its function under Section 47 of the Children Act 1989. Before any investigation, a strategy discussion or meeting is convened to plan the next steps to be taken to keep the young person safe from harm. The teacher will have valuable information to share on any disclosure as well as knowledge about the young person's development, school attainments, any learning difficulties, school attendance, punctuality, any significant changes in behaviour and knowledge of family and peer relationships. In addition, teachers have an important contribution to make based on their professional and specialist expertise in assisting in the analysis of information. It is important that teachers feel confident to question other professionals' contributions and enter into the debate regarding any plan of intervention for keeping a young person safe. Agencies are required to share information to ensure that children and young people are protected and do not suffer significant harm.

The strategy meeting or discussion will formulate a plan of intervention to investigate any child protection concerns. The investigation of these concerns could lead to a child protection conference. The child protection conference will determine the category for any child abuse and whether there is a need for a formal child protection plan for the young person and how this will be enacted. The teacher would be expected to present a report to the conference, contribute to the discussion and be part of the decision-making process. Any child protection plan for a young person is conducted through the activities of a core group of professionals and it is normal practice for a teacher to be part of this group. Periodically, the core group is required to report progress to a reconvened child protection conference to review the effectiveness of the child protection plan.

Task 20.1

The scenarios below depict the four categories of child protection: physical abuse, emotional abuse, sexual abuse, and neglect.

Based on your reading of this chapter, decide how you would respond to each scenario. Then check your responses against the probable route that the teacher involved in the investigation would follow, given below.

Scenario 1: Physical abuse
Andrew is a Year 8 pupil and his form tutor notices at registration that he has bruising around his left eye. The tutor asks him casually what has happened and he explains that he banged himself against a cupboard door the previous night. The tutor then notices that tears start to build up in Andrew's eyes and he looks away. Andrew is an outgoing and confident young man who will normally hold his tutor's gaze in any conversation. The tutor further enquires if he is okay and Andrew bursts into tears. The tutor finds a quiet area to sit with Andrew to learn more of the story.

Andrew starts to disclose that the previous evening he had a row with his father who went into a rage and lashed out at him, hitting his left eye. The teacher then enquires if he has any other injuries and Andrew shows the teacher some finger bruising to both arms where he was restrained.

Scenario 2: Emotional abuse
Emily is a Year 9 pupil who is quiet and shy at school. Recently teachers have noticed that she has become more withdrawn from school activities and her self-esteem is giving concern. She lives at home with her mother and stepfather. There is not a great deal of contact between the school and Emily's parents but, on those occasions when there has been contact, Emily's mother was derogatory about Emily's abilities and efforts to achieve better grades. The form teacher is completing a number of one-to-one meetings with pupils in her form and decides to check how Emily is feeling as well as mentioning concerns that she appears to be increasingly isolated in school.

At the one-to-one meeting, Emily starts to share her home circumstances. She relates that she is often sent to her bedroom for long periods and her mum shows little interest in her. She cannot remember the last time her mum praised her or gave her a hug. She also describes incidents of domestic violence between her mum and stepfather that she has overheard while in her bedroom. There have been occasions when she was frightened because of the shouting and banging she could hear from downstairs. However, Emily tells the teacher that she does not want anyone to do anything about home, as her mum would be very angry if she knew that Emily had shared what was going on with a teacher.

Scenario 3: Sexual abuse

Rashpal is a Year 10 pupil and is nearly 15 years old. She is outgoing, academically able and popular with her peers. One day at school a girlfriend of Rashpal approaches a teacher to say that she thinks someone should talk to Rashpal, as she is distressed and says she can't go home at the end of the day. The teacher arranges to see Rashpal in a confidential setting to find out if there is a problem.

Rashpal is very tearful and starts to disclose that the previous evening her uncle, who is staying with the family, walked into her bedroom and made suggestive remarks to her of a sexual nature. Rashpal states that he appeared to have been consuming alcohol and was slightly drunk. He had groped her breasts over her clothes until she had managed to push him away and run out of the bedroom to find her mother. She told her mother what had happened but her mother downplayed the incident, saying that her brother would never do such a thing and Rashpal was probably exaggerating but she would speak to him. Later in the evening Rashpal's mum told her she had spoken to her brother who denied the incident but said that Rashpal had brushed against him provocatively. As far as Rashpal's mum was concerned, this was an end to the matter. Rashpal was upset that her mother had not believed her version of events.

Scenario 4: Neglect

John, aged 11, has just started secondary school. During the first term in Year 7 teachers became concerned about him. Several times he has arrived at school hungry and unkempt. Teachers have noticed that at lunchtime he gobbles his food but still seems hungry. He is a small, thin boy with a pale complexion. He has explained to a teacher that he often misses breakfast when he oversleeps and has to rush to get to school on time. He says that he often has to get himself up and off to school, as his mum and dad often sleep in until late morning. He also explained that he has to help his younger brothers aged 7 and 9 to get ready for school as well. He says money is tight at home and his mum often shops on a daily basis to buy food for the day.

Scenario 1: Action taken by the teacher

The teacher will need to make a referral to children's social care, as clearly a physical assault has taken place involving some force by the parent. The teacher should speak to the designated teacher for child protection in the school to share the information and decide on the process to alert the local children's social care office. It is also important for the teacher to make some notes on the conversation that has taken place with Andrew as soon as possible. Andrew will need to have a medical examination because of the bruising. Unless it is considered that there is an urgent need for medical attention, it can be organized during the investigation process coordinated by the social worker. The advice of the school nurse, if available, could be sought. Once a referral has been made to children's social care, the teacher will be involved in any strategy discussions with the social worker and the information recorded on the incident will form an important part of the strategy drawn up. The strategy discussion will decide a plan for the investigation of the incident and it could progress to calling an initial child protection conference to which the teacher would be invited. The police will be involved in the process and may well wish to take a statement from the teacher that could be used in any court case.

In such cases, teachers need to be supported themselves, either by the designated teacher for child protection or a peer/colleague, as it can be a stressful and traumatic experience for them to relay the information disclosed by a child.

Scenario 2: Action taken by the teacher
It is always difficult for a teacher who receives information from a pupil in confidence. The teacher will not wish to breach the relationship of trust with the pupil. However, a teacher has to balance the need to maintain confidences with their statutory responsibility to ensure that a young person is not placed in a harmful situation. In this instance, there is growing evidence that Emily could be suffering emotional abuse and the evidence suggests that other teachers are noticing her becoming withdrawn and lacking confidence. Thus, maintaining confidentiality must always be balanced against the requirement to keep young people safe. In this case, the teacher should make a written record, as soon as possible, of the information disclosed to her by Emily as well as sharing the content of the discussion with Emily with the designated teacher for child protection. It is likely that the outcome from this discussion will be the need to investigate the situation further and, since domestic violence is occurring in the household as well, contact with the local children's social care office would be applicable. At a later stage, the teacher would need to explain to Emily that there is a duty on teachers to report any concerns they might have that a child is at risk of harm and this obligation overrides the issue of confidentiality.

Scenario 3: Action taken by the teacher
The incident needs to be investigated, so the teacher needs to discuss how to progress the matter with the designated teacher for child protection. The teacher should make a written record, as soon as possible, of the information disclosed to her by Rashpal. The incident should be reported to the local children's social care office, which will arrange a strategy discussion or meeting involving the police and the school to determine a plan on how to manage the disclosure and progress an investigation. It is likely that the social worker and police, after interviewing Rashpal, would make a home visit to gather information and assess any evidence.

Scenario 4: Action taken by the teacher
Clearly, concerns are starting to emerge about the functioning of the family. The school may need to make further enquiries, possibly at the primary school, to ascertain if this type of problem has occurred in that setting. When there are concerns emerging that do not necessarily require an immediate response, the teacher and the school could consider using the CAF to instigate a gathering together of information. In this situation, there are signs that John is being neglected and if, on gathering information from the primary school, it emerges that this has been happening for some time, a referral to the local children's social care office would be applicable to investigate the situation under child protection procedures. Similar to other kinds of suspected abuse, the start of an investigation would be a strategy discussion or meeting to plan the investigation across the different agencies. Again, input from the teacher of the observations and information obtained from John would be crucial for the strategic plan of intervention.

Task 20.2

A child wishes to confide in you but insists that you promise not to tell anyone what they are about to disclose. Consider how you would respond to such a request in ways that enable the child to share their concerns but avoids you making a promise of confidentiality that you are unable to keep.

Task 20.3

Prompts and open questions are important to clarify what has happened without leading a young person. Here are a few examples of prompts/open questions:

- Explain to me what is worrying you (or what is worrying you?)
- Tell me what happened (or what happened?)
- Describe how that happened (or how did that happen?)

Suggest other questions that could be useful in dealing with a child protection disclosure.

20.6 Recommendations for further reading

Davies, J., Ryan, J., Tarr, J., Last, K., Kushner, S. and Rose, R. (2009) *Preparing Teachers for Management and Leadership of Multi-agency Assessment of Vulnerability: Building Capacity in ITT, TDA. Project Report.* Bristol: Teacher Development Agency. Available at: http://eprints.uwe.ac.uk/12563/ (Appendix A contains a useful list of children's services occupational roles and responsibilities.)

Department for Children, Schools and Families (DCSF) (2010) *Working Together to Safeguard Children.* Nottingham: DCSF. Available at: www.dcsf.gov.uk/publications

Department for Education and Skills (DfES) (2003) *Every Child Matters.* London: DfES. Available online at: www.everychildmatters.gov.uk/publications

21

Special educational needs and inclusive schooling

Jan Warner

21.1 Introduction

> Under the 1944 Education Act, children with special educational needs . . . were considered to be 'uneducable' and pupils were labelled into categories such as 'maladjusted' or 'educationally sub-normal' and given 'special educational treatment' in special schools.
>
> (House of Commons Education and Skills Committee 2006: para. 1)

It is no longer regarded as good practice for children with special educational needs (SEN) to be treated as 'different' from their peers and educated in separate schools. Pupils with SEN are now included in mainstream schools wherever possible and taught in classes alongside others in their age group.

By the end of this chapter, you should be able to:

- track the evolution of the main principles and concepts informing SEN provision over time;
- understand how these principles are put into practice including the key roles of the special education needs coordinator (SENCo) and support staff in a SEN department in a mainstream school;
- identify the key issues and challenges raised by past practice and possible future directions.

At the time of writing, policy on provision for pupils with SEN is subject to consultation. This chapter will therefore focus on identifying key issues arising from past policy and practice and likely future directions for SEN provision.

21.2 Principles and concepts in SEN

The term 'special educational needs' was introduced by the Warnock Report (DES 1978). This report, followed by the 1981 Education Act, radically altered the conceptualization of special education by emphasizing that a child's educational needs should be prioritized – not their disability or impairment.

> To describe someone as handicapped conveys nothing of the type of educational help, and hence provision that is required. We wish to see a more positive approach, and we have adopted the concept of special educational needs, seen not in terms of a particular disability that a child may be deemed to have, but in relation to everything about him, his abilities and his disabilities – indeed all the factors which may impinge on his educational progress.
>
> (DES 1978: 37)

Thus a 'whole-school approach' to SEN was born. The needs of pupils with SEN became the responsibility of all teachers and a graduated response to identified SEN was enshrined in the SEN Code of Practice (DfES 2001b). This provided a framework for SEN policy, practice and provision based on principles that included recognition of a continuum of needs and provision, full access to the National Curriculum, and giving SEN pupils access to mainstream provision where practical.

Government reports and other recent research reports on SEN and inclusion

There has been a plethora of reports on SEN and inclusion, particularly in the last ten years. The majority of these seek to clarify the definitions of SEN and inclusion, as well as reviewing and reflecting upon whether the government's SEN framework and inclusion policy are actually working. This section considers major issues that have been highlighted by recent research and reports, the impact these have had on practice and what the latest green paper (DfE 2011a) says about how these issues might be dealt with in the future.

A recent report stated that: 'Effective teaching for children with SEN shares most of the characteristics of effective teaching for *all* children. But as schools become more inclusive, so teachers must be able to respond to a wider range of needs in the classroom' (DfES 2004g: para. 3.2). It continued: 'We will work collaboratively with the national strategies . . . to further develop the knowledge base and capacity of schools to improve the quality of teaching and learning of children with SEN' (para. 3.7). This encouraged schools to incorporate issues associated with SEN and inclusion within their management of 'whole-school' initiatives rather than viewing them as the exclusive domain of the SEN department. The national strategies Inclusion Development Programme (IDP), launched in 2008, continued to emphasize a generic strengthening of teaching and learning, rather than focusing exclusively on specialist approaches. Nevertheless, the IDP's information on removing barriers to learning does identify specific strategies relevant to each particular type of SEN.

The IDP was designed to increase the confidence and expertise of teachers in mainstream schools in meeting high-incidence SEN. The programme offers web-based materials that include: teaching and learning resources; practical continuing professional development (CPD) activities; guidance on effective classroom strategies; models of good practice; and information about sources of more specialist advice. It was an important milestone in recognizing that all teachers, including those new to the role, need to be better prepared to teach SEN pupils. These materials can be found in the National Archives (at http://webarchive.nationalarchives.gov. uk/20110202093118/ and http://nationalstrategies.standards.dcsf.gov.uk/search/ inclusion/results/nav:46335).

Two other recent government initiatives that influenced approaches to teaching and learning in relation to pupils with SEN were the National Strategy directives concerning personalized learning (see Chapter 6) and assessment for learning (see Chapter 9). These have reinforced a 'whole-school' approach to meeting the needs of all children, including those with SEN. For pupils with SEN in particular, this has entailed a move away from the use of individual education plans (IEPs) on the grounds that schools which had introduced a robust provision-mapping system that entailed individual pupil target setting, planning, tracking and recording as well as reviewing progress and outcomes for *all* pupils, were unlikely to need IEPs for pupils with SEN.

One other report that needs to be considered in relation to SEN and inclusion is *Breaking the Link Between Special Educational Needs and Low Attainment: Everyone's Business* (DCSF 2010a). This report asserts that: 'Good progress, attainment and high aspirations for children with SEN can be found in *any setting*. Inclusion is not about a place, but about how a child with SEN is helped to learn and take part in school life' (DSCF 2010a: para. 3.15). The evidence for this claim is Ofsted's (2006b) observation that the most important factor in determining outcomes for pupils with learning difficulties and disabilities is not the type but the quality of provision. 'The best practice in schools indicates that when personalised learning is part of the culture of a whole school approach to curriculum development, the systems for assessing, planning and teaching match the needs of all pupils, reducing the need to define children according to category of need' (DSCF 2010c: para. 3.15). The report emphasizes a 'whole-school approach to curriculum development' as the means by which schools can best provide for pupils with SEN, alongside all other pupils, thereby diminishing the need for categorization by SEN. It also emphasizes the need for high expectations to close the attainment gap for all low-achieving pupils. 'In short, the identification of SEN should be seen as a challenge to all concerned – to put in the extra resources and effort so that even the minority of pupils maintain **good** progress relative to their starting point – and not as a justification for assuming and accepting **slow** progress' (DSCF 2010a: para. 3.4). Thus, SEN and inclusion have been increasingly subsumed into a concern for the progress of all pupils rather than being narrowly defined as involving specialist provision and extra resources. The Green Paper (DfE 2011a) states the case for change as follows:

- Every child deserves a fair start in life, with the very best opportunity to succeed. Currently life chances for … children and young people in England who are identified as having SEN, or who are disabled, are disproportionately poor.

- Disabled children and children with SEN tell us that they can feel frustrated by a lack of help at school or from other services … Parents say that the system is bureaucratic, bewildering and adversarial and that it does not sufficiently reflect the needs of their child and their family life.

- Children's support needs can be identified late; families are made to put up with a culture of low expectations about what their child can achieve at school; and parents have limited choices about the best schools and care for their child.

(DfE 2011a: 4)

The issues raised above will be explored in terms of their background and past history and the plans for the future that might lead to change.

The practice of assessing children to determine whether their needs justify the issuing of a statement of SEN leading to the provision of additional funding to provide extra resources has been the subject of severe criticism. Concerns include a lack of clarity in the criteria used to determine which children received a statement, inequalities in the provision available across local authorities, and a slow and overly bureaucratic statementing system (Warnock 2005). Warnock called for a review of the statementing system and the inclusion framework, arguing that the meaning of inclusion was unclear. She considered that the concept of inclusion was more about 'hearts in the right place', and children being involved in a common enterprise of learning, rather than necessarily being under the same roof. She urged the government to consider creating smaller specialist schools that could cater for children with specific disabilities who might not be able to function in larger schools. The Green Paper (DfE 2011a) reflects these on-going concerns, proposing to replace the statementing system with a less bureaucratic and more holistic plan encompassing education, health and care needs.

Where pupils with SEN should be taught is also a matter of ongoing debate (e.g. House of Commons Education and Skills Committee 2006). Ofsted (2006c) examined the factors that promote good outcomes across a range of different provision for pupils with learning difficulties and disabilities (LDD). It identified the most successful provision as being in additionally resourced mainstream schools where pupils with LDD had the benefit of carefully planned mainstream lessons and small group teaching. The key factors identified by Ofsted for ensuring good progress of pupils with LDD were: involvement of a specialist teacher; good assessment; work tailored to challenge LDD sufficiently; and a commitment from school leaders to ensure good progress for all pupils. These factors are also identified in the latest Green Paper (DfE 2011a), where the recommendations include tackling the underachievement of pupils with SEN and the involvement of specialist teachers wherever possible. The Green Paper also promotes the view that schooling for pupils with SEN should be flexible in order to meet a variety of needs and not always in a mainstream setting.

Another recurring theme concerns the need for systematic, high-quality SEN training for students as part of initial training and for practising teachers as part of CPD (House of Commons Education and Skills Committee 2006). One extensive research study (Ellis *et al.* 2008) found that teachers have real concerns about the practicalities of inclusion and that their attitudes and values are crucial to the success of inclusion in mainstream schools. It recommended that training to meet the needs of SEN pupils must be more substantial and reflective for teachers, and build their confidence, competence and preparedness for classroom experiences. The latest Green Paper also identifies the need for sufficient training for teachers so that pupils with SEN are identified early and that teachers feel confident in teaching these pupils and are able to challenge them sufficiently.

A final concern about the operation of the system was that pupils with SEN made up the majority of those excluded, expelled or suspended from school, as well as those with unauthorized or persistent absences from school (Leslie and Skidmore 2007). These findings were seen as evidence that children's needs were not being met and that the government's inclusion policy was not working. This highlights concerns about the number of children with SEN placed in inappropriate schools (i.e. those retained in mainstream schools), who would formerly have gone to special schools, and who experience personal isolation and social exclusion as a result. The report indicates that systematic reform must encompass a spectrum of provision to meet a spectrum of needs. The latest Green Paper also emphasizes that inclusion is not just teaching all pupils with SEN in mainstream schools and recommends that a variety of schools should be made available for these pupils.

Thus, it can be seen that the major issues raised by reports commissioned by the previous government are now the concern of the present coalition. The final section of this chapter considers the direction this government intends to take in relation to SEN and inclusion.

Special Educational Needs Code of Practice

The SEN Code of Practice (DfES 2001b) defines SEN as: 'difficulties and/or disabilities in children that are significantly greater than in the majority of their peers, that prevent or hinder them from making use of education facilities of a kind generally provided for children in schools, and that require special educational provision to be made for them'. The Code also acknowledges that children and young people with SEN make progress at different rates and have different ways they learn best. However, it must not be assumed that children who are making slower progress or experiencing difficulties in one area necessarily have a special educational need. Furthermore, Section 7.52 of the Code provides practical advice to local authorities and maintained schools on how to identify, assess and make provision for children's SEN. It recognizes that there are no hard and fast categories of SEN and that there is a wide spectrum of needs that are frequently interrelated. The Code does however indicate that a child's needs and requirements may fall into at least one of four areas:

- communication and interaction;
- cognition and learning;
- behavioural, emotional and social development;
- sensory and/or physical.

The Code sets out guidance on policies and procedures aimed at enabling children and young people with SEN to reach their full potential, to be fully included in their school's community and to make a successful transition through to adulthood.

The fundamental principles of the SEN Code of Practice are:

- Children with SEN should have their needs met.
- The SEN of children will normally be met in mainstream schools.
- The views of the child should be sought and taken into account.
- Parents have a vital role to play in supporting their child's education.
- Children with SEN should be offered full access to a broad, balanced and relevant education, including the National Curriculum.

The Code of Practice emphasizes that provision for pupils with SEN is the responsibility of every teacher. In practice, this means that they should:

- identify and reduce the barriers to pupils' learning and participation;
- differentiate the curriculum to provide maximum access;
- follow the guidance of the National Curriculum (as it stands at the present time) for including pupils with SEN;
- discuss the progress of pupils with SEN with the SENCo and other colleagues working with the same pupil, including external practitioners;
- ensure teacher planning clarifies the deployment and role of additional adults such as teaching assistants;
- ensure that personalized learning approaches meet the needs of pupils with SEN;
- monitor the progress of the pupils with SEN whom they teach;
- measure the progress of pupils with SEN at the end of a Key Stage or academic year against National Curriculum levels;
- work in partnership with the parents/carers of pupils with SEN, keeping them informed about their child's progress.

At present, the SEN Code of Practice adopts a graduated response to meeting the needs of pupils with SEN, which includes the following stages: School Action; School Action Plus; and, following a successful statutory assessment outcome, a Statement of SEN. These stages concern provision and interventions that are *additional to* or *different from* those provided as part of the school's usual differentiated curriculum offer and differentiated learning opportunities. This means that whatever is provided is above and beyond what the school does to personalize learning for all pupils, set individual learning targets and ensure that all teaching takes into account that all pupils learn in different ways. The latest Green Paper recommends that these stages are removed and that responses are no longer graduated. A Statement of Special Educational Needs is to be replaced by a combined education, health and care plan.

Inclusion for all pupils is based upon the following principles (expanded in Figure 21.1):

- to set suitable learning challenges;
- to respond to pupils' diverse learning needs;

Setting suitable learning challenges	Responding to pupils' diverse learning needs	Overcoming potential barriers to learning and assessment
Teachers should:	Teachers should:	Teachers should:
• give every learner the opportunity to experience success in learning and achieve as high a standard as possible • teach the knowledge, skills, and understanding in ways that match and suit pupils' different abilities • adopt a flexible approach to take account of any gaps in pupils' learning	• create effective learning environments • secure pupils' motivation and concentration • provide equality of opportunity through teaching approaches • use appropriate assessment techniques • set appropriate targets for learning	• support pupils to enable them to participate effectively in curriculum and assessment activities • plan the curriculum and assessment for pupils with SEN by taking account of the type and extent of the difficulty and disability experienced by the pupil

Figure 21.1 Inclusion principles in practice (from Cheminais 2010: 17)

- to overcome potential barriers to learning and assessment for individuals and groups of pupils.

Code of Practice for Schools – Disability Discrimination Act 1995 (Part IV)

The Disability Discrimination Act (DDA) (Part IV), as amended by the Special Educational Needs and Disability Act (SENDA) 2001, Code of Practice for Schools, which became effective in September 2002, set out new duties that local authorities, maintained and independent schools must follow. These duties are as follows:

1. not to discriminate against disabled children and prospective pupils in admissions, exclusions, education and associated services which include:
    - preparation for entry to school and preparation for moving on to the next phase of education;
    - the curriculum, homework, timetabling and activities to supplement the curriculum;
    - teaching and learning, classroom organisation, grouping of pupils, assessment and examination arrangements, interaction with peers;
    - school policies, access to school facilities, breaks and lunchtimes, the serving of school meals, the school's arrangements for working with other agencies;
    - school discipline and sanctions, exclusion procedures;
    - school clubs and activities, school sports, school trips;

2. not to treat disabled children less favourably, without justification, for a reason which relates to their disability or impairment.
3. to take reasonable steps and make reasonable adjustments to policies, practice and procedures in order to ensure that children and young people with disabilities are not placed at a substantial disadvantage compared to other children/young people who are not disabled.
4. to plan strategically for, and make progress in, improving the physical environment of schools for children with disabilities, increasing their participation in the curriculum and improving the ways in which written information is provided to children, young people and adults with disabilities, in a range of formats, such as Braille, large print type formats, on audio tape, using signing and symbols to convey information.

21.3 The SEN department

The role of the special educational needs coordinator

The SENCo is a vital point of contact for all trainee and newly qualified teachers. SENCOs have a wealth of experience, skills and knowledge in working with pupils with SEN. The following list identifies the key responsibilities of the SENCo. To exemplify what these responsibilities might mean in practical terms, they have been linked to practice in a comprehensive school.

The SENCo's key responsibilities are as follows:

- to identify pupils' special educational needs and maintain a list of these pupils;
  - o pupils with SEN are identified from liaison with feeder schools
  - o the responsibility of one member of the SEN team in school is to test pupils' reading and spelling ability in order to identify weaknesses
  - o testing is also carried out in order to identify which pupils may need exam concessions
- to inform parents/carers that their child has SEN and is on the school's maintained list;
- to coordinate SEN provision for pupils with SEN to meet their needs;
  - o managing the support from all the teaching assistants across the school
  - o training the teaching assistants to run interventions for those pupils who need extra help with literacy skills
  - o holding half-termly liaison meetings with SEN representatives from all departments to ensure that all teachers are aware of the identified needs of pupils with SEN and the strategies that need to be used in relation to these pupils
  - o all those with specific needs are withdrawn from lessons once or twice a week to be given extra help with literacy skills
- to monitor the effectiveness of SEN provision made for pupils with SEN;
  - o all SEN provision is mapped across the school and every intervention is monitored for its effectiveness

- all those pupils who are withdrawn are tested to identify which particular intervention suits their needs and then re-tested at the end of the planned intervention to monitor the success of the help that has been given
- all pupils in the school are tested on a 10-weekly cycle and targets are set accordingly. The SENCo has access to all the data concerning levels achieved and targets set so that the progress of all pupils on the SEN Register can be monitored

- to secure relevant services for pupils with SEN where necessary;
  - monthly meetings are held with all outside agencies working with the school to review the progress of pupils already referred and to discuss the needs of others who may require more help
- to maintain and keep up-to-date records on pupils with SEN and the SEN provision to meet those needs;
  - all data on progress made for each of the interventions used is noted
  - the progress of all statemented pupils is reviewed annually and annual review reports are kept
- on a regular basis to liaise with, and provide information to, the parents/carers of pupils with SEN;
  - reports are sent to parents about interventions used and progress made
  - the SENCo attends all parents' evenings to see any parents of pupils with SEN
- to ensure all relevant information about a pupil's SEN and SEN provision made to meet those needs is conveyed to the next school or educational institution on transfer and transition;
- to promote the inclusion of pupils with SEN in the school community, the curriculum, facilities and extra-curricula activities;
  - regular meetings with departmental SEN representatives ensures that there is a two-way flow of information between the SEN department and the rest of the school
  - these meetings are also used for training purposes concerning the types of needs of pupils with SEN and how to meet those needs
  - termly meetings with Heads of Year and pastoral teams about each year group in the school where all pupils' needs are discussed and action planning for the next term takes place
  - the engagement of pupils with SEN with extra-curricular activities is monitored
- to recruit, supervise and train teaching assistants who work with pupils with SEN;
- to advise teachers at the school about differentiated teaching methods appropriate to individual pupils with SEN;
  - as well as delivering specific training on differentiation, all teachers receive information about the needs of pupils with SEN, including their spelling and reading ages, and recommended strategies to use with these pupils, as well as

information sheets on types of needs such as autistic spectrum disorder, dyslexia, dyspraxia and dyscalculia.

The SENCo is the main point of contact for all members of staff and teaching assistants when there are queries about pupils who are already identified as having SEN or where there are concerns regarding possible SEN. The SENCo is also responsible for ensuring that SEN practices are consistent across departments. However, the SENCo will expect all members of staff to be proactive in noting pupils on the SEN Register in the classes they teach, noting the SEN information profile provided and using the strategies suggested according to pupils' needs. The SENCo who was interviewed prioritized how she viewed the role of the teachers in the school as follows:

- take note of the reading ages of pupils on the register in order to be prepared for the types of texts they can read independently (a computer program is available in the school that calculates the reading age of a text when an extract from it is typed in);
- introduce subject vocabulary for each lesson and ensure pupils with SEN have access to this vocabulary at all times;
- prepare worksheets that match the reading abilities of the pupils and include pictorial information as well as text;
- be familiar with the link teaching assistant for the pupils with SEN in the particular classes and liaise with them over difficulties that may arise.

Teachers have a responsibility to their pupils in terms of inclusion. Ofsted (2004b: paras. 63–64) identified the features of inclusive teaching for pupils with SEN as follows:

- effective teamwork among teachers and teaching assistants;
- specially devised/adapted materials and methods of teaching tailored well to pupils' needs;
- activities capturing pupils' interest and participation;
- careful grouping of pupils with SEN to ensure productive working with others;
- staff showing positive attitudes and having high expectations of pupils with SEN;
- adequate information and communications technology (ICT) support should be available;
- multi-sensory resources in all parts of lessons;
- personal targets incorporated into learning objectives;
- opportunities for independent learning;
- next steps in learning carefully spelled out.

It is also the responsibility of teachers to differentiate the National Curriculum for pupils with SEN (see Chapter 6) and work closely with any other adults who may support these pupils in the classroom.

Task 21.1

The aim of ensuring the package of duties works as a seamless whole is to give pupils the opportunity to learn successfully alongside their peers. Consider how School A might respond to Pupil B's needs.

School A knows that disabled Pupil B is going to be admitted next term. Pupil B has a hearing impairment. He will need hearing aids that are set up and regularly maintained by a specialist teacher (SEN framework). His teachers need to adapt their teaching style to suit him (reasonable adjustments) and pay particular attention to his physical location in the learning environment (reasonable adjustments). To enable him to gain access to all communications across the school, a loop system will need to be in place in all teaching areas (planning duties).

Task 21.2

1. Decide which of the categories of need identified above (communication and interaction; cognition and learning; behaviour, emotional and social development; sensory and/or physical) best describe the pupils in the two case studies below.

Case Study 21.1

Asif is an 11-year-old child who transferred to secondary school from a small, rural primary school. He is an articulate child who is a well-liked member of his class. Asif, however, has difficulties in activities that involve reading, writing and spelling and his teachers have been unable to help him make progress with his school work. Recently, he has become increasingly frustrated with his inability to keep up with the rest of the class, especially in English lessons. In light of Asif's continuing difficulties, he was referred to an educational psychologist for an assessment of his needs. After completing several tests, the educational psychologist judged that Asif was some 36 months behind in his spelling and reading ability for a child of his age. It is interesting to note that, when questioned, Asif's father stated that he had had similar difficulties with his English work when he was at school.

Case Study 21.2

Joanne is a happy, polite and well-motivated pupil who is due to sit her GCSEs next year. She is an avid reader who likes nothing better than sharing her favourite stories with her friends. She is a well-liked pupil and teachers had expected her to do well in forthcoming exams. However, recently Joanne's handwriting has become untidy and she has become increasingly slow at copying work from the board during lessons. Her teachers have also noticed that she is finding it more and more difficult to navigate around the school. At a recent hospital assessment, Joanne was found to have a deteriorating eye condition.

In terms of government legislation, Asif requires SEN provision because he has a 'significantly greater difficulty in learning' than other children of the same age. His SEN would be described as a specific learning difficulty that would be classified as being concerned with cognition and learning.

Joanne would be classified as having a SEN that is sensory in nature. This is because her deteriorating eyesight is adversely affecting her ability to learn and her educational progress is being restricted because of this.

2. Based on your readings, list actions you would take in preparing to teach classes attended by Asif and Joanne.

21.4 Concluding reflections

At the time of writing, the Coalition government has published a consultation document concerning SEN and inclusion that is likely to have implications for how SEN is organized in schools in the future. Following a consultation on the Green Paper (DfE 2011a), the government is to formulate detailed plans that will form the basis for any necessary legislative changes to be taken forward from May 2012. By the time you read this book, some key deadlines are likely to have passed.

The recommendations the Green Paper makes are far-reaching and include a great number of proposals concerning SEN and disability ranging from identification in the early years to preparing for adulthood and post-16 education. The areas of this document highlighted below have been chosen for their relevance to possible changes in the way SEN and inclusion are currently managed and how these changes might affect practice previously documented in this chapter.

Inclusion – where pupils are taught

The report is explicit about how the government views inclusion, including the idea that pupils should be taught in mainstream schools wherever possible. It refers to 'giving parents a real choice of school' in the following ways:

> We will remove the bias towards inclusion and propose to strengthen parental choice by improving the range and diversity of schools from which parents can choose ... Parents of children with statements of SEN will be able to express a preference for any state-funded school – including special schools, Academies and Free Schools ... We will also prevent the unnecessary closure of special schools by giving parents and community groups the power to take them over.
>
> (DfE 2011a: 5)

These proposals are likely to strengthen the position of special schools and how they might fit into a continuum of provision for pupils with SEN in the future. With reference to special schools, the report also refers to flexible placements in more than one type of provision over time or simultaneously as being 'beneficial for children with SEN ... It may be helpful for some children attending mainstream school to spend some time in a specialist setting for their learning needs to be thoroughly assessed, or for specialist support or to help them to catch up. Stronger links between schools improve support for the child and develop the skills of staff in both settings' (DfE 2011a: 6).

Learning and achieving

The government's perspective on a theme in previous reports, the barriers to learning faced by pupils with SEN, is that: 'Previous measures of school performance created perverse incentives to over-identify children as having SEN. There is compelling evidence that these labels of SEN have perpetuated a culture of low expectations and have not led to the right support being in place' (DfE 2011a: 9).

The report refers to the Schools White Paper, *The Importance of Teaching* (DfE 2010), as the place where the government has set out its vision 'to match the best education systems in the world' (DfE 2011a: 5). The Green Paper intends to builds on that by proposing that:

- teachers and other staff in schools and colleges are well trained and confident to identify and overcome a range of barriers to learning;
- schools will have additional flexibility to support the needs of all pupils, and additional funding to support disadvantaged pupils through the pupil premium;
- teachers feel able to identify effectively what a child needs to help them to learn and plan support to help every child progress well, reflecting the specific needs of children with SEN and those who may just be struggling with learning and need school-based catch-up support which is normally available (DfE 2011a: 9).

Thus, the view of this report is that current practices, designed to support pupils with SEN in mainstream schools, lead to over-identification due to lack of clarity about the nature of pupils' difficulties and how they should be dealt with. The report identifies the need to help teachers 'to spot quickly and accurately any barriers to learning and provide the right support to help each child progress' (DfE 2011a: 9). The government therefore intends to: 'replace the current SEN identification levels of School Action and School Action Plus with a new single school-based SEN category for children whose needs exceed what is normally available in schools; revising statutory guidance on SEN identification to make it clearer for professionals; and supporting the best schools to share their practices' (DfE 2011a: 58). The implication is that too many pupils are identified with SEN in the first place and that this number will be reduced in the future.

A new approach to statutory assessment and statements

According to the research leading up to the Green Paper, parents find the statutory assessment process slow and 'like a battle' to secure the help required. It can be complicated, including several assessments that are not always necessary. By 2014, it is proposed that 'all children who would currently have a statement of SEN or learning difficulty assessment would be entitled to a new single assessment process and "Education, Health and Care Plan" to identify their support needs' (DfE 2011a: 7). The intentions are to make the process less time-consuming and bureaucratic and that all the services involved will work together to agree the plan and commit to provide their services from birth to age 25. Like a Statement, the plan should specify in detail the child's needs and support required, but would then go further to 'set out the learning and life outcomes sought for young people, with reviews focused on their progress towards life outcomes across education, health, employment, and an independent life' (DfE 2011a: 59).

Developing excellent teaching practice for SEN in schools and colleges

According to the Green Paper: 'Recent evidence highlights gaps in teachers' initial training in supporting pupils with SEN' (DfE 2011a: 59). To address this, the government has set out plans to provide a stronger focus on support for children with additional needs, including those with SEN, in the Standards for Qualified Teacher Status (DfE 2010). These include the view that: 'Working in special schools can also provide a unique opportunity for teachers to develop their skills in teaching children with particular needs' (DfE 2011a: 59). With this in mind, the government proposes to provide additional funding for initial teacher training providers to secure a greater number of placements for trainee teachers in special school settings as well as to fund scholarships for serving teachers to develop their practice in supporting disabled pupils and pupils with SEN, including specific impairments.

The report stresses that: 'Teaching assistant time should never be a substitute for teaching from a qualified teacher ... too often, the most vulnerable pupils are supported almost exclusively by teaching assistants' (DfE 2011a: 63). It states emphatically that: 'this practice is not acceptable ... children with SEN need more, not less, time with the school's most skilled and qualified teachers' (DfE 2011a: 63). It sets out how schools will be enabled to make use of the talents of support staff by being given the freedom to decide how to deploy them and on their responsibilities and their pay. The Green Paper, likewise, emphasizes that teaching assistants need to be trained, supported, deployed and managed effectively if they are to have a positive impact on pupil progress.

The Achievement for All Approach

The Labour government introduced the Achievement for All initiative in 2010 and, as has already been stated in this chapter, the 'whole-school approach' promoted by this approach involves improved outcomes for all pupils through clear target setting, careful tracking of pupils' progress, high expectations and greater and more constructive involvement of parents. The Coalition government intends to build upon the positive impact this approach has been shown to have on pupils by launching a tender for bids from external organizations to spread the practices that those involved with Achievement for All have developed and, in so doing, to develop a quality mark for those schools that are developing excellent and innovative SEN support.

According to the Coalition government, the SEN system 'needs radical reform'. The Green Paper is adamant that: 'Today's system for supporting children with SEN is based on a model introduced 30 years ago. It is no longer fit for purpose and has not kept pace with wider reforms; it fails children and undermines the effective use of resources' (DfE 2011a: 15). It remains to be seen how the system will change once new legislation has been introduced and whether the needs of SEN pupils will be better met in the future. The key test will be whether future policy and practice meet the challenges and issues raised at the beginning of this chapter.

21.5 Recommendations for further reading and webliography

Cheminais, R. (2010) *Special Educational Needs for Qualified Teachers and Teaching Assistants*, 2nd edn. London: Routledge.

Department for Children Schools and Families (DCSF) (2008) *The Education of Children and Young People with Behavioural, Emotional and Social Difficulties as a Special Educational Need*. Nottingham: DCSF.

Department for Children Schools and Families (DCSF) (2008) *Initial Teacher Training Inclusion Development Programme: Primary/Secondary – Dyslexia and Speech, Language and Communication Needs. An Interactive Resource to Support Initial Teacher Training Institutions and Trainee Teachers*. Nottingham: DCSF.

Department for Children Schools and Families (DCSF) (2009) *Initial Teacher Training Inclusion Development Programme: Primary/Secondary – Dyslexia and Autistic Spectrum Disorders. An Interactive Resource to Support Initial Teacher Training Institutions and Trainee Teachers*. Nottingham: DCSF.

Department for Children Schools and Families (DCSF) (2010) *Breaking the Link Between Special Educational Needs and Low Attainment: Everyone's Business*. Nottingham: DCSF.

Training and Development Agency for Schools (TDA) (2006) *Special Educational Needs in Mainstream Schools: A Guide for the Beginner Teacher*. London: TDA.

Websites

Introduction – Special Educational Needs and/or Disabilities: A Training Resource for Secondary Undergraduate ITT courses. This resource is one of the most comprehensive teaching tool-kits for SEN. It includes eighteen taught sessions on topics that include: inclusive planning and assessment, and learning and teaching, for pupils with dyslexia, autistic spectrum disorders, speech and language needs, and behavioural, emotional, and social difficulties. It is available at www.education.gov.uk

Making SENse of CPD is a resource provided by the General Teaching Council for England (GTCE). It provides a link to many useful organizations relating to SEN. It can be found at http://www.gtce.org.uk/networks/sen/

22

Schooling, ethnicity and English as an additional language

Sandra Howard

22.1   Introduction and background to the issues

By the end of this chapter, you should:

- know about legislation and other initiatives aimed at raising the achievement of minority ethnic pupils;
- have an understanding of the range of issues impacting on pupils of minority ethnic backgrounds;
- have an awareness of the needs of pupils with English as an additional language, including newly arrived pupils;
- be familiar with appropriate strategies to support pupils with English as an additional language in the classroom.

The publication of the Stephen Lawrence Inquiry Report (Macpherson 1999) following the murder of the black teenager in 1993 was a significant event in race relations in this country. It demonstrated that there had been a time lag between the experiences of minority ethnic communities in Britain and recognition of those experiences by the state and its institutions. In the words of Doreen Lawrence, Stephen's mother, 'The time is right for change, don't let this opportunity pass you by, cling to it with both hands' (Richardson and Wood 1999: v).

People from minority ethnic heritage have been in Britain for a very long time. However, their numbers were relatively small until the period of reconstruction after the Second World War when people migrated from the New Commonwealth in response to the 'Mother Country's' call for labour. Post-war industrial expansion had created a need for cheap labour, and effective recruitment campaigns in the 'former colonies' lured people from the Caribbean, India and Pakistan to take up work in badly paid jobs that the indigenous population did not want. Few of these workers intended to stay in Britain for long and the aim of most was to improve their status so that they could return home assured of a better standard of living for themselves and their families. However, for many this was not to be the case until they reached the age of retirement and, gradually, as minority ethnic families settled initially in the poor housing of Britain's large cities, their children entered the education system. The colonial experience had not prepared Britain to cope with a multiracial society. However, from 1960 some schools had an increasingly multiracial population. While official policies acknowledged the need for teachers to be aware of the backgrounds of minority ethnic pupils, and the Bullock Report (DES 1975) promoted the importance of language across the curriculum, the educational needs of minority ethnic pupils were not a priority and the state hoped to assimilate these 'immigrant' pupils with as little disruption as possible into the school system.

Section 11 of the Local Government Act 1966 provided additional funding to local education authorities (LEAs) with 2 per cent or more of Commonwealth immigrant pupils and this funding was used predominantly for the teaching of English. Initially, this took place in language centres where pupils were withdrawn from the mainstream. Gradually, the language centres were phased out and pupils with English language needs were first supported in schools in withdrawal groups and then more inclusively within mainstream classrooms. This additional funding continued until 1999 when the DfES introduced the Ethnic Minority Achievement Grant (EMAG) and placed responsibility for the achievement of minority ethnic pupils on schools. In the same year, the Stephen Lawrence Inquiry Report (Macpherson 1999) made a number of recommendations for education and emphasized the need to address institutionalized racism. It stated that LEAs and school governors had a duty to create and implement strategies in their schools to prevent and address racism. The Report also stated that consideration should be given to amending the National Curriculum (NC) to better reflect the needs of a diverse society and prevent racism. The following year saw the publication of Curriculum 2000, which made statutory the duty to ensure that teaching is inclusive. Also in 2000 the Race Relations Act of 1976 was amended to place both general and specific duties upon schools. The general duty required schools to be proactive in eliminating racial discrimination and in the promotion of equality of opportunity and good relations between people of different racial groups. For example, if patterns of racial inequality exist within a school, it is not enough simply to identify them – action must be taken to remove them. The specific duties required English schools to prepare and publish a race equality policy and monitor and assess how their policies affected ethnic minority pupils, staff and parents, placing the emphasis on pupils' achievements.

22.2 Analysing achievement

As attention focused on raising levels of achievement of all pupils during the 1990s, reports by Ofsted (1996b, 1999) indicated that, while the achievement of minority ethnic pupils as a whole was improving, the gap between the highest and lowest achieving ethnic groups was growing. Particular concerns about the performance of Caribbean, Bangladeshi and Pakistani pupils were raised, as well as the level of exclusions of Black Caribbean boys. In their report on *Raising the Attainment of Minority Ethnic Pupils*, Ofsted (1999) recommended that schools should monitor pupils' achievement and behaviour, including attendance and exclusions, by ethnic group. These data should then be used to set targets for raising the attainment and improving the attendance and behaviour of under-achieving groups.

1966	Section 11 of Local Government Act
1975/6	Race Relations Act Bullock Report *A Language for Life*
1981	Rampton Report *West Indian Children in our Schools*
1985	Swann Report *Education for All*
1996	*Recent Research on the Achievements of Ethnic Pupils* Ofsted *Teaching EAL: A Framework for Policy* SCAA
1998	*Teaching and Learning Strategies in Successful Multi-ethnic Schools* DfEE/OU
1999	*Raising the Attainment of Minority Ethnic Pupils – School and LEA Responses* Ofsted Macpherson Report Home Office Introduction of Ethnic Minority Achievement Grant (EMAG)
2000	*Removing the Barriers* DfEE Race Relations Amendment Act Curriculum 2000 *Learning For All Standards for Racial Equality in Schools* CRE *A Language in Common* QCA
2001	*Managing Support for the Attainment of Pupils from Minority Ethnic Groups* HMI *Evaluating Educational Inclusion* Ofsted
2002	*Achievement of Black Caribbean Pupils* HMI
2003	*Aiming High: Raising the Achievement of Minority Ethnic Pupils* DfES
2004	*Minority Ethnic Pupils in Mainly White Schools* DfES

Figure 22.1 Summary of influential legislation and publications   *(Continued)*

2006	*Ethnictly and Education: the Evidence on Minority Ethnic Pupils aged 5–18* DfES
2007	*New Arrivals Excellence Programme* DCSF
2007	*Ensuring the Attainment of Black Pupils* DCSF
2008	*Raising the Attainment of Pakistani, Bangladeshi, Somali and Turkish Heritage Pupils: Guidance for developing inclusive practice* DCSF
2009	*Moving Forward Together: Raising Gypsy, Roma and Traveller Achievement* DCSF

Figure 22.1 *(Continued)*

In March 2003, the government released statistics showing the percentage of pupils with five or more A*–C grades at GCSE across ethnic groups. This was the first time such data had been placed in the public domain and it served to illustrate the concerns expressed by Ofsted four years previously. Only 30 per cent of Black Caribbean pupils achieved five or more good GCSE passes, compared with more than half of White pupils and 64 per cent of Indian pupils. In 2002, the highest achieving ethnic group was the 12,000 Chinese pupils. The release of these data coincided with the launch of a consultation document entitled *Aiming High* (DfES 2003d), which set out specific proposals for:

- a national framework to support bilingual pupils;
- raising achievement and reducing exclusions of African Caribbean pupils;
- meeting the needs of highly mobile pupils.

In the Foreword to the document, the Schools Minister, Stephen Twigg, made it clear that the 'long tail of underachievement for many Black and Pakistani pupils in particular' was unacceptable. He continued:

> The best schools already show us the way to deliver high standards for their minority ethnic pupils. They employ several complementary strategies. High expectations are matched by strong parental and community support. Data is monitored and used to improve teaching and learning. There is a clear whole school approach with a consistent approach to racism, bullying and bad behaviour.
>
> (DfES 2003d: 1)

Over the next seven years, the focus was very firmly on narrowing attainment gaps. Data show that for some minority ethnic pupils the gaps start wide and, although they narrow by the end of schooling, the reality for many Black and minority ethnic (BME) pupils is that their attainment by the end of Key Stage 4 (KS4) is still below the national average. The National Strategies produced guidance and resources to support work to narrow attainment gaps for BME pupils, and local authorities were tasked with producing challenging performance targets for BME pupils as well as other vulnerable under-achieving groups.

While the achievement of BME pupils overall has improved, we can see that the gap between the lower and higher attaining groups remains wide. Of most concern is the very low attainment of pupils of Irish Traveller and Gypsy Roma heritage, particularly at a time when increasing numbers of Roma pupils from Eastern European countries are entering our schools (see Figure 22.2).

Ethnic Group	%
White British	55.0
Irish	63.4
Traveller of Irish Heritage	21.8
Gypsy/Roma	8.3
Any White other background	50.6
White and Black Caribbean	45.3
White and Black African	55.6
White and Asian	65.2
Any other mixed background	57.8
Indian	71.3
Pakistani	49.1
Bangladeshi	53.7
Any other Asian background	57.6
Black Caribbean	43.5
Black African	52.8
Any other Black background	45.8
Chinese	75.1
Any other ethnic group	51.2
All pupils	54.8

Figure 22.2 2010 GCSE results – percentage of pupils in the 5+ A*–C group including A*–C passes in English and Mathematics

22.3 Cultural and religious issues

Pupils in schools, even predominantly white schools, come from a range of cultural backgrounds. For some, there may be conflict between the culture of home or 'the street' and the culture of school. For pupils from minority ethnic groups, there may be other potential areas of tension connected with their cultural, religious or linguistic identity: 'Inclusive schools respect the identities of their pupils and students and their experiences, histories and concerns. They know where their pupils are coming from, and the tensions, difficulties and struggles in which they are engaged' (Richardson and Wood 1999: 17).

In their research into the characteristics of successful multi-ethnic schools, Blair and Bourne develop the concept of 'the listening school', claiming that effective schools listen to and learn from pupils and their parents. They refer to interviews with secondary pupils, in which 'all young people interviewed stressed the importance of being treated with respect by teachers' (Blair and Bourne 1998: 54). Being treated with respect is a powerful message that also comes out of specific research by Her Majesty's Inspectors into secondary schools that had been successful in raising the achievement of Black Caribbean pupils: 'What the pupils interviewed for the study appreciated most about their schools was being listened to, valued and supported. They saw the response to Black people in wider society as often marked by negativity and discrimination and the notion of "respect" in school was of critical importance to them' (HMI 2002: 4).

Racism has a powerful impact on the lives of those pupils who experience it, as the Black Year 10 pupil in Case Study 22.1 illustrates.

Case Study 22.1

'It makes me feel angry, really mad inside like nothing else does'. Michael talks about the name-calling and comments on his skin colour that he has experienced ever since starting school. He describes how this kind of abuse continues. He talks about the 'new kids' who are refugees. 'They call everyone who's a refugee Kosovan. It's like we used to get called Paki even though we weren't'. Michael talks about his concerns regarding one particular teacher who he feels is treating him in a racist way. He feels that he gets into trouble for doing exactly the same things that white boys in his group do and don't get into trouble for. He is the only Black boy in this group. He feels that there is no-one in the school he can talk to about this and that his new year head won't take his perspective seriously. He used to enjoy this subject and thought he was quite good at it. Now he is worried that he's going to get 'chucked out' because he's always on report.

The Commission for Racial Equality (CRE) has developed a set of standards to help schools address race issues and develop a socially inclusive ethos and environment. They advise that schools should have 'clear procedures in place to ensure that racist incidents, racial discrimination and racial harassment are dealt with promptly, firmly and consistently' (CRE 2000: 41). This section of the standards continues by listing a number of ways this can be achieved by schools, among which is that a named teacher has overall responsibility for dealing with such incidents and that this teacher's role is widely publicized. Clearly, whoever fills this role must be able to demonstrate that they are prepared to listen to and learn from pupils.

The curriculum provides an opportunity to show respect for pupils' cultural, religious, and linguistic heritage by drawing on the backgrounds of all pupils. Resources in all curriculum areas should be inclusive with positive images of people from different ethnic groups and different religious backgrounds. The choice of content in subject areas and the teaching methods used should encourage positive attitudes to cultural diversity and race equality. Schools quite often forget to tap into the human resource that their parents and local minority ethnic communities provide. Some secondary schools have made good use of positive role models from their minority ethnic communities, particularly in terms of mentoring older pupils. Schools with pupils from backgrounds where a language other than English is spoken at home have made arrangements for those pupils to study their first language to GCSE and A level standard. In the best of practice these languages are timetabled as modern foreign language options rather than extra-curricular activities. Some schools have liaised with their local Mosque regarding test and exam timetables and have set aside an appropriate space for Muslim pupils to use for prayer, particularly during the period of Ramadan (the Muslim month of fasting). Further good practice involves the monitoring of pupils' optional subject choices by ethnicity and the allocation of pupils to sets, bands and streams.

Task 22.1

Consider how well the schools you've worked in have reflected ethnic diversity in curricular or pastoral policies and practice. What would you do if a group of pupils started to make fun of an image of a person from a minority ethnic background during one of your lessons?

22.4 Meeting the needs of pupils with English as an additional language

Pupils learning English as an additional language (EAL) are by no means a homogenous group, and while they share some characteristics with pupils whose first or only language is English, their needs are very different. The process of learning a second or other language is intertwined with the pupil's cultural, social, and first language development. You are likely to come across two main categories of pupils learning EAL:

- those who were born in Britain and who have progressed through the education system – some of these pupils may have entered school with little or no English;

- those who have recently arrived in this country either because their families are seeking asylum or because one or both of their parents is studying or working in the UK.

Clearly, pupils' cultural and social experiences will influence their learning experiences in school. The acquisition of EAL is also dependent on the pupil's proficiency in their first language. It is vital that teachers find out as much information as possible about the individual pupils they teach rather than make assumptions based on stereotypes. Student teachers will need to take account of this broad range of factors when planning lessons.

The length of time it takes for a pupil learning EAL to acquire English to an academic level comparable to their peers will vary. Research has shown that it can take between five and seven years (Collier 1989; Wong Fillmore 1991). However, a range of factors will contribute to this and for some pupils, particularly those who have a lack of appropriate support at school and at home, it may take a lot longer. It is important not to confuse pupils' ability to converse socially with their ability in using academic language. Cummins (1984) distinguishes between basic interpersonal communication skills (BICS) and cognitive academic language proficiency (CALP). He explains that fluent use of English in social situations, for example the playground and corridor conversations, does not necessarily equip pupils to use the academic language of the curriculum. As pupils move through school, the language of the curriculum becomes increasingly complex. By the time pupils reach KS3, they are expected to make sense of texts that are both cognitively and linguistically demanding and use this kind of language in an accurate way in their own writing. Many pupils, not just those with EAL, will require support to do this. Student teachers often feel overwhelmed by the amount of curriculum content they need to cover with their pupils. However, it is important that you also consider the language demands of your lessons, ask what pupils are expected to do with language during the course of the lesson, and structure tasks appropriately so that language is used to aid pupils' learning.

Task 22.2

Choose a lesson that you have taught recently and consider what oral, written and reading tasks your pupils have needed to engage in. How did you support any pupils with EAL to complete these tasks effectively? Would they have benefited from any additional support?

Checklist

You may have asked your pupils to:

- give or justify an opinion;
- agree or disagree with something;

- pronounce words in a way that could be understood by others;
- challenge another view;
- understand both general and subject-specific vocabulary and use it appropriately;
- make notes;
- write grammatically correct sentences;
- form paragraphs and order them logically; and
- use an appropriate style.

Pupils for whom English is an additional language are likely to need support with some or all of these tasks depending on their level of English language development. It is also important to remember that pupils who appear to be quite fluent English speakers will need continuing support with understanding more abstract concepts and completing linguistically demanding tasks such as the kind of extended writing activities generated by exam questions.

In the absence of a nationally recognized framework for assessing EAL, most LEAs created their own individual systems. This not only meant that it was impossible to monitor the progress of pupils nationally but it also presented difficulties for teachers in understanding pupils' progress should a pupil move from one part of the country to another. In 2000, the Qualifications and Curriculum Authority (QCA) published *A Language in Common*, which stated that the: 'assessment of English as an additional language should follow the same principles of effective assessment of all pupils' (QCA 2000a: 7). The QCA recommended the use of a common scale of assessment for pupils learning EAL that is based on NC levels of attainment in English. Additional assessment criteria have been developed at two steps before NC Level 1, and Level 1 has been divided into 'threshold' and 'secure'.

The following case studies provide an opportunity for you to consider two EAL learner profiles.

Case Study 22.2

Atif, who is in Year 9, was born in Britain and is of Pakistani heritage and speaks Urdu as his first language. Speaking Urdu is an important part of Atif's life and he can switch easily between Urdu and English. He uses both languages when talking with his siblings, his father, and other pupils of Pakistani heritage at school but always speaks in Urdu to his mother and grandparents. Atif's family is Muslim and after school he attends a class at the local Mosque from 4.30 p.m. to 7.30 p.m. Here he studies the Arabic text of the Quran. When Atif began nursery in his local primary school, he knew very little English. He received specialist language support and made good progress. He obtained

Level 4 in his end-of-KS2 tests in maths and Level 3 in science and English. This language sample is taken from a piece of written work Atif did in history on the effects of the agricultural revolution. All class members were asked to complete a written answer to two questions written on the board. This is part of his answer.

'William Read probably liked[2] the agricultural revolution and enclosure because he was always[1] well off anyway. He could use machinery which would make[1] farming easier and faster. He would make more money from crop[3] because he has[1] an estate which is big enough for machinery. It would be[1] more efficient and would benefit[1] him.'

'The agricultural revolution and enclosure wouldn't do much for Thomas Goddard because he was poor so he would probably be more[4] less[5] off than he was even though he was hard working[1] all his life. A landless labourer wouldn't be benefited by the agricultural revolution because they would be[1] moved out of their huts and become poor labourers working[6] hard.'

While it would be inappropriate to consider only one sample of written work when judging a pupil, this individual piece of work does give us an indication of some problems Atif has. This piece of writing was considered to be at NC Level 3. Atif's writing conveys meaning in non-narrative form, using some appropriate vocabulary. Ideas are developed in a sequence of sentences, demarcated by capital letters and full stops. However, the confusion over tense and the grammatical construction of some of his sentences indicates that he is not secure at Level 3.

The following errors were noted:

1. Tense
2. Colloquial register
3. Plural
4. Inappropriate use of comparative
5. Word omission
6. Sentence order.

It appears that Atif has made little progress in his written work since KS2. This often happens to pupils at this stage of linguistic development, who may appear to be doing well orally and 'surviving' in the classroom. Also, additional support from EMAG-funded teachers (see p. 96) may not have been available for Atif. However, if Atif is going to cope with the more complex writing tasks expected of him as he enters KS4, and embarks on examination coursework, he will need significant support.

Atif would benefit from:

- support with understanding questions used for writing tasks, such as elucidation of terms like compare, explain, describe, summarize;
- modelling of paragraphs and sentence patterns;
- highlighting contextualized phrases and vocabulary;
- support in using grammatical structures accurately, which could be done by oral rehearsal before writing or individual/paired re-drafting;
- support in writing different forms using writing frames;
- support in developing a greater range of language by the use of synonym and antonym word banks.

Case Study 22.3

Maria arrived in Britain three weeks after the start of the autumn term when she was 12 years old. Her family is from Brazil and they are planning to stay in Britain for three or four years while her father completes his PhD. Maria speaks, reads, and writes Portuguese and has attended school for five years in Brazil where, according to her parents, she was doing well. Maria has had very limited experience of hearing and/or using English and is having difficulty in 'tuning in' to British English.

The following language sample was taken from Maria's geography notebook. Class members were answering a question on the water cycle having seen a diagram with key words in their textbook.

'The average Britain consume[1] use[2] each day of water is 200 litre[4]. 4,400 litre[3] of water people in our class use[3]. After you use water it is use[5] again to be[6] treated first than goes to been clean[5].'

Maria has tried hard to explain a process without receiving any support. This piece of writing was considered to be at NC Level 1 secure. She has attempted to use phrases to convey her ideas with some use of full stops and capital letters. However, the amount she has been able to write is limited and she has problems with word order and grammar. Maria has tried to use key vocabulary taken from the diagram but without support in structuring, her writing has run into difficulties.

The following errors were noted:

1. Subject/verb agreement
2. Additional verb

3. Sentence structure
4. Plural omission
5. Tense
6. Sentence structure/verb choice.

Maria would benefit from:

- using a Portuguese/English dictionary;
- bilingual teaching assistant support if available;
- the opportunity to participate in paired or small group talk to clarify her ideas and hear good role models, and rehearse in preparation for written work;
- oral and written modelling of sentence structures;
- the use of writing frames;
- the use of cloze procedures (text with deleted words that the pupil fills in). These can be key vocabulary or structured words. To help the pupil you can initially list the missing words at the side.

It is important that teachers and pupils have high expectations of pupils and that 'commonly perceived setbacks such as poor command of English are regarded as challenges to be met rather than excuses for underachievement' (DfEE 2000a: 8). Given appropriate support, both Atif and Maria have the potential to achieve so much more.

22.5 Supporting newly arrived pupils

Although the majority of pupils from minority ethnic backgrounds will have been born in this country, you may find yourself teaching a pupil or pupils who are newly arrived in Britain. Their families may be seeking asylum in this country, they may be economic migrants – particularly from other countries in the EU – or they may be studying here. Entering schooling in a new country where you are unfamiliar with the system, teaching and learning styles, and language and, in addition, have no friends, is a challenge for all youngsters regardless of their reasons for being here. For children of families seeking asylum (applying for refugee status), their experiences before arriving in Britain, and while waiting for a decision on their application, which could take over a year, are likely to make schooling an even greater challenge. Although many asylum-seeker and refugee families are living in London and the South East, the system of dispersal introduced under the 2002 Nationality, Immigration and Asylum Act means that families are housed all over the country, sometimes in areas that are hostile to their presence. Children who may have experienced trauma due to their experiences of persecution, of possibly seeing a parent or family members killed, of leaving relatives behind as well as their home, possessions, and friends are not necessarily able to feel safe once in Britain. For some, the experience of victimization will continue at home, on the way to and from school, and at school. For these children, it is hard to know whom they can trust and teachers can help to give children some security.

Case Study 22.4 features Ornelo, who shared her story when she was in Year 11.

Case Study 22.4

'My name is Ornelo and I came from Gjakova in Kosovo. My family and I are Muslims. I will share with you that I have a sister and two brothers. I now live in Coventry with my brothers and my mum. At this point I don't live with my dad and one of my brothers because they went missing during the war in Kosovo. When the war started my family was still together. It was the war that split my family apart and it's the worst thing that could happen to anyone. There wasn't a second without a bullet on the sky, there wasn't an hour without a bomb exploding. It was truly horrifying for me. My family and I ran away from this to a camp in Macedonia. This is the point where my family was destroyed.

Ornelo describes her traumatic journey to 'somewhere safe' and being found somewhere to live and attend school in London before being moved to the Midlands and another house and another school. She continues:

'I'm doing my very best in school and teachers tell me that I'm doing well with the amount of English that I know. I think the people back home were kinder and nicer – they helped you when you needed help and it didn't matter what gender or colour you were. That was the best thing about school at home. It helped you to be more confident. But here in England the students bully each other. Me! I'm fine. I can't wait for weekends to be over just to go to school to be with my friends but mostly to learn. I really want a good future, not just for myself but for my family – especially after what they've been through. Today there is still no sign of my dad or my brother. Sometimes people do tell me that I am brave and clever. Brave because I always tell my story to people without a tear on my eye. I don't like people to see me cry. And clever because I have learnt English in just three years now. When I came to England I didn't know one word of English. Now I'm here writing my story for you to read.'

Ornelo's story illustrates how important being successful at school is for asylum-seeking and refugee children and their families. It also demonstrates the progress that Ornelo has made in terms of her English language acquisition. Like Ornelo, some newly arrived pupils will have no previous knowledge of English, while some may have had the opportunity to learn to read and write English in their home country.

Some children may have had limited or disrupted experiences of schooling and for a few no experience of schooling at all. These pupils will need a great deal of support to settle into the school environment but, once settled, are likely to make rapid progress. When working with newly arrived pupils, it is important to remember that, while they may be limited in their use of English, they may in fact be very able pupils who are likely to be experiencing frustration on a daily basis as they struggle with the linguistic and cultural demands of the curriculum.

Task 22.5

The following checklist provides some suggestions for creating a learning environment that is supportive to the needs of pupils who are newly arrived in this country. When you have read it, consider how you might adapt your teaching style to incorporate some of the points.

Checklist for supporting newly arrived pupils

- ensure that you pronounce and spell their name correctly;
- establish a buddy system that is supervised and monitored and is the focus of classroom work;
- make use of any additional support from specialist/bilingual staff;
- if the pupil is literate in their first language, provide a bilingual dictionary;
- show you value the pupil's first language skills by giving them the chance to write in their preferred language;
- maximize the use of information and communications technology (ICT), including on-line translation sites;
- respect the pupil's right to a 'silent period', which could last for a number of months while they 'tune-in' to the language of the classroom and gain confidence;
- continue to communicate with pupils even if they do not speak, and provide a range of opportunities for speaking and listening in pairs or small groups;
- prioritize activities that encourage collaboration between pupils and help to speed up the acquisition of English;
- consider how you group pupils for particular activities: (i) with same language speaking pupils; and/or (ii) with positive role models for behaviour and/or language;
- use 'key visuals', for example, diagrams, tables, timelines and so on whenever possible;
- identify areas of strength and give praise to pupils' strengths and successes;
- remember pupils need cognitive challenge with structured language support – don't just ask them to copy paragraphs of text.

22.6   Conclusion

As in the previous chapter on special educational needs (SEN), the underlying principles that should inform provision for children from different ethnic backgrounds are enshrined in the ideal of inclusive schooling. Inclusion insists that whatever children's ethnic background or educational needs, they should be recognized as individuals, their rights should be respected, their potential should be harnessed and their needs should be met. Inclusion also dictates that all pupils should be prepared for life in an inclusive, pluralist society and the challenge is for schools to reflect that inclusivity.

22.7   Recommendations for further reading and webliography

Gravelle, M. (2000) *Planning for Bilingual Learners: An Inclusive Curriculum*. Stoke-on-Trent: Trentham Books.

Mundi Global Education Centre (2010) *Global and Anti-Racist Perspectives within the Secondary Curriculum*. Nottingham: Mundi.

National Key Stage 3 Strategy (2002) *Access and Engagement in: Science; Maths; English; Information Communication Technology; History; Geography; Physical Education; and Design Technology*. London: DfES.

Richardson, R. and Wood, A. (1999) *Inclusive Schools, Inclusive Society: Race and Identity on the Agenda*. Stoke-on-Trent: Trentham Books.

Rutter, J. (2003) *Supporting Refugee Children in 21st Century Britain*. Stoke-on-Trent: Trentham Books.

Websites
http://uk.babelfish.yahoo.com/translate
www.naldic.org.uk
www.insted.co.uk
www.rewind.org.uk
www.foreignword.com

23

Schooling and gender
Kate Shilvock and Jenni Ingram

23.1 Background

Any reader of the national press during recent years could not fail to be aware of the concern being expressed about the difference in attainment of girls and boys. Each summer, when GCSE and AS/A2 results are announced, attention is paid to the differences in relative performance between boys and girls.

A generation ago, it was a very different story. Under-achievement by girls was highlighted as a national concern. Research published in the 1970s suggested that girls were marginalized in the classroom, resulting in their low representation in higher education. Measures were taken to address girls' perception of themselves as achievers, to increase girls' interest in traditionally 'male' subjects such as maths and science, and to ensure equal opportunities within, and access to, the school curriculum. In addition, schools began to adopt teaching strategies designed to suit girls' learning styles and examination boards adapted assessment methods to shift the emphasis from terminal examinations towards the inclusion of more continuous assessment. The inclusion of coursework at GCSE was part of this. At the same time, changes in society resulted in more women entering the workforce and changes in law resulted in equal access to some jobs that had hitherto remained male preserves.

In the 1990s, the government of the day focused on raising standards of achievement by making schools more explicitly accountable. Also, the introduction of the National Curriculum (NC) prescribed what should be studied and obliged girls to continue with science subjects, which previously many had dropped at Key Stage 4 (KS4). Against this background, girls have steadily improved their performance in areas of the curriculum once thought to be 'male' preserves, matching boys' performance in maths and science at GCSE for the first time in 1995. By 2001, girls outperformed boys at GCSE in all subjects except physics (Ofsted 2003a). It remains the case, however, that women earn less than men at all levels, even compared with those who have the same qualifications and work in the same industries. In 2010, eighteen FTSE 100 companies had no female directors and less than 4 per cent of executive directors in the FTSE 250 were female.

In this chapter, you will:

- be introduced to the debate surrounding academic achievement and gender;
- learn about current patterns of achievement and choice for boys and girls;
- consider the likely reasons for differences in achievement between the sexes;
- consider the research evidence for differences in achievement between the sexes;
- consider current strategies for addressing differences in achievement related to gender;
- reflect upon the implications for your practice as a classroom teacher.

23.2   The global picture

Britain is not alone in its concern about male achievement. *Literacy Skills for the World of Tomorrow*, a report by the Organization for Economic Cooperation and Development and UNESCO (OECD/UNESCO 2003), noted that at age 15 girls had higher reading scores than boys in every one of the 43 countries surveyed. The survey tested three forms of literacy – reading, mathematical and scientific – to assess how well pupils applied knowledge and skills to tasks that were relevant to their future lives. The executive summary of the report noted that 'reading is an increasingly essential prerequisite for success in today's societies' (OECD/UNESCO 2003: 6). The report linked reading under-performance by boys to 'lack of engagement', with more than half of boys saying they read only to obtain information. Given the importance attached to reading, and its relevance to examination performance, under-performance in reading by boys is likely to have a major impact on their overall achievement. On the positive side, Britain performed significantly above the OECD average in all three areas covered – reading, maths and science. British pupils rated the support they received from their teachers more highly than in any other country in the survey.

23.3   Patterns of achievement

'When boys enter secondary school they are already well behind girls in English, although they achieve marginally better than girls in mathematics. Except in a small number of schools, the gap does not close during the secondary years' (Ofsted 2003a: 3).

   Differences in achievement are evident very early in a child's schooling. By the end of KS1, a higher proportion of girls than boys achieves Level 2 in all subjects, and a higher proportion of girls than boys achieves Level 3 or above in speaking and listening, reading and writing, while a higher proportion of boys than girls achieve Level 3 or above in maths and science. By the end of KS2, girls continue to score more highly than boys in English (reading and writing), the sexes achieve roughly equally in science and mathematics, though a higher proportion of boys than girls achieves Level 5 in mathematics.

   At GCSE, girls gain more A*–C grades than boys in nearly all subjects, though boys do marginally better in maths, physics, and economics. The difference between the sexes is greatest in language-based and creative subjects. Subject choices for GCSE,

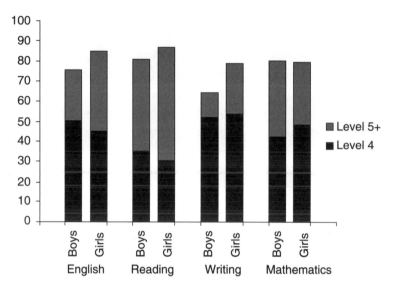

Figure 23.1 Key Stage 3: percentage of pupils achieving Level 4 or above, 2011

diplomas and A Levels also reflect gender preferences and stereotypes with girls pre-dominating in language and creative subjects such as English, art, and modern foreign languages, while boys opt in greater numbers for maths, economics, physics, and chemistry. Diploma programmes in engineering, information technology, and the built environment and construction often have fewer girls than the industry averages for employees, while hair and beauty, and society, health and development often have fewer boys. These gender differences continue into higher education. A greater proportion of students in university are female (59%); however, this is not the case within individual subjects. Only 15 per cent of students studying engineering, 21 per cent of those studying physics, and 37 per cent of those studying mathematics are female. While the differences between the subject choices of boys and girls are becoming less marked, girls are more likely to attempt subjects perceived as high status and 'masculine' than boys are to attempt 'feminine' subjects (Ofsted 2010d).

It is important to stress that boys' achievement is not getting worse in absolute terms. Boys are improving their performance, as are girls. Reporting on the findings of a four-year research project, *Raising Boys' Achievement*, Younger and Warrington (2005: 8) commented:

Achievement levels in primary and secondary schools, as measured by national tests at the end of each key stage, are rising through time. In some schools and LEAs [local education authorities], this has widened the 'gender gap', at least in the short term, as girls' performances have 'taken off' at a more dramatic level than those of boys. Overall, however, evidence suggests that the gap has stabilised, against a background of a rising trajectory of achievement for both girls *and* boys.

It should also be noted that differences in achievement by gender are not as pronounced as differences associated with ethnic origin or social class.

Some groups of boys and girls are particularly vulnerable. These include African Caribbean boys and white, working-class boys and girls. Of course, not all boys are under-achieving, just as not all girls are achieving to their potential.

Task 23.1

When you are in school, look at attainment data analysed by gender to identify trends in achievement over recent years. Are there particular issues in particular subjects for your school?

23.4   Reasons for differences in attainment

It is difficult to isolate any one reason or area that could be responsible for differences in attainment between girls and boys: 'The overwhelming message from research is that there are no simple explanations for the gender gap in performance nor any simple solutions' (Arnot *et al.* 1998: 90).

Some attempts at explaining the gender gap focus on biological factors. There are biological differences between boys and girls that can affect their learning. Boys are more likely to be colour blind, and visually boys are better at distinguishing moving objects against a background, while girls are more able to make distinctions between colours. Boys also have more difficulty hearing high-pitched or soft sounds. When pupils enter school at age 5, girls are already more competent users of language than boys. Psychologists have suggested differences in the way the two sexes think (Kohn 1995; Gurian 2001) and research by neurologists has found that areas of the brain associated with language are more highly developed in females, which may contribute to their better aptitude for language and social skills (Marrin 1997). Bleach (1998), however, cautions against assuming that differences are innate and so nothing can be done. The 'nature versus nurture' debate is recognized as being too simplistic to be of any real help in understanding the causes of gender differences in achievement. The situation is far more complex.

By the time children enter playgroup, they already have clear ideas about what girls and boys do. Observers note that boys tend towards physical activity, rushing around, while girls play quieter games and involve themselves more in discussion-based talk. From an early age, literacy is perceived by many to be feminine in nature, while mathematics, technology, and physical education (PE) are perceived to be masculine. By the age of 7, different attitudes to school are evident:

> Girls are more conscientious and concerned about presentation, they listen and pay attention . . . They tend to play without supervision, establishing their own rules and roles for each other in a way that mimics adult behaviour. Boys, by

contrast, are more noisy and attention-seeking; they find it difficult to sit still and pay attention.

(Bleach 1998: 4)

Other explanations focus more on social factors. Younger and Warrington (2005) point to the importance for boys of conforming to group norms, which are often in conflict with the expectations of the school. There is a narrower range of behaviour acceptable to the peer group for boys than for girls. Avoidance of the feminine and of the stigma of homosexuality is of major concern for boys. Whether this pattern of behaviour is innate or learned is open to question. It is likely to be the result of a mix of these factors.

Task 23.2

The following are some commonly expressed views about the differences between boys' and girls' aptitudes and preferences:

- Boys are loud and demanding in the classroom and get more attention from teachers.
- Boys don't like writing.
- Girls prefer to work in groups.
- Girls find it difficult to think logically.
- Boys find it difficult to express themselves.
- Girls do not perform well under pressure of timed exams.
- Boys prefer physical activity to academic work.
- Girls underestimate their abilities.

Consider your reaction to them. Note your responses for later reference.

At the start of their secondary school career, girls are more mature than boys. They are more likely to remain on-task and to set themselves high standards. Bleach (1998), referring to an article by Lightfoot (1997), comments that the concentration span of a typical 13- to 14-year-old boy is 4–5 minutes, compared with 13 minutes for girls. Boys' need for frequent interaction with the teacher if they are to remain on-task has relevance for you as a teacher when planning tasks.

Teachers often comment that girls are more compliant, seeking to please by getting on with tasks, endeavouring to do their best, and prepared to stick at tasks to complete them while boys rush to do things quickly and prefer short-term tasks. A survey of schools in Wales undertaken by HMI found that boys were less tolerant of poor or lacklustre teaching, quickly becoming off-task, indifferent and sometimes disruptive when they were bored or did not see the point of the activity (Ofsted 2003b). This reinforces the point that boys' learning is more teacher-dependent than that of girls.

There are nearly three times as many boys as girls with Statements of Special Education Needs (Ofsted 2010c). There is much debate as to why this might be. One possible explanation is that boys' higher activity levels and their frequent physical and verbal contributions result in the identification of attention difficulties or other learning difficulties. Another is that girls are under-identified.

In the home, it is often the mother who reads and engages in literacy activities with the children, while the father engages in outdoor activities or playing computer games with his sons, or helps with information and communications technology (ICT) and maths schoolwork. This reinforces the gender perception of literacy as 'female' and ICT or maths as 'male'. Adolescent girls are likely to spend their leisure time reading, doing homework, and chatting to friends, while boys' activities have an emphasis on doing rather than talking. Thus boys, having a learning style that is experiential, fail to develop the reflective abilities of analysing, discussing, and expressing feelings. While these are stereotypical statements, and will not be the experience of all pupils – indeed, may not be your own experience – research has shown it to be broadly the case.

Society's attitudes towards males are also cited as a cause for boys' underachievement. Traditional patterns of male employment have undergone radical change in recent decades, leading to uncertainty about what it is to be male. The decline of manufacturing industries with the loss of unskilled and semi-skilled jobs and their replacement by new technologies and service industries leads at once to a need for a better qualified workforce and to the replacement of traditional 'male' jobs with 'female' jobs. In addition, an increase in family breakdown leaves many boys without a strong positive male role model in their everyday lives. This is compounded by a decline in the number of male teachers in primary schools and, increasingly, in secondary schools, especially in subjects that are 'language-based'.

In response to these changes and to male images as portrayed in the media, many boys have a 'macho' peer culture that affects, often negatively, their attitude to school and to academic achievement. Shipman and Hicks (1998) found that both pupils and teachers identified peer group culture as having the greatest negative influence on the motivation of boys. Teachers need to be aware of, and able to counter, this peer culture, making academic success and being seen to work in class acceptable.

23.5 Approaches to raising achievement for all

The first thing to emphasize here is that, as the heading suggests, measures that a school might consider must be aimed at raising achievement for *all* pupils, both girls and boys. Girls should not be disadvantaged by actions taken to raise the standards of boys. Indeed, there is the possibility that girls' achievement will be raised and the gender gap will not be decreased by any measures that a school adopts. Second, it is important for schools to adopt a strategy that suits its circumstances.

23.6 Building an achievement culture

Building a culture where achievement in all forms is valued and celebrated is crucial to raising standards. On a whole-school level, this includes ensuring that a positive learning and achievement culture is developed among both pupils and staff. As regards gender, it is important that staff members understand the issues surrounding boys' and girls' achievement and that school and departmental policies pay explicit attention to gender issues. This includes analysis of pupil performance data by gender, including gender issues in departmental action plans and taking account of gender in lesson planning and delivery. Staff need to ensure that gender stereotypes and stereotypical attitudes do not enter their classroom or teaching. The physical environment, including displays, should encourage achievement, reflect the work of both sexes, and give positive signals about the subject's value to both sexes. Enabling pupils to use ICT to present work may help ensure that work is viewed as high quality and be of benefit to boys whose presentational skills may be weak.

Task 23.3

Does your subject have a gender stereotype or an achievement difference? What strategies can be used within your subject to address this?

Reflect upon how you can enable both sexes to access learning in your subject area.

Reward and sanction systems, where rewards are given for progress and effort in addition to attainment, and where sanctions are perceived to be fairly applied to both sexes, are important. Rewards, however, need to be of a type that boys value. Teachers know that praise is an important motivational tool but many adolescents, and particularly boys, prefer praise to be given privately rather than publicly.

School assemblies can be used to celebrate achievement, both academic and sporting. Research suggests that schools that place the same emphasis on celebrating academic or non-sporting achievement as on sporting achievement are effective in promoting a climate where standards are raised. In this way, boys learn to value academic success equally with sporting prowess, although there needs to be a balance between the numbers of girls and boys receiving each type of award. Speakers who provide positive role models and challenge gender stereotypes are also used effectively.

Schools' pastoral structures offer many opportunities to support the academic curriculum and build a culture of achievement. Personal, Social, Health and Economic Education (PSHEE) lessons offer opportunities to address gender issues, including the roles of males and females in today's society, career choices, and stereo-typing. Within a supportive environment, the macho culture can be countered and strategies for resisting peer pressure developed. Many schools use PSHEE to prepare pupils for subject choices at GCSE and post-16 education, providing further opportunities to counter gender stereotypes in subjects, for both girls and boys. Furthermore, PSHEE can be used to teach study skills and organizational skills, benefiting all pupils.

The pastoral system provides opportunities to support pupils. Increasingly, tutors are involved in target-setting with pupils and have an overview of the individual pupil's development and learning. Target-setting is an important tool in raising standards and has been discussed in Chapters 9 and 10. An important point in addressing boys' achievement is the active involvement of the pupil throughout the process; regular reviews of progress are believed to be of particular benefit to boys. The tutor is often the secondary school equivalent of the class teacher in the primary school – the teacher who, because of their detailed knowledge of and daily involvement with the pupil, has most frequent contact and is well placed to pick up early signs of disaffection and provide individual support and encouragement. The role of the tutor and the relationships the tutor develops with tutees is crucial here. Pupils value being seen as individuals with individual needs. Tutors are also well placed to mediate between home and school, bringing an awareness of the pupil's home circumstances, which may affect learning and enable, through the use of pupil diaries, communication with parents or carers to promote pupils' achievement. Many teachers are involved in delivering the PSHEE curriculum and so this has relevance for your classroom practice. Commenting on schools that are successfully closing the gender gap in achievement, Younger says: 'Where it's working is where the pastoral system in the school has as its aim the fulfillment of academic objectives'(in the *Independent* 2002). More is said about the role of the tutor and the PSHEE curriculum in Chapters 24 and 25.

A further strategy for raising standards through developing pupils' self-esteem and awareness of learning potential is the use of mentors. Mentors are used to target and support pupils who are identified as under-achieving. Younger and Warrington (2005) reported how targeting mentoring on pupils who were seen as 'key leaders', or particularly influential in their peer group, proved especially effective when combined with other strategies for building an achievement culture. Although mentors can be used with either sex, the disproportionate number of male under-achievers results in more boys than girls taking part. Two main forms of mentoring exist – both have at their heart the objective of building the pupil's confidence as a learner and enhancing self-esteem.

1. *Mentors taken from the business or commerce community*. Under-achieving pupils, who may be of any ability level, are paired with an individual mentor. These volunteers meet with their pupil partner on a regular basis. Their remit is to act as a role model and sounding board, to encourage the young person to consider the value of learning and to raise aspirations. On a practical level, they might also provide advice on career choices or discuss strategies to resolve barriers to learning the young person might have (for example, organizational skills or countering the 'anti-swot' culture). Meetings may take place off the school site. The mentor does not have a duty to assess the pupil or report back on the meetings.

2. *Mentors taken from the school staff*. Again, individual pupils who are felt to be under-achieving are selected for the scheme. Each is assigned a member of staff – frequently a member of senior management. The mentor's role is to meet with the pupil regularly to review achievement in subject areas, to encourage and give positive reinforcement, to help the pupil set targets and to discuss strategies for resolving

difficulties. The aim is to raise aspirations and expectations. This is a heavy commitment on staff time, so in some schools pupils are mentored in small groups.

A final point to consider in building a culture of success is that opportunities to succeed outside the classroom by taking part in extra-curricular activities can be beneficial in building self-esteem and in developing a less hostile view of school for some pupils. Extra-curricular activities help to build a school ethos, promote good relationships between teachers and pupils and encourage a feeling of belonging to an achieving community.

23.7 Groupings

A quick perusal of the league tables published following GCSE results shows that single-sex schools are highly placed. Many of these schools have a selective intake and a history and tradition of achievement. Research shows that it is difficult to separate the effects of single-sex teaching from other factors. The picture that emerges is very mixed and the proportion of pupils in single-sex schools is relatively small, so results should be treated with caution.

There is some evidence that girls' schools have a positive effect in encouraging girls to study subjects considered to be 'masculine' and in challenging stereotypical views, and girls in single-sex comprehensives achieve more highly than those in mixed-sex comprehensives. Boys in single-sex grammar schools perform better than those in mixed-sex grammar schools. Boys of low attainment perform better in single-sex comprehensives but for boys of middle or higher attainment, whether the school is single- or mixed-sex does not appear to make a significant difference. The school's size, pupils' social class, prior attainment levels, history and tradition of achievement may all impact upon achievement: league tables are far too crude to give a picture that schools could use to make decisions. In addition, one needs to be aware that schools are concerned to develop pupils' social skills in addition to their academic skills and there are disadvantages in single-sex schooling. Consider, for example, the consequence of having the views of only one sex represented in discussion, or drama, and there is often a negative behavioural effect on all-boys' low-attaining groups.

However, some mixed schools have experimented with single-sex teaching, often in a few subject areas such as English and science. Single-sex teaching in a subject that sets by ability may avoid the problem of sets that are dominated by one sex. Many schools find that in English, higher ability sets are predominantly female, while in maths, higher ability sets are predominantly male. Such a situation can have negative effects upon the self-esteem of boys and girls and lead to reinforcement of the idea that subjects are 'male' or 'female'. Younger and Warrington (2005) reported an evaluation of examples of single-sex grouping in three mixed comprehensive schools. The effects on pupils' achievements, on the whole, appeared to be positive, but it was very difficult to isolate the effect of the intervention. Their work, though, provided strong evidence that pupils felt more relaxed about contributing to lessons without the pressure of having members of the opposite sex in the class and that they felt better able to concentrate. They concluded that the success of single-sex grouping depended on the teacher developing a relationship with the class that provided a basis for collaborative effort.

Sukhanandan *et al.* (2000) found that when teachers adapted their teaching for single-sex groups, boys responded well to fast-paced, highly structured lessons. However, many teachers did not adapt their teaching style for the all-girl groups and there was little effect on girls' achievement.

Task 23.4

What has been your experience, if any, of single-sex teaching? Reflect upon the classroom situation and the advantages and disadvantages of the grouping adopted.

If you have no experience of single-sex teaching, consider your own schooldays and the way the two sexes behaved and learnt in the classroom. What differences can you discern?

What is your experience of the distribution of the sexes in ability sets and what impact did this have on the classroom environment?

You will need to think carefully about grouping in the classroom so that it enables both sexes to achieve. It is not uncommon for teachers to seat pupils with a view to behaviour management, but as Bleach (1998: 33)comments, 'the teacher should take the initiative in deciding where individuals should sit, based not on their behaviour but on optimising their learning'. Within classrooms there are many choices for gender-based seating, such as girl/boy pairings, mixed-sex groups or same-sex groups.

23.8 Teaching and learning

You may have read about learning styles and positive approaches to behaviour management in earlier chapters. Many schools are focusing their attention on a whole-school approach to raising the quality of teaching and learning with a consequent effect for all pupils but particularly for those who are under-achieving, many of whom will be boys. Contributions from boys in lessons are prominent, both physically and verbally, and they often have more experience than girls of having their contributions evaluated by a teacher. Boys also show greater adaptability to approaches to learning that require memorizing facts, rules and procedures. They appear willing to sacrifice deep understanding in exchange for fast answers. Girls, on the other hand, do better on sustained, open-ended tasks, related to real-life situations and that require pupils to think for themselves.

There have been suggestions that boys are more likely to prefer more kinaes-thetic, active, fast-paced and competitive teaching and learning styles. However, the picture is complex. In the interim report of their four-year research project referred to earlier in this chapter, Younger and Warrington found little overall difference in the learning styles favoured by boys and girls. Younger and Warrington (2003: 5) reported that:

- girls are more likely than boys to have a good grasp of effective learning strategies;
- there is a marked preference for visual-kinaesthetic modes of learning among boys identified as potential under-achievers or potentially disruptive;
- under-achieving boys showed a predominance of interpersonal, mathematical/ logical and musical intelligences.

In the final project report Younger and Warrington (2005) found that teaching styles targeted at preferred learning styles and at areas of weakness (for example, working explicitly on collaboration with groups of 'competitive' boys) can enhance learning opportunities for pupils. There was also evidence that simplistic approaches to learning styles were ineffective and genuine change in teaching practices difficult to achieve.

23.9 Assessment

It is widely believed that terminal examinations favour boys' learning styles emphasizing flair, risk-taking and short-burst effort, whereas continuous assessment and coursework, which demand reflection and sustained effort over a considerable length of time, favour girls. There may be some truth in this. However, when the proportion of coursework at GCSE was lowered or, as in the case of mathematics, removed, the gap between the sexes did not decrease. Girls currently outperform boys in both coursework and examination components. Differences may reflect the type of questions asked. For example, questions that demand discussion and reflection and require high-level language skills favour girls, whereas multiple-choice questions and ones that do not require written English favour boys. It has also been shown that boys believe that a last minute burst of revision will suffice, while girls work more conscientiously over a longer period. Encouraging self-assessment may help boys to develop a more realistic assessment of their learning and potential.

This has relevance for teachers. You have learned about formative assessment and the benefits it has for pupils' learning in Chapter 9. Assessment that provides quick feedback and targeted advice is helpful for all pupils but particularly for under-achieving boys who need close monitoring and to feel that their efforts are rewarded. It is important that the relevance of homework tasks is evident to pupils, since whereas girls may conscientiously complete the work whether it appears relevant or not, boys are less likely to adopt this attitude.

Boys can be helped more than girls by being given structures that enable them to succeed in tasks. This might include essay plans, mind maps and writing frames or being given short tasks that build towards creating an extended piece of work. They also benefit from being taught organizational skills, test-taking skills and revision strategies.

23.10   Literacy

Literacy is an area to which many schools are paying particular attention to raise standards. Pupils entering secondary school face heavy new demands on their literacy skills. Reading competence is particularly important. The quantity of reading they are expected to do increases while the time devoted to teaching literacy skills decreases. Most pupils will already be aware of their difficulties with literacy and the effect of this on their achievement and many of these pupils will be boys. When a pupil whose literacy skills are insufficient begins secondary school, the demands on their ability to read and write can be overwhelming and decrease motivation. Many pupils fail to progress in Year 7 and teachers note that demotivation and resultant disaffection often begins in Year 8 (Barber 1994).

23.11   Conclusion

In this chapter, you have learnt about the patterns of achievement shown by boys and girls and examined some of the reasons for the differences. Research evidence for the under-achievement of boys has been discussed. Strategies for addressing under-achievement have been outlined and related to the features of effective teaching examined elsewhere in this book.

Achievement by boys in recent decades is a complex matter involving changes in society's attitudes and understanding of the male role, economic and workplace change, and changes in schooling and assessment procedures. Schools that have set out to raise the standards achieved by all pupils and tackle under-achievement in general are most successful in narrowing the gender gap. Girls' learning should not be jeopardized by strategies to address lower achievement by boys.

23.12   Recommendations for further reading and webliography

Department for Children Schools and Families (DCSF) (2009) *Gender and Education – Mythbusters: Addressing Gender and Achievement: Myths and Realities*. Nottingham: DCSF.

Francis, B. (2001) *Boys, Girls and Achievement: Addressing the Classroom Issues*. London: RoutledgeFalmer.

Sukhnandan, L., Lee, B. and Kelleher, S. (2000) *An Investigation into Gender Differences in Achievement*. Slough: NFER.

Younger, M. and Warrington, M. (2005) *Raising Boys' Achievement*, DfES Research Report No.636. London: HMSO.

Websites

www.ofsted.gov.uk/publications (for text of *Boys' Achievement in Secondary Schools*)

www-rba.educ.cam.ac.uk/ (the home page for the *Raising Boys' Achievement* research project)

http://www.education.gov.uk/publications/standard/Equalityanddiversitysch/Page1/ (the gender and achievement section of the government's standards website, including a lot of background data and links to research reports and development projects)

24

Pastoral care and the role of the tutor
Cheryl Cane

24.1 Introduction

There has been a concept of pastoral care in English secondary schools for over 40 years, yet its aims and practice remain among the less examined areas of secondary school activity. Indeed, the term 'pastoral care' only entered general use in schools in the late 1960s and the term 'tutor' was not used in the maintained sector much before this time (Power 1991). Nevertheless, pastoral care is a vital and pervasive part of professional work in schools. Secondary schools today are as likely to promote 'excellent provision for pastoral care' as they are 'outstanding examination results', but there is also confusion about the nature of 'pastoral' care. Policy initiatives regarding workforce re-modelling (see Chapter 3) have created a 'blurring of boundaries between previously distinct roles' (Edmond and Price 2009: 302). These changes have resulted in a wide range of new roles within pastoral care, including 'associate professional' roles such as learning mentors, parent support advisors alongside (in some settings) non-teaching pastoral leaders. Also, because the role of the form tutor continues to evolve, some have suggested that there are instances where it is 'scarcely recognizable as such' (Roberts 2011). Rather than viewing pastoral care as diminishing in some way, there is, alternatively, the suggestion that a 'wider workforce at all levels is allowing schools to provide more care, guidance and support for pupils' (Ofsted 2008b: 308). This appears to be supported by emerging evidence that pupils today are spending more time than their predecessors accessing 'pastoral activity' (Symonds and Hagell 2011), although it is not possible here to evaluate the quality of that additional activity. Whatever your personal views on the status of 'pastoral' work in schools or on the particular titles given to various pastoral roles, it is the case that pastoral care will be an important aspect of your professional role whether as a form tutor or within your subject teaching.

By the end of this chapter, you should:

- understand the nature of pastoral care and the way it has developed;
- be aware of the relationship between pastoral care subject teaching and other related areas, in particular PSHEE/SEAL/learning-to-learn;

- understand the different dimensions of your potential role as a form tutor;
- have thought critically and reflectively about pastoral care.

24.2 The nature of pastoral care

As outlined in the Introduction, a fixed definition of pastoral care is problematic because of its evolving nature. However, there are many descriptions of pastoral care available and these can offer clues to the way that pastoral care has developed over time.

Task 24.1

Read and consider the following descriptions of pastoral care:

Pastoral care is:
- that part of the curriculum that caters for the 'social/emotional' aspects of the pupil, as opposed to their 'cognitive' needs. (Power 1991: 193)
- the heart of the work of a secondary school . . . enabling a child to become a student and develop fully as a person. (Marland and Rogers 2004: 1)
- providing the appropriate emotional support alongside learning support. (Weare 2004, cited in Schofield 2007: 31)
- concerned with the wellbeing and development of pupils in ways beyond the purely academic. (Lang 2007: 314)
- the vision of education as a moral endeavor, one that is aimed at human development in its widest sense. (Wortley and Harrison 2008: 241)
- concerned with the welfare of the person as an individual. That is, there is an implicit recognition that each person is unique and that care . . . should thus recognise individual and not merely communal need. (Carroll 2010: 147)

Consider the descriptions again. Are there particular aspects that you are drawn to? Can you find further descriptions from other sources or from your own experience? Do you notice any differences across time? What might these differences suggest? What aspects of school life today do you think might fit under the term 'pastoral care'?

Despite the lack of a fixed definition for pastoral care, there are sources that have offered explanations regarding the range of activity that could feature under the term 'pastoral'. A popular and often-cited explanation by Best (1999) suggested that pastoral work might engage staff in: (1) reactive activity responding to individual need; (2) proactive activity that anticipates 'critical incidents' for pupils; (3) developing specific curriculum in relation to PSHEE (or, more recently, SEAL, PLTS or 'learning-to-learn' programmes); (4) promoting a supportive environment with an ethos of mutual care and concern; (5) management or administration. While these five tasks remain relevant today, and might relate to the suggestions you made for

Task 24.1, Wortley and Harrison (2008: 250) point out that they 'do not take account of one of the recent developments . . . namely, tutoring to support students' academic progress and achievement'. This provision of support for pupils' academic work and achievement, now commonly known as 'academic tutoring', is an important feature of the pastoral care system in schools today. Academic tutors can be seen to represent a synthesis between pastoral and academic roles. This has not always been the case though, and a brief look at the history of pastoral care can lead to greater understanding of the current situation.

24.3 The origins of pastoral care

Lang (2007) described the beginnings of pastoral care in England in the public schools of the first half of the nineteenth century. Using examples of 'reforming headmasters of whom Thomas Arnold of Rugby School is the best known' (Lang 2007: 316), Lang recounted Arnold's ideals of religious, moral, and 'gentlemanly' conduct alongside intellectual ability. Thus, almost two hundred years ago, we find a perception of education that goes well beyond the purely academic to encompass morality and principled behaviour (Lang 2007). By the middle of the nineteenth century, it seems that these perceptions had been developed further to include consideration of how pastoral organization and the structure of the school might respond to these needs. In 1860, the Clarendon Commission collected examples from prestigious public schools of the day. They found that, at Eton, each pupil had a tutor 'whose connection with him remains unbroken during his whole stay in the school and whose duty it is to bestow that attention on him and undertake that responsibility for him that cannot be expected of the class teacher' (cited in Lang 2007: 316). Such a system was designed to provide each pupil with a link to an adult responsible for their overall welfare in school, but it also offered a structure for referring discipline issues. The relationship between pastoral 'care' and 'control' can thus be traced back to the nineteenth century.

The spread of comprehensive schooling from the late 1940s created fresh challenges for pastoral care, particularly regarding the size and organization of schools. Comprehensive schools tended to be much larger than previous secondary schools and required new systems to ensure that each 'individual pupil is made to feel that he belongs (even in a large school of 1500) and in which careful supervision of progress of the individual is the responsibility of someone who has under his care a manageable number of pupils' (Chinn, Chief Education Officer for Coventry, 1949: quoted in Lang 2007: 317). As a result, Coventry comprehensive schools were established using house systems. House systems were, of course, an important feature of the way public schools were organized. However, as Power (1991) suggested, a 'house' system was also an appropriate fit because it encapsulated the 'comprehensive spirit'. This organization of pupils by means other than the 'academic' promoted a sense of 'inclusion' rather than selection: 'it is there for all pupils from their first days to their leaving' (Power 1991: 197).

24.4 Organization of pastoral care

By the 1970s, comprehensive schools had been established in many local education authorities (LEAs) and often operated a house system following the Coventry model. These systems are normally described as 'vertical', in that pupils entering a house remain in it until they leave the school, with the house head and tutorial team also working in that house on a permanent basis. Some key advantages of a house system are:

- An all-age grouping whereby it is easier to introduce both collaborative activities between year groups within the house and competitive activities between houses.
- Pupils from different years groups can support other pupils at critical points.
- All the siblings from a particular family can join the same house and thus a stronger relationship with the family will be formed.

Over the years, preferences have been cited for a move away from house systems to year group or 'horizontal' systems for some schools. The arguments for year-group systems were partly administrative, but also pastoral. If all the pupils in a pastoral grouping are at the same stage, both administrative and personal issues are likely to be similar. Hamblin (1978) presented the idea of 'critical incidents' and suggested that a priority for pastoral care was to support pupils at key points in their development. A horizontal system allows for significant focus on the specific stage of development and critical events for each year group. It also allows for 'Head of Year' or 'Learning Manager' roles specialized in particular aspects of development such as transition from primary to secondary school or choosing options for Key Stage 4 (KS4) or KS5 study. Workforce remodelling has also encouraged some schools to re-invent the Head of Year role, assigning it to non-teaching managers who can be 'on-call' throughout the school day.

There are other important dimensions to the way pastoral care is organized and these can be common to both vertical and horizontal systems. For example, the degree of continuity in staff–pupil relationships is significant with schools needing to decide whether pupils should remain with a tutor and pastoral manager over a long period of time. Schools also need to consider the general organization of the day and where and when to place 'form tutor' activity, with most schools providing daily contact. In recent years, the allocation of pastoral time within the school day appears to have increased (Symonds and Hagell 2011). Their study of adolescents suggested that this increase might be in response to 'the increased prominence of wellbeing indicators used in Ofsted inspections' (Symonds and Hagell 2011: 299) and also following the 2004 Children's Act and the 'extended schooling' agenda (see Chapter 3).

Most schools today use either vertical or horizontal pastoral systems but some schools are challenging these traditional systems with new initiatives such as 'mentor groups'. Many schools use learning mentors alongside other forms of tutoring but for some schools, traditional form or house groups have been abandoned in favour of an exclusive focus on small mentor groups led by *all* staff (both teaching and non-teaching). The move from class-size tutor or house groups (approximately 30 pupils) towards small mentor groups (approximately 5–10 pupils) could be said to promote a greater focus on the individuals within the group. Such systems are very recent and require further research but are perhaps indicative of further changes for secondary pastoral care. New policies such as *Achievement for All* (Humphrey and Squires 2011), a new National Curriculum (2012–13) and new Standards for teachers (2012) are also likely to impact further on the organization of pastoral care within secondary schools.

24.5 Relationships between pastoral care, subject teaching and other aspects of the curriculum

Pastoral care can be seen as having strong relationships with other aspects of the school's work. There is a relationship with the academic curriculum and the academic structure of the school. Pastoral care supports the work of subject departments and the school as a whole but it also relies on support from subject departments and senior management to work effectively. It was suggested earlier that the role of 'academic tutoring' has supported schools in bringing pastoral and academic systems together. Having pastoral roles that encompass academic monitoring and support relies on curriculum systems that display awareness of the affective dimension within each subject.

Pastoral care can be seen as one manifestation of a broader concern with pupils' affective education. Thus, pastoral care is part of a broader concept. Affective education is not confined to pastoral care and all curriculum subjects, whether explicitly or implicitly, have an affective dimension. There is not the scope here to discuss this in detail but it is important to note that all curriculum areas impact on pupils' understanding of the world and can influence their developing sense of 'being' and 'belonging'. Whether it is through the choice of curriculum content, the way that learning takes place or the pupils' perceptions of how they are treated, every experience within school plays a part in their developing sense of identity and morality.

Alongside the affective dimension of subject teaching, there are specific areas of the curriculum labelled as 'pastoral education'. For many schools, these are led by form tutors who deliver PSHEE or SEAL programmes in lesson time or through specified tutorial times. In other schools, this is done by semispecialist teams. It is also commonplace for schools to incorporate 'learning' and 'leadership' into their pastoral programme with pupils learning 'how to learn' and 'how to lead' key aspects of their general development. The school's understanding of the nature of affective education, then, is important, and can influence the relationship between the pastoral and other manifestations of affective education within the school.

24.6 The role of form tutor

Many student teachers experience the role of form tutor either as an observer or through sole responsibility as part of their training. Even if your programme does not require you to take on the role of 'form tutor', it is still useful to consider the role in detail to understand the support available for both pupils and teachers.

Task 24.2

Personal vision for pastoral care
Imagine yourself as a form tutor. How will you present yourself to pupils? What will the experience of being in your form group feel like for them?

Decide upon a series of images for the sort of form tutor you intend to be and the sort of environment or atmosphere that you wish to promote. This might change from moment to moment depending on the context but what images does this role bring to mind? The following are some examples from trainee teachers:

- a cushion
- a piece of scaffolding
- an umbrella
- a set of traffic lights
- a pair of wings.

Save your images and return to them after you have (a) read the rest of this chapter and (b) experienced or observed the role of the form tutor, to reflect on any changes or challenges.

There are many aspects to a form tutor's role. Marland and Rogers (2004: 1) have described the tutor as 'the integrative centre for the school's efforts in personal development, from attendance to welfare, study skills to behaviour'. The form tutor role, then, is multi-dimensional. It is important to differentiate here 'form tutor' from 'tutor', as the latter can refer to one-to-one tutoring in a specific aspect of the curriculum. It is also useful to note that the title 'form tutor' may differ from school to school but it is used here to denote a significant adult to whom a pupil is accountable and who 'knows them well and gives them personal support and challenge' (Ofsted 2010a: 10). For many schools, this significant adult is the form tutor – an adult who knows a specific group of pupils very well, who sets high expectations for them but also provides a sense of belonging and 'home'.

The academic and caring aspects of the role are drawn together by the notion that there is nothing more caring than offering *all* young people the opportunity to reach their full potential in *every* aspect of their development. Rather than being seen as a divide, the academic and pastoral aspects of the tutor's role can work well together through a focus on 'all' and 'every'. This does place high demands on tutors though – you need to know your pupils well enough to offer them advice and support and to notice when they have difficulties. It also demands that pupils know you well enough to trust you and to rely on your guidance. Many of the activities that tutor groups and tutors undertake can support the development of trust and mutual respect. You can get to know your form through working with them on collecting money for charity, organizing a form assembly, planning a tutor group outing, and peer-coaching with other tutor groups. It is also important to provide regular opportunities when there is no formal agenda and when individual pupils can raise issues if they want to.

Task 24.3

The term 'unconditional positive regard' (Lodge 2002: 36) is sometimes used to denote the culture to be promoted within a tutor group. A key role here for the tutor is to ensure that all members of the tutor group are treated positively and understand their responsibility in treating others positively.

Consider how you might promote such a culture within your own tutor group. If you are using a reflective journal or a blog, you could focus an entry on strategies that you might use to encourage the tutor behaviours described below by experienced tutors who took part in Lodge's (2002) study, 'Tutors Talking':

- Be fair, open and honest
- Be positive and constructive
- Value them all as worthwhile individuals
- Provide guidance rather than control
- Be non-judgemental
- Establish trust
- Avoid favouritism or a perception of 'dislike' for any individual.

One example you might use for listening to, and valuing, individual voice and opinion is a Voice Box strategy. This is a simple postal box where all individuals are asked to deposit anonymous comments about how they feel about a situation or an aspect of their learning. It is a simple device that ensures that everyone's voice is heard when considering content and form of tutor sessions. Although you might expect that pupils would be able to discuss issues openly, I have never failed to be surprised by something I have learnt through the Voice Box that I would have been unlikely to hear in other ways.

What strategies might you employ with your tutor group and why?

The important aspects of pastoral support were explored by Schofield (2007) in a small study based on the perceptions of post-16 pupils and their form tutors. The study found agreement between form tutors and pupils that (a) offering emotional support, (b) monitoring academic progress, and (c) supporting academic progress were three of the most important aspects. Other aspects highlighted included: monitoring attendance, negotiating with other teachers or adults, and dealing with discipline. Thus Schofield found that while advocacy, accountability, and administration were important parts of the tutor role, support and monitoring of academic progress were seen as the most important aspects.

As a form tutor, you are likely to be involved in scrutinizing performance data, setting and reviewing targets with pupils and, most importantly, helping pupils to understand their own learning processes in order to develop themselves. Working with data is increasingly important within schools and a helpful quote that also suggests a note of caution is that data should be treated as 'a signpost, not a destination' (Ofsted 2010a: 12). A form tutor can bring together information from across the curriculum and, alongside subject specialists, can ask questions when a pupil is not attaining at a level that might be expected of them. Improving results is not the only goal of academic tutoring, however, and you will also be called on to talk to pupils about important curriculum decisions (particularly at the end of KS3 and KS4).

Communication with pupils themselves and their parents or carers will also be an important part of your tutor role. It is common for the form tutor to take a key role in holding 'learning conversations' with pupils and their parents/carers where progress and target-setting across the curriculum are the focus. In many schools, these longer 'overview' conversations have replaced the traditional curriculum evenings where parents meet with each subject teacher for a few minutes.

Schools and tutors take various approaches to the organization of progress discussions and to building relationships with pupils, parents, and carers. Many set one or two whole days aside in the year when an individual tutor undertakes tutee interviews (parents are often involved in this). Alternatively, for some schools, tutees are withdrawn from classes for individual interviews. Such approaches provide an opportunity to develop your tutorial role to the full. Though a key task of the interviews is likely to be target-setting and review, it is also an opportunity to gain a fuller understanding of your tutees and to strengthen your relationship with them. If you are in a school that does not provide time for working with pupils individually, it is still important to find time for individual discussions. This can provide opportunities to identify pupils who are in particular need of your support in one way or another.

Advocacy is an important aspect of the tutor's role. Most schools have school councils and some also have peer mentoring or leadership schemes, but these do not always provide a way for pupils to express an individual view or to seek individual support. There are circumstances in which pupils benefit from the support of an adult who knows them well and can speak on their behalf, particularly with other teachers or sometimes with family members. Taking this role demands care and judgement and also, for a new teacher, needs to be negotiated with a more experienced school colleague such as an induction mentor. Pupils who come to you for help will need to have their concerns recognized and not dismissed; they need to be listened to. They may also need reassurance or space to deal with anger. Don't be tempted, though, to promise to sort out the problem for them or to promise confidentiality, as this will not be possible. What you can commit to is partnership – you can be there for them as a listener, as an adviser, and as a member of a wider support network. Make it clear to them that they are not alone.

Many schools also look to form tutors to enforce school rules on matters such as dress, equipment, and completion of homework, seeing it as both a pastoral responsibility and a subject teacher's role to make sure that pupils are, in this sense, fit for the school day. Blending roles such as advocate and academic adviser needs skill and sensitivity. A confrontation over non-completion of homework is not the best way to start a conversation about option choices!

As a form tutor you will also be responsible for recording and monitoring attendance and punctuality. School attendance is a legal issue, as parents or carers are legally responsible for ensuring that their children attend school. It is also an important issue for school targets. Schools have strict procedures for recording and following up absence and you need to make sure that you understand and follow these procedures. For some new schools, a simple thumb impression from each pupil, on an electronic reader on entry to class, will make attendance monitoring relatively straightforward. For other schools, the form tutor and class teachers fill in electronic registers and submit them to a central system. Many schools also have robust policies for improving attendance in the form of rewards and praise for good attendance plus quick follow-up on absences particularly through text messaging directly to parents. The most important aspect though is ensuring that there is a coordinated response to any individuals who develop patterns of absence.

The role of a form tutor today, then, is wide and varied. Even when engaging in 'academic tutoring', we can see that this aspect encompasses more than just 'cognitive' needs. An Ofsted report exploring good practice in re-engaging disaffected and reluctant students in secondary schools identified the importance of 'Robust monitoring of academic, personal and social progress' (Ofsted 2008b: 22) in order to identify and intervene where there is a possibility of pupils becoming disaffected. The same report identified that best practice demonstrated regular communication with pupils and their families to ensure that they were fully involved and in agreement. Perhaps the term 'academic tutoring', then, also needs some revision to respond to current manifestations of the role. A term such as 'progress tutor' could represent the focus on academic, personal, and social progress. Today's form tutor does not just bring together the pastoral and the academic aspects; they recognize that these aspects are inextricably intertwined in an understanding of individual progress.

24.7 Conclusion

The intention of this chapter has been to provide a thoughtful starting point for your pastoral role in school. The pastoral role is central to the work of secondary schools, particularly in terms of the contribution it makes to support the personal, academic, and social progress of pupils. Schools vary enormously in terms of the time and resources they allocate to pastoral care, the importance they attach to it, and their interpretation of what it entails. This chapter recognizes that pastoral care is an important part of any teacher's role. Whether as a form tutor or as a subject teacher, all teachers will be committed to all 'pupils' achievements and wellbeing' (DfE 2011c: 8). The new Standards for teachers that will come into force in September 2012 state that all teachers are required to treat pupils 'with dignity, building relationships rooted in mutual respect' (DfE 2011c: 8) and to promote values of democracy, the rule of law, individual liberty, and tolerance. The tutor group, then, can be an important place to set and reinforce these expectations and to work in partnership with pupils as they make sense of, and create, their world. The form tutor is an adviser, advocate and academic challenger, but most importantly they are in partnership with tutees as they make their way through their secondary school journey together.

24.8   Recommendations for further reading

Carnell, E. and Lodge, C. (2002) Support for students' learning: what the form tutor can do. *Pastoral Care in Education*, 20(4): 12–20.

Carnell, E. and Lodge, C. (2002) *Supporting Effective Learning*. London: Paul Chapman.

Lodge, C. (2002) Tutors talking. *Pastoral Care in Education*, 20(4): 35–7.

Rosenblatt, M. (2002) Effective tutoring and school improvement. *Pastoral Care in Education*, 20(4): 21–6.

Watson-Davies, R. (2005) *Form Tutor's Pocket Book*. Alresford: Teachers' Pocketbooks.

25

Personal, social, health and economic education

Faith Muir, Nick Zafar and Chris Husbands

25.1 Introduction

There is an old saying that suggests that the most important things we learn
are learnt in nursery school – to line up, take turns and, most important of all, always
to flush the toilet. It's a reminder that schools are not simply concerned with the
formal, academic curriculum of subjects, but also with pupils' wider development –
with their personal, social, health and economic education (PSHEE). We expect
schools to play a leading role in the socialization of pupils, preparing them in the
most general terms for the demands of adult life, and this involves learning to interact
effectively with others in a range of settings. It is also about learning to negotiate
a path through the intricacies of life in a diverse and rapidly changing society.
More than this, we understand that while pupils' academic attainments may be powerfully influenced by their cognitive skills and dispositions and the quality of teaching
they receive, it is also the case that educational success is affected by self-esteem,
resilience, and the ability to negotiate one's way through the emotional and psychological complexities of childhood and adolescence. These considerations surround
schools' work in PSHEE.

Although Personal, Social, and Health Education (PSHE – note the absence of
'Economic') has been a required part of the secondary curriculum since the National
Curriculum (NC) review of 2000, underpinned by non-statutory national guidance
and closely aligned to citizenship, the publication of *Every Child Matters* (DfES
2003e) prompted a major shift in thinking about its potential role and how it could
help schools contribute to the five *Every Child Matters* outcomes (see Chapter 20).
Following a further NC review (2006/07), it was renamed Personal, Social, Health,
and Economic Education and restructured to comprise two new non-statutory
programmes of study at Key Stage 3 (KS3) and KS4: 'Personal wellbeing' and
'Economic wellbeing and financial capability'. In 2008, the government announced
its intention to make PSHEE statutory across KS1–4 but this decision has since been
rescinded; at the time of writing, the subject's future structure and content are again
under review.

By the end of this chapter, you should:

- understand the aims and content of PSHEE;
- know the main methods of and issues in the organization of PSHEE in schools;
- be aware of pedagogic issues in the teaching of PSHEE.

Task 25.1

Consider each part of the term 'PSHE education'. Reflect upon what you think 'Personal' may mean, then 'Social', and so on; try to relate it to situations you anticipate your learners may encounter as they reach maturity and beyond. Now note what you think personal, social, health and economic education should involve and how it differs from pastoral care.

25.2 The aims and content of PSHEE

The school curriculum is one of the main ways in which schools set out to provide opportunities for all pupils to learn and achieve. The 1988 Education Reform Act saw the overarching aim of the school curriculum as being to promote pupils' spiritual, moral, social, and cultural development and to prepare pupils for the opportunities, responsibilities, and experiences of adult life. These are ambitious aims that go to the heart of the purposes of schooling in a modern, complex society. If schools are to succeed in achieving these aims, they need to suffuse the whole academic curriculum. This is a challenging task, and one way of thinking about PSHEE is that it provides the framework that draws together the full range of schools' curriculum work: dealing with issues of pupils' confidence and motivation, supporting them in making the most of their abilities, helping them develop fully as individuals and as members of families and social and economic communities (Ofsted 2010a). In this context, schools' curricula for PSHEE have wide-ranging aims and objectives, but they can generally be grouped into four main areas:

1. Aims in respect of supporting pupils' social and emotional development, including addressing issues of self-awareness and change, managing feelings, empathy, diversity and prejudice reduction, building relationships and working with others.
2. Aims in respect of supporting pupils' social and health education, including addressing areas of content such as developing a healthy lifestyle, understanding substance use and misuse, making appropriate sexual decisions, and understanding and managing risk in personal, work-related, and social contexts.
3. Aims in respect of pupils' abilities to take advantage of learning opportunities across the school and in their life outside school, addressing issues of

decision-making, using critical reflection to clarify values and attitudes, learning and target-setting across the curriculum, developing a 'can-do', enterprising approach, and making informed career choices.

4. Aims in respect of supporting pupils' development as critical and informed consumers, producers, and citizens, including addressing issues of money management, personal budgeting and financial responsibility, employability, learning in work-related contexts, and basic business and economic understanding.

Task 25.2

Every Child Matters identified five outcomes for all children:

- enjoy and achieve
- achieve economic wellbeing
- stay safe
- be healthy
- make a positive contribution.

How do you see the aims of PSHEE contributing to these outcomes?

It is apparent from this range of aims that the potential scope of PSHEE programmes in schools is enormous. The non-statutory programmes of study for 'Personal wellbeing' and 'Economic wellbeing and financial capability' acknowledge this, identifying no less than eight strands for the teaching of PSHEE: sex and relationships education; drug and alcohol education; emotional health and wellbeing; diet and healthy lifestyle; safety education; careers education; financial capability; and work-related learning including enterprise (Macdonald 2009). Guidance is given, in line with all other NC subjects, as to the key concepts, processes, range and content and curriculum opportunities to be covered. However, each school is invited to develop its own approach to PSHEE, setting priorities within the broad framework that relate to pupils' own needs given the community the school serves. In some schools, the task of building a coherent, balanced, and well-structured PSHEE curriculum, often in very limited time, has proved challenging; programmes often appear to be made up of loosely related tasks each with their own implicit mini-objective. In a crowded curriculum, it is very difficult to cover everything and attempts to synthesize mini-objectives into broad, holistic aims, which themselves serve as the basis for robust curriculum planning remain rare (Ofsted 2002). In many schools, there is a taken-for-granted approach to the way PSHEE is planned and delivered, with more concern for timetabling and fitting in all the topics that have become traditionally associated with the subject, rather than evidence of an agreed set of overarching aims.

Pring (1984) tried to provide a systematic approach to thinking about the place of PSHE that still holds true today. He began by noting some of the difficulties teachers face:

> Too often teachers react to the consequences of the essentially controversial nature of PSE either by reducing it to trivia, or by saying that it is what they are doing all the time in helping each individual to realise his or her potential. There is rarely any systematic reflection upon the values which should be promoted in the school or in each classroom, or detailed analysis of what is defensible as personal development. Education, or the process whereby individuals are helped to grow as persons, requires a clear idea of what counts as being a person. It is difficult to see how anyone can claim to be an educator (as opposed to trainer) unless he or she has addressed him or herself to such an examination.
>
> (Pring 1984: 43)

Pring went on to suggest four underlying philosophical issues for PSHE curricula, conceived in terms of education of the person:

> First, one characteristic of being a person is the capacity to think, to reflect, to make sense of one's experience, to engage critically with the received values, beliefs, and assumptions that one is confronted with – the development in other words, of the powers of mind. A second characteristic of being a person is the capacity to recognise others as persons. Hence it is a peculiarity of being a person that one is able to relate to others in a person-like way, not using them as instruments of one's own ends, but as deserving of respect in their own right, worthy of being listened to, able to contribute a distinctive point of view. Third, it is a characteristic of being a person that one acts intentionally, deliberately, and thus can be held responsible for what one does. Finally, what is distinctive of personhood is the consciousness not only of others as persons but of oneself – a sense of one's own unity as a person, one's own values and dignity, one's own capacity to think through a problem etc.
>
> (Pring 1984: 43–4)

Personal social education, as it was then known, was ignored in the first version of the NC in 1988; attempts to develop it in the 1990 NC as a 'cross-curricular dimension' underpinned by 'themes' (economic and industrial understanding; careers education and guidance; health education; education for citizenship; environmental education) were largely stillborn as schools devoted energies to implementing the NC and its associated testing regimes. Since the early 1990s there has been a continuous, dramatic improvement in the status and position of PSHEE in schools for a number of reasons. In the first place, a widespread view developed that the academic curriculum of the NC was insufficient as a framework for thinking about the curriculum as a whole and its relationship to pupils' wider development. These views were linked to general concerns about the place of values in society and the effectiveness of schools in developing young people's values (Haydon 1997). In 1994, Ofsted published general guidance on *Spiritual, Moral, Social and Cultural Education* (Ofsted 1994). Three years later, the Schools Curriculum and Assessment Authority (SCAA) established a national forum on education and values in order to develop general guidance for schools on personal and values education (SCAA 1997). These developments fed into the review of the NC in 2000 and to the development of national frameworks for PSHE. At their most general, these sought to help schools steer a curriculum course through the multiple demands of delivering education for citizenship, health, sex and relationships, alongside a concern to support young people's moral, emotional and personal development. These developments were supplemented by resurgent interest in schools in the nature of learning across the curriculum and, in particular, interest in ideas such as thinking skills (McGuiness 1998), emotional literacy (Goleman 1996) and, in some schools, the development of what the Campaign for Learning called 'learnacy' (Rodd 2002).

More recently, in addition to *Every Child Matters*, a range of initiatives including the SEAL Framework (Social and Emotional Aspects of Learning – in secondary schools since 2007), the National Healthy Schools Programme, and the National PSHE CPD Programme have all made a positive impact on schools. As a result, schools now are probably more aware of their responsibilities in PSHEE than ever before.

Task 25.3

Draw up a list of topics you might include in a Year 9 PSHEE course.

Reflect on what influenced your choice, and consider the impact of the following factors: pupils' emotional development; pupils' physical development; the impact of pupils' social experience outside school; and the issues Year 9 pupils may be dealing with in terms of money management and career aspirations.

Ask some teachers and pupils to do the same and compare their results with yours.

The following website for Banbury School in Oxfordshire gives you an example of how one school structures its PSHEE provision:
http://www.banbury.oxon.sch.uk/pshe/index.htm

25.3 The organization of PSHEE in schools

Schools vary enormously in terms of the time, resources, and importance they attach to PSHEE. In most schools, its coordination has been improved by the identification of formal positions of responsibility, and the support of a designated member of the Senior Leadership Team. However, the allocation of time, resources and staffing to PSHEE remains difficult in many schools. One obvious reason for this is that in most – although not all – schools, PSHEE is taught by non-specialist teachers who are not organized into the sort of strong faculties that predominate elsewhere in the curriculum; teaching PSHEE is a part-time commitment for many teachers and student teachers may receive no training to teach it. Although some schools have specialist or semi-specialist PSHEE teams, it remains the case that almost all teachers can expect to find themselves teaching it at some point in their career – often to pupils for whom they also act as form tutors, which can make PSHEE very much part of the pastoral offering in schools. Given the complexity of the PSHEE curriculum, the range of topics that may need to be covered, the need to relate those topics to the needs and expectations of demanding adolescents with complex lives, and the sensitivity of many issues in health and particularly sexual health education, this is a daunting prospect. Beverley Labbett famously described preparing to teach PSHE as 'learning to handle your own ignorance in public'.

In many respects, the teaching of PSHEE can seem quite different from the teaching of other curriculum subjects. However, this difference can be more apparent than real. PSHEE may have its own discrete lessons and curriculum guidance, but it is also obvious that all subjects contribute to pupils' personal and social education as well as to their preparation for adult and working life. In all subjects, pupils need to learn to cooperate in groups, to manage their time effectively, and to make effective connections between their cognitive and emotional or 'affective' development. This means that there should be strong links between the overall curriculum and the PSHEE curriculum, not just in terms of content (for example, in the teaching of financial capability in mathematics and PSHEE) but also in terms of developing learning processes and achieving standards. Successful schools will have considered the ways in which learning demands are made on pupils across the curriculum and developed PSHEE programmes that support this – for example, timing work on homework skills or how to present oneself effectively in a work placement when they are most helpful for pupils. Schools that are most successful in managing the relationship between the wider curriculum and PSHEE will have gone further to explore the effectiveness of learning processes and styles across the curriculum and may have used lessons to support pupils in reflecting on their own approaches to learning. Paradoxically, the national focus on target-setting and on maximizing academic attainment potentially strengthens rather than weakens the place of PSHEE, opening a new role for it in providing a framework in which teachers and pupils can work together on identifying barriers to pupil achievement and developing cross-curricular and integrated approaches to addressing and removing these. Schools that have successfully diagnosed this issue and developed plans to address it have established robust relationships between their academic, pastoral, and social missions for pupils. The concept of the 'affective school' has also been elaborated to describe schools that have developed strong structures for supporting pupils' acquisition of 'emotional literacy' – that is, an understanding of how emotions affect our decisions and actions (Lang 1999).

25.4 Teaching PSHEE

A further challenge in relation to teaching PSHEE for many teachers relates to pedagogy. Mark Twain once said, 'I have never let my schooling interfere with my education'. His experience of 'schooling' was one of teachers, expert in particular subjects, teaching facts. However, unlike other areas of the curriculum, teachers are not 'experts' in PSHEE. The interrelated programmes of study refer to the knowledge, skills, understanding, and attributes to be developed. Clearly, these are not things that should be developed separately, because all are essential parts of effective personal, social, health, and economic education. Critically, though, these are not just things to learn, like facts – they have to be internalized, and this is more likely to be possible as a result of active experience rather than passive assimilation. It is equally clear that teaching pupils to work collaboratively and to make effective contributions to group work demands teaching methods that are themselves based on collaborative and group-based planning.

However, the difficulties are more deep-rooted than this. The outcomes of teaching history or mathematics are frequently clear in terms of pupils' understandings and ability to put into practice what has been taught. The outcomes of a teaching session on HIV/AIDS are more difficult to assess: pupils' understanding of the biology and epidemiology of HIV could be assessed but, in PSHEE, the concern is more likely to be with pupils' ability to make informed decisions about their behaviour some years after the teaching session. More complex still, in many PSHEE teaching sessions, teachers find themselves dealing with pupils' experiences of life situations which they have not experienced themselves and where they lack confidence – particularly in the light of the complex family and personal circumstances of many young people. Finally, the content of PSHEE differs from much of the conventional academic curriculum in some important respects. First, it is frequently process-based – that is, the content of the curriculum is also its medium: concerns with group work, with learning how to learn, and with personal decision-making are both the vehicle and the purpose of the curriculum. Second, it is highly learner-dependent in ways that the content of the English or science curriculum is not. Third, it is sensitive in many respects. This is obvious in the case of developing pupils' capacities to make appropriate decisions about their sexual behaviour, but less obvious in relation to issues about healthy eating or career choices, where there may be tension between teachers' values and those of pupils, parents or powerful social groups. Fourth, it may involve areas that are not touched upon elsewhere in the curriculum, such as drug education. The responsibility falls upon the PSHEE teacher to deliver this, creating considerable challenge for them unless they are able to call upon the expertise of other subject teachers or external support agencies.

PSHEE lessons are likely to feature specific techniques, including thought showering, ranking, values continuum, role-play or hot-seating, trust exercises, discussions and debates, interactive whiteboard, and imaginative use of the internet. In addition, resources devised by external providers may be used (although assessing the integrity of such resources can also pose a problem for teachers). Although these techniques are used in most subjects, they are likely to feature more strongly in PSHEE because of their focus on values issues and, in particular, on what has been called 'values-clarification': the intended outcome of exploring issues through these activities is not a class agreement on a best course of action, but a clearer sense of what is at stake. It follows that in PSHEE, more than anywhere else in the curriculum, a teacher's role may be to ask pupils to clarify their thinking and refine ideas rather than to correct misconceptions and errors. In PSHEE, it is a teacher's responsibility to allow diversity of views and to protect dissent. In PSHEE, exploring the debate may be more important than reaching a particular outcome.

25.5   PSHEE pedagogies

Generally, people recall:

- 10% of what they read
- 20% of what they hear
- 30% of what they see
- 50% of what they both see and hear
- 70% of what they say
- 90% of what they simultaneously say and do.

(Ekwall and Shanker 1988)

Arguably, the pedagogies applied to the teaching of PSHEE need to be particularly mindful of these findings, given that pupils are required to recall not just facts but experiences, feelings, and emotional evaluations.

Question Time

More than most other subjects, perhaps, PSHEE requires participants to be pro-active in setting the agenda for a lesson. Question Time is a useful activity for developing this type of lesson. It involves scattering a range of visual stimuli/resources relating to the lesson topic around the classroom. Pupils take five minutes to visit each item and devise a question about each one. In a circle, they then raise their questions to stimulate discussion.

Centre of the Universe

A technique used to involve the whole class in discussion. Arrange chairs in a circle and in the middle mark out a circle to represent the Centre of the Universe. A volunteer stands in the centre and is asked to make a comment about a particular subject; for example, that Birmingham is the centre of the universe because Birmingham City Football Club plays there. Anyone agreeing will stand as close to him/her as they feel their strength of agreement to be. If they totally agree, they will stand in the centre of the universe. Those disagreeing remain seated. Either the original pupil or any other in the centre of the universe makes another statement and so on. This will establish how the members of the class feel about a specific topic.

Thought showering

This can be undertaken as a whole-class activity or with smaller groups who then pool their results. It involves making a list of related ideas without thinking carefully about what springs to mind. Everything that participants suggest is recorded without discussion. No ideas are rejected. A thought-showering exercise should be spontaneous and brief. Some advantages of the technique are:

*   everybody is equal and has a contribution to make;
*   all ideas are accepted;
*   it is a quick way of gaining a lot of information;
*   it can help a group leader to assess the level of understanding;
*   it is cooperative and open-minded;
*   it can help with problem-solving;
*   it helps develop self-confidence.

Ranking

There are various methods of ranking and a wide range of topics/issues that can be addressed. Ranking entails listing a series of statements or pictures according to the demands of the task; for example, ranking a series of statements from agreement to disagreement or ranking a series of photographs from the most to the least stereotypical images. It is important to have each statement or picture on a separate sheet so that they can be manoeuvred during discussion. Items can be ranked in order, or 'diamond ranked' using nine separate sheets. This is useful with, for example, value statements where it may not be possible to create a strict hierarchy. A variation, known as 'twos and fours', involves giving pairs of pupils a set of six statements/points. They have to decide which four are the most important and discard two. They then form a group of four who have to agree on the four most important out of eight. The process is repeated with a group of eight after which groups report back and discuss their choices.

Values continuum

Individuals consider where they stand on particular issues and then rank themselves physically, in a line. This can also be done using statements on pieces of paper but the act of taking a 'standpoint' may be more thought-provoking or committed, for instance, 'Strongly agree' through to 'Strongly disagree'. Having established their relative viewpoints, pupils can be moved into structured discussion groups.

Role-play

Role-play allows students to explore a situation (through the feelings and attitudes they might experience) by assuming the persona of a participant in a situation. Role-play means presenting a set of attitudes rather than any physical change or characterization. It is a way in which teachers can give pupils quick access to a topic or generate more concern for an issue. This can take place in small groups possibly followed by a reporting back session, but it can also be an excellent medium for whole-group activities where the outcome need not be anticipated in advance. Role-play can help individuals to share emotions or concerns that they feel unable to express normally, since it allows them to say how they feel and, at the same time, distance themselves from the emotions by putting themselves in a fictional situation. Role-play can be part of an ongoing scenario.

Circle time

Although there is no definitive PSHEE pedagogy, it is nonetheless true that PSHEE has been particularly influenced by 'circle time'. Participants work in a circle, usually seated on chairs, with the teacher acting as a facilitator. Activities usually start with a round where pupils pass an object and take it in turns to complete a statement, such as 'I feel happy when . . .' or 'Something I find upsetting is . . .', or make comments on a particular theme. Ground rules normally include 'only one person talks', 'everyone else listens', and 'no negative statements about other individuals in the circle are allowed'. From this basis a wide range of activities, pair work, games, and small and larger group discussions are often developed. The process is normally seen as democratic and unthreatening, with no participant having to speak if they do not want to. However, there are considerable variations in what teachers perceive the outcomes to be, and therefore also in practice, ranging from development of speaking and listening skills, through improved behaviour to increased self-esteem and emotional maturity. One important aspect of circle time is that ways are found of getting pupils to change places (which is much easier to organize if pupils are sitting on chairs) so that everyone is sitting next to someone other than the person they chose to sit next to. This means that pupils get to know and work with a wider group of classmates than might otherwise be the case.

Debates

These can be formal affairs governed by the rules and regulations of debating, or more active, such as 'verbal boxing': desks are organized in the shape of a boxing ring and pupils are divided into two groups, taking up position outside either side of the 'boxing ring'. The two groups hold diametrically opposed views on a particular issue and will send one representative into the boxing ring to argue their point of view in turn. As each contestant exhausts their argument, they tag another team member to continue. As the debate progresses, pupils may change sides if their views alter. The verbal boxing match ends when either all pupils adopt the same point of view or a pre-defined time period comes to an end. To encourage participation by all, rules can be introduced limiting the number of times a pupil can be tagged.

Task 25.4

Think about the range of teaching strategies above and any other active learning techniques you know. Using one or a combination of them, plan a 30-minute lesson for pupils in Year 9 on a theme in health or sex education, or designed to promote pupils' thinking skills. Include a starter activity, active involvement, and some sort of conclusion that protects divergence of views and pupils' self-esteem.

25.6 Conclusion

PSHEE is one of a school's most important responsibilities. In this area more than in any other, perhaps, there is a strong connection between the subject matter and the way it is taught. In PSHEE, teachers are required to work directly with pupils on issues that raise complex moral and values difficulties. They need to do so in ways that are structured and professional so that values can be clarified and principles protected. PSHEE is not just something teachers teach to other people; if it is given the commitment it deserves, it affects and possibly changes teachers as much as pupils. For many new teachers, this makes PSHEE a challenging prospect. However, it also offers the opportunity to work directly with young people on the issues they see affecting their lives. As a result, engagement with both the content matter of PSHEE and, perhaps as important, the pedagogic approaches with which it is associated, has the potential to contribute strongly to teachers' own personal and professional development.

25.7 Recommendations for further reading and webliography

Hornby, G. and Atkinson, M. (2003) A framework for promoting mental health in school. *Pastoral Care in Education*, 21(2): 3–9.

Lang, P. (1999) Counselling, counselling skills and encouraging pupils to talk: clarifying and addressing confusion. *British Journal of Guidance and Counselling*, 27(1): 23–33.

Radford, M. (2002) Educating the emotions: interior and exterior realities. *Pastoral Care in Education*, 20(2): 24–9.

Websites
Personal wellbeing
www.pshe-association.org.uk/ (PSHE education content/policy)
www.antidote.org.uk/ (charity working towards an emotionally literate society)
eqi.org/elit.htm (emotional intelligence; parenting; relationships; abuse)
http://www.kenttrustweb.org.uk/children/kenthealthyschools_home.cfm
www.brook.org.uk (Brook Advisory, information for young people on sexual health)
www.tht.org.uk (Terence Higgins Trust, combating the spread of HIV/AIDS)
www.drugeducationforum.com/ (Drug Education Forum)
www.ncb.org.uk/sef/home.aspx (Sex Education Forum)
www.antibullying.net/circletimeinfo.htm (circle time information)

Economic wellbeing and financial capability
www.enterprisevillage.org.uk/ (WRL/enterprise resources)
www.pfeg.org/ (Personal Finance Education Group, financial capability: KS1–4)
www.cegnet.co.uk/ (resources for careers education)

26

Government policy

Ian Abbott

26.1 Introduction

Task 26.1

Before you start to read this chapter, list five recent education issues that have been in the news. Why do you think education is so important to the government?

As a student teacher you should be aware that the present Coalition government, elected in 2010, and the previous Labour government, has devoted a great deal of time and effort to a major reform of the education system. Even if you attended secondary school as a pupil fairly recently, you will have noticed a great deal of change when you went back into school as a student teacher. Teachers are always complaining about the amount and pace of change they have to deal with. You've probably heard teachers make comments such as: 'Why did they have to change that?' or 'Not another government initiative!'

Alongside the reform of the National Health Service, education has been at the forefront of the policy agenda for the government. Every part of the system, ranging from nursery education to adult education, has been subject to scrutiny and change. The secondary sector has been at the forefront of these changes, with policy shifts in areas such as inspection, management, curriculum content, teaching methods, and assessment. The pace of change has been so rapid that many teachers have felt unable to accommodate each initiative before the next arrived. Given this rate of change, there is a danger that a chapter about government initiatives will become dated very quickly as policy continues to be developed and implemented. However, it is important that you are aware of some of the most important changes and have an understanding of the reasons for government's emphasis on education. Therefore, we need to analyse the reasons for the government's approach to education, to use some recent policy initiatives as exemplars of government strategy, and to consider whether the policies have been successful.

By the end of this chapter, you should have:

- an understanding of the rationale for the recent reform of the education system;
- an awareness of overall government policy for secondary education;
- an understanding of the specific pattern of reform;
- an awareness of the impact of recent reforms on secondary teachers' lives.

26.2 What's the problem with our education system?

According to the government, the simple answer to this question has to be standards, which have been considered too low in this country. *The Importance of Teaching*, the first education White Paper published by the Coalition government (DfE 2010), claimed that the education system had considerable room for improvement and failed to perform to its potential. Since the publication of the White Paper, numerous policies have been introduced to raise standards for individual pupils and for schools. So, why has the government placed this emphasis on standards?

Most commentators would agree that access to education is a basic human right and it is clearly important in a civilized democracy that opportunities for a high-quality education are made available to all young people. While the government accepts this argument, it also believes that education has a key role in dealing with a range of social and economic issues. Reducing social exclusion is a key factor and the economic consequences of globalization and the technological developments of the last decade have increased the need for Britain to have a highly educated and skilled workforce. To compete with other industrialized and developing nations, Britain must have well-educated and adaptable workers who are able to respond to the demands of the twenty-first century. The economic argument for improving school standards can be viewed as straightforward:

1. In a global economy, Britain must be able to compete effectively with other countries.
2. Given Britain is not able to compete solely on the basis of cost because of the emergence of low-cost economies, we have to focus on ideas, innovation, and high skill sectors (the so-called 'knowledge economy').
3. To enable Britain to compete, standards in our schools have to be high and rising at least as fast as those of our competitors.
4. The government has a responsibility to ensure that standards in schools and colleges continue to rise and to develop strategies and systems that produce skilled and motivated young people.
5. To maintain our economic competitiveness, this will involve major changes in the education system.

6. A successful education system will produce young people who are able to make a positive contribution to the economic wellbeing of the country.
7. A flexible and skilled workforce will enable Britain to compete successfully in a global economy.

(Abbott *et al.*, 2012)

The Prime Minister, David Cameron, and Deputy Prime Minister, Nick Clegg, strongly support education reform and argued that:

> So much of the education debate in this country is backward looking: have standards fallen? Have exams got easier? These debates will continue, but what really matters is how we're doing compared with our international competitors. That is what will define our economic growth and our country's future. The truth is, at the moment we are standing still while others race past.
>
> (DfE 2010: 3)

There is a strong emphasis by the Coalition government on the importance of international comparisons. Many of the most recent policy initiatives have been 'borrowed' from other countries where they have been considered to be successful. For example, Free Schools are based on the Charter Schools in the USA. There is a recognition that even successful education systems aim for continual improvement:

> Even the best school systems in the world are constantly striving to get better – Singapore is looking again at further improving its curriculum, while Hong Kong is looking at ways in which it can improve its teacher training.
>
> (DfE 2010: 8)

While there are obvious advantages to looking at other successful school systems, there are also some potential problems. It is important to remember that what is successful in one country might not be easily transferred to another. There will be cultural, social, and economic differences that make it difficult to implement particular policies. International comparisons are useful but have to be treated with some caution and it is essential to recognize the particular features of the English education system.

However, the government has instigated fundamental reform of the education system, and it has introduced a range of specific policies to raise standards. You might disagree with the policies, but it is difficult to disagree with the Coalition government's drive to raise standards in education. Earlier in this book, you will have read about strategies to raise standards in areas such as literacy and numeracy, to reduce truancy, and combat social exclusion. Targets have been set for pupils and schools, and performance indicators are used to gauge the success of policy. The results of these have been published in an attempt to drive up standards across the board. Probably the best examples of this are the annual publication of league tables for schools and the regular Ofsted inspection process. If you are undertaking a school placement, or are looking for a teaching job, you will almost certainly have consulted the school's Ofsted report and looked at the various measures of school performance that are publicly available. An army of inspectors and statisticians is employed to collect these data. All of this effort will clearly result in better information and should enable clear identification of problem areas. As a consequence, remedial action can be taken to address particular issues. The collection and the publication of data by the government is a valuable means of evaluating particular policy initiatives. However, what we need to do now is to consider in broad terms what policies have been implemented and how they are likely to impact on you as a new secondary school teacher.

26.3 Government policies

A central feature of the previous government's commitment to education was the increased resources made available to schools. The proportion of national income spent on education increased from 4.7 per cent when the Labour government came to power to 5.6 per cent in 2007–08 (DfES 2006b). Average real terms expenditure per secondary pupil in England increased from £3300 in 1997–98 to £4530 in 2005–06. There has been massive capital expenditure on education with a £45 billion building programme to rebuild or renew every one of England's 3500 secondary schools over a 15-year period (Partnership for Schools 2007). The composition of the workforce has changed as the overall size of the workforce has increased:

> Teacher numbers have grown by 36,200 since 1997. There are now 435,400 full-time equivalent (FTE) teachers in the maintained schools sector in England, the highest level since 1981. Support staff numbers have also risen with 287,100 FTE support staff in schools, including 152,800 teaching assistants, an increase of 162,800 since 1997.
>
> (DfES 2006b: 11)

Since the onset of the global financial crisis, however, the growth in resources devoted to education has stalled. According to the Institute of Fiscal Studies, there will be a 13 per cent cut in real terms in expenditure on education between 2010–11 and 2014–15 (Chowdry and Sibieta 2011). All sectors of education are affected by the cuts in funding, but the major impact will fall on capital expenditure, 16–19 education, and early years' provision. Spending on schools has received some protection but most schools will see real cuts in revenue. This is a major change to the earlier part of the century, which was a period of unprecedented growth. The cuts in education funding are predicted to be the largest for over fifty years.

Against a background of reduced resources, the government aims to develop a radical new school system that is supported by improved choice and access for all. The first White Paper published by the Coalition government; *The Importance of Teaching* (DfE 2010), strongly suggests that the teaching profession is seen as central to the government's aim to improve the education system. In Chapter 2, we considered the introduction of new teachers' Standards, which are designed to raise the professional status of teachers. The recently appointed head of Ofsted stated that 'an outstanding school will have outstanding teaching' (Wilshaw 2012). While teachers are central to the drive to improve education standards, other aspects of the system are also being reformed:

- the curriculum, assessment, and qualifications
- school funding
- behaviour policies
- school improvement policies
- school leadership
- the school system.

There will be ongoing reform of the National Curriculum (NC) and greater emphasis on academic standards. Vocational programmes will be strengthened to ensure progression to further education and employment routes. The emphasis will be on high-quality and rigorous qualifications. Schools will be encouraged to offer a broad range of academic subjects and the introduction of the English Baccalaureate will be an important part of this process. The English Baccalaureate will be awarded to students who obtain A*–C GCSE or iGCSE passes in English, mathematics, two sciences, a modern or ancient foreign language, and a humanities subject. This is part of the drive to provide a more rounded educational experience and to promote academic achievement.

Task 26.2

What have been the major curriculum reforms in your subject area? What is the likely impact of curriculum reform on your subject area?

At the time of writing, it is too early to judge the impact of the reforms that are being implemented, but as you begin your teaching career you will be affected by the many reforms taking place. In particular, you are likely to find yourself working in different types of school that are structured and controlled in a variety of ways. A central part of the reform process is the belief that schools can make a significant difference to raising standards and this can be achieved by giving greater independence to individual schools. The government has placed strong emphasis on school autonomy:

13. Across the world, the case for the benefits of school autonomy has been established beyond doubt. In a school system with good quality teachers, flexibility in the curriculum and clearly established accountability measures, it makes sense to devolve as much day-to-day decision-making as possible to the front line.
14. In this country, the ability of schools to decide their own ethos and chart their own destiny has been severely constrained by government guidance,

Ministerial interference and too much bureaucracy. While Academies and City Technology Colleges (CTCs) have taken advantage of greater freedoms to innovate and raise standards, these freedoms too have been curtailed in recent years. Meanwhile, it has been virtually impossible to establish a new state-funded school without local authority support, despite convincing international evidence of the galvanising effect on the whole school system of allowing new entrants in areas where parents are dissatisfied with what is available.

(DfE 2010: 11)

Given this belief that school autonomy will lead to a stronger education system, the Coalition government is attempting to introduce a new schools system based around different types of school. These include:

- Academies
- Maintained Schools: Community/Foundation
- Technical Academies, University Technical Colleges (UTCs) and Studio Schools
- Voluntary and Faith Schools
- Free Schools
- Trust Schools
- Specialist Schools.

According to the Coalition government, allowing different types of school to open will encourage innovation and lead to rising standards of pupil achievement. For example, parents, teachers, charities, and interested groups will be able to open a Free School if there is evidence of parental demand in a particular locality. Another example of an alternative type of school is the UTC, which will be established by a partnership of universities, colleges, and businesses. University Technical Colleges will offer a combination of technical and academic education and are designed to raise overall standards in vocational education.

However, the major area of expansion in the system proposed by the Coalition government will be the number of schools becoming Academies. Originally, Academies were a New Labour policy initiative and the first Academy schools opened in 2003. Initially, they were designed to deal with the problems facing a number of failing schools in inner cities (Gorard 2009). In effect, Academies were new schools that provided the opportunity for a fresh start and a break from past failures (Abbott *et al.* 2012). Academies were freed from many regulations, removed from local authority control, and sponsored by an external organization that brought fresh ideas and enthusiasm. Initially, evidence of the success of Academies was mixed but there were some notable success stories with some schools being transformed. The Coalition government aims to build on the successes of the Academy programme and the eventual aim is that every school in England should become an Academy. In 2010, the first stage of this process enabled outstanding schools to become Academies and these schools would provide leadership and inspiration for the wider education system. At the other end of the spectrum, the weakest schools would also convert to Academy status with the support of an out-standing school or a strong sponsor to provide the stimulus for change. The sponsor plays a significant role in the operation of an Academy and can provide a range of common services and approaches to leadership and professional development. A number of sponsors such as ARK (Absolute Return for Kids – a UK education char-ity) are associated with a range of schools and provide a common approach across all their Academy schools.

The Coalition government envisages that Academy status will 'be the norm for all state schools, with schools enjoying direct funding and full independence from central and local bureaucracy' (DfE 2010: 52). The move to greater school autonomy through the establishment of Academies and other types of new school organization is designed to have a positive impact on standards and to improve the overall quality of teaching and learning. As part of a package of policy measures, it is designed to encourage the development of a quasi market in education aimed at promoting choice and competition.

Task 26.3

Do you agree with the argument that giving schools greater autonomy will lead to improvements in the system? Find out the status of the school where you are training or working.

There is a strong desire on the part of the Coalition government to provide the high-est educational opportunities for all children. Against a background of cuts in public expenditure, additional funding has been made available through the introduction of the Pupil Premium, which provides additional money to pupils from deprived back-grounds. The amount of money allocated for the Pupil Premium is £2.5 billion by 2014–15. This is money additional to existing expenditure on schools. The intention is to raise educational standards among the poorest sections of society and to reduce the attainment gap between rich and poor pupils. The drive to improve the perfor-mance of the poorest group of school pupils is a significant part of Coalition policy and is reflected in a number of initiatives. For example, the number of teachers train-ing through the Teach First route has increased significantly. Teach First is a charity that aims to address educational disadvantage by transforming exceptional graduates into effective, inspirational teachers and leaders in all fields. They work in disadvan-taged inner-city schools in challenging circumstances with a high level of poverty and/or under-achievement.

26.4   Impact of government policies

The government has placed a great deal of emphasis on the drive to raise standards in schools and to improve the education system. It is important to remember that the notion of educational standards is open to more than one interpretation, an ambiguity that complicates any attempt to measure educational standards. Moreover, statistics are also open to interpretation and different groups will put a different emphasis on the same data. You need to be aware that there are conflicting agendas and messages in the daily output of government statistics and information relating to education.

For you as a beginning teacher, the significance of any government initiative is the impact it has on your school and your classroom teaching. Polices will directly affect you in your subject area as you are compelled by the government to adopt particular approaches, introduce new subject content or assessment procedures. In a wider school context, government initiatives will directly affect the amount of resource available, staffing levels, and your conditions of service. If you are training or working in a specialist school or in an Academy School, there is a strong likelihood that you will have greater access to additional resources and more specialized equipment. If, however, you find yourself teaching in a rural school, you might have significantly fewer resources to deal with similar issues. However, the key significance of all education initiatives is the impact they have on the individual school pupil and your ability to operate effectively as a classroom teacher.

Task 26.4

During your school placement, find out what new initiatives the school has been involved in over the past five years. How were these initiatives evaluated and how successful have they been in improving standards?

26.5 Conclusion

There is general agreement on the importance of education for the individual and for the wider community. All political parties recognize the need to improve educational standards and to create a more educated workforce to enable the creation of:

- a fair and just society that gives equal opportunities to all regardless of background;
- a safe society that enables young people to make a positive contribution;
- a prosperous society that contributes to economic wellbeing for all.

There is no general agreement, however, about how these objectives can be achieved. In political terms, education remains a key battleground between the main parties. All governments will be keen to be seen to be improving education and it is very easy to confuse change with improvement. Whether or not they can be unambiguously viewed as improvements, changes in policy are set to continue. The policy debate taking place in Parliament and in the media might seem far removed from your day-to-day responsibilities as a classroom teacher. However, you cannot close your classroom door and ignore the latest policy initiatives. Ultimately, policy initiatives filter down to the classroom and affect the way you teach. You will be in the best position to make the changes effective in a positive way if you have taken the time to understand where they are coming from and why.

It is rather early to judge the success or failure of many recent government policies. The pace of change continues at a rapid rate and you will need to keep up-to-date with current developments. At times this can be daunting given the sheer volume of legislation and the demands placed on you as you begin your teaching career. Education policies often take a great deal of time to produce results and numerous questions about ongoing government reform remain unanswered. For instance:

- Even if standards are improving, are they rising at a fast enough rate or in the right areas?
- Should the emphasis be on developing skills for employment or on more general education?
- Are the changes being suggested for the secondary curriculum right?
- Should the government develop a radical new school system?
- Is the pace of change right?
- Is the level of funding right?

Imagine this scene. The year is 2020. It is Monday morning. You arrive at your newly built school, sponsored by a local software company. The first thing you do is to download the homework that has been emailed to you over the weekend, along with one or two excuse messages. You check over the slide presentation that has been put together for you from your notes by the department's information and communications technology (ICT) assistant and set out to greet your Year 10 tutor group, who have been working on their personalized learning programme. The group is busy checking the e-conference notice-board while you talk to a few individuals about arrangements for the modular exams they will be sitting next month. At 9.00 a.m. you dismiss the group and go to deliver your presentation to your class and, by video link, to the other Academies in your group. After the small-group follow-up seminars, you use the video phone to contact your colleague at your partner Academy in another city to discuss timetabling for next year.

This may seem far-fetched, but it is just as likely to be a very conservative assessment of the changes that will take place before 2020. Every aspect of this scenario is a foreseeable result of government policy initiatives current at the time of writing. Some of these changes will seem more desirable to you than others. More than ever, teachers, through their schools, professional associations, subject associations, and research networks, have the chance to influence the policies that impact on their work at local, regional, and national level. Teachers are being placed at the forefront of the current policy reforms and in this sense, as well as others, the future of teaching is in your hands.

26.6 Recommendations for further reading and webliography

Abbott, I., Rathbone, M. and Whitehead, P. (2012) *Education Policy*. London: Sage.

Benn, M. (2011) *School Wars: The Battle for Britain's Education*. London: Verso.

Chowdry, H. and Sibieta, L. (2011) *Trends in Education and Schools Spending*. London: IFS.

Department for Education (DfE) (2010) *The Importance of Teaching: The Schools White Paper 2010*. London: HMSO.

Gorard, S. (2009) What are Academies the answer to? *Journal of Education Policy*, 24(1): 101–13.

Website

http://www.education.gov.uk/ (Department for Education website)

Bibliography

Abbott, I., Rathbone, M. and Whitehead, P. (2012) *Education Policy*. London: Sage.

Adey, K. and Biddulph, M. (2001) The influence of pupil perceptions on subject choice at 14+ in geography and history, *Educational Studies*, 27(4): 439–47.

Adey, R.S. and Shayer, M. (eds.), (2002) *Learning Intelligence: Cognitive Acceleration Across the Curriculum from 5 to 15 years,* Buckingham: Open University Press.

Ainley, J. (2008) *Task Design Based on Purpose and Utility, Topic Study Group 34: Research and Development in Task Design and Analysis*. Paper presented at the Eleventh International Congress on Mathematical Education, Monterrey, Mexico, 6–13 July.

Alexander, R. (2005) *Towards Dialogic Teaching: Rethinking Classroom Talk*, 2nd edn. Cambridge: Dialogos.

Arnot, M., Gray, J., James, M., Ruddock, J. with Duveen, G. (1998) *Recent Research on Gender and Educational Performance*. London: HMSO.

Arthur, J., Davies, I., Wrenn, A., Haydn, H. and Kerr, D. (2001) *Citizenship Through Secondary History*. London: RoutledgeFalmer.

Askew, M., Brown, M., Rhodes, V., Wiliam, D. and Johnson, D. (1997) *Effective teachers of numeracy*. Report of a study for the Teacher Training Agency. London: King's College, University of London.

Ausubel, D. (1968) *Educational Psychology: A Cognitive View*. New York: Holt, Rinehart & Winston.

Ayers, H., Clarke, D. and Murray, A. (2000) *Perspectives on Behaviour: A Practical Guide to Effective Interventions for Teachers*, 2nd edn. London: David Fulton.

Bandura, A. (1985) *Social Foundations of Thought and Action*. Englewood Cliffs, NJ: Prentice-Hall.

Barber, M. (1994) *Young People and Their Attitudes to School*. Keele: Keele University.

Barnes, D., Britton, J., Rosen, H. and the LATE (1969) *Language, the Learner and the School*. Harmondsworth: Pelican.

Bassett, D.S., Wymbs, N.F., Porter, M.A., Mucha, P.J., Carlson, J.M. and Grafton, S.T. (2010) *Dynamic reconfiguration of human brain networks during learning*, Paper presented at the Conference on New Horizons in Human Brain Imaging: A Focus on Brain Networks and Connectivity, Oahu, Hawaii, 1–3 December.

Bell, M., Cordingley, P. and Goodchild, L. (2008) *Map of Research Review QCA Building Evidence Based Project: September 2007–March 2011*, CUREE. Available online at: http://dera.ioe.ac.uk/1208/1/CUREE_Map_of_research_ reviews_FINAL.pdf [accessed October 2011].

Bennett, N. and Carré, C. (1993) *Learning to Teach*. London: Routledge.

Best, R. (1999) The impact of a decade of educational change on pastoral care and PSE: a survey of teacher perceptions, *Pastoral Care in Education*, 17(2): 3–13.

Bigger, S. and Brown, E. (eds.) (1999) *Spiritual, Moral, Social and Cultural Education: Exploring Values in the Curriculum*. London: David Fulton.

Black, P. (1998) *Testing: Friend or Foe? Theory and Practice of Assessment and Testing*. London: Falmer Press.

Black, P. and Wiliam, D. (1998a) Assessment and classroom learning, *Assessment in Education*, 5(1): 7–78.

Black, P. and Wiliam, D. (1998b) *Inside the Black Box: Raising Standards through Classroom Assessment*. London: King's College.

Black, P., Harrison, C., Lee, C., Marshall, B. and Wiliam, D. (2002) *Working Inside the Black Box: Assessment for Learning in the Classroom*. London: King's College.

Blair, M. and Bourne, J. (1998) *Making the Difference: Teaching and Learning Strategies in Successful Multi-ethnic Schools*. London: DfEE and Open University.

Bleach, K. (ed.) (1998) *Raising Boys' Achievement in Schools*. Stoke-on-Trent: Trentham Books.

Bloom, B.S. (ed.) (1956) *Taxonomy of Educational Objectives*. New York: Longmans Green.

Bloom, B.S., Englehart, M., Furst, E., Hill, W. and Krathwohl, D. (1956) *Taxonomy of Educational Objectives: The Classification of Educational Goals, Handbook 1: Cognitive Domain*. New York: Longmans Green.

Blum, L. (1980) *Friendship, Altruism, and Morality*. Boston, MA: Routledge & Kegan Paul.

Boaler, J. (1997) Setting, social class and survival of the quickest, *British Educational Research Journal*, 23(5): 575–95.

Board of Education (1905) *Suggestions for the Consideration of Teachers and Others Concerned with the Work of Public Elementary Schools*. London: HMSO.

Board of Education (1921) *The Teaching of English in England* (The Newbolt Report). London: HMSO.

Brett, P. (2007) *Identity and Diversity: Citizenship Education and Looking Forwards from the Ajegbo Report*. Available online at: http://www.citized.info/pdf/commarticles/Peter%20 Brett%20-%20Identity%20and%20Diversity.pdf [last accessed 2 April 2011].

Bromfield, C. (2005) PGCE secondary trainee teachers and effective behaviour management: an evaluation and commentary, *Support for Learning*, 21(4): 188–93.

Brooks, V. and Fancourt, N. (2012) Is self-assessment in religious education unique? *British Journal of Religious Education* 34(2): 123–137.

Brown, G. (2006) Address to the Fabian Society, London, 14 January.

Carroll, M. (2010) The practice of pastoral care of teachers: a summary analysis of published outlines, *Pastoral Care in Education*, 28(2): 145–54.

Cassen, R. and Kingdon, G. (2007) *Tackling Low Educational Achievement*. York: Joseph Rowntree Foundation.

Cassen, R., Feinstein, L. and Graham, P. (2009) Educational outcomes: adversity and resilience, *Social Policy and Society*, 8: 73–85.

Cheminais, R. (2010) *Special Educational Needs for Qualified Teachers and Teaching Assistants*, 2nd edn. London: Routledge.

Children and Young People's Unit (2000) *Children's Fund Guidance*. London: DfES.

Chitty, C. (2002) *Understanding Schools and Society*. London: Routledge.

Chowdry, H. and Sibieta, L. (2011) *Trends in Education and Schools Spending*. London: IFS.

Clark, C. (1989) Asking the right questions about teacher education: contributions of research on teacher thinking, in J. Lowyck and C. Clark (eds.) *Teacher Thinking and Professional Action*. Leuven: Leuven University Press.

Claxton, G. (1984) The psychology of teacher training: inaccuracies and improvements, *Educational Psychology*, 4(2): 167–74.

Clegg, S. and McNulty, K. (2002) Partnership working in delivering social inclusion: organizational and gender dynamics, *Journal of Education Policy*, 17(5): 587–601.

Cockroft, W.H. (1982) *Mathematics Counts*. London: HMSO.

Cofield, F.J., Moseley, D.V., Hall, E. and Ecclestone, K. (2004) *Should We Be Using Learning Styles? What Research has to Say to Practice*. London: Learning and Skills Research Centre/ University of Newcastle upon Tyne.

Collier, V. (1989) How long? A synthesis of research on academic achievement in a second language, *TESOL Quarterly*, 23(3): 509–31.

Comber, C., Watling, R., Lawson, T., Cavendish, S., McEune, R. and Paterson, F. (2002) *ImpaCT2 – Learning at Home and School: Case Studies*. Coventry: Becta.

Commission for Racial Equality (2000) *Learning For All, Standards for Racial Equality in Schools*. London: CRE.

Cope, B. and Kalantzis, M. (2003) A multiliteracies pedagogy: a pedagogical supplement, in B. Cope and M. Kalantzis (eds.) *Multiliteracies*. London: Routledge.

Cowley, S. (2006) *Getting the Buggers to Behave*. London: Continuum.

Cox, B. (ed.) (1998) *Literacy is not Enough*. Manchester: Manchester University Press.

Cuban, L., Kirkpatrick, H. and Peck, C. (2001) High access and low use of technologies in high school classrooms: explaining an apparent paradox, *American Education Research Journal*, 38(4): 313–34.

Cummings, C., Todd, L. and Dyson, A. (2004) *Evaluation of the Extended Schools Pathfinder Projects*. London: DfES.

Cummins, J. (1984) *Bilingualism and Special Education: Issues in Assessment and Pedagogy*. Bristol: Multilingual Matters.

Dall'Alba, G. (2006) Learning strategies and the learner's approach to a problem solving task, *Research in Science Education*, 16(1): 11–20.

Daloz, L. (1986) *Effective Teaching and Mentoring*. San Francisco, CA: Jossey-Bass.

Davies, H. (2002) *Review of Enterprise and the Economy in Education*. London: HMSO.

Dawkins, R. (1989) *The Selfish Gene*. Oxford: Oxford University Press.

Day, C. (1999) *Developing Teachers: The Challenges of Lifelong Learning*. London: Falmer Press.

Department for Children Schools and Families (DCSF) (2007) *Smoking Out Underachievement*. London: DCSF.

Department for Children Schools and Families (2008) *The Education and Skills Act 2008*. London: DCSF.

Department for Children Schools and Families (DCSF) (2009a) *Learning Behaviour: Lessons Learned – A Review of Behaviour Standards and Practices in Our Schools* (DCSF-00453-2009). Nottingham: DCSF.

Department for Children Schools and Families (DCSF) (2009b) *Getting to Grips with Assessing Pupils' Progress*. London: HMSO.

Department for Children Schools and Families (DCSF) (2009c) *Breaking the Link Between Disadvantage and Low Attainment: Everyone's Business* (DCSF-00357-2009). Nottingham: DCSF.

Department for Children Schools and Families (DCSF) (2010a) *Breaking the Link Between Special Educational Needs and Low Attainment: Everyone's Business*. Nottingham: DCSF.

Department for Children Schools and Families (DCSF) (2010b) *Working Together to Safeguard Children*. Nottingham: DCSF.

Department for Children Schools and Families (DCSF) (2010c) *Smoking Out Underachievement*. Nottingham: DCSF.

Department for Education (DfE) (2010) *The Importance of Teaching: The Schools White Paper 2010*, Cm 7980. London: DfE. Available at: http://www.education.gov.uk/publications/standard/publicationdetail/page1/CM%207980

Department for Education (DfE) (2011a) *Support and Aspiration: A New Approach to Special Educational Needs and Disability: A Consultation*, Cm. 8027 (Green Paper). London: HMSO.

Department for Education (DfE) (2011b) *Participation in Education, Training and Employment by 16–18 Year Olds in England*, Statistical First Release SFR 15/2011, June. Available online at: http://www.education.gov.uk/rsgateway/DB/SFR/s001011/index.shtml [accessed 13 December 2011].

Department for Education (DfE) (2011c) *Teachers' Standards*. London: HMSO.

Department for Education (DfE) (2011d) *Home–School Agreements*, updated 23 June. Available at: http://www.education.gov.uk/schools/pupilsupport/parents/ involvement/hsa/a0014718/homeschoolagreements

Department for Education (DfE) (2011e) *Foundation Learning*. Available at: http://www.education.gov.uk/schools/teachingandlearning/qualifications/foundationlearning [accessed 19 August 2011].

Department for Education (DfE) (2011f) *Review of Vocational Education* (The Wolf Report), DFE-00031-2011. London: DfE.

Department for Education and Employment (DfEE) (1996) *Education Act*. London: DfEE Publications.

Department for Education and Employment (DfEE) (1997a) *Excellence in Schools* (White Paper), Cmnd 3681. London: HMSO.

Department for Education and Employment (DfEE) (1997b) *From Targets to Action: Guidance to Support Effective Target-setting in Schools*. London: DfEE.

Department for Education and Employment (DfEE) (1997c) *Literary Task Force: The Implementation of the National Literary Strategy*. London: DfEE.

Department for Education and Employment (DfEE) (1997d) *Excellence for All Children: Meeting Special Educational Needs*. London: DfEE.

Department for Education and Employment (DfEE) (1999) *The National Numeracy Strategy: Framework for Teaching Mathematics from Reception to Year 6*. London: DfEE.

Department for Education and Employment (DfEE) (2000a) *Removing the Barriers*. London: DfEE.

Department for Education and Employment (DfEE) (2000b) *SEN Code of Practice on the Identification and Assessment of Pupils with Special Educational Needs and SEN Thresholds Good Practice Guidelines on Identification and Provision for Pupils with Special Educational Needs*. London: DfEE Publications.

Department for Education and Employment (DfEE) (2001a) *Key Stage 3 National Strategy. Framework for Teaching English: Years 7, 8 and 9*. London: DfEE Publications. Available at: www.standards.dfes.gov.uk/keystage3/publications.

Department for Education and Employment/Qualifications and Curriculum Authority (DfEE/QCA) (1999) *The National Curriculum: Values, Aims and Purposes*. London: DfEE/QCA. Available online at: www.nc.uk.net/nc_resources/html/ valuesAimsPurposes.shtml

Department for Education and Employment/Qualifications and Curriculum Authority (DfEE/QCA) (2000) *The National Curriculum Handbook for Secondary Teachers in England: Key Stage 3 and 4*. London: DfEE/QCA.

Department for Education and Skills (DfES) (2001a) *Schools: Achieving Success*. London: DfES.

Department for Education and Skills (DfES) (2001b) *Special Education Needs Code of Practice*. London: DfES.

Department for Education and Skills (DfES) (2001c) *Key Stage 3 National Strategy. Numeracy Across the Curriculum: Notes for School-based Training*. London: DfES Publications. Available online at: www.standards.dfes.gov.uk/keystage3/ publications

Department for Education and Skills (DfES) (2001d) *Inclusive Schooling: Children with Special Educational Needs*. London: DfES.

Department for Education and Skills (DfES) (2002a) *Effective Lessons in Science. Notes for Tutors*. London: DfES.

Department for Education and Skills (DfES) (2002b) *Extending Opportunities: Raising Standards*. London: DfES.

Department for Education and Skills (DfES) (2002c) *National Strategy for Key Stage 3: Managing the Second Year*. London: DfES.

Department for Education and Skills (DfES) (2002d) *Developing the Role of School Support Staff*. London: HMSO.

Department for Education and Skills (DfES) (2003a) *14–19 Opportunity and Excellence*. London: DfES.

Department for Education and Skills (DfES) (2003b) *Working Group on 14–19 Reform: Principles for Reform of 14–19 Learning Programmes and Qualifications*. London: DfES.

Department for Education and Skills (DfES) (2003c) *Effective Teaching and Learning in Science*. London: DfES.

Department for Education and Skills (DfES) (2003d) *Aiming High: Raising the Achievement of Minority Ethnic Pupils*. London: DfES.

Department for Education and Skills (DfES) (2003e) *Every Child Matters*. London: DfES.

Department for Education and Skills (DfES) (2003f) *The Learning Challenge*. London: DfES.

Department for Education and Skills (DfES) (2004a) *A National Conversation about Personalised Learning*. London: DfES.

Department for Education and Skills (DfES) (2004b) *Working Group on 14–19 Reform: Interim Report*. London: DfES.

Department for Education and Skills (DfES) (2004c) *Strengthening Teaching and Learning in Science Through Using Different Pedagogies. Unit 1: Using Group Talk and Argument*. London: DfES.

Department for Education and Skills (DfES) (2004d) *Pedagogy and Practice: Teaching and Learning in Secondary School. Unit 1: Structure and Learning*. London: DfES Publications.

Department for Education and Skills (DfES) (2004e) *Pedagogy and Practice: Teaching and Learning in Secondary School. Unit 3: Lesson Design for Lower Attainers*. London: DfES Publications.

Department for Education and Skills (DfES) (2004f) *Pedagogy and Practice: Teaching and Learning in Secondary School. Unit 5: Starters and Plenaries*. London: DfES Publications.

Department for Education and Skills (DfES) (2004g) *Removing Barriers to Achievement. The Government's Strategy for SEN*. Nottingham: DfES.

Department for Education and Skills (DfES) (2005a) *Learning Behaviour: The Report of the Practitioners Group on School Behaviour and Discipline* (The Steer Report). London: DfES.

Department for Education and Skills (DfES) (2005b) *Leading in Learning: Developing Thinking Skills at Key Stage Three*. London: DfES.

Department for Education and Skills (DfES) (2005c) *14–19 Education and Skills*. London: DfES.

Department for Education and Skills (DfES) (2005d) *Leading on Inclusion: Primary National Strategy*. London: DfES.

Department for Education and Skills (DfES) (2005e) *Higher Standards, Better Schools for All: More Choice for Parents and Pupils* (White Paper), Cm. 6677. London: DfES.

Department for Education and Skills (DfES) (2006a) *The Offer to Schools for 2006*. London: DfES.

Department for Education and Skills (DfES) (2006b) *The Five Year Strategy for Children and Learners: Maintaining the Excellent Progress*. London: DfES.

Department for Education and Skills (DfES) (2006c) *A Guide to the Law for School Governors*. London: DfES.

Department for Education and Skills (DfES) (2006d) *Primary National Strategy: Leading an Intervention: Summary of Research on Commonly used Provision – Teaching Assistant (TA) Support*. London: DfES.

Department for Education and Skills (DfES) (2007a) *2020 Vision: Report of the Teaching and Learning in 2020 Review Group* (The Gilbert Review). London: DfES.

Department for Education and Skills (DfES) (2007b) *Making Good Progress: How Can We Help Every Pupil to Make Good Progress?* London: HMSO.

Department for Education and Skills (DfES) (2007c) *Diversity and Citizenship: Curriculum Review* (The Ajegbo Report). London: DfES.

Department of Education and Science (DES) (1975) *A Language for Life* (The Bullock Report). London: HMSO.

Department of Education and Science (DES) (1978) *Special Educational Need* (Report of the Warnock Committee). London: HMSO.

Department of Education and Science (DES) (1988) *The Education Reform Act 1988*. London: HMSO.

Department of Education and Science (DES) (1989) *Discipline in Schools: Report of the Committee of Enquiry Chaired by Lord Elton*. London: HMSO.

Department of Health (DH) (2003) *The Victoria Climbié Inquiry: Report of an Inquiry by Lord Laming*. Cm 5730. London: Department of Health.

Desforges, C. and Abouchaar, A. (2003) *The Impact of Parental Involvement, Parental Support and Family Education on Pupil Achievements and Adjustments: A Literature Review*. Research Report #443. London: DfES.

Dessent, T. (2006) Will Mrs Thatcher have her way? Future options for children's services, in B. Norwich (ed.), *Taking Stock: Integrated Children's Services, Improvement and Inclusion*. SEN Policy Options Group, Policy Paper 1, 6th Series. Available online at: www.nasen.org.uk

Dias-Ferreira, E., Sousa, J.C., Melo, I. *et al.* (2009) Chronic stress causes frontostriatal reorganization and affects decision-making, *Science*, 325(5940): 621–5.

Docking, J. (ed.) (2000) *New Labour's Policies for Schools: Raising the Standard*. London: David Fulton.

Doyle, W. (1986) Classroom management and organisation, in M.C. Wittrock (ed.), *Handbook of Research on Teaching*. New York: Macmillan.

Dunn, R. (1990) Understanding the Dunn and Dunn learning styles model and the need for individual diagnosis and prescription, *Reading: Writing and Learning Disabilities*, 6: 223–47.

Dyson, A., Cummings, C. and Todd, C. (2004) *Evaluation of the Extended Schools Pathfinder Projects*. London: DfES.

Edmond, N. and Price, M. (2009) Workforce re-modelling and pastoral care in schools: a diversification of roles or a de-professionalisation of functions? *Pastoral Care in Education*, 27(4): 301–11.

Edwards, A., Lunt, I. and Stamou, E. (2010) Inter-professional work and expertise: new roles at the boundaries of schools, *British Educational Research Journal*, 36(1): 27–45.

Eichenbaum, H. (1997) How does the brain organize memories? *Science*, 277(5324): 330–2.

Ekwall, E.E. and Shanker, J.L. (1988) *Diagnosis and Remediation of the Disabled Reader*, 3rd edn. Boston, MA: Allyn & Bacon.

Elliott, B. and Calderhead, J. (1993) Mentoring for teacher development: possibilities and caveats, in D. Mcintyre, H. Hagger and M. Wilkinson (eds.); *Mentoring: Perspectives on School-based Teacher Education*. London: Kogan Page.

Elliott, J. (1997) *The Curriculum Experiment: Meeting the Challenge of Social Change*. Buckingham: Open University Press.

Ellis, S. and Tod, J. (2009) *Behaviour for Learning: Proactive Approaches to Behaviour Management*. London: Routledge.

Ellis, S., Tod, J. and Graham-Matheson, L. (2008) *Special Educational Needs and Inclusion: Reflection and Renewal*. Birmingham: NASUWT.

Ellis, V. (ed.), (2002) *Learning and Teaching in Secondary Schools*. Exeter: Learning Matters.

Ellis, V., Butler, R. and Simpson, D. (2002) Planning for learning, in V. Ellis (ed.), *Learning and Teaching in Secondary Schools*. Exeter: Learning Matters.

Feinstein, L., Duckworth, K. and Sabates, R. (2008) *Education and the Family: Passing Success across the Generations*. London: Routledge.

Flutter, J. and Rudduck, J. (2004) *Consulting Pupils: What's in it for Schools?* London: Routledge.

Flynn, J.R. (1994) IQ gains over time, in R.J. Sternberg (ed.), *Encyclopaedia of Human Intelligence*. New York: Macmillan.

Fones, D. (2001) Blocking them in to free them to act, *English in Education*, 36(3): 21–31.

Frater, G. (1997) *Improving Boys' Literacy*. London: The Basic Skills Agency.

Fredricks, J., Blumenfeld, P.C. and Paris, A.H. (2004) School engagement: potential of the concept, state of the evidence, *Review of Educational Research*, 74(1): 59–109.

Freeman, R. and Lewis, R. (1998) *Planning and Implementing Assessment*. London: Kogan Page.

Furlong, J. and Maynard, T. (1995) *Mentoring Student Teachers: The Growth of Professional Knowledge*. London: Routledge.

Galloway, S. (2000) Issues and challenges in continuing professional development, in S. Galloway (ed.), *Continuous Professional Development: Looking Ahead*. Proceedings of a Symposium by the Centre on Skills, Knowledge and Organisational Performance, Oxford, May.

Gardner, H. (1983) *Frames of Mind*. New York: Basic Books.

Gardner, H. (1993) *Multiple Intelligences: The Theory in Practice*. New York: Basic Books.

Gardner, H. (1995) Reflections on the multiple intelligences: myths and messages, *Phi Delta Kappan*, 77(3): 200–9.

Gardner, H. (2003) *Multiple intelligences after 20 years*. Paper presented at the Annual Meeting of the American Educational Research Association, Chicago, IL, 21 April.

Gipps, C. (1994) *Beyond Testing: Towards a Theory of Educational Assessment*. London: Falmer Press.

Gipps, C. and Murphy, P. (1994) *A Fair Test? Assessment, Achievement and Equity*. Buckingham: Open University Press.

Goleman, D. (1996) *Emotional Intelligence: Why it can Matter More than IQ*. London: Bloomsbury.

Gorard, S. (2009) What are Academies the answer to? *Journal of Education Policy*, 24(1): 101–13.

Gorard, S. (2010) Education can compensate for society (a bit), *British Journal of Educational Studies*, 58(1): 47–65.

Gorard, S. and Smith, E. (2008) The impact of school experience on students' sense of justice: an international study of student voice, *Orbis Scholae*, 2(2): 87–105.

Gould, J. (1983) *The Mismeasure of Man*. New York: Norton.

Gouseti, G. (2010) Web 2.0 and education: not just another case of hype, hope and disappointment? *Learning, Media and Technology*, 35(3): 351–6.

Graham, D. (1993) *A Lesson for All of Us? Making the National Curriculum*. London: Routledge.

Guild, P. (1994) The culture/learning style connection, *Educational Leadership*, 51(8): 16–21.

Guppy, P. and Hughes, M. (1999) *The Development of Independent Reading*. Buckingham: Open University Press.

Gurian, M. (2001) *Boys and Girls Learn Differently!* San Francisco, CA: Jossey-Bass.

Hamblin, D. (1978) *The Teacher and Pastoral Care*. Oxford: Basil Blackwell.

Hammond, M., Ingram, J. and Reynolds, L. (2011) How and why do student teachers use ICT? *Journal of Computer Assisted Learning*, 27(3): 191–203.

Hardiker, P., Exton, K. and Barker, M. (1991) *Policies and Practices in Preventive Child Care*. Aldershot: Avebury.

Hargreaves, D.H. (2003) *From improvement to transformation*. Keynote address to the 16th International Congress for School Effectiveness and Improvement, Sydney, NSW, January.

Hargreaves, D.H., Hestor, S. and Mellor, F. (1975) *Deviance in Classrooms*. London: Routledge & Kegan Paul.

Harlen, W. and Deakin Crick, R. (2002) A systematic review of the impact of summative assessment and tests on students' motivation for learning (EPPI-Centre Review, version 1.1*), in *Research Evidence in Education Library*. London: EPPI-Centre, Social Science Research Unit, Institute of Education. Available at: http://www.eppi.ioe.ac.uk

Harris, A. (1998) Effective teaching: a review of the literature, *School Leadership and Management*, 18(2): 169–83.

Harris, A. (2002) *School Improvement: What's in it for Schools?* London: Routledge.

Harrison, C., Comber, C., Fisher, T. *et al.* (2002) *ImpaCT2 – The Impact of Information and Communication Technologies on Pupil Learning and Attainment*. Coventry: Becta.

Haydn, T. (2007) *Managing Pupil Behaviour: Key Issues in Teaching and Learning*. London: Routledge.

Haydon, G. (1997) *Teaching About Values: A New Approach*. London: Cassell.

Hayes, S.G. and Clay, J. (2007) *Progression from Key Stage 2 to 4: Understanding the Context and Nature of Performance and Underperformance between the Ages 11–16*. Paper presented at the British Educational Research Association Annual Conference, Institute of Education, University of London, 5–8 September. Available online at: http://www.leeds.ac.uk/educol/documents/167840.htm

Hayes, S.G., Shaw, H., McGrath, G. and Bonel, F. (2009) *Using RAISEonline as a Research Tool to Analyse the Link Between Attainment, Social Class and Ethnicity*. London: Information, Research and Statistics Team, Greenwich Children's Service (British Education Index Reference 184218).

Head, J. (1995) *Gender identity and cognitive style*, Paper presented at the UNESCO colloquium: 'Is there a Pedagogy for Girls?', London.

Heater, D. (2001) The history of citizenship education, *The Curriculum Journal*, 12(1): 103–24.

Higgins, S., Beauchamp, G. and Miller, D. (2007) Reviewing the literature on interactive whiteboards, *Learning, Media and Technology*, 32(3): 213–25.

Hilgard, E. (1995) *Theories of Learning*. New York: Appleton.

Hircsh, E.D. (1996) *The Schools We Need and Why We Don't Have Them*. New York: Anchor Books.

Her Majesty's Inspectorate (HMI) (2002) *Achievement of Black Caribbean Pupils: Good Practice in Secondary Schools*. London: HMSO.

HMSO (1999) *Highly Able Children: Third Report of the Education and Employment Committee 1998–99*. London: HMSO.

HMSO (2002) *Education Act*. London: HMSO.

Hopkins, D. (2003) *Transforming schools*. Keynote address to DfES 'Transforming Schools Conference', London, September.

House of Commons Education and Skills Committee (2006) *Special Educational Needs, Third Report of Session 2005–06. Volume 1*. London: The Stationery Office.

Howe, M.J.A. (1997) *IQ in Question: The Truth about Intelligence*. London: Sage.

Howes, A. (2003) Teaching reforms and the impact of paid adult support on participation and learning in mainstream schools, *Support for Learning*, 18(4): 147–53.

Huddleston, P. (2002) Uncertain destinies: student recruitment and retention on GNVQ intermediate programmes, *SKOPE Research Paper*, 37, Winter.

Humphrey, N. and Squires, G.T. (2011) *Achievement for All, National Evaluation: Final report* (Research Report DfE RR176). London: HMSO.

Jama, D. and Dugdale, G. (2010) *Literacy: State of the Nation – A Picture of Literacy in the UK Today*. London: National Literacy Trust.

Jewitt, C., Hadjithoma-Garstka, C., Clark, W., Banaji, S. and Selwyn, N. (2010) *School Use of Learning Platforms and Associated Technologies*. Coventry: Becta.

Joyce, B., Calhoun, E. and Hopkins, D. (1998) *Models of Teaching: Tools for Learning*. Buckingham: Open University Press.

Kaufman, D. and Moss, D. (2010) A new look at pre-service teachers' conceptions of classroom management and organization: uncovering complexity and dissonance, *The Teacher Educator*, 45: 118–36.

Kerr, D. (1999) *Re-examining Citizenship Education: The Case of England*. Slough: NFER.

Kerr, D. (2005) 'England's teenagers fail the patriotic test': the lessons from England's participation in the IEA Civic Education Study, in S. Wilde (ed.), *Political and Citizenship Education: International Perspectives*. London: Symposium.

Kerr, D., Cleaver, E., Ireland, E. and Blenkinsop, S. (2003) *Citizenship Education Longitudinal Study: First Cross-sectional Survey 2001–2002*. London: DfES.

Kerr, K. and West, M. (eds.) (2010) *Social Inequality: Can Schools Narrow the Gap?* London: British Educational Research Association.

Kirschner, P.A., Sweller, J. and Clark, R.E. (2006) Why minimal guidance during instruction does not work: an analysis of the failure of constructivist, discovery, problem-based, experiential, and inquiry based teaching, *Educational Psychologist*, 41(2): 75–86.

Klein, P.D. (1997) Multiplying the problems of intelligence by eight: a critique of Gardner's theory, *Canadian Journal of Education*, 22(4): 377–94.

Kohn, M. (1995) In two minds, *Guardian Weekend*, 5 August.

Kotulak, R. (1996) *Inside the Brain*. Kansas City, KS: Universal Press Syndicate.

Kress, G. (2003) *Literacy in the New Media Age*. London: Routledge.

Lackney, J.A. (1999) Twelve design principles for schools derived from brain-based learning research, *Schoolhouse Journal*, 2(2): 1–12.

Lang, P. (1999) Counselling, counselling skills and encouraging pupils to talk: clarifying and addressing confusion, *British Journal of Guidance and Counselling*, 27(1): 23–33.

Lang, P. (2007) Pastoral care and the role of the tutor, in V. Brooks, I. Abbott and L. Bills (eds.), *Preparing to Teach in Secondary Schools*. Maidenhead: Open University Press.

Lave, J. and Wenger, E. (1991) *Situated Learning: Legitimate Peripheral Participation*. Cambridge: Cambridge University Press.

Learning and Skills Improvement Service (2011) *Supporting Teaching and Learning in Schools (England)*, Framework ID FR00799, 22 July. London: LSIS. Available at: http://www.afo.sscalliance.org/frameworkslibrary/index.cfm?id= FR00799 [accessed October 2011].

Leask, M. (ed.) (2001) *Issues in Teaching Using ICT*. London: RoutledgeFalmer.

Leitch, A. (2006) *Prosperity for All in the Global Economy – World Class Skills*, Final Report. London: HM Treasury.

Leslie, C. and Skidmore, C. (2007) *SEN: The Truth about Inclusion*. London: The Bow Group.

Lewin, C., Mavers, D. and Somekh, B. (2003) Broadening access to the curriculum through using technology to link home and school: a critical analysis of reforms intended to improve students' educational attainment, *Curriculum Journal*, 14(1): 23–53.

Lewin, C., Mavers, D., Saxon, D., Twining, P. and Woodrow, D. (2006) *Evaluation of the ICT Test Bed Project: Annual Report*. Coventry: Becta. Available online at: www.evaluation.icttestbed.org.uk/reports

Lewis, M. and Wray, D. (1998) *Writing Across the Curriculum*. Reading: Reading Language Information Centre.

Lewis, M. and Wray, D. (eds.) (2000) *Literacy in the Secondary School*. London: David Fulton.

Lightfoot, L. (1997) Attention span of boys' only five minutes, *Daily Telegraph*, 26 April.

Little, J.W. (1993) Teachers' professional development in a climate of educational reform, *Educational Evaluation and Policy Analysis*, 15(2): 129–51.

Lodge, C. (2002) Tutors talking, *Pastoral Care in Education*, 20(4): 35–7.

Macdonald, A. (2009) *Independent Review of the Proposal to Make Personal, Social, Health and Economic Education Statutory*. London: DCSF.

MacGrath, M. (1998) *The Art of Teaching Peacefully*. London: David Fulton.

Macpherson, W. (1999) *The Stephen Lawrence Inquiry: Report of an Inquiry by Sir William Macpherson* (The Macpherson Report). London: HMSO.

Margo, J. and Dixon, M. (2006) *Freedom's Orphans: Raising Youth in a Changing World*. London: Institute for Public Policy Research.

Marland, M. and Rogers, R. (2004) *How to be a Successful Form Tutor*. London: Continuum.

Marrin, M. (1997) Mr Evans is right about women MPs, *Sunday Telegraph*, 9 March.

Marshall, T.H. (1950) *Citizenship and Social Class, and Other Essays*. Cambridge: Cambridge University Press.

McGuiness, C. (1998) *From Thinking Skills to Thinking Classrooms*. London: DfEE.

McIntyre, D., Pedder, D. and Rudduck, J. (2005) Pupil voice: comfortable and uncomfortable learnings for teachers. *Research Papers in Education*, 20(2): 149–68.

McNally, J., I'anson, J., Whewell, C. and Wilson, G. (2005) 'They think swearing is OK': first lessons in behaviour management, *Journal of Education for Teaching*, 31(3): 169–85.

McWilliam, N. (1998) *What's in a World?* Stoke-on-Trent: Trentham Books.

Midgley, P., Beskeen, L., Egginton, N. *et al.* (1999) *Promoting Students' Spiritual, Moral, Social and Cultural Development Through Specific Teaching and Learning Strategies Across the Curriculum*. Available online at: www.becal.net/toolkit/smrtvalues/documents/values_interventions_summary_ report.pdf

Milbourne, L., Macrae, S. and Maguire, M. (2003) Collaborative solutions or new policy problems: exploring multi-agency partnerships in education and health work, *Journal of Education Policy*, 18(1): 19–35.

Mishra, P. and Koehler, M.J. (2006) Technological pedagogical content knowledge: a framework for teacher knowledge, *Teachers College Record*, 108(6): 1017–54.

Molfese, V., Molfese, P., Molfese, D., Rudasill, K., Armstrong, N. and Starkey, G. (2010) Executive function skills of 6 to 8 year olds: brain and behavioral evidence and implications for school achievement, *Contemporary Educational Psychology*, 30(3): 116–53 (Special Issue on Brain and Academic Development).

Moll, L. (1992) Literacy research in community and classrooms: a sociocultural approach, in R. Beach, J. Green, M. Kamil and T. Shanahan (eds.), *Multidisciplinary Perspectives on Literacy Research*. Urbana, IL: National Council of Teachers of English.

Morgan, H. (1996) An analysis of Gardner's theory of multiple intelligence, *Roeper Review*, 18: 263–9.

Muijs, D. (2004) *Doing Quantitative Research in Education*. London: Sage.

Muijs, D. and Reynolds, D. (2002) Teachers' beliefs and behaviors: what really matters, *Journal of Classroom Interaction*, 37(2): 3–15.

Muijs, D. and Reynolds, D. (2003) Student background and teacher effects on achievement and attainment in mathematics, *Educational Review and Evaluation*, 9(1): 289–313.

Muijs, D. and Reynolds, D. (2010) *Effective Teaching: Evidence and Practice*. London: Sage.

Muijs, D., Day, C., Harris, A. and Lindsay, G. (2004) Evaluating CPD: an overview, in C. Day, and J. Sachs (eds.), *International Handbook on the Continuing Professional Development of Teachers*. Maidenhead: Open University Press.

Muijs, R.D. (1997) *Self, School and Media: A Longitudinal Study of Media Use, Self-concept, School Achievement and Peer Relations Among Primary School Children*. Leuven: Catholic University of Leuven, Department of Communication Science.

National Advisory Committee on Creative and Cultural Education (1999) *All Our Futures: Creativity, Culture and Education*. London: DfEE/DCMS.

National Curriculum Council (NCC) (1990) *Curriculum Guidance Eight: Education for Citizenship*. York: NCC.

National Foundation for Educational Research (NFER) (2003) *Consultation on Proposed Changes to the Key Stage 4 Curriculum*. Slough: NFER.

National Institute of Adult Continuing Education (NIACE) (2011) *Numeracy Counts: Final Report of the NIACE Committee on Inquiry on Adult Numeracy Learning*. Leicester: NIACE.

National Endowment for Science, Technology and the Arts (NESTA) (2004) *The Good Guide to Interactive Whiteboards*. Hull: University of Hull.

Neill, S. and Caswell, C. (1993) *Body Language for Competent Teachers*. London: Routledge.

Newton, L. and Rogers, L. (2001) *Teaching Science with ICT*. London: Continuum.

Newton, P.E. (2007) Clarifying the purposes of educational assessment, *Assessment in Education: Principles, Policy and Practice*, 14(2): 149–70.

Nolan, Lord (1996) *Second Report of the Committee on Standards in Public Life*. London: HMSO.

Norman, K. (ed.) (1992) *Thinking Voices: The Work of the National Oracy Project*. London: Hodder & Stoughton.

Norwich Area Schools Consortium (NASC) (2002) *Pupil Perceptions of School Subjects*. Available online at: www.uea.ac.uk/~m242/nasc/cross/cman/leaste.ort.htm

Norwich Area Schools Consortium (NASC) (2002) *Researching Classroom Dissaffection: The Classroom Management Strand*. Available online at: http://www.uea.ac.uk/~m242/nasc/welcome.htm [last accessed 7 February 2012].

O'Donohue, W. and Ferguson, K. (2001) *The Psychology of B.F. Skinner*. Thousand Oaks, CA: Sage.

O'Neill, O. (2002) *Reith Lectures*. Available online at: www.bbc.co.uk/radio4/reith2002

Oates, T. (2010) *Could Do Better: Using International Comparisons to Refine the National Curriculum in England*. Cambridge: Cambridge Assessment.

OECD (2003) *The PISA 2003 Assessment Framework: Mathematics, Reading, Science and Problem Solving Knowledge and Skills*. OECD: Paris. Available online at: http://www.pisa.oecd.org/dataoecd/46/14/33694881.pdf [accessed October 2011].

OECD/UNESCO (2003) *Literacy Skills for the World of Tomorrow*. Available online at: www.oecd.org

Office for Standards in Education (Ofsted) (1993) *Access and Achievement in Urban Education*. London: Ofsted.

Office for Standards in Education (Ofsted) (1994) *Spiritual, Moral, Social and Cultural Education: A Discussion Paper*. London: Ofsted.

Office for Standards in Education (Ofsted) (1996a) *The Annual Report of Her Majesty's Chief Inspector of Schools.* London: HMSO.

Office for Standards in Education (Ofsted) (1996b) *Recent Research on the Achievements of Minority Ethnic Pupils.* London: HMI.

Office for Standards in Education (Ofsted) (1998) *Secondary Education 1993–1997: A Review of Secondary Schools in England.* London: HMSO.

Office for Standards in Education (Ofsted) (1999) *Raising the Attainment of Minority Ethnic Pupils.* London: HMI.

Office for Standards in Education (Ofsted) (2002) *Inspecting Spiritual, Moral, Social and Cultural Education: Guidance for Inspectors.* London: Ofsted.

Office for Standards in Education (Ofsted) (2003a) *Boys' Achievement in Secondary Schools.* London: HMSO.

Office for Standards in Education (Ofsted) (2003b) *Quality and Standards in Secondary Initial Teacher Training.* London: Ofsted.

Office for Standards in Education (Ofsted) (2004a) *Promoting and Evaluating Pupils' Spiritual, Moral, Social and Cultural Development.* London: Ofsted.

Office for Standards in Education (Ofsted) (2004b) *Special Educational Needs and Disability. Towards Inclusive Schools.* London: Ofsted.

Office for Standards in Education (Ofsted) (2005a) *Framework for the Inspection of Schools from September 2005.* London: Ofsted.

Office for Standards in Education (Ofsted) (2005b) *Annual Report of Her Majesty's Chief Inspector for Schools.* London: Ofsted.

Office for Standards in Education (Ofsted) (2005c) *Managing Challenging Behaviour.* HMI 2363. London: Ofsted.

Office for Standards in Education (Ofsted) (2005d) *Personal, Social and Health Education in Secondary Schools.* HMI 2311. London: Ofsted.

Office for Standards in Education (Ofsted) (2006a) *Towards Consensus? Citizenship in Secondary Schools.* London: Ofsted.

Office for Standards in Education (Ofsted) (2006b) *Annual Report of Her Majesty's Chief Inspector of Schools.* London: Ofsted.

Office for Standards in Education (Ofsted) (2006c) *Inclusion: Does it Matter Where Pupils Are Taught? Provision and Outcomes in Different Settings for Pupils with Learning Difficulties.* London: Ofsted.

Office for Standards in Education (Ofsted) (2008a) *Using Data, Improving Schools.* London: Ofsted.

Office for Standards in Education (Ofsted) (2008b) *Good Practice in Re-engaging Disaffected and Reluctant Students in Secondary Schools.* London: Ofsted.

Office for Standards in Education (Ofsted) (2009a) *The Annual Report of Her Majesty's Chief Inspector of Education, Children's Services and Skills 2008/09.* London: The Stationery Office.

Office for Standards in Education Ofsted (2009b) *Citizenship Established? Citizenship in Schools 2006-09.* London: Ofsted.

Office for Standards in Education (Ofsted) (2010a) *Personal, Social, Health and Economic Education in Schools.* Ref. 090222. London: Ofsted.

Office for Standards in Education (Ofsted) (2010b) *Steady Progress for Citizenship Education.* DfES Press Release 2010-02, 22 January. London: Ofsted.

Office for Standards in Education (Ofsted) (2010c) *The Annual Report of Her Majesty's Chief Inspector of Education, Children's Services and Skills 2009/10.* London: The Stationery Office.

Office for Standards in Education (Ofsted) (2010d) *Diplomas: The Second Year.* London: Ofsted.

Office for Standards in Education (Ofsted) (2011a) *Removing Barriers to Literacy*. Manchester: Ofsted.

Office for Standards in Education (Ofsted) (2011b) *Tackling the Challenge of Low Numeracy Skills in Young People and Adults*. London: Ofsted. Available online at: http://www.ofsted. gov.uk/resources/tackling-challenge-of-low-numeracy-skills-young-people-and-adults [accessed October 2011].

Offices for Standards in Education (Ofsted) (2011c) *Inspection 2012: Proposals for Inspection Arrangements for Maintained Schools and Academics from January 2012 – For Consultation*. Manchester: Ofdted. Available online at: www.osted.gov.uk/publications/110025

Partnership for Schools (2007) *Partnerships for Schools*. Available online at: www.p4s.org.uk/

Paton, G. (2010) Education White Paper: Ofsted inspections to be overhauled, *Daily Telegraph*, 24 November.

Piaget, J. (2001) *The Child's Conception of Physical Causality*. New Brunswick, NJ: Transaction Publishers.

Pollard, A. and James, M. (2004) *Personalised Learning: A Commentary by the Teaching and Learning Research Programme*. London: DfES. Available online at: wwwfitlrp.org/ documents/ESRCPerson.pdf.

Porter, L. (2000) *Behaviour in Schools: Theory and Practice for Teachers*. Buckingham: Open University Press.

Power, S. (1991): 'Pastoral care' as curriculum discourse: a study in the reformation of 'academic' schooling, *International Studies in Sociology of Education*, 1(1–2): 193–208.

Pring, R. (1984) Personal and social education in the primary school, in P. Lang (ed.), *Thinking about ... Personal and Social Education in the Primary School*. Oxford: Blackwell.

Qualifications and Curriculum Authority (QCA) (1998) *Education for Citizenship and the Teaching of Democracy in Schools: Final Report of the Advisory Group on Citizenship*. London: QCA.

Qualifications and Curriculum Authority (QCA) (1999a) *The National Numeracy Strategy: Teaching Mental Calculation Strategies: Guidance for Teachers at Key Stages 1 and 2*. London: QCA.

Qualifications and Curriculum Authority (QCA) (1999b) *The National Numeracy Strategy: Teaching Written Calculations: Guidance for Teachers at Key Stages 1 and 2*. London: QCA.

Qualifications and Curriculum Authority (QCA) (1999c) *Qualifications 16–19: A Guide to the Changes Resulting from the Qualifying for Success Consultation*. London: QCA.

Qualifications and Curriculum Authority (QCA) (2000a) *A Language in Common: Assessing English as an Additional Language*. London: QCA.

Qualifications and Curriculum Authority (QCA) (2000b) *Personal, Social and Health Education at Key Stages 3 and 4: Initial Guidance for Schools*. London: QCA.

Qualifications and Curriculum Authority (QCA) (2001) *Citizenship: A Scheme of Work for Key Stage 3: Teacher's Guide*. London: QCA.

Qualifications and Curriculum Authority (QCA) (2003) *Non Statutory Guidelines for PSHE at Key Stages 3 and 4*. London: QCA.

Qualifications and Curriculum Authority/Department for Education and Employment (QCA/ DfEE) (1999) *The National Curriculum*. London: HMSO.

Qualifications and Curriculum Development Agency (QCDA) (2007a) *National Curriculum for Citizenship*. London: QCDA. Available online at: http://curriculum.qcda.gov.uk/ uploads/QCA-07-3329-pCitizenship3_tcm8-396.pdf [last accessed 1 April 2011].

Qualifications and Curriculum Development Agency (QCDA) (2007b) *National Curriculum for England: Aims, Values and Purposes*. London: QCDA. Available online at: http:// curriculum.qcda.gov.uk/key-stages-3-and-4/aims-values-and-purposes/index.aspx [last accessed 1 April 2011].

Race Relations (Amendment) Act (2000) *New Laws for a Successful Multi-racial Britain*. London: Home Office.

Renshaw, P.D. (1992) The psychology of learning and small group work, in R. Maclean (ed.), *Classroom Oral Language*. Deakin, VIC: Deakin University Press.

Reynolds, D., Treharne, D. and Tripp, H. (2003) ICT – the hopes and the reality, *British Journal of Educational Technology*, 34(2): 151–67.

Richardson, R. and Wood, A. (1999) *Inclusive Schools, Inclusive Society*. Stoke-on-Trent: Trentham Books.

Riding, R. and Cheema, I. (1991) Cognitive style – an overview and integration, *Educational Psychology*, 65: 113–24.

Roberts, M. (2011) www.napce.org.uk/ [accessed 26 October 2011].

Rodd, J. (2002) *Learning to Learn in Schools*. Crediton: Campaign for Learning.

Roehrig, A.D., Turner, J.E., Grove, C.M., Schneider, N. and Liu, Z. (2009) Degree of alignment between beginning teachers' practices and beliefs about effective classroom practices. *The Teacher Educator*, 44: 164–87.

Roffey, S. (2011) *The New Teacher's Survival Guide to Behaviour*, 2nd edn. London: Sage.

Rogers, B. (1998) *You Know the Fair Rule*. London: Prentice-Hall.

Rogers, B. (2011) *Classroom Behaviour: A Practical Guide to Effective Teaching, Behaviour Management and Colleague Support*, 3nd edn. London: Paul Chapman.

Rosas, C. and West, M. (2009) Teachers' beliefs about classroom management: pre-service and in-service teachers' beliefs about classroom management, *International Journal of Applied Educational Studies*, 5(1): 55–61.

Rose, D. and Meyer, A. (2002) *Teaching in the Digital Age*. Alexandria, VA: ASCD.

Rudd, T. (2007) *Do Whiteboards have a Future in the UK Classroom?* Bristol: Futurelab. Available at: http://www.futurelab.org.uk/events/listing/whiteboards/report

Sammons, P., Thomas, S. and Mortimore, P. (1997). *Forging Links: Effective Schools and Effective Departments*. London: Paul Chapman.

Sampson, G. (1921) *English for the English*. Cambridge: Cambridge University Press.

Schofield, T. (2007) Student and tutor perceptions of the role of the tutor in a sixth form college, *Pastoral Care in Education*, 25(1): 26–32.

Schön, D. (1983) *The Reflective Practitioner*. New York: Basic Books.

Schools Curriculum and Assessment Authority (SCAA) (1995) *Spiritual and Moral Development*. London: SCAA.

Schools Curriculum and Assessment Authority (SCAA) (1997) *Consultation on Values in Education and the Community*. London: SCAA.

Selwyn, N. (2001) Why the computer is not dominating schools: a failure of policy or a failure of practice? *Cambridge Journal of Education*, 29(1): 77–92.

Shayer, M. and Adey, P. (2002) (eds.) Learning Intelligence: Cognitive Acceleration across the Curriculum from 5 to 15 years. Open University Press.

Shephard, J. (2011) Don't scrap citizenship lessons, plead teachers, *The Guardian*, 20 January.

Shipman, K. and Hicks, K. (1998) *How Can Teachers Motivate Less Able Boys?* London: TTA.

Shulman, L.S. (1986) Those who understand: knowledge growth in teaching, *Educational Researcher*, 15: 4–14.

Skinner, B.F. (1974) *About Behaviorism*. New York: Random House.

Smith, A. (2004) *Making Mathematics Count*. London: The Stationery Office.

Smith, R. and Alred, G. (1994) The impersonation of wisdom, in D. McIntyre, H. Hagger and M. Wilkin (eds.), *Mentoring: Perspectives on School-based Teacher Education*. London: Kogan Page.

Somekh, B. (2008) Factors affecting teachers' pedagogical adoption of ICT, in J. Voogt and G. Knezek (eds.), *International Handbook of Information Technology in Primary and Secondary Education*. New York: Springer.

Somekh, B., Lewin, C., Mavers, D. *et al.* (2002) *ImpaCT2 – Pupils' and Teachers' Perceptions of ICT in the Home, School and Community*. Coventry: Becta.

Somekh, B., Underwood, J., Convery, A. *et al.* (2006) *Evaluation of the ICT Test Bed Project, Annual Report*. Coventry: Becta.

Sousa, D. (1998) Brain research can help principals reform secondary schools, *NASSP Bulletin*, 82(598): 21–8.

Strand, S. (2006) Comparing the predictive validity of reasoning tests and national end of Key Stage 2 tests: which tests are the best? *British Educational Research Journal*, 32(2): 209–25.

Strand, S. and Winston, J. (2008) Educational aspirations in inner city schools, *Educational Studies*, 34(4): 249–67.

Sukhanandan, L., Lee, B., and Kelleher, S. (2000) *An Investigation into Gender Differences in Achievement*, Slough: NFER.

Symonds, J.E. and Hagell, A. (2011) Adolescents and the organisation of their school time: a review of changes over recent decades in England, *Educational Review*, 63(3): 291–312.

Tennant, G. 2001 The rhetoric and reality of learning support in the classroom: towards a synthesis, *Support for Learning*, 16(4): 178–82.

Tett, T., Crowther, J. and O'Hara, P. (2003) Collaborative partnerships in community education, *Journal of Education Policy*, 18(1): 37–51.

The National Strategies (Secondary) (2009) *Key Leaflet: Reading for Real, Purposeful and Relevant Contexts*. London: DfES.

Tomlinson, M. (2002) *Inquiry into A Level Standards: Final Report*. London: QCA.

Tomlinson, P. (1995) *Understanding Mentoring*. Buckingham: Open University Press.

Tosh, J. (2008) *Why History Matters*. Basingstoke: Palgrave Macmillan.

Training and Development Agency for Schools (TDA) (2007a) *Professional Standards for Teachers*. London: TDA.

Training and Development Agency (TDA) (2007b) *Professional Standards for Qualified Teacher Status and Requirements for Initial Teacher Training*. London: TDA.

Tyler, K. and Jones, B.D. (2002) Teachers' responses to the ecosystemic approach to changing chronic problem behaviour in schools, *Pastoral Care in Education*, 20(2): 30–9.

Uhden, O., Karam, R., Pietrocola, M. and Pospiech, G. (2011) Modelling mathematical reasoning in physics education, *Science and Education* (DOI: 10.1007/s11191-011-9396-6) [accessed October 2011].

Unsworth, L. (2001) *Teaching Multiliteracies Across the Curriculum*. Maidenhead: Open University Press.

Vygotsky, L.S. (1978) *Mind in Society: The Development of Higher Psychological Processes*. Cambridge, MA: Harvard University Press.

Vygotsky, L.S. (1986) *Thought and Language*. Cambridge, MA: The MIT Press.

Walsh, B. (2003) Building learning packages: integrating virtual resources with the real world of teaching and learning, in T. Haydn and C. Counsell (eds.) *History, ICT and Learning*. London, RoutledgeFalmer.

Warnock, M. (2005) *Special Educational Needs: A New Look*. IMPACT Number 11 in a series of policy discussions. London: Philosophy of Education Society of Great Britain.

Watkins, C. and Wagner, P. (2000) *Improving School Behaviour*. London: Paul Chapman.

Watson, D. (2001) Pedagogy before technology: re-thinking the relationship between ICT and teaching, *Education and Information Technologies*, 6(4): 251–66.

Wells, G. (1999) *Dialogic Inquiry: Towards a Sociocultural Practice and Theory of Education.* Cambridge: Cambridge University Press.

Wertsch, J.V. (1985) *Vygotsky and the Social Formation of Mind.* Cambridge, MA: Harvard University Press.

Wertsch, J. and Tulviste, P. (1992) L.S. Vygotsky and contemporary developmental psychology, *Developmental Psychology*, 28(4): 548–57.

White, J. (1998) *Do Howard Gardner's Multiple Intelligences Add Up?* London: Institute of Education, University of London.

White, J. (2010) The coalition and the curriculum, *Forum*, 52(3): 299–309.

Wiggins, G. and McTighe, J. (2005) *Understanding by Design.* Alexandria, VA: Association for Supervision and Curriculum Development.

Wiliam, D. and Black, P. (1996) Meanings and consequences: a basis for distinguishing formative and summative functions of assessment? *British Educational Research Journal*, 22(5): 537–48.

Wilshaw, M. (2012) Successful schools are all about good teaching, *The Times*, 30 November, p. 29.

Wintersgill, B. (2002) *Spiritual development – what do teenagers think it is?* Unpublished MA Field Study, University of Warwick.

Wong Fillmore, L. (1991) Second language learning in children, a model of language learning in social context, in E. Bialystock (ed.), *Language Processing in Bilingual Children.* Cambridge: Cambridge University Press.

Wortley, A. and Harrison, J. (2008) Pastoral care and tutorial roles, in S. Dymoke and J. Harrison (eds.), *Reflective Teaching and Learning: A Guide to Professional Issues for Beginning Secondary Teachers.* London: Sage.

Wubbels, T. (1992) Taking account of student teachers' preconceptions, *Teaching and Teacher Education*, 8: 47–58.

Younger, M. and Warrington, M. (2003) *Raising Boys' Achievement: Interim Report.* London: DfES.

Younger, M. and Warrington, M. (2005) *Raising Boys' Achievement*, DfES Research Report No. 636. London: HMSO.

Index

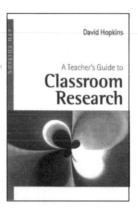

A TEACHER'S GUIDE TO CLASSROOM RESEARCH 4/E

David Hopkins

978-0-335-22174-5 (Paperback)
2008

The fourth edition of this bestselling book is a practical guide for teachers that wish to conduct research in their classrooms and for schools that wish to improve their practice. Classroom research, as described in this book, will enable teachers to enhance their own or their colleagues' teaching, to test the assumptions of educational theory in practice and to implement and evaluate whole school developments.

Changes to the new edition include:

- A major re-working of the last four chapters
- Comprehensive description of how to conduct classroom research
- Two new chapters on analyzing and reporting research
- Updated case study examples and cameos
- The contribution of teacher research in enhancing personalized learning and school transformation

OPEN UNIVERSITY PRESS
McGraw - Hill Education

www.openup.co.uk